THE SUFFERING SERVANT IN DEUTERO-ISAIAH

THE SUFFERING SERVANT IN DEUTERO-ISAIAH

An Historical and Critical Study

BY

CHRISTOPHER R. NORTH

EMERITUS PROFESSOR OF HEBREW
UNIVERSITY COLLEGE OF WALES, BANGOR
HON. D.D. (ABERDEEN)

SECOND EDITION

Wipf & Stock
PUBLISHERS
Eugene, Oregon

Wipf and Stock Publishers
199 W 8th Ave, Suite 3
Eugene, OR 97401

The Suffering Servant in Deutero-Isaiah
An Historical and Critical Study
By North, Christopher R.

ISBN: 1-59752-097-7
Publication date 3/3/2005
Previously published by Oxford University Press, 1956

PREFACE TO THE SECOND EDITION

THE call for a Second Edition of this book does not appear to demand any drastic revision. The most numerous and significant contributions to the subject in recent years have been by Scandinavian scholars. I have therefore contented myself with correcting a few slips, tidying up and supplementing the bibliography, and substituting for the Postscript to the First Edition what is substantially my article on 'Current Scandinavian Discussions' in *The Scottish Journal of Theology*, 3, 1950; this with the kind permission of the editors of the *Journal*.

When the book was first published I was quite prepared to be taken to task for proposing what is essentially a return to the traditional interpretation of the identity of the Servant. Instead, subsequent discussion has on the whole proceeded along the lines I suggested. On one point I should like to clear myself of misunderstanding. Professor H. H. Rowley has said (*The Servant of the Lord and other Essays on the Old Testament*, p. 54) that he and I 'differ . . . in our conception of the nature of the fluidity of the prophet's thought. Professor North finds only linear progress and rejects the idea of oscillation, whereas I find development from the thought of Israel as the Servant to the thought of an individual Servant *par excellence*, without abandoning the thought of Israel as still the Servant'. I quite agree with Professor Rowley that Israel does not cease to be Yahweh's servant. When I wrote (*infra*, p. 216): 'As I see it, the direction (of the Prophet's thought) was rather from collective Israel to an individual who was neither himself nor anyone else who had lived hitherto', I was criticizing Wheeler Robinson, who appeared to say that the direction of the Prophet's thought 'was from Israel to his own prophetic consciousness, *and back to Israel*'. I should have been better understood if I had disposed the italics differently: 'from Israel *to his own prophetic consciousness*, and back to Israel'. This I have done in the present edition.

C. R. N.

BANGOR
August, 1955

PREFACE TO THE FIRST EDITION

THE present work has been prompted by the conviction that the time is opportune for a presentation of the problem of the Servant of Yahweh in all its manifold complexities. During the past fifty years many solutions of the problem have been proposed, most of them new, one or two of them old but long forgotten, and revived by writers who may even betray no awareness that they have ever been suggested before. For nearly twenty years no new theory has been forthcoming, and the only fresh approaches to the subject are in the two Swedish articles which are dealt with in the Postscript. It would seem as if for the time being the impetus of speculation has exhausted itself. Indeed, so many expedients have been tried that it is hard to imagine that any more remain to be thought of.

It has often seemed to me, in reading discussions of the problem, that the critic, sometimes perhaps unconsciously, arranges the various theories at a kind of round table, and then, by the expedient of beginning at the place next to the one at which he himself wishes to arrive, and working round in the opposite direction, comes at last to the theory of his choice. I have tried to avoid doing that. In the historical summary I begin with the type of theory that is new, or most prominent, at any given period in the discussion, and in the final critical summary I deal first with the historical-individual theories, because they have been the most persistently advocated during the past half-century. If my own conclusions do not begin to appear clearly until towards the end of the book, that is not with any intention of mystifying the reader, but simply that the treatment may be as objective and impartial as possible. Like most British students I was brought up on the Collective theory, and when I set out on the present inquiry it was not even that I had become dissatisfied with that theory, but simply that I had become interested in the subject. Nor had I any idea to what conclusions I should come. The stage at which I disclose my own views corresponds roughly with the stage at which, in a preliminary reading of the most important works on the subject, I came to make up my mind.

The Bibliography, extensive though it is, is of course not exhaustive. No bibliography on the subject could be, and any attempt to make it exhaustive would only submerge what is important in a welter of what is not. I do not think I have omitted anything of major importance, and I have only listed works which I have actually seen. In order to reduce the number of footnotes I have occasionally mentioned a writer without any specific reference to his work. In such cases the reader should consult the Bibliography. Titles of books and articles have usually been abbreviated in the footnotes; if ever they are obscure full details will again be found in the Bibliography.

My grateful thanks are due especially to three scholars. First, to the Rev. Professor H. H. Rowley, D.D., F.B.A., to whom, during the war, I used to send, for safe custody, a copy of the manuscript, part by part as it was written, and who offered me much in the way of criticism and suggestion. Next, to the Rev. W. F. Lofthouse, M.A., D.D., my colleague and Principal at Handsworth College during fifteen years, with whom I have frequently discussed the subject. Thirdly, to Emeritus Professor S. A. Cook, Litt.D., D.D., F.B.A., who read the manuscript in its first draft, and to whom, like most workers in the Old Testament field, I am much indebted for stimulus and encouragement. My present colleagues, Mr. D. R. Ap-Thomas, M.A., B.D., and the Rev. Bleddyn J. Roberts, M.A., B.D., have read the proofs and compiled the Indexes of Authors and Scripture References. My wife has helped me with the copy and the proofs at all stages, and without her encouragement and patience the work could hardly have been written at all.

Finally, I wish to express my gratitude to the Delegates of the Clarendon Press for their acceptance of the book for publication, and to the readers of the Press for the care and courtesy with which they have handled the proofs.

C. R. N.

BANGOR
Ascensiontide, 1948

CONTENTS

PRINCIPAL ABBREVIATIONS EMPLOYED . . . xii

CHAPTER I. INTRODUCTION 1

PART I. HISTORICAL

CHAPTER II. JEWISH INTERPRETATIONS

1. In Pre-Christian Times 6
   (a) In the Old Testament 6
   (b) Apocrypha and Pseudepigrapha 7
   (c) The Septuagint 8
   (d) The New Testament 9
2. Since the Beginning of the Christian Era 9
   (a) The Righteous 9
   (b) Messianic 11
   (c) Collective 17
   (d) Individual (Jeremiah, Josiah, Hezekiah, Job) . . 20

CHAPTER III. CHRISTIAN INTERPRETATIONS: TO THE EIGHTEENTH CENTURY

1. In the New Testament 23
2. From the Sub-apostolic Period 26

CHAPTER IV. CHRISTIAN INTERPRETATIONS: FROM DÖDERLEIN TO DUHM

1. Collective 28
   (a) Collective Israel . 28
   (b) Ideal Israel . . 31
   (c) The Remnant . 35
   (d) The Prophets . . 37
   (e) The Priests . . 39
2. Historical Individual 39
   (a) Hezekiah . . 39
   (b) Isaiah. . . 40
   (c) Uzziah . . 41
   (d) Jeremiah . . 41
   (e) Deutero-Isaiah . . 41
   (f) Zerubbabel . . 42
   (g) Anonymous . . 42
3. Messianic 42

CHAPTER V. CHRISTIAN INTERPRETATIONS: FROM DUHM TO MOWINCKEL

1. Historical Individual 47
   (a) Unknown Teacher of the Law . . 47
   (b) Eleazar . . 49
   (c) Zerubbabel . . 49
   (d) Jehoiachin . . 50
   (e) Moses . . 53
   (f) Historico-Messianic . 55
   (g) Ezekiel . . . 56
   (h) Hezekiah: Jeremiah: Uzziah . . . 56
   (i) Cyrus . . . 57

2. Collective 57
(*a*) Collective Israel . 57 (*c*) Ideal Israel . . 63
(*b*) Pious Remnant . 62
3. Messianic 64
(*a*) Protestant . . 64 (*b*) Catholic . . . 67
4. Mythological 69

CHAPTER VI. CHRISTIAN INTERPRETATIONS: FROM MOWINCKEL TO THE PRESENT DAY
1. Autobiographical 72
2. Historico-Messianic 85
3. Historical Individual 89
(*a*) Uzziah . . 89 (*b*) Meshullam . . 89
4. Messianic 90
(*a*) Protestant . . 90 (*b*) Catholic . . . 94
5. Ideal 99
6. Mythological 101
7. Collective 103

PART II. CRITICAL

CHAPTER VII. THE SONGS: TEXT AND TRANSLATION
1. xlii. 1–4 . . . 117 3. l. 4–9 . . . 120
2. xlix. 1–6 . . . 118 4. lii. 13–liii. 12 . . 121
Are any other Passages to be reckoned as 'Songs'? xlix. 7–13; xlii. 5–9; l. 10–11; xlii. 19–21; xlviii. 14–16; li. 4–(6)8; li. 9(12)–16; lxi. 1 ff. 127

CHAPTER VIII. THE SERVANT AS DEPICTED IN THE SONGS
1. xlii. 1–4. Is the Servant a Kingly or a Prophetic Figure? Meanings of *mišpāṭ* and *tôrâh*. Begrich's Interpretation . . 139
2. xlix. 1–6. The Servant's Ministry to Israel—Political or Spiritual? 143
3. l. 4–9 146
4. lii. 13–liii. 12. Did the Servant die? How did he die? Who are the Speakers in liii. 1 ff.? Is the Portrait of the Servant consistent? 147

CHAPTER IX. AUTHORSHIP OF THE SONGS
1. Their Formal Relation to their Contexts. Gressmann's Theory of Independent Short Oracles. Mowinckel's 'Catchword' Theory 156
2. Language of the Songs. xlii. 1–4; xlix. 1–6; l. 4–9; lii. 13–liii. 12. The Problem of the Fourth Song. Elliger's Theory examined 161

3. Style and Metre of the Songs 177
4. Theological Standpoint of the Songs 178
(*a*) Anonymity of the Servant 178
(*b*) Heightened Individualization of the Portrait . . . 180
(*c*) Character of the Servant 181
(*d*) His Active Mission 182
(*e*) Attitude to the Heathen 184
(*f*) Conceptions of Salvation and Atonement . . . 185
Conclusion: The Songs by Deutero-Isaiah; later than Main Prophecy; composed at Intervals 186
Note on the Language of the Secondary Songs: xlii. 5–9; xlix. 7–13; l. 10–11 189

CHAPTER X. CRITICAL SUMMARY AND CONCLUSION
1. Historical–Individual Interpretations 192
(*a*) That the Servant is a known Individual . . . 192
(*b*) Historico-Messianic 194
(*c*) Autobiographical 195
2. Mythological Interpretation 201
3. Collective Interpretation 202
Remnant and Ideal Israel Theories 202
Corporate Personality Theory 204
4. Messianic Interpretation 207
Conclusion 211

POSTSCRIPT 220

LIST OF WORKS CONSULTED 240

INDEX OF AUTHORS 254

INDEX OF SUBJECTS 258

INDEX OF SCRIPTURE PASSAGES 260

PRINCIPAL ABBREVIATIONS EMPLOYED

AT = Alte Testament.

BDB = Brown–Driver–Briggs, *A Hebrew and English Lexicon of the Old Testament*, Oxford, 1907.

BZAW = *Beihefte zur Zeitschrift für die alttestamentliche Wissenschaft*, Giessen.

BZWANT = *Beiträge zur Wissenschaft vom Alten und Neuen Testament*, Stuttgart.

DI = Deutero-Isaiah.

DJ = Deuterojesaja.

DN = Driver and Neubauer, *The Fifty-third Chapter of Isaiah according to the Jewish Interpreters.*

EB = *Études Bibliques*, Paris.

EJ = Ebed-Jahwe.

EJL = Ebed-Jahwe-Lieder.

ET = *Expository Times.*

ET = English Translation.

GK = Gottesknecht.

G-K = Gesenius–Kautzsch, *Hebrew Grammar*, ET Cowley, Oxford, 1910.

JBL = *Journal of Biblical Literature*, Newhaven, Conn.

JTS = *Journal of Theological Studies*, Oxford.

KG = Knecht Gottes.

KJ = Knecht Jahwes.

NKZ = *Neue Kirchliche Zeitschrift*, Erlangen and Leipzig.

RB = *Revue Biblique*, Paris and Rome.

RGG = *Die Religion in Geschichte und Gegenwart.*

TI = Trito-Isaiah.

TJ = Tritojesaja.

TSK = *Theologische Studien und Kritiken*, Stuttgart and Gotha.

ZAW = *Zeitschrift für die alttestamentliche Wissenschaft*, Giessen.

ZNW = *Zeitschrift für die neutestamentliche Wissenschaft*, Giessen.

ZST = *Zeitschrift für systematische Theologie*, Gütersloh.

ZWT = *Zeitschrift für wissenschaftliche Theologie*, Jena, Halle, Leipzig.

In cases of uncertainty, reference should be made to the full Bibliography.

I

INTRODUCTION

THE question which this book attempts to answer is at least as old as the first Christian century, when the Ethiopian eunuch asked the evangelist Philip, 'Of whom speaketh the prophet this? of himself, or of some other?' (Acts viii. 34). The answers that have been given to it are numerous, and bewildering in their variety. The literature on the subject is immense, and Dr. Wheeler Robinson has recorded[1] that 'a well-known commentator is said to have abandoned his projected commentary on Isaiah because this part of his subject overwhelmed him'. It is an open secret that he was referring to Professor S. R. Driver. Even so long ago as the year 1800 the German scholar, J. C. W. Augusti, stated[2] that an annotated bibliography on Isa. liii would make a fair-sized treatise. Since then there has been a continuous stream of books and articles in well-nigh a dozen languages. Since this study is concerned only with the question 'Who was the Servant?', not with the theological significance of the conception, I have not felt it necessary to consult many works earlier than the last quarter of the eighteenth century, when the traditional Messianic interpretation began to be seriously challenged. For the period of undivided opinion only the two or three writers who dissented from the prevailing orthodoxy seem to call for mention. For the opinions of Jewish scholars, scattered as they are over a vast literature, I have relied mainly upon the texts collected and translated by Driver and Neubauer.[3]

Until the close of the eighteenth century Christian writers—with almost the sole exception of Grotius, who thought of Jeremiah—were unanimous that Isa. liii was Messianic prophecy. This was natural enough, since no one then doubted that the passage, even if its exilic background had been perceived, was written by a prophet who lived some two centuries before the exile. The principle that a prophecy must be relevant to the

[1] *The Cross of the Servant*, p. 18.

[2] *Exegetisches Handbuch des ATs*, 7te Stück, p. 153.

[3] See also, more recently, J. J. Brierre-Narbonne, *Le Messie souffrant dans la littérature rabbinique*, 1940; H. A. Fischel, 'Die deuterojesajanischen Gottesknechtlieder in der jüdischen Auslegung', *HUCA* 18, pp. 53–76.

immediate circumstances of those to whom it was addressed was not yet recognized, and the fulfilment of the prophecy could therefore equally well be seven centuries distant as two. But no sooner was there talk of a 'Second-Isaiah', with the inevitable corollary that the chapters were addressed to the circumstances of the Jews in exile, than Christian scholars very naturally began to adopt the view that had long prevailed among the Jews, namely, that the Servant was the nation Israel. This collective theory, in one form or another, held the field until 1892, when Duhm published his commentary on Isaiah, in which he argued that the Servant 'Songs', as he called them, were not the work of the Second Isaiah, and that the figure portrayed in them was an historical individual. No one, so far as I know, has ever adopted Duhm's 'leprous rabbi' theory; but ever since he wrote, scholarship, particularly in Germany, has tended to move away from the collective to some form or other of individual interpretation.

Many candidates for the title of Servant have been put forward, among them, in the last fifty years, Zerubbabel, Meshullam the son of Zerubbabel, Sheshbazzar, Jehoiachin, Moses, Uzziah, Ezekiel, Eleazar—a martyr in the time of the Maccabees, and even Cyrus. Most of these theories have either been abandoned by, or have died with, their authors. In 1921 the Norwegian scholar, Sigmund Mowinckel, published a brochure which has been almost as influential upon the discussion as Duhm's Commentary. Let us cease, he said, to play blindman's buff among all the known and unknown figures of the exilic and post-exilic periods, and recognize that the answer to the enigma is implicit in the question of the Ethiopian eunuch. Of whom should the Prophet be speaking if not of himself? The suggestion was at once hailed by a number of famous scholars, all of them German, and including the redoubtable Ernst Sellin, who had already three times, and each time finally, settled the problem by proposing in turn Zerubbabel, Jehoiachin, and Moses. In 1931, ten years after he had made it, Mowinckel abandoned his own theory because it had committed him to the extremely hazardous assumption that the Prophet wrote the account of his own death. To conclude this brief initial summary, during the last century and a half the Messianic interpretation has never been without advocacy, whether by Catholic or Protestant, fundamentalist or critic.

And, as we might expect, there are not wanting those who have seen in the Servant a figure akin to Tammuz, a refinement of the myth of the dying and rising god.

To-day only four of these theories still hold the field. They are:

1. That the Servant was an anonymous contemporary of the Second Isaiah, a man who, the Prophet believed, was destined to be the Messiah. This solution, which may be termed historico-messianic, was first proposed by Rudolf Kittel, and elaborated by Wilhelm Rudolph, in Germany, and is represented in this country by Dr. W. O. E. Oesterley.

2. That the Servant was the Prophet himself. We may call this for convenience the autobiographical theory. It is true that Mowinckel, who originated it, no longer believes that the last Song was composed by the Prophet. Indeed, he now denies that any of the Songs is by the Prophet, and in so far as he has any positive opinion about the identity of the Servant it is only that the figure described in Isa. liii is a 'cult-hero delineated with mythological colouring', possibly reminiscent of the presumably martyred Deutero-Isaiah. Nevertheless, in 1938 Joachim Begrich, of Leipzig, published a volume of studies in Deutero-Isaiah, in which he so far revived Mowinckel's original thesis, that he regarded the Servant as the Prophet, and the Prophet as the author of all the Songs. But the most confident exposition of the autobiographical theory is that of Sellin, elaborated by Karl Elliger. These two scholars think that the last Song was written by Trito-Isaiah, the disciple of Deutero-Isaiah, as a threnody upon his martyred master.

3. The collective theory. This is the theory still most widely held in this country, largely owing to the powerful advocacy of it by the late Dr. Peake and by Dr. Wheeler Robinson, and to the fact that our three commentaries on Isaiah, the Cambridge, the Century, and the Westminster, all present it, though in different forms. The theory, indeed, has taken many forms, empirical Israel, ideal Israel, the pious remnant of the true Israel, the order of prophets, together with combinations of these elements in different proportions. The most recent, as well as the most attractive, form of the theory is that associated with the names of Dr. H. Wheeler Robinson and Professor Otto Eissfeldt of Halle, whose views, published independently, are nevertheless strikingly similar. In their restatement of the

collective theory they lay great stress upon the ancient idea of corporate personality. The concept of corporate personality was appealed to in support of the collective interpretation as long ago as 1794 by Schuster; but Wheeler Robinson and Eissfeldt give it a new cogency in the light especially of the researches of the French socio-anthropological school of writers.

4. The Messianic theory. This is to be distinguished from theories that would make the Servant a purely ideal or imaginary figure, the product of a deep concern about the problem of unmerited suffering. Such a solution has, indeed, albeit somewhat hesitantly, been proposed in recent years, though it seems strangely remote from the historical realism of the ancient Hebrews. Somewhat related to the ideal theory is Gressmann's exposition of the Messianic theory, which stands outside the main stream of what is still, speaking generally, conservative Christian tradition. Gressmann thought that the true original of the Servant was King Josiah, who was slain at Megiddo. The Servant was thus, with some accretions, largely mythological, a kind of Josiah redivivus. There is nothing to indicate that Gressmann was in the least concerned that such an expectation was obviously never fulfilled. There was for him nothing ultimate or final about the portrait of the Servant in Isa. liii. It was but one of a series of developing conceptions, and it did not do more than permanently incorporate thoughts of sacrifice and martyrdom into the conception of the Messiah. The great majority of defenders of the Messianic interpretation have been conservative in their theological outlook. Catholic writers, with but one or two exceptions,[1] have held firmly to the traditional interpretation. For a century after the rise of criticism the defenders of the Messianic theory were almost, if not quite, without exception fundamentalists, whether Catholic or Protestant. During the past fifty years, however, a number of works have appeared advocating a Messianic interpretation, while at the same time often frankly admitting that the writer of the Servant passages lived during the exile. Most of them, though

[1] I know of only the late Fr. Eric Burrows (*The Gospel of the Infancy and other Essays*, pp. 59–80), and two writers mentioned by Fischer (*Isaias 40–55 und die Perikopen vom GK*, p. 16 f.) whose works I have not seen. They are S. Minocchi (*Le profezie d'Isaia*, Bologna, 1907), whose position seems similar to that of Duhm, and K. Holzhey (*Kurzgefasstes Lehrbuch der speziellen Einleitung in das AT*, Paderborn, 1912, p. 150 f.), who thought it possible that the Prophet saw in the Servant a type of the suffering righteous man and of the people in its ideal calling.

not all, have sought to prove that the Servant of the Songs is none other than the Davidic Messiah of Isa. ix and xi. This is to run the risk of over-emphasizing the political features in the portrait, and the protagonists for the Messianic interpretation would seem to be on safer ground if they admit that the Servant of Isa. liii differs as much from the traditional political Messiah of Isa. ix and xi as Jesus subsequently did. It is generally agreed that the Messianic consciousness of Jesus combined elements from two different sources, the Messianic Son, and the Suffering Servant, and that the voice that He heard at His Baptism, 'Thou art my beloved Son, in thee I am well pleased' (Mark i. 11), was a conflation of the 'Thou art my son' of Ps. ii. 7, which by His time had come to be interpreted Messianically, and the 'In whom my soul delighteth' of the first Servant-Song (Isa. xlii. 1).

This outline of the history and present state of the discussion is given in the hope that the reader may be better able to take and keep his bearings in the more detailed description that follows.

PART I

HISTORICAL

II

JEWISH INTERPRETATIONS

I. IN PRE-CHRISTIAN TIMES

REFERENCES to the Servant passages in pre-Christian Jewish literature are few, and sometimes obscure. The following is a summary of those that have been alleged:

(*a*) *In the Old Testament itself*

It is probable[1] that xlii. 6*b* and xlix. 8*bα*, 'And I form thee, and make thee to be a covenant-bond of the people (a light to the nations)', are later insertions into their contexts, and that they were intended to change what were originally passages about Israel into passages about the Servant. This surmise, if correct, does not prove that the glossator thought the Servant was an individual, but it makes it very probable. Much the same conclusion follows from l. 10 f., which is generally regarded as a later expansion of the Song to which it is appended. Further, since lxi. 1 ff. undoubtedly refers to an individual, and is probably reminiscent of the Songs, the conclusion is almost inescapable that its author understood the Servant to be an individual.

It is possible that the description of the Messianic King in Zech. ix. 9 is reminiscent of the Servant in Isa. liii. He is said to be 'righteous' (*ṣaddîq*, cf. liii. 11, though the text there is probably corrupt), and 'lowly' (*'ānî*, cf. *na'ᵃnēh*, 'afflicted', liii. 7). But, as Vincent Taylor[2] points out, 'the inference is far from being certain, and in no sense is the King a vicarious sufferer'. Nor can anything be based upon the rather remote verbal similarity between Zech. xii. 10—where the Hebrew word for 'pierced' is *dāqārû*—and the *mᵉḥôlāl*, 'pierced', of liii. 5. Correspondences between Ps. xxii and Isa. liii are too general to justify any inference.

The words of Dan. xii. 3: 'And they that be wise (*ham-maśkî-*

[1] See *infra*, pp. 130, 134.

[2] *Jesus and His Sacrifice*, p. 44.

lîm, cf. *yaśkîl*, lii. 13) shall shine as the brightness of the firmament; and they that turn many to righteousness (*maṣdîqê hā-rabbîm*, cf. *yaṣdîq . . . lā-rabbîm*, liii. 11) as the stars for ever and ever' (cf. Dan. xi. 33 ff.), can hardly be accounted for by literary reminiscence. So close is the correspondence that some medieval Jewish writers[1] concluded that the Servant was the 'wise' men (*maśkîlîm*), evidently assuming Dan. xii. 3 to be a deliberate attempt at interpretation. This it may well have been, and there is a fair amount of evidence[2] that before the rise to prominence of the Messianic interpretation the Servant was identified with the community of the righteous. This was the view of Dalman: 'The *maṣdîqê hā-rabbîm* are certainly to be considered as the concrete manifestation of the Servant of God in Isa. liii. . . . Isa. liii was then understood of the fate of those who were teachers of the law in the time of violent opposition preceding the end of things.'[3]

(*b*) *In the Apocrypha and Pseudepigrapha*

In the Greek text of Ecclus. xlviii. 10 we read of Elijah that he was 'to turn the heart of the father unto the son (Heb. "fathers . . . sons") and to restore (Heb. "give understanding to") the tribes of Israel'. This is clearly a conflation of Mal. iii. 24 (EV iv. 6) and Isa. xlix. 6. But it would be hazardous to conclude from it that Ben Sira thought of the Servant as an individual, still less as a Messianic figure. The language may have been dictated simply by literary reminiscence. In any case there is nothing to indicate that Ben Sira thought of Elijah in connexion with Isa. lii–liii.

The similarities between the descriptions of the Servant in Isaiah and the Son of Man in the Parables of Enoch are certainly more than verbal. Thus the Son of Man is the Elect One (Enoch xl. 5, xlv. 3, xlvi. 3, xlix. 2, &c., cf. Isa. xlii. 1), the Righteous One (Enoch xxxviii. 2, xlvi. 3, cf. *ṣaddîq*, Isa. liii. 11), the light of the Gentiles (Enoch xlviii. 4, cf. Isa. xlii. 6, xlix. 6). With Isa. xlix. 2 we may compare 'For from the beginning the Son of Man was hidden, and the Most High preserved him in the presence of His might, and revealed him to the elect' (Enoch lxii. 7), and 'For this reason hath he been chosen and hidden before Him, before the creation of the world

[1] See *infra*, p. 10. [2] See *infra*, p. 9.
[3] *Der leidende und der sterbende Messias*, p. 31.

and for evermore' (Enoch xlviii. 6). Further, 'This Son of Man whom thou hast seen shall raise up the kings and the mighty from their seats' (Enoch xlvi. 4), and 'There shall stand up in that day all the kings and the mighty, and the exalted and those who hold the earth, and they shall see and recognize how he sits on the throne of his glory' (Enoch lxii. 3, cf. Isa. lii. 15, xlix. 7). These passages are so interspersed with others reminiscent of the Messianic oracles in Isa. ix and xi, that it seems clear that the author of the 'Parables' identified the Servant with the Messianic Son of Man. At the same time it is doubtful whether he fully realized the implications of the identification, since there is nowhere any hint that the Son of Man is to suffer.

That the writer of the Wisdom of Solomon was familiar with Isa. xl–lxvi needs no proof, and his description of the sufferings of the righteous man in v. 1–7 reads like a paraphrase of Isa. lii. 15–liii. 6. The righteous man is called *παῖς κυρίου* in ii. 13, *υἱὸς θεοῦ* in ii. 18, the two terms being apparently interchangeable (cf. ix. 4, 7 and xii. 19 f.). Since *παῖς* is used in the LXX to translate the Heb. *'ebed* (Isa. xlii. 1, lii. 13, &c.), it may be that the author of Wisdom identified the Servant with the (community of the) righteous. But there the similarity ends. There is no suggestion in Wisdom that the righteous suffer for or on behalf of others. The ungodly are troubled with terrible fear, and acknowledge their error. For the rest, the righteous have been tried and found worthy, and their souls are in the hand of God (Wisd. iii. 1–6).

(*c*) *In the Septuagint*

The LXX[1] interpreted xlii. 1 of Jacob-Israel, and in xlix. 3 it read 'Israel' with the MT. There is nothing to indicate decisively whether it understood the Servant in lii. 13–liii. 12 to be Israel or an individual; but Euler,[2] after a minute examination of the passage in the LXX, has argued that an individual martyr is depicted who is indeed none other than Isaiah himself. Dalman[3] thought that the LXX interpreted it of the righteous man, as did the Book of Wisdom.

[1] Cf. Zillessen, 'Jes. 52, 13–53, 12 hebräisch nach LXX', *ZAW* 25, pp. 261–84.
[2] *Die Verkündigung vom leidenden GK aus Jes. 53 in der griechischen Bibel.*
[3] Op. cit., p. 32.

(*d*) *In the New Testament*

The words of the *Nunc Dimittis* quite clearly have the Songs of the Servant in mind (Luke ii. 29–32, cf. Isa. xlix. 6), and interpret them of the coming Messiah. It may be argued that they are of Christian, not Jewish, provenance, though it is difficult to believe that the intensely Jewish poems in the first two chapters of St. Luke can have been composed by a Gentile evangelist. A similar question may be asked, whether the words of John the Baptist, 'Behold, the Lamb of God, which taketh away the sin of the world' (John i. 29), have been coloured by the thought of the evangelist. As they stand they appear clearly to have in mind Isa. liii. 4, 11.

2. SINCE THE BEGINNING OF THE CHRISTIAN ERA

(*a*) *The Servant is the Righteous*

In the early Christian era, before the Messianic interpretation became general, the Servant was sometimes identified with the righteous, along the lines of Dan. xii. 3 and the Wisdom of Solomon. A typical passage is:

'Rab Huna (d. 297) said, When God has pleasure in a man, He bruises him with chastisements, as it is said, It pleased the Lord to bruise him, &c. (Isa. liii. 10). But what if that man does not accept the chastisements willingly? Then the Scripture teaches, If his soul brings a guilt-offering: as a guilt-offering is to be brought with the understanding and the will, so also are chastisements to be accepted with the understanding and the will. If he so accepts them, what shall be his reward? He shall see seed, prolong days; and not only so, but what he has gained from experience shall endure in his hand, as it is said, The pleasure of the Lord shall prosper in his hand.'[1]

Sometimes individual righteous men were singled out for special mention. Especially have there been from time to time those who have interpreted the concluding verse or verses of chap. liii of Moses,[2] though none has ever affirmed that the whole passage relates to him. In the Jerusalem Talmud (*Sheqalim*, v. 1) it is stated that Rabbi Jonah said: 'It is written, "I will allot him a portion with the many": this refers to Rabbi Akiba, who introduced the study of the *Midrash*, the *Halakhoth*, and the

[1] Strack-Billerbeck, i, p. 484.
[2] See DN, *passim*; Strack-Billerbeck, i, p. 483 f.

Haggadoth.'[1] This, presumably, can only have been intended for edification, as if to say that Akiba was such a one as the Servant. The same applies to the reference to Phinehas in *Siphre* Num. xxv. 13, based upon the similarity of the verse to Isa. liii. 10–12.[2]

After the Messianic interpretation became general, there were writers who continued to think of the Servant as the righteous; even later, when the collective and righteous Israel theories gained the ascendancy, there were still those who saw in the Servant the righteous, without any stated relation to the nation Israel as such. Thus, Jacob ben Reuben (Qaraite, 12 c.),[3] Eliezer of Beaujenci,[4] and Aaron ben Joseph (Qaraite)[5] concluded from Dan. xii. 3[6] that the Servant was 'the wise'. According to Jephet ibn 'Ali 'some of the learned Qaraites apply the prophecy to the pious of their own sect, resting their view upon two arguments: in the first place, because their history answers to the descriptions given in this section; and secondly, because of the word *lamô*, which is plural'.[7] Solomon Levi (Salonica, 1600), after lamenting that the commentators are at no small variance, confesses that

'the thirst of my desire has not been satisfied with what the net of my speculation has brought up for me out of the springs which extend themselves at the foundations of their writings. . . . To me the object of the prophet seems to be to describe in general the varied forms of suffering to which the righteous are exposed, and, after having done this, to exhibit to us in particular how they all ultimately result in the greater perfection of the sufferer.'[8]

In the 'humble opinion' of Samuel Lanyado, 'the parashah must be supposed to describe the righteous worshipper of God'.[9] A still more universalistic, not to say mystico-theosophical, note is struck in a passage which Driver-Neubauer[10] gives as 'from the *Midrash Ne'lam*, according to the *Yalkut Rubeni* (Wilhermsdorf, 1681)': it reads:

'Who is it that carried our sicknesses and bare our pains? Man himself, who first brought death into the world. Now learn what is secret from that which is revealed: Because he carried our sicknesses

[1] DN, p. 7.
[2] Strack-Billerbeck, i, p. 483.
[3] See DN, pp. 61 ff.
[4] Ibid., p. 66.
[5] Ibid., p. 86.
[6] See *supra*, p. 6 f.
[7] DN, p. 19.
[8] Ibid., p. 275.
[9] Ibid., p. 304.
[10] p. xvii.

—for man himself by the rotation (of souls, i.e. in accordance with the doctrine of transmigration) is Adam, David, and the Messiah—therefore he suffered in order to atone for the sin of our first parent who brought death into the world.'[1]

(*b*) *Messianic Interpretation*

The earliest witness to the Messianic interpretation of Isa. liii after the beginning of the Christian era is perhaps the Targum of Jonathan ben Uzziel. The date of this cannot be exactly determined. Jonathan himself lived in the first century B.C., but, since some portions of the Targum are in the Talmud assigned to Joseph ben Chija (*c.* A.D. 300), the text now extant is presumably the result of an editorial process. Since, however, the Targum identifies the Servant with the Messiah, it seems likely that its main content must go back to the early Christian era, since the Jews would hardly have begun to interpret the passage of the Messiah—even in the qualified manner of the Targum—after the Christians had already claimed it for Christ.[2]

The Targum identifies the Servant in xlii. 1 with the Messiah; similarly xliii. 10. A Messianic interpretation of xlix. 1 ff. was excluded by the 'Israel' of ver. 3. In l. 4 ff. the Servant is the Prophet himself. In lii. 13 he is expressly identified with the Messiah—'Behold, my Servant the Messiah shall prosper.' That the Targum understood the whole of lii. 13–liii. 12 to relate to the Messiah seems clear. But, by what seems to us a strange exegetical perversity, all the sufferings are transferred elsewhere. Aytoun[3] would except one clause in ver. 12, which he translates: 'Therefore will I divide for him the spoil of many nations. And the goods of the strong cities will he divide as plunder, *because he delivered up his soul to death* and brought rebels into subjection to the Law, and he will make supplication for many sins and rebels will be forgiven for his sake.' But Dalman[4] and Seidelin[5] make out a strong case for taking the italicized words as meaning, in Aramaic idiom, 'Because he exposed himself to the risk of death.' This, too, is antecedently more probable than that the Targum, in what is evidently a carefully

[1] Ibid., p. 396.

[2] Cf. Aytoun, 'The Servant of the Lord in the Targum', *JTS* 23, pp. 172–80; Seidelin, 'Der 'Ebed Jahwe und die Messiasgestalt im Jesajatargum', *ZNW* 35, pp. 194–231.

[3] Op. cit., p. 177.

[4] *Der leidende . . . Messias*, p. 48 f.

[5] Op. cit., p. 215.

wrought composition, was guilty of inconsistency or oversight. The first clause in liii. 3 is best rendered: 'Then he will be despised.' This is quite in accord with Jewish expectations that the Messiah, on his first appearance, would be met with hostility. Apart from this, no sufferings are predicated of the Messiah, and the picture presented of him is entirely consistent with what was usual in the messianology of the Talmudic era. The sufferings of the Servant are distributed elsewhere. They fall mainly upon Israel; sometimes upon the Gentiles—e.g. 'The mighty of the peoples he will deliver up as a lamb to the slaughter, and as a ewe that before her shearers is dumb' (liii. 7); or upon the wicked generally—'And he shall deliver up the wicked to Gehenna, and the oppressors that are rich in possessions to mortal perdition, so that those who commit sin may not be preserved, nor speak deceits with their mouth' (liii. 9).

Even after the doctrine of a suffering Messiah had found acceptance among the Jews, there were still those who interpreted the passage along the lines of Targum Jonathan. Thus Jephet ibn 'Ali (10 c.) says that some of the Qaraites 'think the subject of it to be David and the Messiah, saying that all the expressions of contempt, such as "many were desolated at thee", refer to the seed of David who are in exile; and all the glorious things, such as "behold my servant will be prosperous" and "so shall he sprinkle", refer to the Messiah'.[1] Jephet, himself a Messianist, wrote on liii. 9: 'This means that he sometimes despaired so much of his life as either to dig for himself a grave amongst the wicked, or at least desire to be buried amongst them. The general sense is that he resigned himself to die in exile.'[2] Moses ben Nahman (13 c.), while otherwise consistent, had it that the Messiah only *expected* to die.[3] Similarly, Moses Kohen ibn Crispin could not bring himself to apply liii. 9 to the Messiah.[4] Another way out of the difficulty was to say that the Servant was both the Messiah and the people as a whole. Thus Solomon Astruc (14 c.) argued that when the Prophet 'speaks of the people, the King Messiah is included in it; and when he speaks of the King Messiah, the people is comprehended with him'.[5] In this way liii. 9 declares 'how the people of the King Messiah were buried in the same place with the wicked'.[6] Moses el-Shaikh (16 c.) announces that he in-

[1] DN, p. 19. [2] Ibid., p. 27. [3] Ibid., p. 84.
[4] Ibid., p. 111. [5] Ibid., p. 139. [6] Ibid., p. 134.

tends, with the rabbis, to interpret the passage of the Messiah.[1] But when it comes to the sufferings of chap. liii he observes, somewhat ambiguously,

'From the fact of the Rabbis expounding the previous verses of the Messiah, it may be seen that these speak of the righteous who endures in the present world the chastisements of love; and therefore I maintain that up to this point we have had the words of God announcing the greatness of the Messiah in return for his sufferings, and designed to set forth the exalted dignity of him by whom these chastisements were borne.'[2]

Whether by the 'righteous' he means the Messiah is not clear—probably not. Finally, he interprets liii. 9–12 of Moses. Naphtali ben Asher Altschuler, after expressing surprise that Rashi and Kimchi did not explain the paragraph of the Messiah, nevertheless interprets nearly all chap. liii of the sufferings of Israel, and attempts to cover up his confusion by saying that 'the prophet uses the singular, referring to the Messiah who is their king: thus the Messiah is termed "despised" as representing Israel'.[3] As recently as 1791, Joshua Segre maintained that the division between chaps. lii and liii ought to be preserved, that lii referred to the Messiah, and liii to Israel.[4] Finally, Herz Homberg, in the *Korem* (Vienna, 1818),[5] said that the enemies of the Messiah 'will not actually kill him . . . but . . . will devise to do so, and will *decree* that he is to have his grave with the wicked: God will deliver him, and not leave him in their power: *nigzar* (ver. 8) thus signifies *was decreed*, as Esth. ii. 1'.

It is often supposed that the interpretation of Targum Jonathan is unique, that in the Middle Ages the Messianic interpretation was either abandoned altogether, or rigorously applied. The truth is that there is not a single full-length exposition on Messianic lines in which the principle embodied in the Targum is not in some degree adhered to. Without exception the commentators begin to equivocate when they come to the words 'They made his grave with the wicked'. While the Jews allowed that the Messiah, son of David, would suffer, it was no part of their expectation that his sufferings would end in a violent death. They were the more easily able to gloss over liii. 9, and so make the Messiah-Servant fit into their general

[1] Ibid., p. 258. [2] Ibid., p. 263 f. [3] Ibid., pp. 318–23.
[4] Ibid., pp. 360 ff. [5] Quoted in ibid., pp. 400–5.

conception of the Messiah, because vv. 10–12 do not speak unambiguously of a resurrection of the Servant.

There are, of course, a number of shorter passages in which the Servant is said to be the Messiah, beginning with the Talmud and early Midrashim, but continuing sporadically even down to synagogue rites at the present day.[1] Most of them are homiletical, and it is questionable whether their authors would have been any more consistent than the Targum if they had set out to write a full commentary on Isa. lii–liii. The following are fairly typical: the Midrash Rabbah, writing on Ruth ii. 14, says, 'He is speaking of the King Messiah: "Come hither", draw near to the throne; "and eat of the bread", that is the bread of the kingdom; "and dip thy morsel in the vinegar", this refers to the chastisements, as it is said, "But he was wounded for our transgressions, bruised for our iniquities".'[2] Or this, from the *Pesiqta*:[3] 'The Holy One brought forth the soul of the Messiah, and said to him, "Art thou willing to be created and to redeem my sons after 6,000 years?" He replied, "I am". God replied, "If so, thou must take upon thyself chastisements in order to wipe away their iniquity", as it is written, "Surely our sicknesses he hath carried". The Messiah answered, "I will take them upon me gladly".' The most famous passage is one from the Talmud:[4] 'The Messiah —what is his name? . . . The rabbis say, The leprous one; those of the house of Rabbi (Judah han-Nasi) say, The sick one, as it is said, Surely he hath borne our sicknesses, &c.'

Many of the medieval commentators, whatever their own views might be, began their expositions of lii. 13 by quoting the Midrash to the effect that it refers to the Messiah, who will be 'higher than Abraham, more exalted than Moses, and loftier than the ministering angels'. They had great reverence for the opinions of the fathers, but they sometimes felt constrained to explain them away. The commonest way of doing this was to say that the equation of the Servant with the Messiah was only intended as allegory. This is argued at some length by Abarbanel:

'In a word, the interpretation of Jonathan, and of those who follow

[1] Cf. Wünsche, *Die Leiden des Messias*; Dalman, *Jes. 53*, 2 Aufl.; Strack-Billerbeck, i, pp. 481 ff.; also DN.

[2] DN, p. 9.

[3] Wünsche, op. cit., p. 68 f.; DN, p. 11.

[4] *Sanhedrin*, Edit. Venet., fol. 98*b*, quoted by DN, p. 7; Wünsche, op. cit., p. 63.

him in the same opinion, can never be considered to be the true one, in a literal sense, because the character and drift of the passage as a whole will not bear it: these learned men were only concerned with allegorical or adventitious expositions, and hence merely applied the traditions they had received respecting the Messiah to the present passage, without in the least imagining such to be its actual meaning';[1]

similarly Samuel Lanyado.[2] Abarbanel and Lanyado were not just trying to extricate themselves from a difficult position. There is a good deal of truth in their contention. There are features in the passage which accord ill with Jewish conceptions of the Messiah. Moreover, the writers of Talmud and Midrash had little idea of the unity of the paragraph; they would, when engaged in haggadic edification, illustrate anything from any- and everywhere.

The question may naturally be asked, Was the Messiah with whom the Servant was identified perchance the so-called Messiah son of Joseph (or Ephraim)? When and how the conception of the two Messiahs originated is obscure. It appears in the Babylonian Talmud, and its beginnings may date from about the end of the second century A.D. Briefly, Messiah ben Joseph was expected to appear before Messiah ben David. He would rally the children of Israel, march to Jerusalem, and, after overcoming the hostile powers, re-establish the Temple-worship. Later he would be slain in battle with the hosts of 'Armilus', or, as other texts have it, of Gog and Magog. Finally, Messiah ben David would come and resurrect him.[3]

It might seem obvious that those Jews who thought the Servant was the Messiah would further identify him with Messiah ben Joseph. He was slain. What else was wanting? Simply this, as Dalman[4] and Klausner[5] point out, that the Messiah ben Joseph was a purely political figure, a *Kriegsmessias*, whose death had no atoning significance. Nor do the texts, taken as a whole, bear out the supposition that the Messiah of Isa. lii–liii was thought to be ben Joseph. The subject was obscure even to the Jews themselves. Thus Abarbanel observed: 'I do not

[1] DN, p. 163. [2] Ibid., p. 300.

[3] Cf. *Jewish Encyclopaedia*, viii, p. 511 f.; Dalman, *Der leidende . . . Messias*, pp. 1–26; Klausner, *Die mess. Vorstellungen des jüd. Volkes im Zeitalter der Tannaiten*, ch. ix; Lagrange, *Le Messianisme chez les Juifs*, pp. 251–6; Brièrre-Narbonne, op. cit., part i, section i, chap. 2 *et passim*.

[4] Op. cit., p. 9 f., 23. [5] Op. cit., pp. 86–97.

know whether . . . they mean Messiah the son of Joseph . . . or whether they intend Messiah the son of David.'[1] Similarly Lanyado: 'We do not gather clearly from their language whether they are speaking of Messiah son of Ephraim, or of Messiah son of David,'[2] and he supposes that they must intend to refer lii. 13 to ben David, and much of the rest of the passage to ben Ephraim.[3] Naphtali ben Asher Altschuler, who apparently referred lii. 13–15 to the Messiah ben David, and most of liii to Israel, nevertheless interjects at liii. 4 a note that the prophet means to speak here of ben Joseph.[4] A passage in the cabbalistic *Asereth Memroth* of Menahem Azariah (17 c.) concludes from the fact that the Messiah makes his soul an *'āšām* (guilt-offering, liii. 10) that he must be Menahem ben 'Ammiel —one of the many names of Messiah ben Joseph.[5] The ground for this astonishing assumption is that the numerical values of the consonants in *'āšām* and *Menahem ben 'Ammiel* are the same, namely, 341! Dalman[6] quotes from the late (ninth-century?) Midrash *Pesiqta Rabbathi* passages in which sufferings similar to those of the Servant in Isa. liii are to be borne by 'Ephraim my righteous Messiah'. From this it has sometimes, quite naturally, been assumed that the Messiah-Servant was Messiah ben Joseph. But Dalman[7] points out that elsewhere in the *Pesiqta* 'Ephraim' is called 'Son of David', that 'Ephraim is for the *Pesiqta* the sole and final real saviour of Israel, and therefore the Son of David', and, finally, that the Messiah ben Ephraim is never called Ephraim simply. It may be that the original warrior-vocation of the Messiah ben Joseph could, in late mystical speculation, like that of the *Asereth Memroth*, become modified to embrace something more soteriological. So many eccentricities are associated with the Ephraimite Messiah that one need not be surprised at anything that was said of him. Even so, any passages that may seem to identify the Servant of Isa. liii with the Messiah ben Joseph are late, and outside the main stream of orthodox tradition. A passage from the *Book of Secrets* (? thirteenth century) mentions both Messiahs, and defi-

[1] DN, p. 162. [2] Ibid., p. 300. [3] Ibid., pp. 301 ff.

[4] Ibid., p. 321.

[5] Ibid., p. 394 f.; Dalman, *Jes. 53*, p. 9.

[6] *Der leidende . . . Messias*, pp. 52–64; *Jes. 53*, pp. 3–6.

[7] *Messias*, p. 59. Similarly Brierre-Narbonne (op. cit., p. 41) says that in the *Pesiqta* there is only one Messiah, and that in one place he (Ephraim) 'is even called Son of David'.

nitely relates the Servant to the Messiah ben David.[1] This, despite occasional vagaries, must be considered to have been the usual opinion among those who interpreted Isa. liii of the Messiah. To sum up: the Messiah ben David suffers, but does not die; the Messiah ben Joseph is slain, but no preceding sufferings are related of him. During the first Christian millennium the Messiah-Servant is always ben David, but Isa. liii. 9 was never interpreted of his death. Later, and then only in cabbalistic speculation, the Servant was occasionally associated with the Messiah ben Joseph.[2]

(*c*) *Collective Interpretation*

The earliest witness to the collective interpretation among the Jews is to be found in the famous passage in Origen *Contra Celsum*, Book I, chap. 55:

'Now I remember that on one occasion at a disputation held with certain Jews, who were reckoned wise men, I quoted these prophecies (viz. Isa. lii–liii). To which my Jewish opponent replied that these predictions bore reference to the whole people regarded as one individual as being in a state of dispersion and suffering, in order that many proselytes might be gained, on account of the dispersion of the Jews among numerous heathen nations. And this is the way he explained the words "Thy form shall be of no reputation among men" and "a man under suffering". Many arguments were employed on that occasion during the discussion to prove that these predictions regarding one particular person were not rightly applied by them to the whole nation. And I asked to what character the expression would be appropriate, "this man bears our sins and suffers pain on our behalf", etc. But we seemed to press them hardest with the expression, "Because of the iniquities of *my people* was he led away to death".'[3]

There is little further evidence for the collective interpretation until we come to the great medieval commentators, beyond an occasional haggadah like that in the *Midrash Rabbah* which interprets 'I have eaten my honeycomb (Heb. *ya'ar*) with my honey' (Song v. 1): 'because the Israelites poured out (*hε'εrâ*) their soul to die in the captivity, as it is said, Because he poured

[1] DN, p. 32; Levy, *Deutero-Isaiah*, p. 106.

[2] The suggestion of Marmorstein, 'Zur Erklärung von Jes. 53', *ZAW* 44, pp. 260–5, that the Messiah ben Joseph speculations grew out of Isa. liii, does not seem to be borne out by the evidence.

[3] Translation in Aytoun, op. cit., p. 173.

out his soul to die'.[1] Such a play upon words is not evidence that the Midrash would have expounded the whole of Isa. lii. 13–liii. 12 of Israel, any more than similar haggadoth which expounded odd verses of the Messiah necessitated a thoroughgoing Messianic interpretation.

Since the twelfth century the collective interpretation has been usual. The best-known names are those of Rashi (d. 1105), Ibn Ezra, Joseph and David Kimchi, Jacob ben Reuben the Rabbanite (12 c.), Joseph ben Nathan (Sens, 13 c.), Isaiah ben Mali (13 c.), Shem Tob ben Shaprut (Toledo, 14 c.), Abarbanel (d. 1508), Abraham Farissol (Avignon, 1503), Isaac Troki (Qaraite, 1593), Abraham of Cordova (Proselyte, *c.* 1600), Isaac Orobio de Castro (17 c.).[2]

It is often thought that the Jews abandoned the Messianic in favour of the collective interpretation as a means of defence against the Christians. To admit that the Servant was the Messiah was to lay themselves the more open to the assaults of Christian propaganda. There may be something in this. Certain it is that their exposition of the collective theory has, ever since Origen's time, been associated with polemics against Christianity, e.g. in Ibn Ezra, David Kimchi, Abarbanel, and Orobio. It is not, perhaps, without significance that the most biting attack upon the Christian Messianic interpretation comes from the proselyte Abraham of Cordova, who wrote of 'the craft and guile of the lying Hieronymus, who, in his version, so misused his inkpot as to trample on the word *lāmô*' (liii. 8—referring to the plural form of the word). At the same time it should be recognized that with Rashi we enter upon a period of more literal and scientific, as opposed to 'allegorical and adventitious' expositions, together with a fuller recognition of the principle of the unity of the paragraph and its relation to its context. If we set Isa. lii–liii against the background of Jewish, as distinct from Christian, Messianic doctrine on the one hand, and the Old Testament concept of corporate personality on the other, it need occasion no surprise that Jewish opinion, put on its guard and made self-conscious by Christianity, came to rest where it did. The way in which, since the rise of criticism, even Christian interpretation has gone over to the collective theory, is sufficient testimony to the essential soundness of the collective theory, at any rate from the Jewish

[1] DN, p. 9.

[2] See DN, *passim*.

standpoint. It will not do, then, to say that the abandonment of the Messianic interpretation was due to mere opportunism, especially since, as we have seen, Judaism has never been able to apply the Messianic interpretation with absolute and uncompromising rigour.

In one important particular the Jewish exposition of the collective theory differs from that subsequently adopted by Christians: the captivity in which the Servant is taken is not the Babylonian captivity of the sixth century B.C., but the wide dispersion and persecution of the Jews up to and including the times in which the several rabbis happened to be living. It was common to argue from the plural forms *lāmô* (lit. 'for them', liii. 8) and *b^{e}môṯâw* (lit. 'in his deaths', liii. 9) that the Servant must comprise more than a single individual. Thus Jephet ibn 'Ali already records this as a contention of some of the Qaraites of his own time.[1] David Kimchi said that the phrase 'in his deaths' was 'employed because they used to be put to death in many ways: some were burnt, some were slain, and others were stoned'.[2] Lippmann (15 c.) remarked that 'a single man cannot die more than once'.[3] Abarbanel's comment is that *lamô* is 'in order to render it clear that the individual mentioned throughout is not some isolated man, but the whole nation collectively'.[4] Abraham of Cordova's accusation of dishonesty against Jerome has already been mentioned.[5] The fact is, of course, that the plurals are unintelligible in their context, that to attempt to reproduce them in a translation would only add to the obscurity, and that both words are almost certainly corrupt. In the early days of the Christian advocacy of the collective theory it was likewise not uncommon for stress to be laid upon *lāmô* and *b^{e}môṯâw*.[6] Later, it came to be recognized that this was forced and unnatural, or, alternatively, that the text should be emended; but as recently as 1883 Feilchenfeld,[7] rabbi of the synagogue community in Posen, argued along traditional Jewish lines, and even maintained that the words 'pierced through' (*m^{e}ḥôlāl*) and 'crushed' (*m^{e}ḏukkā'*) cannot both refer to one individual.

The righteous remnant of Israel theory has a lineage as old as the collective theory itself, if we accept the testimony in

[1] Ibid., p. 19.
[2] Ibid., p. 53.
[3] Ibid., p. 149.
[4] Ibid., p. 180.
[5] *Supra*, p. 18.
[6] See *infra*, pp. 30, 36 f.
[7] *Das stellvertretende Sühneleiden.*

Origen. It goes back even to Rashi, who interpreted lii. 13 of 'My Servant Jacob, that is the righteous who are in him'. Ibn Ezra has a similar note, but says that 'Israel as a whole' is 'more probable'.[1] Moses hak-Kohen of Torresilas (14 c.) wrote that 'the prophet describes what the nations will say of Israel generally . . . and what the nations and the multitudes of Israel will say of the righteous in particular'.[2] Lippmann thought that 'the term does not include *all* Israel, but only the righteous among them'.[3] In one writer, Eliezer of Beaujenci (?), there is approximation to a theory which has had several advocates in modern times, namely, that the Servant was the Order of Prophets. Starting from Dan. xii. 2, he said that the Servant was 'those who correct and make many wise'. Such were 'Elijah, Jeremiah, and, in fact, all the prophets—even Moses. . . . The prophets also were despised and of no estimation in the eyes of the nations . . . even their own people despised them.'[4] The one form of the collective theory which is not represented in medieval Judaism is that which would make the Servant the Ideal Israel. So far as I have been able to discover, the only Jew who has declared himself an adherent of the Ideal theory is the contemporary scholar Reuben Levy, who regards the Servant 'not as the entire, ordinary, everyday, historical Israel, but rather as the idealized Israel who suffered and died in the early days of its exile, but whose characteristic elements remained to provide the life and motive force of new generations that came into being'.[5] Whether he really intends by this the righteous element in Israel is not clear, but his 'idealized Israel' is probably not the Ideal Israel of Beck and Kleinert,[6] nor even of Davidson and Skinner.[7]

(*d*) *Individual Interpretations*

Several of the modern historical-individual theories were anticipated by Jewish writers. Saadyah Gaon (d. 942) thought the Servant was Jeremiah. Among his reasons for doing so, according to Abarbanel,[8] were that 'the word *sucker* (*yônēq*, liii. 2) is an allusion to his youth (Jer. i. 6) . . . that he was "like a sheep led to the slaughter", as he says himself (Jer. xi. 19), and that the words "I will divide him a portion with

[1] DN, p. 44.
[2] Ibid., p. 116.
[3] Ibid., p. 150.
[4] Ibid., p. 66.
[5] *Deutero-Isaiah*, p. 16.
[6] See *infra*, p. 32 f.
[7] See *infra*, pp. 33 f., 63 f.
[8] DN, p. 153.

the great" have reference to the provisions with which he was every day supplied' (Jer. xl. 5). Ibn Ezra[1] mentions the Gaon's interpretation as 'attractive', and Judah ben Balaam (*c.* 1080) said that the description of the Servant is 'quite consistent with such an interpretation'.[2] Abarbanel, after a detailed exposition of the collective theory, offers an alternative 'which has suggested itself to me, of supposing the whole prophecy to have reference to Josiah, king of Judah'.[3] Saadyah ibn Danân (Grenada, *c.* 1600) made known 'what has been communicated to me from heaven, how, namely, the Parashah was originally uttered with reference to Hezekiah'.[4] Jacob Joseph Mordekai Hayyim Passani, chief rabbi at Rome (A.D. 1852–67), was also 'led to the conviction that the Parashah may after all be referred intelligibly and naturally to Hezekiah'.[5] According to Samuel David Luzzatto (Padua, 1867), 'Rabbi Eliezer, the German, author of the "Works of the Lord", interprets it of Job'.[6] Arthur S. Weissmann, in an 'earnest reply' to Delitzsch,[7] argued that 'the picture suits Nehemiah the son of Hacaliah'.

It is evident that the Jews themselves have been almost as perplexed about the Servant as Christians have been ever since, a century and a half ago, they abandoned the Messianic interpretation. Well might Ibn Crispin confess that 'it seemed to me that the doors of the literal interpretation of the Parashah were shut in their face, and that "they wearied themselves to find the entrance" '.[8] Many of the modern theories have their counterparts among the rabbis, and, as if to show the complexity of the problem, the rabbis, like some moderns, occasionally attempted to hold more than one theory at once. It might be that the collective and Messianic theories were held together, without any attempt to co-ordinate them, as by Nachmanides,[9] Solomon Astruc,[10] and Meir ben Simeon;[11] or the collective theory and Josiah, by Abarbanel;[12] or Ibn Danân might discern behind 'the revealed and open-to-all' reference to Hezekiah, a 'secret one, sealed and treasured up in its midst, which sees throughout allusions to the King Messiah'.[13] Even Delitzsch, with his 'pyramid' theory, had a forerunner in Solomon de Morini (Padua, end of 17 c.), who wrote: 'It should

[1] Ibid., p. 43. [2] Ibid., p. 551. [3] Ibid., pp. 165, 187–97.
[4] Ibid., p. 203. [5] Ibid., p. 407. [6] Ibid., p. 413.
[7] *Ernste Antworten auf ernste Fragen*, 2. Aufl., p. 34.
[8] DN, p. 99. [9] Ibid., p. 78. [10] Ibid., p. 129.
[11] Ibid., p. 376 f. [12] Ibid., p. 164 f. [13] Ibid., p. 215 f.

be remembered that this prophecy not only speaks at once both of the Israelitish nation and of the Messiah, but at the same time alludes also to any righteous one amongst them who may have been "a sign and a portent" of what happened to the people at large . . . all three are styled "my servant"'.[1]

[1] DN, p. 324 f.

III

CHRISTIAN INTERPRETATIONS: TO THE EIGHTEENTH CENTURY

I. IN THE NEW TESTAMENT

THERE is no doubt that the Christian Church early interpreted Isa. liii as a prophecy of Christ. This conviction, which is sufficiently evidenced in the New Testament, was derived from the consciousness of Jesus Himself, and Moffatt's view[1] 'that the suffering Servant conception was organic to the consciousness of Jesus, and that He often regarded His vocation in the light of this supremely suggestive prophecy', is generally accepted.[2]

There would be no need to pursue the matter farther, were it not that this majority opinion has in recent years been challenged. The editors of *The Beginnings of Christianity*,[3] in their discussion of passages in which Jesus is represented as speaking of the sufferings of the Son of Man, say, 'The question is whether the predictions in these passages are the *ipsissima verba* of Jesus, or the later interpretation of his words'.[4] The student of tradition is 'aware that predictions are often given explicit precision by an *ex post facto* knowledge of the event'. Hence it may be that 'the records as we have them give not the *ipsissima verba* of Jesus, but the meaning put upon them by the disciples or by the evangelists. The recognition of this fact suggests that though Jesus did speak to his disciples of his coming rejection by the Jewish leaders, and of his ultimate triumph, he did not define the details of either with the accuracy of the present documents'.[5] They think it probable that 'the connexion of Son of Man with the predictions of suffering belongs to Greek Christians, who had failed to appreciate the full meaning of the phrase'.[6] With this view Burkitt[7] substantially agreed.

[1] *The Theology of the Gospels*, p. 149.

[2] See also H. Wheeler Robinson, *The Cross of the Servant*, pp. 64 ff., and further references; F. R. M. Hitchcock, 'The "Servant" in Isaiah and the N.T.', *Expositor*, 8th ser., 14, 1917, pp. 309–20; L. L. Carpenter, *Primitive Christian Application of the Doctrine of the Servant*, 1929.

[3] Ed. F. J. Foakes-Jackson and Kirsopp Lake, part i, 1920.

[4] Ibid., p. 381. [5] Ibid., p. 381 f. [6] Ibid., p. 383.

[7] *Christian Beginnings*, 1924, pp. 35–9.

On the question whether the amplification of the connotation of Son of Man is due to the literary influence of the figure of the Suffering Servant, or to the actual facts of the Passion, the editors of *The Beginnings of Christianity* argue that 'there is no clear reference to the Suffering Servant in the early strata of the Gospels'. They think 'that it was the knowledge of the Passion, whether prophetic or historic, not the interpretation of Isa. liii, which produced the Gospel narrative', and they conclude: 'The most probable theory seems to be that Jesus spoke of his future sufferings in general terms, and that his disciples developed his sayings in accordance with the event'.[1]

Very similarly, R. Bultmann[2] admits the influence of the Old Testament, including Isa. liii, upon the Gospel narratives; but instead of its being the thought of Jesus Himself that was influenced by the Old Testament, the story as told by the evangelists was influenced by the Old Testament after the events. W. Bousset[3] takes substantially the same view, and nevertheless finds it remarkable that Isa. liii exerted at first so little influence upon the Christian imagination.

It may be conceded that the evangelists, especially Matthew, do sometimes give rein to their imagination when they point to examples of the fulfilment of prophecy (e.g. Matt. ii. 15, xxi. 4–7), and we cannot assume that they have never expanded sayings of Jesus about His approaching sufferings. But even if we are suspicious of, and write off, all sayings which are introduced by 'It is written . . .', we are still left with the sayings about the 'cup' and the 'baptism', which, Jesus seems to say, are part of His destiny (Mark x. 38 f., xiv. 36, Luke xii. 50, and parallels; cf. also Mark xiv. 41, 'the hour is come', and parallels). As He saw it, His death was neither a result of the circumstances in which He found Himself, nor of the course of action He had taken. It was an irrevocable destiny, ordained for Him by His Father. And if we ask how this conviction came to Him, the simplest and most likely answer is that He found it written in the Scripture, as the evangelists report of Him. The authors of *The Beginnings of Christianity* do not, indeed, deny that Jesus spoke of His future sufferings 'in general terms'. What they do say is that the disciples 'developed his sayings in

[1] Op. cit., p. 383 f.
[2] *Die Geschichte der synoptischen Tradition*, 2. Aufl., 1931, p. 303 f.
[3] *Kyrios Christos*, 1921, pp. 69–72.

accordance with the event'. There are passages of which this may be true, but it is not inconsistent with the belief that Jesus did see His way more clearly in the light of the Old Testament, that what He read there helped to shape His conviction of His destiny. On this point the words at the Baptism, in the original form that they have in Mark i. 11, 'Thou art my beloved Son, in thee I am well pleased', seem decisive, and determinative of the whole course of Jesus' ministry. They were probably heard by Jesus only, and at some time later communicated by Him to the disciples. However that may be, it is inconceivable that the disciples or the evangelists had the insight to invent them. They are a conflation of Ps. ii. 7, 'Thou art my son', and Isa. xlii. 1, 'in whom I am well pleased' (lit. 'in whom my soul delighteth, or is well pleased').[1] True, Isa. xlii. 1 is not Isa. liii, but it belongs to the same complex of passages, as also does Isa. lxi. 1, of which Jesus said at Nazareth, 'To-day hath this scripture been fulfilled in your ears' (Luke iv. 21). And if Mark i. 11 is genuine, it would seem that Jesus, from the moment of His baptism, conceived of His person and mission in terms of the Old Testament Messiah, developed by His own time into that of the Messianic Son of Man, and the Servant. The rest follows: even if Jesus does not indisputably refer to Isa. liii, and even if disciples and evangelists sometimes amplified His sayings, Wheeler Robinson[2] is right when he says:

> 'Even if some of the references of this kind are due to the later attestation of the Gospel story by the interpretative faith of the early Christians, yet we have still to account for the acceptance of death by Jesus as part of the Messianic mission, and there is no explanation so simple and direct as that He was profoundly influenced by "the Servant of Yahweh" before and in and after the baptismal hour. Here, in Isaiah liii, there was the one indubitable and sufficient basis for the faith of the disciples that Christ died for our sins "according to the Scriptures", when once the application to the Messiah was made; but that which explains the faith of the disciples might with equal justice be used to explain the shaping of the conviction in the mind of their Master'.

Robinson goes on to point out that this general line of argument gives a new force to passages which are allusive, rather than

[1] H. Wheeler Robinson, *The Cross of the Servant*, p. 67 n., notes that the same verb ηὐδόκησεν is used in the Theodotion version of Isa. xlii. 1.

[2] Ibid., p. 68.

direct citations from Isa. liii, such as those in which Jesus refers to His death as a 'ransom' and a 'covenant' *for many* (Mark x. 45, xiv. 24).

When we turn to the New Testament outside the Gospels it is surprising that the relation of the Servant idea to the sufferings of Jesus is neither so clear, nor so frequent, as we might have expected. Passages like Acts viii. 27–39 and 1 Pet. ii. 22–5 seem decisive that the early Church did interpret the cross in the light of Isa. liii,[1] and it is difficult to see how the early Christian preachers could 'show by the scriptures that Jesus was the Christ' without appealing to the same crucial passage. Nevertheless, there is some justification for Bousset's statement that Isa. liii exerted at first comparatively little influence upon Christian imagination. This, however, need not mean that the Christians were at first unconscious of a relation between the cross of Christ and the sufferings of the Servant, and that later they discovered it and altogether overdid it in their reports of the sayings of Jesus. The facts are patient of another explanation, as Dr. Vincent Taylor[2] urges, namely, that 'in the records of primitive Christian belief we can trace a diminishing emphasis upon an idea which for Jesus Himself was central and determinative'.

2. FROM THE SUB-APOSTOLIC PERIOD TO THE EIGHTEENTH CENTURY

In the sub-apostolic[3] and patristic[4] periods the Messianic interpretation of Isa. liii was regnant, and even unchallenged. Chrysostom might interpret l. 4–9 of the Prophet, but about chap. liii there was complete unanimity of opinion. Nor did the Reformation bring any immediate change. If a heretic like Servetus[5] maintained that Isa. liii referred to Cyrus, that only went to show the more clearly what a mischievous person he

[1] Notwithstanding H. J. Cadbury's suggestion in *The Beginnings of Christianity*, part i, vol. v, pp. 365–9, that Peter's use of the word παῖς, 'Servant', as applied to Jesus in Acts iii. 13, 26, iv. 27–30, is not reminiscent of the Servant in Isaiah, but 'a somewhat archaic term not so much redolent of a given section of Scripture as suggestive of the language in which the notable figures of sacred history are described'.

[2] *The Atonement in N.T. Teaching*, pp. 95 ff., 150 n. 2, 186, 201 f.

[3] Cf. Euler, op. cit., pp. 132–46.

[4] See Condamin, *Le Livre d'Isaïe*, p. 326 f., for a representative selection of references.

[5] See J. Mackinnon, *Calvin and the Reformation*, 1936, p. 144.

was. Hengstenberg[1] mentions 'a certain Silesian, called Seidel —who, given up to total unbelief, asserted that the Messiah had never yet come, nor ever would come', and who supposed that the Servant was Jeremiah. A similar suggestion, albeit in more orthodox terms, was made by Grotius.[2] He supposed that xlii. 1 ff., xlix. 1 ff., l. 4 ff. referred to Isaiah, and lii–liii to Jeremiah 'as a figure of Christ'. He attempted to apply the details of the passage to Jeremiah's life and circumstances, very much as Abarbanel[3] relates that Saadyah Gaon had done. Thus, 'he shall divide the spoil with the strong' (liii. 12) refers to the provision made for the Prophet by Nebuzaradan (Jer. xl. 5). Grotius was closely followed by the English deist Anthony Collins,[4] who affirmed that the words of liii. 12 'are not in the least applicable to Jesus, who never had a portion with the great, nor divided the spoil with the strong'. Reinke[5] refers to Samuel Parvish[6] for the view that the Servant was Hezekiah. Parvish, however, did not actually say this. His treatise was in the form of a 'Dialogue between an Indian and a Christian', and the statement that God's Servant was probably 'King Hezekiah, who was lately recovered from a dangerous Illness', was put into the mouth of the Indian. The Christian's reply to it is a model of orthodoxy, and we should probably give to Parvish the benefit of the assumption that it represented his own views. He says in his Preface that it was only the approbation of those who were reputed pillars in the Church that decided him to publish his *Inquiry*. On the other hand, it may be significant that he also says: 'I have only ranged all the Arguments I could form, one against another, and left them, without Conclusion, to the Judgment of every Reader'. Clearly the spirit of free inquiry was beginning to stir.

[1] *Christology of the O.T.*, ET, vol. ii, p. 319.
[2] *Annotata ad Vetus Testamentum*, Tomus II, Paris, 1644.
[3] See *supra*, p. 20 f.
[4] *The Scheme of Literal Prophecy Considered*, 1727, pp. 208–20.
[5] *Exegesis critica in Jes. cap. LII, 13–LIII, 12*, p. 30.
[6] *An Inquiry into the Jewish and Christian Revelation*, 1739, p. 227.

IV

CHRISTIAN INTERPRETATIONS: FROM DÖDERLEIN TO DUHM

The interpretations proposed in the century preceding Duhm's *Isaiah* (1892) may be arranged in three groups.

I. COLLECTIVE INTERPRETATION

As long as it was believed that the Book of Isaiah was entirely the work of an eighth-century prophet, it was natural to assume that those portions of it which have an exilic background must be prophecy in the predictive sense of the word. Accordingly, the Messianic interpretation of the Servant seemed obvious. But no sooner was there talk of a Babylonian Isaiah than Christian scholars began to adopt the view that had long prevailed among the Jews, namely, that the Servant was the nation Israel. This collective theory has taken many forms.

(*a*) *The Servant is the Entire Nation Israel*

According to Reinke[1] the first to deny the Isaianic authorship of chaps. xl ff. was J. S. Semler.[2] Semler was followed by J. B. Koppe,[3] J. C. Döderlein,[4] and J. G. Eichhorn.[5] It was not long before the logical consequences of the new criticism began to manifest themselves in discussions about the Servant. In 1787 Heinrich Stephani[6] stated that the Servant was 'none other than the Servant Jacob (xlviii. 20) or the Israelitish people'. There is nothing in his book to indicate that he was prompted by ideas that were beginning to be current about a Deutero-Isaiah; he took his stand simply upon the principle that the portrait of the Servant is entirely different from prophetic anticipations of the Davidic Messiah. Döderlein, in the third edition of his *Esaias* (1789) was plainly following along

[1] *Die mess. Weissagungen*, 2. Bd, p. 484.

[2] *Abhandlung von freier Untersuchung des Canons*, 4 Theile, 1771–5. I have not been able to get access to this.

[3] *D. Robert Lowth's Jesaias neu übersetzt*, 4 Bde, 1779–81.

[4] *Auserlesene theol. Biblioth.*, 1. Bd, St. XI, 1780, p. 832.

[5] *Allgemeine Biblioth. der bibl. Litteratur*, 2. Bd, 1790, pp. 1044–6.

[6] *Meine Gedanken über die Entstehung und Ausbildung der Idee von einem Messias*, pp. 89 ff.

the lines of the criticism he had helped to inaugurate. In the first and second editions (1775 and 1780) he had adhered to the traditional Messianic interpretation. In the third edition he referred xlii. 1 ff. to Cyrus,[1] and xlix. 1 ff., and lii. 13–liii. 12 to 'the entire Jewish people',[2] as being 'more appropriate to the context'. But as if to suggest that he had not finally made up his mind, he printed two versions of lii. 13–liii. 12, a *versio christiana* and a *versio antechristiana et Judaica*, with separate notes on each. Döderlein was followed in 1794 by C. G. Schuster,[3] who saw in the passage an 'allegory' of the fortunes of collective Israel. Jehovah takes His seat as World-Judge; the Hebrews are represented by a scourged slave, and the rest of the peoples by their kings and ambassadors. After Jehovah has announced his intention to pardon and restore Israel, a proselyte, speaking for the heathen peoples, expresses the hope that the excessive punishment of the Hebrews may avail to atone for the rest of mankind. Jehovah assures them that it shall be so on condition of their unquestioning obedience. For this application of the idea of 'corporate personality', as it has come to be called, Schuster referred to passages like Isa. i. 5 f. and Ps. cxxix.

Eichhorn,[4] in a review of Schuster, described the theory of the latter as 'rather too artificial in some of its details', but as 'unquestionably the best that has yet been written on this *locus vexatissimus*'. In the same volume of the *Allgemeine Bibliothek*[5] there appeared seven 'Letters', by a writer unnamed, defending the full collective theory against the 'Pious Kernel' and 'Ideal Israel' theories that were already gaining currency. Eichhorn himself returned to the subject in *Die hebräischen Propheten*,[6] in which he interpreted xlii. 1 ff. of Cyrus,[7] xlix. 1 ff. and l. 4 ff. of the Prophet,[8] and lii. 13–liii. 12 of Israel.[9] Meanwhile J. F. Telge had contributed to G. A. Ruperti's *Theologische Miscellen*, three articles under the title 'Meletemata in carmen fatidicum Jes. LII, 13–LIII, 12'.[10] They contained a review of the various theories, an exegetical commentary, and a declaration that no other identification of the Servant except

[1] Op. cit., p. 196.
[2] Op. cit., pp. 225 f., 241 ff.
[3] *Jesaiae Orationem Propheticam cap. LII, 7–LIII, 12.*
[4] *Allgemeine Bibliothek d. bibl. Litteratur*, 6. Bd, pp. 153–63.
[5] pp. 919–95.
[6] 3. Bd, 1819.
[7] Ibid., p. 286 f.
[8] Ibid., pp. 142–6, 179 ff.
[9] Ibid., pp. 189 ff.
[10] 1. Bd, pp. 315–38, 2. Bd, pp. 289–356, 3. Bd, pp. 356–93.

that with Israel could have been understood by those to whom the passage was addressed.

Next E. F. C. Rosenmüller, who had earlier[1] initiated the theory that the Servant was a personification of the Order of Prophets, in the second edition of his *Scholia in Vetus Testamentum* (1820) abandoned it in favour of the wider equation, which he applied to all the three passages xlii. 1 ff, xlix. 1 ff., and lii. 13–liii. 12. Like some other writers of the period, notably Gesenius, he argued that the collective personality of the Servant was apparent from the plural expression *lāmô* in the Hebrew text at the end of liii. 8. The commentary of Hitzig (1833) and a short monograph by F. Köster[2] followed along the now familiar lines. Two things in Hitzig deserve mention: it was he who first proposed to remove the difficulty presented by the apparent mission of the Servant to Israel in xlix. 5 f. by taking the infinitives there as gerundives,[3] with Yahweh as subject—a contention later revived by Budde;[4] and he ended his discussion of the whole subject with a remark which shows how deeply the newer criticism had been influenced by the rationalistic spirit of the *Aufklärung*: 'The Messianic interpretation is altogether contrary to the character of prophecy, which excludes prediction.'[5]

The collective Israel theory was adopted, without much discussion, by J. Wellhausen.[6] 'There is no God save Yahweh, and Israel is His Prophet.' Stade[7] dealt with the subject somewhat more fully. Although he was conscious of the difficulty of reconciling the view that the martyred Servant was the Israel of the exile with the unquestioned severity of some of the Prophet's references to Israel, he would not take refuge in the supposition that the Servant-passages were from another hand,[8] nor would he countenance any pious remnant theory. The apparent contradiction is resolved 'if we consider that Deutero-Isaiah's ideas are built up throughout on a retrospect over the past history of his people. In this retrospect he directs his view now more to the idea which Israel was to serve and realise, now more to its actual performances.'[9] There is thus a certain contrast—of which the Prophet was not conscious—between

[1] See *infra*, p. 37.
[2] *De Servo Jehovae*, 1838.
[3] Op. cit., p. 540 f.
[4] See *infra*, p. 58 f.
[5] Op. cit., p. 577.
[6] *Prolegomena z. Gesch. Israels*; *Israel. u. jüd. Geschichte.*
[7] *Geschichte des Volkes Israel*, 2. Bd; *Bibl. Theol. des ATs.*
[8] *Bibl. Theol.*, p. 307 f.
[9] *Geschichte*, ii, p. 79.

the 'ideal' and 'empirical' Israel; but it would be an exaggeration of Stade's position to put him in the category of those who think that the Servant was the ideal as opposed to the empirical Israel.

(b) *The Servant is the Ideal Israel*

The first to advocate the view that the Servant was the Ideal Israel was J. C. R. Eckermann.[1] He did so on the basis of a distinction between the state and its citizens. The citizens have sinned and the state has suffered. The 'He' in chap. liii is 'the people, as people, as a civic unity; the State as State'. The 'We' are the individual citizens of the state, from its foundation to the time of the Prophet.[2] The state was politically dead. The citizens also had experienced a measure of suffering, but they had built houses, engaged in trade, and even preferred to remain where they were.[3] Jehovah will gladden the state with new kindnesses, as a proof that His purpose was not its total destruction, but the recovery of its citizens.[4]

This rather unpromising beginning does not seem to have been followed up until 1835, when W. Vatke[5] in a brief discussion said that the Servant was Israel 'according to its higher religious unity and divine calling'. In 1840 the theory enlisted the powerful support of Ewald.[6] The Servant is 'Israel according to its true idea'. So conceived

'Israel shall restore Israel, that is the spiritual Israel shall restore the dead Israel, or the handful already moved by the higher spirit, in whom Israel even now shows himself to be the true Servant of Jehovah, shall quicken the remaining large multitude who are still dead. However, this is not only conceivable, but this prophet feels clearly and powerfully within himself, and perceives in those who are likeminded with him, how necessarily the restoration must take this course. . . . The animated conception of what the Servant of Jehovah should be . . . was indeed supplied to him chiefly by his own prophetic feeling and labours, as well as by reference to the great earlier prophets'.[7]

[1] *Theol. Beyträge*, 1790; 2. Aufl., 1794, 1. Bd., Erstes Stück, pp. 209–40.
[2] Ibid., p. 220.
[3] Ibid., p. 221 f.
[4] Ibid., p. 227.
[5] *Die Religion des ATs*, 1. Th., pp. 528 ff.
[6] *Die Propheten des Alten Bundes*, 1. Ausg., 1840, 2. Ausg., 1867–8; ET by F. J. Smith, *Commentary on the Prophets of the O.T.*, 5 vols., 1875–81.
[7] Ibid., ET, iv, p. 250.

This statement is illuminating as showing how difficult it is to maintain the Ideal theory in its pure abstractness, and how difficult to draw a sharp line between it and the Pious Remnant theory. The ideal inevitably tends to find concrete expression in a faithful remnant, and it is not always easy to decide in which category a writer should be placed. In Ewald, indeed, there is a fusion of more than two theories. The 'spiritual' Israel becomes the 'handful moved by the higher spirit'. These again tend to be narrowed down to the prophets, and finally to the Prophet himself. The terms are different, but the result is strikingly similar to the theory associated to-day with the name of Dr. Wheeler Robinson.[1]

This wide range of application of the term Servant is nowhere more evident than in Matthew Arnold.[2] Arnold quite frankly borrowed his criticism from Ewald, though, of course, he expressed the matter in his own way.

> 'A German critic elects one out of these several meanings, and will have the text decidedly mean that one and no other. He does not reflect, that in his author's own being all these characters were certainly blended: the ideal Israel, his own personal individuality, the character of representative of his order, the character of representative of the pious and faithful part of the nation, the character (who that knows human nature can doubt it?) of representative of the sinful mass of the nation. How, then, when the prophet came to speak, could God's Servant fail to be all these by turns?'[3]

Two works by Fr. Beck[4] distinguished between the 'empirical' and the 'ideal' Israel. 'How can the people or the order of prophets, which are collectives, be represented as a person? This is only possible of the Idea, which is in itself the unity that appears as personality. But this personality, which exists only as idea, has its manifestation in the people and their historical development. This is the dialectic of the idea itself.'[5] And so on, in language more akin to that of Hegel than to that of the Old Testament, such as 'the postulate of universality', 'the idea in itself', 'self-consciousness'. Less purely abstract was Kleinert,[6] though he felt it necessary to anticipate the charge

[1] See *infra*, pp. 103 ff.

[2] *Isaiah XL–LXVI*, 1875.

[3] Ibid., p. 30.

[4] *De cap. LIII. libri Jesajani*, 1840; *Die Cyro-jesajanischen Weissagungen*, 1844.

[5] Ibid., p. 151.

[6] 'Ueber das Subject der Weiss. Jes. 52, 13–53, 12', *TSK*, 1862, pp. 699–752.

that his conception was 'abstruse'. His answer was that 'in reality it shows how the prophets could treat religious conceptions dialectically, or rather theosophically, in a way that is unusual—though not quite without analogy—in the Old Testament.'[1] 'It is not at all abstruse', he argues, 'to conceive of a whole people as a unity, and accordingly speak of them in the singular'.[2] While this, of course, is a sufficient answer to objections to the collective theory in general, it entirely failed to meet the obvious objection to the 'ideal' form of the theory in particular. Kleinert, however, was more happy when he pointed, as an analogy, to Fichte's remark about the expiation of the sins of the Germans by means of the sufferings of Germany.

The first British scholar to abandon the Messianic interpretation was, so far as I have been able to ascertain, the pioneer critic Samuel Davidson.[3] He referred with approval to Ewald and Beck, and identified the Servant with the Ideal Israel. Some years later, T. K. Cheyne, in his first handling of the problem,[4] likewise wrote of the Servant as 'a purely poetical figure'[5] . . . 'the personified ideal of the Israelitish nation'[6] . . . 'the genius of Israel'.[7]

Very similar to the view of Ewald was that of Ed. Reuss.[8] One quotation will suffice to show how difficult it is to place him in any one category of interpreter: 'The Servant is Israel; not, indeed, the people as they were, with all their faults, but the ideal people, realising the theocratic idea, the healthy nucleus of the nation, which, with its prophets for guides, is to lead the masses into the ways of God and to exercise a saving influence even over the heathen'.[9]

No more lucid and attractive expositions of the Ideal theory have ever been written than by the British scholars A. B. Davidson[10] and S. R. Driver.[11] Both insist that it is inconceivable that the term Servant in Isa. xl ff. should apply to subjects

[1] Ibid., p. 727. [2] Ibid., p. 728.

[3] *An Introduction to the O.T.*, vol. iii, 1863, pp. 62–76.

[4] *Isaiah Chronologically Arranged, 1870.*

[5] Ibid., p. 155.

[6] Ibid., p. 181. [7] Ibid., pp. 142, 176.

[8] *Les Prophètes*, 2. tome, 1876, pp. 236–80; *Die Gesch. d. heil. Schriften A Ts*, 2. Aufl., 1890, p. 458 f.

[9] *Les Prophètes*, p. 236.

[10] 'The Book of Isa.—Ch. XL–LXVI', *Expositor*, 2nd ser., vol. 8, 1884; *O.T. Prophecy*, 1903.

[11] *Isaiah: His Life and Times*; *Introduction to the Lit. of the O.T.*

entirely distinct, while at the same time recognizing that in the passages which have come to be called the 'Songs' it is used with a different emphasis from that found elsewhere in the prophecy. It is not easy to pick out any one passage which represents their almost identical points of view. The following, from the most easily accessible of their works, may suffice:

'. . . the abstract conception of the community, as distinct from the individuals which compose it, is personified and idealised. So Jacob or Israel is distinct from the members; Jacob or Israel, the abstract conception of the nation, personified, and distinguished from Israelites as individuals. Now the Servant of the Lord appears to me a similar abstraction, elevated by the singular idealism of the prophet into a Being, and distinguished from the individuals or the tribes of Jacob, the fragments of the people in all lands.' This Being does not belong to the Israel of any particular age, he is permanent.'[1]

Similarly, Driver speaks of 'Jehovah's ideal Servant, the ideal impersonation of the theocratic attributes of the nation'.[2] Both are at pains to assert that the Servant was 'not a mere conception';[3] 'no abstract character'.[4] Davidson says it 'had embodiments in saints and prophets and martyrs for the truth',[5] but he saves himself from falling over into the Remnant theory by making the happy distinction between 'Israel according to its true idea' and 'those in Israel true to its idea',[6] and further by the remark that 'the prophet does not idealise the actual; he actualises an ideal'.[7] Driver, for his part, spoke of the Prophet's 'own warmth of feeling and imaginative sympathy reflected' in the conception; 'it is human in its completeness'.[8] Davidson, by way of analogy, speaks of

'the Church, to which we attach certain ideal attributes. . . . When we ourselves speak in this way, we do not have in view the actual Church anywhere. . . . And yet the Church is not an abstraction; it exists. . . . And we should say that it has a double task before it, not only to gather together its own scattered fragments and to animate them with a pure and perfect faith, but also to carry the truth to the nations that do not yet know it; a double function, which pretty much corresponds to the double office of the Servant of the Lord.'[9]

[1] Davidson, *O.T. Prophecy*, p. 437.
[2] Driver, *Isaiah*, p. 179.
[3] Davidson, op. cit., p. 441.
[4] Driver, op. cit., p. 179.
[5] Op. cit., p. 442.
[6] *Expositor*, p. 359.
[7] *O.T. Prophecy*, p. 465.
[8] *Isaiah*, p. 179.
[9] *O.T. Prophecy*, p. 441.

Not unlike the foregoing was the view of Dillmann, who edited the fifth edition of Knobel's Commentary (1890). In xlii. 1 ff. the Servant is 'an Ideal, which soars above reality . . . and is neither identical with the empirical Israel of any particular time, nor with an empirical section of it such as prophets or the community of the pious'.[1] This transcendent ideal figure is expressly distinguished from the empirical Israel (xlix. 6). But from chap. xlix onwards the conception of 'Israel according to its true idea' is insufficient, especially in chap. liii, since such a thought-conception cannot suffer and die. We are to think rather of a God-fearing nucleus of the people, which approximates to the ideal, and whose sufferings are the atonement-offering through which pardon will accrue for others.[2] This is tantamount to a recognition of the untenability of the Ideal theory in its earlier uncompromising form.

(*c*) *The Servant is a Pious Minority within Israel*

This view was first put forward in 1792 by H. E. G. Paulus.[3] 'The people as a whole cannot be represented as worshippers of Jehovah. Only that part of them who really were his worshippers is here treated collectively. They suffered because of the rest of the Jews, suffered with them and for them.'[4] No positive reasons are adduced in support of the theory, which appears to be simply a deduction from the obvious difficulty of applying the passages to Israel as a whole. This is practically acknowledged by C. F. Ammon,[5] who, after referring to the difficulty of the full collective theory, says that this disappears if, with Paulus, we consider that the Servant is 'not the entire Jewish nation, but the nobler part of it'.[6] This Servant, now in exile by the Euphrates, is to live in its seed, which shall return to Judah.

It was not until 1832 that the theory was again put forward, by Otto Thenius.[7] 'The conduct of the better portion in the exile, over whom the divine judgement only came on account

[1] Ibid., p. 387. [2] Ibid., p. 472.

[3] Art. 'Zur Erklärung von Jes. K. LIII', in *Memorabilien*, 3. Stück, pp. 175–92; *Philologischer Clavis über das AT*, 1793.

[4] *Memorab.*, p. 176.

[5] *Entwurf einer Christologie des ATs*, 1794, pp. 92–111.

[6] Ibid., p. 108.

[7] 'Neue Beleuchtung des leid. Jehovadieners', in Winer's *Zeitsch. f. wiss. Theol.*, 2. Bd. 1. Heft, pp. 105–30.

of the bad, became the cause of God's renewing his mercy to his people and bringing them back to the fatherland'.[1] F. J. V. D. Maurer[2] attempted to show that xlix. 3, compared with xlix. 5 f., pointed to a distinction between the nation as a whole and the better part of it.[3] According to D. G. C. von Cölln[4] the distinction between the true Servant and the people as a whole may be inferred from xlix. 5 and l. 10. In lii. 13–liii. 3 we may think of a personification of the whole people, but from liii. 4 that is difficult. Hence 'the prophet uses the expression Servant of God now in a wider, now in a narrower sense . . . in the narrower he designates the choicest of the people, the salt of the people . . . especially the prophets'.[5] Here it may be observed that just as the Ideal tended to pass over into the Remnant theory, so this in turn tends to be narrowed down to the Order of Prophets.

The Pious Minority theory gained many supporters from August Knobel's Commentary,[6] which went into three editions during the author's lifetime,[7] and was afterwards edited, with but few changes, by L. Diestel.[8] Knobel's view was that the Servant was 'the theocratic *Kern* of the people, to which especially the priests and prophets belonged'.[9] Mention may be made also of an article by Bleek,[10] which contains a statement to the effect that the Servant was 'the true Israel κατὰ πνεῦμα as distinct from the mass of the people'.[11] Bleek still felt free to argue from the plural forms *nεgaʿ lāmô* and *bᵉmôṯāw* in liii. 8 f. that the Servant must be collective, though he abandoned something of the assurance with which Rosenmüller and Gesenius had handled this argument.[12]

Each variety of the collective theory could number among its adherents one or more of the foremost scholars of the century. The most prominent to be mentioned in this section is A. Kuenen, who identified the Servant with 'the better portion, the flower of the Israelitish people. . . . Especially does it apply to those who proclaim Jahve's will and counsel, that is, to the

[1] Thenius, op. cit., p. 108.
[2] *Jesaiam commentarius*, 1836.
[3] Ibid., p. 399.
[4] *Biblische Theologie*, 1. Bd., AT, 1836, pp. 325–8.
[5] Ibid., p. 327.
[6] *Der Prophet Jesaia.*
[7] 1843, 1854, 1861.
[8] 4. Ausg., 1872; for the 5th ed., extensively revised, by Dillmann, see p. 35.
[9] 1. Ausg., p. 299.
[10] 'Erklärung von Jes. 52, 13–53, 12', *TSK*, 1861, pp. 177–218.
[11] Ibid., p. 182.
[12] Ibid., p. 201 f.

prophets.' The work and glory of the Messiah are, during the exile, transferred 'to the people, or to a portion of the people'.[1]

(*d*) *The Servant is the Order of Prophets*

The theory that the Servant was a personification of the Order of Prophets was first suggested by Rosenmüller.[2] He seems to have been led to it because he noticed that in xliv. 26 the word Servant is parallel with the plural 'his messengers'. Every feature in the portrait of the Servant, he said, is applicable to the prophets, and he referred particularly to the passages now known as the Colloquies of Jeremiah. During the exile the prophets fared little better than they had done in the last years of the kingdom. Their prospects changed with the fall of Babylon, when they were filled with hope, and it was apparent to all the world that they had been sent by God.[3] In 1820 Rosenmüller abandoned this view in favour of the full collective theory.[4]

In the following year Rosenmüller's Prophetic theory was espoused by Gesenius,[5] who said of all the passages now known as Songs, 'The prophets are here viewed as a corporate body or moral person; in accordance with a customary Hebrew mode of expression . . . they are here called collectively the Servant of Jehovah, yet in such a way that the collective signification of the singular is clearly apparent'; this with reference to xliv. 26, where 'his Servant' is parallel with 'his messengers', to liii. 8 'where it is construed with a plural suffix',[6] and to *b*^{e}*môṯāw* (liii. 9) 'with respect to the Servant of Jehovah as a *Collectivum*'.[7] In the *Thesaurus*[8] Gesenius said that in passages like xli. 8 f. the Israelitish people are addressed by this 'honourable and charitable name'; it is then used of the pious or true Israelites, and within these of the prophets. Once again the definition of the term Servant can be narrowed down, and in between the extremes of full collective and individual theories it would seem that the group to which a writer attaches himself is largely a matter of emphasis.

[1] *The Prophets and Prophecy in Israel*, ET by A. Milroy, 1877, pp. 220–4.

[2] 'Leiden u. Hoffnungen der Propheten Jehova's', in Gabler's *Neues theol. Journal*, 13. Bd., 4. Stück, 1799, pp. 333–69.

[3] Ibid., p. 349.

[4] See *supra*, p. 30.

[5] *Der Prophet Jesaia*, 3. Th., 1821.

[6] Ibid., p. 11.

[7] Ibid., p. 185.

[8] 1840 ed., sub *'ɛḇɛḏ*.

F. W. Umbreit[1] sought to combine the Order of Prophets with a Messianic interpretation. In some passages of the prophecy, he said, the Servant is Israel as a whole, in others the better elements in Israel, and in yet others the prophets. If he had to make a choice, it would be of the last.[2] But, he argued, there are elements of the future in the descriptions, as well as of the past and present. This can only be accounted for by supposing that the view of the Prophet passed gradually from the people as a whole to its best representatives, thence to the Order of Prophets, until it finally rose to a modified exilic conception of a suffering Messiah.[3] This last step in the process was possible because there had from the first been an ideal element in the portrait, and also because in all the preceding stages a community had been personified as an individual.

The next writer to adopt the Prophetic theory was G. M. L. de Wette.[4] He was followed in 1836 by Schenkel, one of his own pupils, who, in an article,[5] produced the most elaborate exposition of the *Prophetenstand* theory that had yet appeared. Its main arguments were that the expression Servant of God is a usual predicate of the Prophetic Order; that in xliv. 26 and l. 10 the term seems to refer to the prophets; that it cannot signify Israel according to its prophetic vocation, because Israel is even described as blind and deaf; that the words *bᵉrîṯ ʿām* (xlii. 6) do not mean covenant-people but covenant-mediator; that in xlix. 5 f. the Servant must be distinguished from Israel; and that in chaps. xlii and xlix the experiences and functions of the Servant entirely accord with those of the prophets. With regard to lii. 13–liii. 12, Schenkel suggested that it was 'perhaps' composed in the period of the true Isaiah, that the original subject of it was an individual martyr-prophet, and that it had been inserted into its present context by the Prophet of the exile, who accommodated it to his personification of the Prophetic Order.[6]

Next in order are two composite theories, in both of which the main emphasis is upon the prophets. The general view of

[1] 'Ueber den KG', *TSK*, 1828, pp. 295–330; *Der KG*, 1840; *Praktischer Commentar über den Jes.*, 2. Th., 1842.

[2] *TSK*, p. 300; *Der KG*, p. 12.

[3] *TSK*, p. 316; *Der KG*, p. 34.

[4] *Opuscula theologica; Comm. de morte Jesu Chr.*, 1830, pp. 34–48.

[5] 'Kritischer Versuch über den KG', *TSK*, pp. 982–1004.

[6] Ibid., p. 996 f.; see further *infra*, p. 42.

J. C. K. Hofmann[1] was that the Servant is Israel, but there is some approximation to the view that he was a personification of the Prophetic Order. The speaker in xlix. 1 ff. and l. 4 ff. is the Prophet, though it is not so much in his own person that he speaks, but as a prophet, so that the passages might apply to any prophet. The sufferings in chap. liii. are a deduction from the experiences of the prophets. The Servant is Israel in its prophetic calling, a calling which is fulfilled in a multitude of prophets.[2] The prophets have the same relation to Israel as Israel has to the heathen world.[3] C. L. Hendewerk[4] thought of a 'Messianic Israel', made up of earlier and later prophets, 'of whom the greatest was Christ'.[5] The Prophet does not speak as an individual, but as the representative of his order. He divides the people into two parts, those who had been led into exile, and those who had grown up in the exile. These latter are the *spes melioris aevi*, and 'my people' (liii. 8) for whose transgressions they are stricken are 'the earlier generations'.[6]

(*e*) *The Servant is the Order of Priests*

The theory that the Servant was the Order of Priests was suggested by the anonymous author of *Ausführliche Erklärung der sämmtlichen messianischen Weissagungen des Alten Testaments* (1801). He interpreted xlii. 1–4 of Cyrus, and for lii. 13–liii. 12 he advanced 'a new explanation of my own', namely, that 'it contains a threnody on the priestly order, scattered in the Babylonian exile, brought low, and undeservedly suffering, in the hope of compensation and better fortune in the future'.[7]

2. HISTORICAL INDIVIDUAL INTERPRETATIONS

(*a*) *Hezekiah*

Towards the close of the eighteenth century the suggestion that the Servant was Hezekiah was made by K. F. Bahrdt[8] and J. Konynenburg.[9] 'If I understand the Hebrew text aright',

[1] *Weissagung und Erfüllung*, Erste Hälfte, 1841, pp. 257–76; *Der Schriftbeweis*, Zweite Hälfte, 1. Abt., 1853, pp. 89–102, 124–39.

[2] *Weiss. u. Erfüll.*, p. 275 f.

[3] *Schriftbew.*, ii, 1, p. 139.

[4] *Des Propheten Jes. Weissagungen*, 2. Th., 1843.

[5] Ibid., p. 125.

[6] Ibid., pp. 127–35.

[7] Op. cit., p. 256.

[8] *Die kleine Bibel*, 1. Bd., 1780; *Freymüthige Versuche über verschiedene in Theol. u. bibl. Kritik einschlagende Materien*, 1783, pp. 99–144; both works published anonymously.

[9] *Untersuchung über die Natur der a-t-lichen Weissagungen auf den Messias*, translated from the Dutch, 1795.

wrote Bahrdt, Isa. liii is a narrative of what is past, not a prophecy, and 'I should be very surprised if I were the first to have ventured upon so natural and probable a conjecture' as that it related to Hezekiah.[1] He betrayed no suspicion that the passage was not by Isaiah. He supposed that Hezekiah suffered from cancer, and, if the disease of the Servant appears to be leprosy, 'that was a name which the Jews no doubt gave to any dangerous sore'.[2] Since Hezekiah's life was prolonged, Bahrdt supposed that Isa. liii did not describe the actual death of the Servant, but only that he seemed certain to die. He interpreted the words 'he shall see seed' (ver. 10) of Hezekiah's issue after his recovery (xxxix. 7). The passage can only refer to Christ 'in a mystical sense'.[3]

Konynenburg referred to the number of words in Isa. liii which describe sickness and recovery.[4] It is more natural to interpret the passage of Hezekiah than of the Messiah, since 'elsewhere there is not the least mention of sufferings of the Messiah, but only of his public success and greatness'.[5]

(*b*) *Isaiah*

The theory that the Servant in chaps. xlii, xlix, lii–liii was Isaiah was advanced in 1791 by C. F. Stäudlin.[6] He started from the rabbinical tradition that Isaiah was of royal birth, that he was martyred under Manasseh, and buried by the sepulchres of the kings. He had been condemned to a felon's grave. But even at the time of his execution his innocence was recognized. His death moved his persecutors to reflection, and the best they could now do to honour him was to bury him close by the kings. This is based on liii. 9, which Stäudlin translated: 'My people intended to make his grave with evil-doers, but he found it with the rich.'[7] Stäudlin was aware of Eichhorn's suggestions about a Deutero-Isaiah, and, although he accepted them in the main, he thought that Isa. liii was a threnody written by a prophet-contemporary of Isaiah. This interpretation was applauded by G. L. Bauer,[8] who, however, referred xlii. 1 ff. to Cyrus.

[1] *Frey. Versuche*, p. 135 f.
[2] Ibid., p. 137.
[3] Ibid., p. 141.
[4] Konynenburg, op. cit., p. 302.
[5] Ibid., p. 303.
[6] *Neue Beiträge zur Erläuterung der bibl. Propheten.*
[7] Ibid., p. 10.
[8] *Scholia in Vetus Test.*, vol. ix, 1795, p. 327 f.

(c) *Uzziah*

The identification of the Servant in chaps. lii–liii with the leprous king Uzziah was suggested by J. C. W. Augusti in three works.[1] The subject of xlii. 1 ff. is Cyrus,[2] of xlix. 1 ff. Israel,[3] and of l. 4 ff. the Prophet himself.[4] It has often been remarked that the Servant was a leper, and according to 2 Chron. xxvi. 22 Isaiah wrote 'of the acts of Uzziah, first and last'.[5] Uzziah's punishment was too severe for one small offence, and people must have looked for some other explanation of the great suffering inflicted by Jehovah upon so excellent a prince. They came to the conclusion that he suffered not so much for his own offence, as for that of the whole people, whose representative he was.[6]

(d) *Jeremiah*

Grotius' theory that the Servant in lii. 13–liii. 12 was Jeremiah was revived by Baron C. C. J. Bunsen.[7] He referred to features in the life of Jeremiah, and tried to fit them into the passage, which, he supposed, was written by the Prophet's disciple Baruch. Duhm, too, in his earlier days, thought of Jeremiah.[8] He was already of the opinion that xlii. 1–7, xlix. 1–6, l. 4–9, and lii. 13–liii. 12 were not, in their original form, from the hand of Deutero-Isaiah. They were perhaps a prophetic description of the life and work of Jeremiah, written by a younger contemporary. They were taken over by Deutero-Isaiah, who considerably revised them, and related them to his own Servant of Yahweh, 'the ideal Israel that has God's word'.[9]

(e) *Deutero-Isaiah*

Mowinckel's theory that the Servant was the Prophet himself was in some measure anticipated in 1847 by J. J. Stähelin,[10] who thought that xlii. 1 ff., xlix. 1 ff., and l. 4 ff. could refer to

[1] 'Ueber den König Usia, nebst einer Erläuterung Jes. 53', in Henke's *Magazin für Religionsphilosophie*, 3. Bd, 1795, pp. 282–9; *Exegetisches Handbuch des ATs*, 1797–1800, published anonymously in association with J. G. Ch. Höpfner; *Apologien und Parallelen theol. Inhalts*, 1800, pp. 1–40.
[2] *Handbuch*, p. 94.
[3] Ibid., p. 133 f.
[4] Ibid., p. 140.
[5] Ibid., p. 156.
[6] Ibid.; *Apologien*, p. 15.
[7] *Gott in der Geschichte*, 1. Th., 1857, pp. 201–7; *Vollständiges Bibelwerk*, 2. Bd, 1860, p. 438.
[8] *Die Theologie der Propheten*, 1875, pp. 287 ff.
[9] Ibid., p. 292.
[10] *Die mess. Weissagungen des ATs*, pp. 99–103.

no one but the Prophet himself. He did not press this interpretation to cover chaps. lii–liii. There the Servant is not collective, but an individual, a pious sufferer who was yet to appear. Even so, 'what led the prophet to this Ideal was his own sufferings and hopes, but, inasmuch as he is very conscious of his own sinfulness, he recognizes that for the lasting blessedness of Israel there is need for one who shall be sinless'.[1]

(*f*) *Zerubbabel*

The Zerubbabel theory of Sellin was anticipated by Samuel Sharpe,[2] who also anticipated Duhm by assigning only Isa. xl–lv to 'the Isaiah of the return home', and chaps. lvi–lxvi to various post-exilic writers down to Maccabaean times. His treatment of the subject is of the slightest, and he seems to have been led to his conjecture by a remark of Ibn Ezra, who, in his introduction to Isa. xl, 'quotes R. Moses Hakkohen as thinking that this part of the Book of Isaiah relates to Zerubbabel'.[3] According to Dalman,[4] Friedmann[5] also thought of Zerubbabel, calumniated by his own people, and perhaps condemned to death by the Persian king.

(*g*) *An Unknown Individual*

It has already been noted[6] that Schenkel thought that the section lii. 13–liii. 12 dates from an earlier period than that of Deutero-Isaiah, and that it originally had for its subject the martyrdom of an anonymous saint or prophet. A similar view was held by Ewald,[7] who believed that Deutero-Isaiah could not better express what he wished to say about the Ideal Israel than by utilizing this older material.

3. MESSIANIC INTERPRETATION

If we reckon only by numbers it is probable that the Messianic interpretation was still able to enlist as many supporters as its rivals put together. The majority of those who held to the traditional view, whether Catholic or Protestant, maintained the unity of the book of Isaiah, and, consequently, the predictive

[1] Stähelin, op. cit., p. 103.
[2] *The Book of Isaiah*, 1877.
[3] Ibid., p. 101.
[4] *Jes. 53*, p. 14.
[5] *S'rubbabel, Erläuterung der Weiss.: 'Siehe, es gelingt meinem Knechte'*, Wien, 1890, p. 16: I have not seen this.
[6] See *supra*, p. 38.
[7] *Die Propheten des Alten Bundes*, 1. Ausg., 2. Bd, p. 407 f.

character of the Servant passages. The case is put clearly by Reinke, who devoted nearly seventy pages to defending the genuineness of Isa. xl–lxvi: 'If all the prophecies in the book are genuine and have the prophet Isaiah for their author, it must be taken for granted that the book contains revelations from God about the future. . . . They cannot, therefore, be simply "presentiments, hopes, wishes, and natural conjectures" derived from a naturalistic source.'[1]

A similar standpoint was maintained by G. C. Storr, G. J. L. Vogel, R. Lowth, J. A. Dathe, J. D. Michaelis, J. H. D. Moldenhawer, W. F. Hezel, C. G. Hensler, M. Dodson, J. I. Hansi, H. Braun, J. C. F. Steudel, E. W. Hengstenberg, J. Beck, E. Henderson, A. McCaul, P. Schegg, R. Stier, J. Bade, M. Drechsler, W. Kelly, A. Rohling, B. Neteler, W. Urwick, C. W. E. Nägelsbach, J. Knabenbauer, and J. Forbes.

Writers who maintained that the Servant was the Messiah, without being hostile to the newer literary criticism, were J. B. Koppe, C. D. A. Martini, and J. D. Kruiger. C. J. Bredenkamp agreed that Isa. xl–lxvi is in its present form exilic, but thought that certain parts of it—including chaps. lii–liii—were earlier and Isaianic.

After the middle of the nineteenth century a more liberal attitude to criticism was adopted by Messianic interpreters like V. F. Oehler, C. von Orelli, and Franz Delitzsch,[2] who sought to make a synthesis of the collective and Messianic interpretations. In this they were following closely in the steps of Umbreit. Oehler[3] thought that in chaps. xlii and xlix the Servant is 'the people viewed according to its original vocation . . . the people conceived as Ideal, the people as theocratic-messianic'. In lii. 13–liii. 12 he is an individual, 'and no other individual can be intended than the Messiah himself'.[4] According to von Orelli[5] the conception stands on a 'broad national basis',[6] but 'the

[1] *Die mess. Weissagungen*, 2. Bd, 1860, p. 483; see also his *Exegesis critica in Jes. LII, 13–LIII, 12*, 1836.

[2] Delitzsch in his early days defended the genuineness of chaps. xl. ff., though he later abandoned that view.

[3] *Der KJ im DJ*, 2. Th., 1865, p. 20.

[4] Ibid., p. 63.

[5] *Die at. Weissagung von der Vollendung des Gottesreiches*, 1882, ET by J. S. Banks, *The O.T. Prophecy of the Consummation of God's Kingdom*, 1885; *The Prophecies of Isaiah*, ET by J. S. Banks, 1889; *Der Prophet Jesaja*, 3. Aufl., 1904; *Der KJ im Jesajabuche*, 1908.

[6] *O.T. Prophecy*, p. 379.

more the nation as a whole shows itself incapable of rising to the high calling . . . the more plainly it detaches itself from the national multitude and becomes a personally conceived ideal, which acquires such independence that the nation itself becomes the object of the Servant's redeeming work'.[1] Each of the collective theories 'contains a true element, although all, taken together, do not exhaust the truth'.[2] We must think in the end of an individual; not, indeed, of a pure ideal, like Plato's perfectly righteous man,[3] but 'a figure destined for most real existence, since God assigns to him in the future a positive mission'.[4] He is ultimately identical with the Davidic Messiah, though the two figures arose in the consciousness of the prophets independently and out of different circumstances. 'The fulfilment, which in other things also unites what was divergent in prophecy, has supplied the synthesis.'[5]

The famous Pyramid theory of Delitzsch was first set forth by him in a supplementary note to Drechsler-Hahn, and later in his own commentary.[6] The original, and fullest, expression of it was:

> 'The idea of the Servant of Jehovah—as Umbreit quite rightly says—is rooted in Israel. It is, to put it briefly and clearly, a Pyramid: its lowest basis is the whole of Israel; its middle section, Israel not merely *κατὰ σάρκα* but *κατὰ πνεῦμα*; its summit is the person of the Redeemer. Or to change the figure: the conception consists of two concentric circles with a common centre. The wider circle is the whole of Israel, the narrower Jeshurun (xliv. 2), the centre Christ.'[7]

The idea must thus be 'conceived as constantly changing from a narrower to a wider sense', and 'becomes applied to a person, through limitation of the meaning'.[8]

In the several editions of his Commentary on Isaiah[9] Cheyne came round substantially to the view of Delitzsch, whose 'pyramid' passage he quoted with approval.[10] On liii. 12 he remarked, 'Thus the Servant of Jehovah becomes at last practi-

[1] *Prophecies of Isaiah*, ET, p. 241.
[2] Ibid., p. 294.
[3] *KJ*, p. 7.
[4] *Prophecies of Isaiah*, ET, p. 276.
[5] *O.T. Prophecy*, p. 403.
[6] *Biblical Commentary on the Prophecies of Isaiah*, ET, 1890.
[7] Drechsler-Hahn, p. 306.
[8] *Commentary*, ET, p. 236.
[9] *The Prophecies of Isaiah*, 2 vols., 1880–1 and later eds.
[10] Ibid., i, p. 253; ii, p. 196—references to 1st ed.

cally identical with the Messianic king'.[1] Cheyne's later views —they are almost as kaleidoscopic as Sellin's—may conveniently be indicated here. In *Jewish Religious Life after the Exile*[2] and *The Book of the Prophet Isaiah*[3] he thought of the Servant in the first three Songs as 'an imaginative fusion of all the teachers of the Jewish religion in and after the time of Ezra', and in the last Song as 'a similar fusion of the different nameless martyrs of Israel in recent years into a colossal figure which is identified with the people of Israel'.[4] In his final phase Cheyne advocated a form of minority collective theory, 'a personification of the body of Jewish exiles in N. Arabia'.[5]

In the widely read exposition of George Adam Smith[6] a similar view to that of Delitzsch is advocated. The many suggestions that have been made about the Servant are to be accounted for by the Prophet's 'dissolving views' of his person and work.[7] Outside the passages now known as the Songs the Servant is Israel as a whole. In xlii. 1–7 there are 'the first traces of distinction between the real Servant and the whole nation'.[8] In xlix. 1 ff. the Servant, though still called Israel, is 'the true, effective Israel as distinguished from the mass of the nation—a Personification, but not yet a Person'.[9] The same holds good for l. 4–9, though the Servant, significantly, no longer calls himself Israel. In lii. 13–liii. 12 'the Personification of previous passages is at last . . . presented as a Person'.[10] In the historical circumstances of the exile such a Messiah as Isaiah had promised 'seemed no longer probable or required'. The change of conception is, however, explicable from the history of the intervening centuries, and 'goes powerfully to prove that it is the Messiah, and therefore an individual, whom the prophet so vividly describes'.[11]

Occasionally a synthetic theory was associated with defence of the Isaianic authorship of chaps. xl–lxvi, as by Bruno Bauer[12] and J. A. Alexander.[13] Alexander, a strict fundamentalist,

[1] Ibid., ii, p. 52.
[2] 1898. [3] *SBOT*, 1899. [4] Ibid., p. 127.
[5] Art. 'Servant of the Lord', in *Ency. Bibl.*, col. 4409.
[6] *The Book of Isaiah*, 2 vols., 1890.
[7] Ibid., ii, p. 255. References to the 1st ed.: the 2nd ed., 1927, is nowise different in its treatment of the subject.
[8] Ibid., p. 261 f.
[9] Ibid., p. 266. [10] Ibid., p. 267. [11] Ibid., p. 274.
[12] *Die Religion des ATs in der geschichtlichen Entwicklung*, 2. Bd, 1838.
[13] *The Later Prophecies of Isaiah*, 1847.

revived—presumably independently—a view similar to one which had already been put forward by certain of the rabbis,[1] namely, that the Servant was both the Messiah and Israel. As he put it:[2] 'The Servant of Jehovah . . . is the Messiah and his People, as a complex person, or the Church in indissoluble union with its Head'.

Although all the writers named in this section were agreed in regarding the Servant of lii. 13–liii. 12 as the Messiah, their interpretations of the other Servant passages were not infrequently different. Only since Duhm has it been an almost invariable rule to see the same Servant in all four 'Songs'. Thus xlii. 1 ff. is interpreted of Cyrus by Vogel, Koppe, Hezel, Hensler; of the Prophet by Dathe, and of Israel by Drechsler-Hahn: xlix. 1 ff. is interpreted of Cyrus by Vogel and Hezel, and of the Prophet by Koppe, Dathe, Hensler, and Braun. That l. 4–9 belonged to the Servant-cycle was not universally recognized, and a number of exegetes supposed it to be a fragment of prophetic autobiography.[3]

[1] See *supra*, p. 21 f.

[2] *The Later Prophecies of Isaiah*, p. 203.

[3] See *supra*, p. 41 f. *et passim*.

V

CHRISTIAN INTERPRETATIONS: FROM DUHM TO MOWINCKEL

THE period between Duhm (1892) and Mowinckel (1921) is notable for strong reaction, at least in Germany, against the collective interpretation, and the advocacy of a number of theories identifying the Servant with some historical individual. It seems proper, therefore, to begin this section with a description of these latter.

I. HISTORICAL INDIVIDUAL INTERPRETATIONS

(a) *An Unknown Teacher of the Law*

Duhm's Commentary[1] has rightly been described as epoch-making. In it he limited the first 'Song'—he was the first to use the term—to the first four verses of chap. xlii,[2] and came down decisively on the side of an individual interpretation. He described the collective theory as 'the most superficial of all expedients'.[3] Nothing could be 'more absurd' than for an exilic writer to say that Israel was morning by morning inspired (on l. 4–9), or more 'laughable' than that Israel had not opened its mouth (on liii. 7). The Songs have no connexion with either their preceding or following contexts, though this might equally be asserted of many other passages in the prophecy.[4] It is probable that they once existed as a separate book, and it may be that some of the original pieces have not been preserved.[5] They were inserted where there was sufficient room in the margins, or between paragraphs or separate sheets, by an editor who at the same time composed xlii. 5–7 and l. 10 f.[6] Unity of authorship may be asserted of the Songs,[7] though it may be that the last consists of two originally separate pieces—lii. 13–15 and liii. 11 (from *ṣaddîq*) –12, and liii. 1–11 (to *yaṣdîq*), which have been skilfully dovetailed into one another.[8] The author, who was indebted to Jeremiah, Deutero-Isaiah, and Job, probably wrote during the first half of the fifth

[1] *Das Buch Jes. übersetzt u. erklärt*, 1892.

[2] Earlier he had thought of vv. 1–7, see *supra*, p. 41.

[3] Ibid., p. 286; all references to the 3rd ed., 1914.

[4] Ibid., p. 284.

[5] Ibid., pp. xv, xx.

[6] Ibid., p. 284.

[7] Ibid., p. xv.

[8] Ibid., p. 365.

century,[1] though a later date is possible.[2] The main reason for not attributing the poems to Deutero-Isaiah was their quiet style when contrasted with the dazzling utterances of the Prophet of the exile; another reason was that their chief theme is markedly different from his.[3] Their hero was an historical person,[4] not properly a prophet, but a disciple of the prophets, a teacher of the law and a pastor of souls.[5] The conception of religion in the Songs is also different from that of normal prophecy: the emphasis is on the formal side of religion, on religion as absolute truth, *νόμος*.[6] In his later years the Servant was smitten with leprosy,[7] and of leprosy he died. The 'piercing through' and 'crushing' of liii. 5 are figures for the effects of leprosy, and it is doubtful, notwithstanding liii. 8 f., whether the Servant was done to death by men.[8] To maintain this, Duhm had to take considerable liberties with what are difficult, and probably corrupt, passages in the last Song.

The first monograph to appear after Duhm's Commentary was by Martin Schian.[9] Schian agreed largely with Duhm, though he was not satisfied with the latter's 'too mechanical theory' of the casual way in which the Songs were inserted into the prophecy.[10] That the Songs have no close connexion with their context is no compelling reason for denying them to the Prophet, since his work nowhere has the appearance of an ordered sequence of oracles, but consists rather of single effusions.[11] Schian made an examination of the literary affinities of the Songs with Deutero-Isaiah, and found that except in chap. liii there are striking similarities. He did not lay so much stress as Duhm had done on the individual character of the Servant as depicted in the Songs. What decided him to exclude the Songs from Deutero-Isaiah was that in them the Servant has an *active* calling, whereas the Servant-Israel elsewhere in the prophecy is completely *passive*, except in his sinfulness.[12] The original Songs are xlii. 1–4, xlix. 1–6, l. 4–9, and liii. 2–12. Of them liii. 2–12 is of different authorship from the others, and may be earlier than they, though it cannot be more exactly dated.[13] The subject of it, Schian conjectured,[14] was perhaps

[1] *Das Buch Jes. übersetzt u. erklärt*, p. xx.
[2] Ibid., p. 377.
[3] Ibid., p. 284.
[4] Cf. the notes on xlix. 4 and liii. 2*a* in loc.
[5] Ibid., pp. xx, 284.
[6] Ibid., pp. 285 f., 340.
[7] Ibid., p. 368.
[8] Ibid., p. 371.
[9] *Die EJL in Jes. 40–66*, 1895.
[10] Ibid., p. 55.
[11] Ibid., p. 5.
[12] Ibid., p. 13 f.
[13] Ibid., p. 59.
[14] Cf. Schenkel and Ewald, *supra*, p. 42.

some individual martyr. The author of the other Songs, who wrote not long after the exile, made use of it, thus transforming the collective Servant of Deutero-Isaiah into a figure more individual.[1] The first verse of chap. liii may also be his. A third author is to be sought for xlii. 5–7, l. 10 f., and lii. 13 ff., and his purpose was to lessen the abruptness with which the Songs appear in their contexts.

(*b*) *Eleazar*

A monograph by A. Bertholet[2] followed Schian in maintaining that the four Songs are not only *not* from Deutero-Isaiah, but also that they are not from one author. But he went farther than Schian by breaking up the last into two parts, namely, lii. 13–15, liii. 11*b* (from *ṣaddîq*) –12, and liii. 1–11*a*. The first of these sections he took with the first three Songs, and, following the suggestion of Duhm, saw in the Servant the Teacher of the Law (*Toralehrer*); not, however, a particular *Toralehrer*, but *The Toralehrer* as representative and type of all his kind. The *Toralehrer* were an order intermediate between prophet and scribe, and are best exemplified by Ezekiel. The 'death' of the Servant is the exile (cf. Ezek. xxxvii), and the date of the poems is somewhere between the beginning of the exile and the introduction of the Priests'-Code (444 B.C.), which constituted a victory for the *Toralehrer*. With regard to liii. 1–11*a*, Bertholet thought it was composed and inserted by someone who wished to make the earlier Songs more intelligible to his own generation, and who, for this purpose, illustrated them by reference to the fate of a well-known contemporary. He hazarded the suggestion that the martyr whose sufferings are described was the aged scribe Eleazar, whose cruel death under the persecution of Antiochus Epiphanes is related in 2 Macc. vi. 18–31.

(*c*) *Zerubbabel*

Ernst Sellin, who wrote more on the subject than anyone has ever done, and in the course of his pilgrimage advocated no less than four theories, first entered the lists with a monograph entitled *Serubbabel*, 1898. In it he maintained the unity of Deutero-Isaiah, including the Servant-Songs. The prophecy, in the form in which we now have it, appeared in Jerusalem

[1] Op. cit., p. 59. [2] *Zu Jes. 53*, 1899.

between 515 and 500 B.C. The prophet had laboured thirty years before in Babylon, and now included in his work, by way of encouragement, citations from his own oracles relating to the conquests of Cyrus and the fall of Babylon.[1] These are the 'former things' of xli. 22, &c.[2] The 'new things' of xlii. 9, &c., refer to the approaching exaltation of Zerubbabel, who, shortly before, had suffered martyrdom.[3] The Prophet shared the Messianic expectations that Haggai and Zechariah had entertained of Zerubbabel. None other than Zerubbabel, indeed, was the Messiah-Servant of Yahweh. But any hopes that had been set upon him had for the moment been shattered by a Persian invasion of Judah, in which the ill-fated scion of the house of David had been scourged, mutilated, and crucified.[4]

Hugo Winckler[5] agreed in the main with Sellin's treatment, and with the results at which he had arrived. But he thought that Zerubbabel was too energetic a person to be the subject of Isa. liii. We are rather to think of his predecessor Sheshbazzar, who, Winckler conjectured, was the Shenazzar of 1 Chron. iii. 18, and the oldest surviving son of Jehoiachin. Yet no sooner had Sellin abandoned Zerubbabel for Jehoiachin than Winckler[6] in his turn abandoned Sheshbazzar and went to the rescue of the forsaken Zerubbabel.

(*d*) *Jehoiachin*

Sellin next published two studies on much the same lines as his *Serubbabel*.[7] In them the unity of Deutero-Isaiah was still affirmed, but its publication was assigned to the weeks immediately preceding and following the entry of Cyrus into Babylon.[8] The passages relating to the individual Servant were xlii. 1–7, xlix. 1–6, 8, 9*a*, l. 4–9, lii. 13–liii. 12.[9] They were originally composed in the reign of Amel-Marduk, and the subject of them was the exiled king Jehoiachin. They were later incorporated into the book as we now have it, perhaps with modifications to make them accord with the Prophet's

[1] *Serubbabel*, p. 130.
[2] Ibid., p. 118.
[3] Ibid., p. 169.
[4] Ibid., p. 175.
[5] *Altorientalische Forschungen*, 2. Reihe, 3. Bd, 1901, p. 452 f.
[6] In *Die Keilinschriften u. das AT*, ed. Schrader, 3. Aufl., 1903, p. 295.
[7] *Studien I. Der KJ bei DJ*, 1901; *Das Rätsel des dj-ischen Buches*, 1908.
[8] *Studien*, p. 193.
[9] *Rätsel*, p. 112 f.; in *Serubbabel*, pp. 107 f., 216, and *Studien*, pp. 207–17, a fifth passage, xlii. 19–21, was also taken as referring to the individual Servant, but this contention was withdrawn in *Rätsel*, pp. 122, 125 f.

later conception that Israel was the Servant,[1] a conception undoubtedly present in xli. 8 and other passages. The individual Servant was neither a prophet nor a teacher of the law, but one who was to lead Israel out of exile. He was not a missionary—as xlii. 1 ff. has generally been interpreted—but a ruler who was to publish *mišpāṭ*.[2] A further indication that he was a king is that we cannot otherwise conceive how the reversal of his fortunes was to astonish the rulers of the nations.[3] Also, in the descriptions of him there are features derived from Babylonian court-style.[4] If, then, he is a king, he must, in the light of contemporary Messianic expectations, be of the house of David. The only possible conclusion is that he was the exiled Jehoiachin who, after thirty-five years of confinement, was set free and honoured by Amel-Marduk, and became the father of six or seven sons—hence 'he shall see seed' (liii. 10). The obvious objection to all this is that Jehoiachin was not put to death. Sellin tried to meet this by maintaining that the expressions referring to the death and burial of the Servant are not to be taken literally, but as figures of exile and imprisonment.[5] The resource with which he maintained his Zerubbabel–Jehoiachin thesis was astonishing. He stood by it for more than twenty years, and though he later abandoned it, it is of great interest as a modification of the traditional Messianic theory.

Sellin's *Studien* was the subject of a lengthy review by J. W. Rothstein,[6] who regarded it as not improbable that the fate of Jehoiachin furnished the historical material out of which lii. 13–liii. 12 was fashioned, though he questioned whether the author actually thought of Jehoiachin at the time when he introduced the piece into its present connexion.[7] It is more probable that he thought of the royal family whose representative Jehoiachin was.[8] There is thus a certain collective character about the Servant.[9] Rothstein was unable to agree with Sellin that the

[1] *Studien*, pp. 226–30; *Rätsel*, pp. 119–22: similarly L. H. K. Bleeker, 'Jojachin, der EJ', *ZAW*, 1922, p. 156. According to Bleeker the Jehoiachin theory was first proposed by L. A. Bühler in an inaugural dissertation: *De Messiaansche heilsverwachting en het Israëlietisch Koningschap*, 1896, pp. 64–7.

[2] *Studien*, pp. 80–98.

[3] Ibid., p. 109.

[4] Ibid., pp. 131–5; *Rätsel*, pp. 98–111.

[5] *Studien*, pp. 258–67.

[6] In *TSK*, 1902, pp. 282–336; see also his *Genealogie des Königs Jojachin u. seiner Nachkommen*, 1902.

[7] *TSK*, p. 321.

[8] Ibid., p. 319; *Genealogie*, p. 156.

[9] *Genealogie*, p. 156.

passages in chaps. xlii, xlix, and l referred to Jehoiachin.[1] In his translation of Driver's *Introduction to the Literature of the Old Testament* he, too, like Sellin, believed that the Servant was Zerubbabel.[2]

Another scholar to cast his vote for Sellin's identification of the Servant in Isa. lii–liii with Jehoiachin was W. Staerk.[3] Staerk's theory was bound up with a highly complicated literary criticism of Deutero-Isaiah, and of the relation of the Songs to one another and to the main prophecy. This was largely polemic against the equally vigorous argumentation of Budde, who had insisted upon the unity of the Songs and the prophecy,[4] and it may be well to outline it, if only to indicate the complexity in which the problem of the Servant has sometimes been involved. Briefly, the prophecy, according to Staerk, falls into two parts, chaps. xl–xlviii and xlix–lv, of different authorship and provenance.[5] The Songs, again, are not from Deutero-Isaiah, nor are they all from one hand. The first three are from the age of Jeremiah and Ezekiel, the last probably from 561 B.C. They are all, therefore, older than Isa. xl–lv, into which they were later inserted with short additions to make them accord with the collective interpretation of the Servant in the main prophecy.[6] The Servant in chap. liii was Jehoiachin. Jehoiachin, to be sure, was not put to death, but the expressions relating to death and burial (ver. 8 f.) are no more to be taken literally than are similar expressions in the Psalms, in which a sufferer describes himself as having already gone down to the grave. The Servant in the first three Songs was, in the *Bemerkungen*, the Prophetic Order (*das Prophetentum Israels*).[7] In the *Ebed Jahwe-Lieder* he has become 'a universal saviour-figure . . .

[1] *TSK*, p. 320 f.

[2] A view very similar to that of Rothstein was later put forward, quite independently in 1937, by E. Burrows, in a paper entitled 'The Servant of Yahweh in Isaiah: An Interpretation', read to the Society for Old Testament Study, and subsequently published in *The Gospel of the Infancy and other Biblical Essays*, ed. E. F. Sutcliffe: 'My suggestion is that the Servant is . . . the HOUSE OF DAVID, the messianic house in the past, present, or future as the case may be; his title of Servant of Yahweh being suggested by that of David himself; his vocation to give law to the nations being that indicated by messianic prophecy; his history during the exile being that of Jehoiachin, the representative of the house of David at that time; his future being the messianic king' (p. 60).

[3] 'Bemerkungen zu den EJL in Jes. 40 ff.', *ZWT*, 1909, pp. 28–56; *Die EJL in Jes. 40 ff.*, 1913.

[4] See *infra*, p. 58.

[5] *EJL*, pp. 100 ff.

[6] Ibid., pp. 117, 138 f.

[7] *ZWT*, p. 52.

a Messianic *Grösse* . . . a wholly mysterious ideal person, who belongs to the future . . . already concealed in Yahweh's saving purpose . . . pre-existent'.[1]

Staerk subsequently, like Sellin, abandoned the Jehoiachin theory,[2] and it may be convenient to mention here his later speculations. The element of mystery already present in his 1913 monograph deepened into agnosticism. Everything in Isa. liii is much too 'typical' to permit us to see in the Servant an individual historical figure.[3] 'It is a mystery-song . . . the exegete and historian are reminded, both by its content and form, of the limits of their interpretative skill: *ignoramus et ignorabimus*. But that is no loss, for Isa. lii. 13 ff. has found its explanation in what, viewed *e conspectu crucis*, is beyond the realm of history. And that must suffice us.'[4] Even this is not Staerk's last word. In a private communication dated 5 January 1938, he wrote: 'Aber ich bin auch nicht mehr ganz einverstanden mit dem Inhalt des Aufsatzes in ZATW. Was der Profet im Auge hat, ist doch wohl die Idealgestalt des Gott gehorsamen Israel, dessen Leiden für die Sache Gottes Sühne und Triumph zugleich ist.' This looks like a return to collectivist orthodoxy. The moral would seem to be that interpretations based upon, or—what is perhaps more to the point—needing the support of highly conjectural literary-critical constructions, are likely to be unstable. This is equally true of Sellin, whose criticism, even when he insisted upon the literary unity of Deutero-Isaiah, was essentially speculative.[5]

(*e*) *Moses*

In 1922 Sellin abandoned his theory that the Servant was Jehoiachin, and proposed instead to identify him with Moses.[6] Although this was in the year following Mowinckel's *Knecht* there is much to be said for treating it here, since it really marks the close of a period, both for Sellin himself and for the discus-

[1] *EJL*, pp. 122–5.

[2] 'Zum EJ-Problem', *ZAW* 44, 1926, pp. 242–60.

[3] Ibid., p. 256.

[4] Ibid., p. 260.

[5] The Jehoiachin theory found an echo in the Catholic A. van Hoonacker whose main interpretation was Messianic, but who thought that 'Joiakin, the offspring and representative of the house of David . . . might have served as a model in miniature for the description of the destiny of that mysterious figure of the days to come' (Art. 'The Servant of the Lord in Isa. XL ff.', *Expositor*, 8th ser., vol. 11, p. 210).

[6] *Mose u. seine Bedeutung für die isr.-jüd. Religionsgeschichte.*

sion in general. His thesis was that Moses had been murdered by his own people in Shittim following upon the apostasy at Baal Peor (Num. xxv), that, despite the efforts of the priests to suppress the sordid story, it nevertheless lived on in prophetic circles, and that out of it the Second Isaiah had developed the expectation that the once-slain leader would return from the dead, lead his people back through the desert, and then announce to all the world the salvation of God.[1] For a time this hope even supplanted that of the Messiah. Reminiscences of it are to be seen in Deutero-Zechariah (xi. 4–xiii. 9), where the good shepherd who is 'pierced' (xii. 10, xiii. 7) is Moses, and the shepherds whom he cut off (xi. 8) are Korah, Dathan, and Abiram.[2]

It is obvious that everything depended upon the trustworthiness of the tradition that Moses was murdered. Sellin's inquiries led him to the conclusion that this is the 'scarlet thread'[3] which runs through most of the prophets and binds them one to another. Whence did this surprising discovery come? From three passages in Hosea, namely, v. 1–2, ix. 7–14, and, above all, xii. 14 (EV 13) –xiii. 1. The last of these, with due emendations and rearrangement, was made to read: (xii. 14) 'But by a prophet (i.e. Moses) did "I" lead Israel forth from Egypt, and by a prophet was he preserved. (xii. 15*a*) Ephraim provoked "him" (i.e. the prophet) to anger, "Israel embittered him". (xiii. 1) So long as Israel spoke "my Torah", he (the prophet) was "prince" in Israel; yet he (the prophet) made expiation for Baal, and was slain. (xii. 15*b*) His blood will "I" leave upon "thee", and to "thee" requite his shame'.

Sellin supposed that the original story in Num. xxv had been altered almost out of recognition by the hand of the Priestly writer. How should the death of a single obscure tribal leader suffice to stay a plague in which 24,000 had perished? Actually it was Moses who was slain. Who but he had already besought Yahweh to slay him on account of the sins of the people (Exod. xxxii. 32)?[4] This established, all sorts of parallels were forthcoming between the Servant of the Songs and Moses. Moses is the Servant of Yahweh *par excellence* (Num. xii. 7 ff., Deut. xxxiv. 5, &c.), a title which only David could dispute with him.

[1] Cf. *Introduction to the O.T.*, ET of the 3rd German ed., 1923, p. 143 f.

[2] *Mose*, pp. 7, 117–20.

[3] Ibid., p. 6.

[4] Cf. ibid., p. 46.

Tradition[1] had it that he suffered from a severe Egyptian disease (elephantiasis? cf. Isa. liii. 2 f.). Like the Servant he was the meekest of men (Num. xii. 3, 8). Two catchwords in the Moses saga—Marah (√ to rebel), and Meribah (√ to contend)—are found in the third Song (Isa. l. 5–8). Moses was buried no man knew where, except that it was on the verge of the wilderness: the Servant's grave was with the wilderness-demons (reading *śᵉʿîrîm* for *ʿāšîr* in liii. 9, witn Praetorius). And so on. Needless to say, none of these analogies, nor all of them together, constitutes proof of identification, and many of them would apply equally to Jeremiah or Job.

With regard to the fate of the keystone of the theory, Sellin may speak for himself. In the first edition of his *Zwölfprophetenbuch*, of which the foreword was written in September 1921, there is no mention of Moses in connexion with the three Hosea passages, and the good shepherd in Zechariah is an eschatological figure. *Mose* was published only twelve months later. In the 1929 edition of the *Zwölfprophetenbuch* the claim that Moses was martyred is retained in the notes on xii. 14–xiii. 1, but allowed to lapse in the other two passages,[2] and the pierced shepherd in Zechariah is the high-priest Onias III. In 1930 Sellin transferred his allegiance to a modified form of Mowinckel's autobiographical theory. Such was the fate of yet another theory of which Sellin had announced[3] that it fully and finally solved the whole problem. The only convert to it, so far as I am aware, has been Freud,[4] and he only announced his support years after it had been discarded by its author.

There is no need to attempt a detailed refutation of the Zerubbabel–Jehoiachin–Moses theories. Their significance lies in the persistent endeavour to see in the Servant a royal—in the case of Moses a ruling—figure of semi-Messianic status.

(*f*) *Historico-Messianic Theory*

Similar in principle to the Zerubbabel–Jehoiachin theories of Sellin was a theory consistently advocated by Rudolf Kittel[5]

[1] Cf. Exod. xv. 25 f., freely interpreted by Sellin, op. cit., p. 134 f.

[2] Similarly in an article 'Hosea und das Martyrium des Mose', *ZAW* 46, 1928, pp. 26–33.

[3] *Mose*, p. 82.

[4] *Moses and Monotheism*, ET, 1939.

[5] *Der Prophet Jes.*, 1898; *Zur Theologie des ATs. II. Jes. 53 u. der leidende Messias im AT*, 1899; *Gestalten u. Gedanken in Israel*, 1925, ET by C. A. Knoch and

in a series of publications extending over a period of thirty years. In them Kittel maintained that the Servant was an anonymous contemporary of Deutero-Isaiah, an individual to whom the terms historical and eschatological may equally apply. We are to think, not of a prophet, but of a political and Messianic figure, 'one of the leaders of the exilic community, a man who, like Zerubbabel and Nehemiah later, hoped and laboured for the deliverance of his imprisoned people, was misunderstood and rejected by them, and finally executed by the Babylonian authorities'.[1] The tenses in the Servant passages indicate that the Servant has lived and died, but that his exaltation lies yet in the future. The conception of a suffering Messiah was not one that could possibly be reached by abstract reasoning; but when suffering and death overtook one upon whom his contemporaries had centred their hopes of deliverance, it was born quite naturally out of the exigences of the time.[2] In the two earlier works Kittel felt constrained to deny the Deutero-Isaianic authorship of the Songs;[3] but in *Gestalten und Gedanken* and the *Geschichte* he revised this opinion. In the latter case we must suppose that, in the two passages where the Servant speaks in the first person, the Prophet 'either himself composed the poems in the name of his hero, or took them over from him as a kind of monologue of the Servant, thus becoming his herald'.[4]

(*g*) *Ezekiel*

In a note on Ezek. iv. 4–8 R. Kraetzschmar[5] remarked on the 'extraordinary similarity' between Ezekiel and the Servant of Isa. liii, and thought it strange that no one had so far conjectured that Ezekiel was 'the historical original' of the Servant. He promised a monograph on the subject, but did not live to publish it.[6]

(*h*) *Hezekiah: Jeremiah: Uzziah*

In a study of the metrical forms of Deutero-Isaiah, L. Itkonen[7] suggested that the Servant in xlii. 1–4, xlii. 5–8, xlix. 1–6 was

C. D. Wright, *Great Men and Movements in Israel*, n.d.; *Geschichte des Volkes Israel*, 3. Bd, 1927.

[1] *Jes.*, p. 462.

[2] *Zur Theol. d. AT*, pp. 28 ff.

[3] Ibid., p. 21 f.; *Jes.*, pp. 379, 461.

[4] *Geschichte*, p. 242.

[5] *Das Buch Ezechiel übersetzt u. erklärt*, 1900, p. 46.

[6] See *infra*, p. 98, n. 2.

[7] *DJ metrisch untersucht*, 1916.

Hezekiah, who himself also composed the pieces; the author and subject of l. 4–9 was Jeremiah; while lii. 13–liii. 12, which has been heavily interpolated, was written by Isaiah about the leprous king Uzziah.

(*i*) *Cyrus*

Cyrus has not infrequently been supposed to be the Servant of xlii. 1 ff., and even of xlix. 1 ff.;[1] but it was left to an unexpectedly incautious Scot to make the paradoxical suggestion that Cyrus was the Servant of lii. 13–liii. 12.[2] Taking Isa. xl–lv as 'the Hebrew Cyropaedeia', Weir interpreted the last Servant passage as 'a dirge or elegy upon a fallen hero, whose marvellous career had been unprecedented, both in its splendour and in its eclipse'. All the 'data are applicable in a marked degree to Cyrus. He was, according to popular belief, brought up by a herdsman.[3] His early successes were unparalleled, but it is not known how he came to his end. It is probable that he died of wounds received in battle. . . . The comparison of the slaughtered sheep might mean that his army was ambushed, and the fact that he was defective in stratagem would lend probability to this'. It is only fair to say that Weir felt that 'any new suggestion may be acceptable, even if in the end this key also should not be found to fit the lock'. That he could have ventured upon so hazardous a speculation is proof enough, if proof were needed, of the extreme complexity of the problem.

2. COLLECTIVE INTERPRETATION

In the period from Duhm to Mowinckel the leading protagonists for the collective interpretation were Karl Budde and F. Giesebrecht.

The former[4] throughout his long life set himself, as he himself confessed, 'almost with the consciousness of a preacher in the wilderness', against the ever-rising tide of the individual

[1] See *supra*, p. 46.

[2] T. H. Weir, 'A New Theory of "The Servant of Jehovah" in Isa. 40–55', *Westminster Review*, 169, 1908, pp. 309–14.

[3] Herod. i. 112.

[4] *Die sogenannten EJL u. die Bedeutung des KJ in Jes. 40–55: Ein Minoritätsvotum*, 1900; published in English under title 'The so-called "EJ-Songs" and the Meaning of the Term "Servant of Yahweh" in Isa. 40–55', *American Journal of Theology*, July 1899; *Das Buch Jes. Kap. 40–66*, in *Die heilige Schrift des ATs*, ed. Kautzsch; see also his review of Eissfeldt in *TLZ*, 1933, Nr. 18, cols. 323–6.

interpretation. His argument for the identification of the Servant with the empirical Israel was grounded upon the conviction that the prophecy of Deutero-Isaiah is a unity, the most complete and best arranged of all the prophetic writings.[1] And since in some passages the Servant is explicitly called Israel, it follows that he must be Israel everywhere. Budde was not in the least dismayed by the insistence that the character of the Servant in the Songs is different from what it is in the rest of the prophecy. On the contrary, he accepted almost without qualification Duhm's description of the Deutero-Isaianic Servant as 'Israel, just as it is, chosen and protected of Yahweh, destined to a glorious future, but at present blind and dumb, imprisoned and plundered, a worm, despised by the heathen, full of sins', only remarking that the last item in the catalogue is a little exaggerated. Why should not the Prophet without any illusions describe Israel as at present blind and dumb (xlii. 19), so long as at the same time he comforts and exhorts the nation, by every means in his power, with the object of opening its eyes to its true destiny as a light to lighten the Gentiles? 'We nail the writer whom we call Deutero-Isaiah down to one idea, which he must ever keep repeating, and beyond which he may never go'.[1] There is an inner unity in the two characters that are presented of the Servant. If the Servant were an individual we might wonder whether such contrasts could be. With a people it is different. A people has a long history, and the Prophet looks back to the beginnings of the nation. In the past it has sinned grievously and has, therefore, been punished. Even now it is blind and dumb. It is still Yahweh's Servant, nevertheless, though it has not yet risen to the height of its calling. Again, if, as the nations describe the Servant in chap. liii, he bears but does not commit sin, that is because, as they see it, the sole worshipper of the true God is also the only one innocent.

With regard to the supposed mission of the Servant to Israel (xlix. 5 f.), Budde entered a protest against basing an individual interpretation upon a single passage, and asserted that another possibility ought to be considered, namely, that of Hitzig,[2] that Yahweh, not the Servant, is the subject of the infinitive clauses. He would thus render the passage:

'And now, saith Yahweh, who formed me from the womb to be

[1] *EJL*, p. 38. [2] See *supra*, p. 30.

his Servant, in that he brought back Jacob (out of Egypt) to himself and gathered (in the wilderness) Israel to himself[1]—and so I became honourable[2] in the eyes of Yahweh, and my God became my strength—(referring to the happy years that followed upon the possession of the promised land); yea, he saith, it is too slight a thing that thou shouldest be my Servant, that I should (only) raise up Jacob's tribes and lead back the preserved of Israel (from Babylon): rather will I make thee a light to the heathen, that my salvation may reach to the end of the earth.'

It is generally conceded that this rendering is grammatically possible. On the other hand, it is exceedingly awkward and involved, and the most recent exponents of the collective theory prefer to abandon it.

Giesebrecht had already, in 1890, written an excursus on the subject.[3] This was followed in 1902 by a monograph[4] which is still the most elaborate defence of the collective theory that has ever been offered. The Servant passages are those originally delimited by Duhm. None of them is altogether unrelated to its context, though admittedly the relations of some are more obvious than those of others. With regard to their authorship, they might conceivably be from another hand. But, in view of their close linguistic and stylistic resemblances to the rest of the prophecy, there are no cogent grounds for this theory, which raises more problems than it solves.[5] Such differences as there are between the Songs and the rest of the prophecy may be accounted for by supposing that they were intended for the more intimate circle of the Prophet's disciples, in whose presence he could be more esoteric than with the great mass of those whose faith rendered them incapable of receiving more than hope and comfort.[6] Since the Servant is Israel throughout the prophecy, and what is said of him is addressed to audiences of unequal spiritual capacity, it follows that he must represent Israel 'according to its highest meaning and abiding worth'. So conceived he stands in a certain contrast with the empirical Israel, yet not as a purely imaginary figure (*Luftgebilde*) that has no share in the actual life of the nation. The election of the people, and their present sufferings, are none other than

[1] Reading לוֹ with the Qere, and pointing יֵאָסֵף.

[2] Reading וְאֶכָּבֵד.

[3] 'Die Idee von Jes. 52^{13}–53^{12}', in *Beiträge zur Jesajakritik*, pp. 146–85.

[4] *Der KJ des DJ.*

[5] Ibid., p. 202 f.

[6] Ibid., p. 140 f.

his own.[1] Giesebrecht insisted that the Servant is always set over against the heathen, and that he has no calling at all to Israel.[2] He found Budde's exposition of xlix. 5 f. 'unquestionably ingenious' but 'too subtle', and preferred to get over the difficulties of the passage by taking Yahweh as the subject of the infinitives in verse 6, and deleting verse 5*aβ* and parts of verse 6*a* as glosses,[3] thus reading:

> But now has Yahweh spoken,
> Who formed me from the womb to be his servant;
> Wherefore I stand high in Yahweh's favour,
> And my God is become my strength:
> Too slight is it to raise up Jacob,
> And to lead back the preserved of Israel,
> So I make thee a light to the heathen,
> That my salvation may reach to the end of the world.

The gloss in verse 5 grew out of that in verse 6, which made the Servant the subject of the infinitives there. It was inserted by someone who interpreted the Servant as an individual.[4] This was a dangerous admission for Giesebrecht to make, since it admits that an individual interpretation is the most natural to the text as it stands. And his drastic handling of the text has found little, if any, acceptance.[5]

In common with Budde and other writers, Giesebrecht maintained that the Songs, if they relate to an individual, are full of obscurities and extravagances. For example, how can we think of any individual undertaking such a mission to the ends of the earth as is described in xlii. 1–4, especially if he does not strive or cry? And how, in chap. liii, are we to combine in one person the ideas of leprosy, violent death, and a continuance of life after death upon this earth without any clear indication of a resurrection from the dead? All this is conceivable only in an allegory in which a people is personified.[6]

Karl Marti's exposition[7] was very similar to that of Budde. He rejected all individual and pious minority theories, and concluded: 'It is clear that Deutero-Isaiah does not separate the ideal and the empirical Israel from one another, but sees

[1] *KJ*, p. 65; *Beiträge*, p. 179 f.
[2] *KJ*, pp. 111, 205.
[3] Ibid., pp. 42–5.
[4] Ibid., p. 46.
[5] Peake, *The Problem of Suffering in the O.T.*, p. 47, was at one time attracted to it, though he hesitated to commit himself fully.
[6] *KJ*, p. 205.
[7] *Das Buch Jes. erklärt*, 1900; *Geschichte der israel. Religion*, 1903.

the ideal in the empirical, and ascribes all the high tasks of the Servant to the actual Israel.'[1]

Budde, Giesebrecht, and Marti were closely followed in England by A. S. Peake,[2] whose support had first been given to the Ideal Israel theory, and his colleague W. L. Wardle, by M. G. Glazebrook, with some approximation to a Messianic interpretation, and by G. W. Wade; and in Germany by C. H. Cornill,[3] A. Zillessen,[4] and Max Haller,[5] the last with some approximation to individual, and even Tammuz, ideas.[6]

An independent and highly original presentation of the collective theory was offered by Henri Roy.[7] Roy believed that the Servant is Israel throughout Isa. xl–lv, but he regarded certain passages, which include the commonly recognized Songs, as later than the main body of the prophecy. They are xlii. 1–7, xlix. 1–13, l. 4–li. 8 (excluding l. 10–11), and lii. 13–liii. 12. In them the external relation of Israel to the world, and also its inner relation to God, are different from what they are in the original Deutero-Isaiah. The oppressors are no longer a single political power, Babylon, but the nations generally. They are guilty not of calculated cruelty, but only of a general contempt for Israel.[8] For this they are not greatly blamed; on the contrary, the attitude to them is one of goodwill,[9] and there is no thought of their subjection to Israel.[10] Israel's calling is not now the momentary one of witnessing for Yahweh in His judgement of the heathen gods, but the longer and more arduous task of carrying the true knowledge of Him to the heathen.[11] For this the nation is described as perfectly fitted. It is zealous and believing, not hesitant and doubtful as in the

[1] *Jes.*, p. 361.

[2] *The Problem of Suffering in the O.T.*, 1904.

[3] 'Die neueste Litteratur über Jes. 40–66', *Theol. Rundschau*, iii, pp. 409–20; *Der israel. Prophetismus*, 4. Aufl., 1903, ET by S. F. Corkran, *The Prophets of Israel*, 1907.

[4] 'Israel in Darstellung u. Beurteilung DJ', *ZAW* 24, pp. 251–95.

[5] *Das Judentum*, 1. Ausg., 1914.

[6] See also S. L. Brown, 'Introduction to the Study of Isa. 40–66', in *The Interpreter*, 7, 1910–11, pp. 397–403, with some hesitation as between the nation as a whole, and 'the incarnate conscience of the faithful few'; and W. W. Graf Baudissin, 'Zur Entwicklung des Gebrauchs von 'ebed in religiösem Sinne', *BZAW* 34, 1920, pp. 1–9, who argues that *'ebed* without further definition, such as 'my servant David', always refers to a community.

[7] *Israel und die Welt in Jes. 40–55. Ein Beitrag zur EJ-Frage*, 1903.

[8] Ibid., p. 6.

[9] Ibid., pp. 11, 21.

[10] Ibid., p. 15.

[11] Ibid., pp. 30 f., 39.

Deutero-Isaiah.[1] The passages are, therefore, to be dated from the period of the Diaspora,[2] and the Servant in them is a personification of the post-exilic Jewish community. Roy is the one writer who sees in the Servant the empirical Israel, without any idealizing traits. Deutero-Isaiah described Israel just as he knew it during the period of the exile, and the interpolator likewise described it just as he knew it in his own later time. In both we have to do with the whole and the real people Israel, and it is not necessary, with Budde, to suppose that the Servant is Israel as it should be, the Israel of the future.[3]

During this period the Pious Minority and Ideal theories still had their advocates, though both had markedly declined in popularity. Of the former, the most prominent, as well as the most persistent, was Ed. König. In two articles entitled 'Deuterojesajanisches'[4] he granted, whilst pleading for a collective interpretation, that in xlix. 5 and liii. 8*b* the Servant has a mission to Israel. He accounted for this by saying that a community finds its voice in an individual, and that such individuals are to be found in the prophets, and particularly in the contemporary representative of the order.[5] We may think of a minority having an active (xlix. 6) and passive (liii. 4 f., 8*b*) relation to the rest of Israel.[6] Here and there the author of the prophecy may be speaking in his own person.[7] We have thus an approximation to the theories of a Pious Nucleus, of the Order of Prophets, and of the Prophet himself, somewhat in the manner of Ewald and Matthew Arnold in the preceding period. In his more recent Commentary on Isaiah[8] König distinguished between 'a faithless majority and a faithful and therefore relatively pious minority' within Israel. This minority is the true Servant. In England this theory is represented by O. C. Whitehouse,[9] who identified the Servant of the Songs with 'the purified but afflicted remnant of exiles in Babylonia',[10] and C. F. Burney,[11] who thought of 'an Israel within Israel,

[1] *Israel und die Welt in Jes. 40–55*, pp. 7, 27.

[2] Ibid., p. 25.

[3] Ibid., p. 35.

[4] *NKZ*, 1898, pp. 895–997; see also *The Exiles' Book of Consolation*, ET by J. A. Selbie, 1899.

[5] *NKZ*, p. 911; *Ex. Book Cons.*, p. 50.

[6] *NKZ*, p. 920; *Ex. Book Cons.*, p. 42.

[7] *NKZ*, p. 926; *Ex. Book Cons.*, p. 180 f.

[8] *Das Buch Jes. eingeleitet*, 1926.

[9] *Isaiah*, Cent. Bible, n.d.

[10] Ibid. ii, p. 194.

[11] 'The Book of Isaiah: A New Theory', *Church Qtly. Rev.* 75, pp. 99–139.

the faithful worshippers of Yahweh upon whom the hope of the nation must be centred'.[1]

Brief mention may be made of writers who identified the Servant with specific minority parties. Matheus Lundborg[2] maintained the genuineness of the Servant Songs, which were to be interpreted of the people, particularly of those who were exiled with Jehoiachin. R. H. Kennett[3] suggested that their original application was to the martyrdom of the Hasîdîm in the persecution of Antiochus Epiphanes.[4] W. H. Kosters[5] argued that Isa. xlix–lv is post-exilic, written in Palestine, that lii. 13–liii. 12 is of different authorship from the other three Servant passages, and later than they, and that none of them is from Deutero-Isaiah. The Servant of xlii. 1–4, xlix. 1–6, and l. 4–9 was a personification of the teachers of the Law, who succeeded Deutero-Isaiah and laboured in his spirit, alike among their co-religionists and in the heathen world;[6] the Servant of chaps. lii–liii was 'the community of the pious'.[7]

The best representative of the Ideal Israel theory was J. Skinner.[8] He was of the opinion that 'the most fundamental contrast between rival interpretations of the Servant idea is not that between *collective* and *individual* theories, but between *historical* and *ideal*; i.e. between those which seek the root and origin of the conception in the sphere of phenomenal reality, and those which place it in the region of *noumena*—things ideal, not seen as yet'.[9] But although Skinner came down on the side of the ideal, his Ideal Israel was no longer the pure abstraction of Beck and Kleinert. The texts make it clear that the Ideal Israel has a history, and in the interest of fair historical interpretation it must be insisted that 'the crisis in the Servant's career is somehow bound up with the fortunes of Israel in the age of the Exile'.[10] Moreover, we must freely admit that the

[1] See also J. Halévy, 'Le עֶבֶד יַהְוֶה d'Isaïe', *Rev. sémitique*, 139, 7, 1899, pp. 193–213, 289–312; R. M. Moffat, 'The Servant of the Lord', *ET*, 13, pp. 7–10, 67–9, 174–8; and Otto Roth, a Swiss pastor, 'Die neueste Deutungen vom leidenden GK', *Protestantische Monatshefte*, 7, 1903, pp. 95–106, 141–57.

[2] *Begreppet Herrens Tjänare hos Andre-Esaias*, 1901.

[3] *The Servant of the Lord*, 1911.

[4] Similarly Paul Haupt, 'Understandest thou what thou readest?', *BZAW* 41, 1915, pp. 118–27.

[5] 'Deutero- en Trito-Jezaja', *Theologisch Tijdschrift*, 30, 1896, pp. 577–623.

[6] Ibid., p. 592.

[7] Ibid., p. 595.

[8] *Isaiah XL–LXVI*, Camb. Bible, 1898, revised ed., 1917.

[9] Ibid., ed. 1917, p. 265.

[10] Ibid., p. lxii.

Servant has a mission to fulfil for the people of Israel. Such considerations inevitably led Skinner, as they have led so many others, to approximate his Ideal Israel to 'the godly minority in whom the true ideal of Israel was partly realised'.[1]

3. MESSIANIC INTERPRETATION

(*a*) *Protestant*

The first to essay a reasoned defence of the Messianic interpretation against modern objections was Julius Ley.[2] Although his book was dated in the year following Duhm's commentary, he does not seem to have known it. Ley did not treat the Songs as a separate entity or entities within the prophecy. He recognized that they have no connexion with the preceding contexts, but accounted for this by supposing that the various oracles of which they are parts were composed at intervals over a period of thirty to thirty-five years. Like most scholars, Ley arrived at his own theory by a process of exclusion. The Servant is neither the empirical Israel, nor the Ideal Israel, nor a theocratic *Kern*, nor the Order of Prophets, nor any historical person who has been proposed. He must, therefore, be the Messiah. The Messiah had previously been thought of as a Davidic prince; but Deutero-Isaiah, 'in consequence of a progressive development in the knowledge of God's plan for the salvation of his own people and of all men, saw him as a much more exalted figure than preceding prophets had done'.[3] Ley, therefore, did not attempt to see everywhere in the Servant the features of a king, though naturally he remarked upon such features wherever he conceived them to be found.[4] The features and fortunes of the Servant are based upon those of the prophets, and, naturally, upon those of Deutero-Isaiah himself.[5] Ley was not of those who see in the Servant passages pure prediction, unrelated to historical circumstances. In particular,

[1] *Isaiah XL–LXVI*, Camb. Bible, ed. 1917, p. 113; see also W. H. Cobb, 'The Servant of Jahveh', *JBL* 14, 1895, pp. 95–113, who thought of 'Israel in its ideal totality', and G. C. Workman, *The Servant of Jehovah*, 1907, whose acknowledgements are mainly to Davidson, though he appears equally to think of 'the pious kernel of the nation to which the notion of the true Israel belonged' (p. 213).

[2] *Historische Erklärung des zweiten Teils des Jes.*, 1893; see also 'Die Bedeutung des EJ im Zweiten Teil des Propheten Jes.', *TSK*, 1899, pp. 163–206; and 'Zur Erklärung der Bedeutung des KJ', ibid., 1901, pp. 659–69.

[3] *Hist. Erklärung*, p. 89.

[4] Ibid., p. 95.

[5] Cf. l. 4–9, which Ley thought autobiographical.

it was disappointment in Cyrus that turned the thought of the Prophet to a deliverer whose weapons of warfare should be spiritual. This idea is worked out at some length,[1] thus anticipating later writers like Mowinckel, Haller, and Hempel.[2] The last passage (lii. 13–liii. 12) was composed some years after the Return (*c.* 534–533), and was prompted by the distressful conditions of the time, and by the ineptitude of leaders like Zerubbabel and Joshua. We must therefore not expect to find complete correspondence between the Messianic Servant and Christ. But in all essentials it is true of the Christ who was to come five centuries later.

The next advocate of the Messianic interpretation, L. Laue,[3] had perforce to take account of Duhm and Schian. Like them —and largely under their influence—he regarded the Songs as not from Deutero-Isaiah. He made, following Ley and others, an exception for l. 4–9, which, he thought, originally embodied experiences of the Prophet himself, being later given the appearance of a Song by the addition of the connecting vv. 10–11. The last Song was not originally a unity. Of it lii. 13–15 was a later addition, as also were xlii. 5–7, xlix. 7–9, and l. 10 f. to the Songs they follow. The original of chap. liii was a theodicy-psalm describing the sickness of someone—perhaps a leper— who had later been restored to health. It was worked up by the author of xlii. 1–4 and xlix. 1–6, who transformed the original sufferer into the Servant whose death was to have value as an offering for many. Laue granted that the language of the Songs—except in chap. liii—is very like that of Deutero-Isaiah, but he felt constrained to deny them to the Prophet because of their contents, their want of connexion with the rest of the book, and because they present the appearance, when taken together, of a 'book within the book'. Not that we can affirm unity of authorship for them; but they have a certain artistic unity, and the fact that they have been separated from one another and scattered throughout the prophecy shows that they are interpolations. They are later than Trito-Isaiah, upon which they are partially modelled. The connecting-links between them and the main prophecy are, of course, later still.

The Servant is an individual, indeed none other than the

[1] *Hist. Erklärung*, pp. 62 f., 94–100.

[2] See *infra*, pp. 75–9.

[3] *Die EJL im II Teil des Jes.*, 1898; also 'Nochmals die EJL im DJ', *TSK*, 1904, pp. 319–79.

Messiah; for in xlii. 1 ff. the same functions are given to him as are ascribed in li. 4 ff. to God Himself. Laue granted that outside Isa. liii. the conception of a suffering Messiah does not figure prominently in the Old Testament. But he thought that Zech. ix. 9 and xii. 10 (which he interpreted Messianically) point in that direction, as also do the experiences of the heroes whose sufferings are depicted in the Psalms, and he quoted with approval a sentence of Bredenkamp that 'the suffering of the pious is an important middle-stage in the development of the Messianic idea'.

A second line of development culminating in the suffering Messiah of the Songs is to be found in the sacrificial system, which, even in its later developments, is earlier than they. The High Priest had functions which approximated to the kingly and Messianic, and there are elements of the priestly in the offering of the Servant (cf. *'āšām*, liii. 10). We may, therefore, speak of the sacrificial system as constituting a virtual prophecy in action (*Thatweissagung*), just as the sufferings depicted in the psalmists and prophets constituted a prophecy in word (*Wortweissagung*) of the Messianic Servant.

According to Gerhard Füllkrug[1] none of the Servant passages has any necessary organic relation either with the preceding or the following context. That, however, is no reason for denying them to Deutero-Isaiah, since they may have been composed at intervals, as Ley supposed. The last of them is to be dated after the return from exile.[2] In its present form it is a connected whole, but it is probable that liii. 2–10 was originally from a different author, and that it was freely adapted to his purpose by Deutero-Isaiah.[3] Its original author may well have had a particular man in mind, but in Deutero-Isaiah it has become pure prediction.[4] The Servant in the four passages is an individual. The parallels between the descriptions of the new Exodus in Deutero-Isaiah and the Exodus from Egypt are so close that we are almost forced to the conclusion that the Prophet thought of the Servant as the second Moses of Deut. xviii. 15, 18.[5] He is not a Messianic figure in the traditional sense, since the Prophet expected him to come soon and lead his people out of exile.[6] When he did not appear, the return had to be made without him. The last Song is the result of the disappointments of the

[1] *Der GK des DJ*, 1899. [2] Ibid., p. 69. [3] Ibid., pp. 57–60.
[4] Ibid., p. 61. [5] Ibid., pp. 81–7, 105 f. [6] Ibid., p. 117.

early days of the return, which led the Prophet to hope anew for a Servant who should deliver Israel by his unmerited suffering. Even this hope was disappointed, only to be fulfilled centuries later in Christ. In the circumstances it would be better to speak of the Servant as a soteriological than as a Messianic figure.[1] The description of him contains elements of prophet, priest, and king.[2] A similar view to that of Füllkrug was taken by A. van der Flier.[3]

In the opinion of A. Mäcklenburg[4] the Servant in xlii. 1–7, xlix. 1–9, lii. 13–liii. 12 is quite distinct from the Servant in the rest of Deutero-Isaiah. There is no need to conclude from this that the passages are of different authorship. The contrast is sufficiently explained if we remember that 'in prophetic descriptions of the kingdom of Yahweh the material and spiritual often overlap, and that for the Old Testament consciousness no clear line of division can be drawn'.[5] In the Servant of the Songs we have a clearly defined individual who rises above material aims to a calling that is purely spiritual. The 'perfect' tenses in the description no more refer to the past than do those in the descriptions of the coming downfall of Babylon in chaps. xlvi–xlvii.[6]

The Messianic interpretation was still advocated along strictly fundamentalist lines by Ernst Ziemer,[7] who even went to the length of defending the integrity of the MT to the last detail. The whole of Isa. xl–lxvi is from the pen of Isaiah of Jerusalem. The Songs are, therefore, direct prediction of the Messiah, and have no relation to any historical occasion or circumstances.[8] The Servant is described as prophet, priest, and king.

(*b*) *Catholic*

Catholic scholars, with very few exceptions, have held firmly to the Messianic interpretation. So far as Franz Feldmann[9]

[1] Ibid., p. 119.
[2] Ibid., p. 110.
[3] 'Drieërlei verklaring van den EJ bij DJ', *Theologische Studiën*, 1904, pp. 345–76. I have not seen his later commentary, *Jezaja II Tekst en Uitleg*, 1926.
[4] 'Ueber die Auffassung der Berufsthätigkeit des EJ', *ZWT* 48, pp. 313–43; and 'Ueber die Auffassung des Berufsleidens des EJ', ibid., pp. 483–517.
[5] Ibid., p. 318.
[6] See also F. B. Denio, 'The Servant of Jehovah', *Amer. Jour. Theol.* 5, 1901, pp. 322–7; W. Volck, 'Jes. 52, 13 ff.–53', *Theol. Literaturblatt*, 23, 1902, Nr. 1–3.
[7] *Jes. 53 in der neueren Theologie*, 1912.
[8] Ibid., p. 61.
[9] *Der KG in Isaias Kap. 40–55*, 1907; *Die Weissagungen über den GK im Buche Jes.*,

was aware, no Catholic writer had ever stood for any other. His own work is remarkable for its very full references to the literature as far back as the eighteenth century. Feldmann argued, as against those who disputed the unity of Isa. xl–lv, that all differences are resolved if, in the passages in which the Servant is equated with Israel, the redemption promised is from the Babylonian exile, while in the passages describing the anonymous Servant another salvation was envisaged, a spiritual salvation, to be consummated only after the fall of Babylon.[1] Cyrus is the mediator of the one, the Servant of the other: 'Cyrus, the mighty king of the nations, is to be followed by another ruler, who announces judgement according to truth, and establishes a spiritual kingdom for both Israelites and heathen.'[2]

This somewhat arbitrary attempt to maintain diversity of function of two servants together with unity of authorship of the prophecy was modified, if not made more convincing, by A. Condamin[3] and A. van Hoonacker.[4] These two scholars, who carried on what was at first a lively, but ultimately tedious, discussion in the pages of the *Revue biblique*, did not agree on all points. They were, however, at one in supposing that xlii. 1–7 (9) had been displaced, and that it originally stood at some point after xlix. 1 ff. This done, they were able to take chaps. xl (less xlii. 1 ff.)–xlvii (xlviii) as referring to the mission and work of Cyrus, and xlix (plus xlii. 1 ff.)–lv, lx–lxii—in which Israel is never called the Servant—as referring to the mission and work of the Messiah-Servant. By this means they felt in a position to dismiss the argument, so frequently based upon xlii. 1 ff. in its present context, that the Servant is everywhere Israel. The obvious reply to this is that the complicated strophic theory upon which Condamin originally based his reconstruction was unacceptable even to van Hoonacker.[5]

3. Aufl., 1913; 'Das Frühere u. das Neue', *Festschrift Sachau*, pp. 162–9; *Das Buch Isaias übersetzt u. erklärt*, 1925–6.

[1] *KG*, pp. 47–55.

[2] Ibid., p. 88. Similarly J. Hontheim, 'Bemerkungen zu Isa. 40, 41, 42', *Zeitschr. f. Katholische Theol.* 30, pp. 159–70, 361–75, 745–61.

[3] *Le Livre d'Isaïe*, *EB*, 1905; 'Le Serviteur de Jahvé', *RB*, nouv. sér., 5, pp. 162–81; 'Les Prédications Nouvelles du chap. XLVIII d'Isaïe', ibid. 7, pp. 200–16.

[4] 'L'Ébed Jahvé et la composition littéraire des chap. XL ss. d'Isaïe', ibid., 6, pp. 497–528; 'Questions de critique littéraire et d'exégèse touchant les chap. XL ss. d'Isaïe', ibid. 7, pp. 557–72; 8, pp. 107–14, 279–85; 'The Servant of the Lord in Isa. XL. ff.', *Expositor*, 8th ser., vol. 11, pp. 183–210; *Het Boek Isaias*, 1932.

[5] Condamin and van Hoonacker were closely followed by Vetter, in *Theol. Quartalschrift*, Jg. 87, 1905, pp. 611–13; and E. Tobac, *Les Prophètes d'Israël II–III*,

4. MYTHOLOGICAL INTERPRETATION

After Ley[1] had expounded Deutero-Isaiah against the historical background of the cuneiform inscriptions, and Sellin[2] had dwelt at some length upon the influence of Babylonian court-style upon the Prophet, it was only a question of time before attempts should be made to interpret the figure of the Servant in the light of the myth of the dying and rising god (Tammuz). The first detailed essay in this direction was by Hugo Gressmann.[3]

Gressmann began by remarking on the fragmentariness of the figure of the Servant in Deutero-Isaiah. In particular, the originally mythological character of the conception 'shines through clearly in the fact of his rising again, which in our present text is not indeed related, but yet is necessarily presupposed'.[4] We must, therefore, assume that Deutero-Isaiah did not himself create the figure of the Servant, but borrowed it from an already existing tradition. The exaltation of the Servant follows without any intermediate stage immediately upon his sufferings and death. That is the characteristic situation in the cult-hymn. Such a hymn may be sung at any time, but it is not, therefore, to be supposed that the time of the singer is between the death and resurrection of the god. Isa. liii thus had its origin in the mystery-cults, in a hymn which was sung by the initiated on the day when the god died. What is said of the exaltation of the Servant points to an eschatological figure, not exactly a Davidic Messiah, but a figure parallel to the Messiah. While we cannot give a name to the figure of the Servant, we can state the circle to which he belongs: he belongs to the circle of Adonis–Tammuz figures. Yet we cannot dare to place him or his original in this circle of dying and rising gods, if these gods were nothing more than personifications of the decaying and newly reviving vegetation, or of the seasons of the year; 'For so the expiatory and sacrificial character of the Servant would be altogether unexplained'.[5] This difficulty,

1921; N. Peters, *Das Trostbuch Israels*, 1923; see also A. Crampon, *La Sainte Bible, Traduction . . .*, 1923; Lagrange, *Le Messianisme chez les Juifs*, 1909, pp. 240 ff.; *Le Judaïsme avant Jésus-Christ*, pp. 368–79. Lagrange, though advocating the Messianic interpretation, thought Condamin's transference of xlii. 1 ff. unnecessary.

[1] See *supra*, p. 64 f.

[2] *Studien*, pp. 131–5; *Rätsel*, pp. 98–111.

[3] *Der Ursprung der isr.-jüd. Eschatologie*, 1905.

[4] Ibid., p. 325.

[5] Ibid., p. 331.

however, is lessened if, with the French anthropological school, we suppose that 'the sacrificial animal by its consecration as an offering changes its nature like the Phoenix and becomes exalted to divine power'. We should thus have in the Servant a figure comparable to both Adonis and the Messiah.[1]

Hermann Gunkel[2] likewise stressed the mysterious character of the Servant, who is alike too colourless and on altogether too massive a scale to be an actual historical individual. He is, therefore, an ideal prophetic figure, of gigantic proportions, standing at the very centre of Israel and indeed of the world, embodying the faith of Hebrew religion in its victory over the world, and the brave readiness of the prophets to take upon themselves the suffering of their God-given calling. Many things have contributed to make up this figure: the experiences of Israel in exile, of great prophets like Jeremiah, and the experiences of the Prophet himself; not least the faith that at the end of things—when the primeval time should come again, and there would be a new deliverance comparable with that from Egypt—a new Moses would arise to free Israel and to found a new covenant. External influence is perhaps to be conjectured for the rising of the Servant from the dead, a thought which was otherwise foreign to contemporary Israelite religion. Here we are reminded of Zech. xii. 10 ff.—'this funeral-elegy is compared with that for Hadad-Rimmon, a god like to Tammuz and Adonis, whose premature death and return were celebrated in impressive rites'.[3] Much in these assumptions is conjectural: we do not know in what form the figure of the dying god came to the Jews, nor in what shape Deutero-Isaiah may have encountered it.

Heinrich Zimmern had already[4] placed these aspects of the discussion in a somewhat wider cultic setting. He thought it possible that the prototype of the Suffering Servant was to be sought in Babylonia. It is 'worthy of remark that in Assyria it is the *King* who, on various occasions of worship recites the

[1] A. Jeremias, *Das AT im Lichte des alten Orients*, 1906, p. 575 f., signified his adhesion to Gressmann's theory: in the 4th edition, 1930, p. 685 f., he says only that the Servant is 'a prophetic-Israelite Tammuz-figure, who offers himself willingly. It is possible that the prophet had in mind a definite royal martyr-figure of his own time. Then the tension between actuality and ideal gave to the Songs something of a Messianic character.'

[2] 'Der KJ', *RGG*, 1. Ausg., III, cols. 1540 ff.

[3] Ibid., col. 1543.

[4] In *Die Keilinschriften u. das AT*, 3. Aufl., 1903, p. 384 f.

penitential psalms, in which the penitent appears as the servant (*ardu*) of the god, and thus, so to speak, assumes the role of penitentiary'. Zimmern also referred to the numerous magical texts, and to the 'suffering righteous-man'—sometimes called the Babylonian Job—who, 'apparently a king, gives touching expression to his sense of suffering, and then in a short concluding sentence expresses his certain hope of relief from his suffering'.[1]

It is, of course, always possible to see in the portrait of the Servant traces of Tammuz-conceptions without going to the length of saying that the Servant is simply a Tammuz-figure. This was the position outlined by Haller,[2] who identified the Servant primarily with the collective Israel. But there is nothing to hinder us from assuming that such a figure as that of the Servant of Yahweh, modelled upon the dying gods of the neighbouring peoples, existed side by side with the Son-of-David in Jewish expectations of the future. Deutero-Isaiah used this mysterious figure as a symbol to illustrate the calling of his own people; but, because he did not quite succeed in carrying through the comparison, the old, semi-mythological element still gleams at some points through his presentation.[3]

[1] See further for the relevant texts, Zimmern, *Babylonische Hymnen u. Gebete*, 1905; ibid., Zweite Auswahl, 1911; *Zum babylonischen Neujahrsfest*, Zweiter Beitrag, 1918; *Das babylonische Neujahrsfest*, 1926.

[2] In the 1st ed. of *Das Judentum*, 1914, see *supra*, p. 61.

[3] Ibid., p. 57.

VI

CHRISTIAN INTERPRETATIONS: FROM MOWINCKEL TO THE PRESENT DAY

THE account of the history of the discussion so far has been almost purely descriptive. In dealing with contemporary theories it will save time later if individual presentations are accompanied by some criticism, though criticism of the theories in their entirety will be deferred to a later stage.

1. AUTOBIOGRAPHICAL INTERPRETATION

It is convenient to use the term 'autobiographical'—even though it may not be strictly exact—to denote the theory that the Servant was the prophet Deutero-Isaiah himself. No one supposes that the Songs present a complete autobiography, nor do the most recent exponents of the theory usually imagine that the Prophet-Servant composed them all. According to Gunkel[1] this autobiographical interpretation was anticipated by a certain Pastor Koeppler in an examination essay written during his student days at Giessen. But the real originator of it was the Norwegian scholar Sigmund Mowinckel, in a short monograph entitled *Der Knecht Jahwäs*.[2] Eissfeldt[3] describes this as a work of 'outstanding importance', and says that it 'exercised an influence comparable with that of Duhm's Commentary'.

Mowinckel, who defined the Songs as xlii. 1–7, xlix. 1–6, l. 4–11 (? 9), lii. 13–liii. 12, began by ruling out the collective interpretation. This he did on two grounds: (1) The Servant in the Songs is clearly described as an individual; outside the Songs there is no real but only a 'rhetorical' personification. There is a striking difference between the strongly individual characterization of the Servant in the Songs, and the 'colourless, unindividual, clearly collective' presentation elsewhere. (2) Outside the Songs the Servant (= Israel) is always passive; in the Songs the title has an 'active' signification. When it refers to Israel it is always Israel as elected to fortune and blessedness, and is bound up with the promise of a splendid future which Yahweh is preparing for His people. In the Songs,

[1] *RGG*, 2. Ausg., iii, col. 1101.
[2] Giessen, 1921.
[3] *ET* 44, p. 262.

on the other hand, the Servant is called to an active missionary vocation, a vocation which will in the end bring honour and exaltation, but which of necessity leads through trouble, suffering, and death. Only in the Songs is the Servant entrusted with a mission to the heathen.

Having decided that the Servant is an individual, Mowinckel then proceeded to rule out eschatological interpretations, on the ground that the Songs throughout make the impression that they describe a living person. We are therefore restricted to some form of historical interpretation. Further, it is no use 'playing blind-man's buff, and groping about helplessly among all the known persons of the post-exilic time'.[1] The true answer to the problem is suggested by the question of the Ethiopian eunuch to the evangelist Philip: 'Of whom speaketh the prophet this? of himself, or of some other?' (Acts viii. 34). The second and third Songs are in the first person. The speaker, therefore, must be either Yahweh or the Prophet. The first alternative is naturally excluded. Hence the thesis: 'The Servant of Yahweh in the four Songs is the Prophet, Deutero-Isaiah himself.'[2]

The Servant is 'clearly described as a prophet', and the main stress in Mowinckel's argument from this point was the inner psychological connexion between the consciousness and vocation of the Servant as depicted in the Songs, and what we can glean of the Prophet elsewhere. The difficulty is that it has generally been assumed that we know nothing at all of the personal experiences of the Prophet, except the little that can be based upon the (certainly original) LXX rendering of xl. 6 (cf. RV mg.). Mowinckel thought that this difficulty had been magnified; but even so he was obliged to make a little go a very long way, and to lay what seems exaggerated emphasis upon four passages (xli. 27, xlviii. 16*c*, xlix. 7 ff., li. 16). Of these, xlviii. 16*c* is of very doubtful genuineness; xli. 27 and li. 16 are obscure, besides being in 'odds-and-endish' contexts; while we are left wondering why Mowinckel, on his theory, did not regard xlix. 7 ff. as a Song, instead of playing it off as evidence for the Prophet's experience over against the Songs. Nor are the passages cited to show that the Prophet's task was not easy (xlii. 18, xlviii. 1, 4, 8) an adequate parallel to the sufferings depicted in even the third Song. When all is said, the objection that Mowinckel set out to meet still holds, namely, that 'the

[1] *Der Knecht Jahwäs*, p. 8. [2] Ibid., p. 9.

ever-jubilant Deutero-Isaiah seems to soar over the high places of the earth, unimpeded by empirical reality, its difficulties and hindrances'.

A strong link in Mowinckel's argument was forged out of Isa. lxi. 1–3, in which the speaker is certainly a prophet, perhaps even (?) the Second Isaiah himself, but, if not, certainly a disciple of his. Mowinckel cogently argued that the disciple could hardly have taken words of the Master and transferred them to himself, if he had not believed the Servant to be identical with his master the Prophet. His theory also afforded a reasonable solution of a difficulty to which the ordinary historical theories have always been exposed, and on which eschatological interpreters like Gunkel and Gressmann had naturally seized, namely, the fragmentary character of the Songs. If the Prophet had been describing a contemporary, would there have been so many gaps in his description? But what if he was describing himself? He was not writing an autobiography; he was wrestling with himself, with his calling, with reality, with God. What should we know of Jeremiah, if we had only his Colloquies? In like manner it stands to reason that what the Songs tell us of the Prophet must be fragmentary.

The most obvious and serious objection to Mowinckel's theory is that it made the Prophet describe, in anticipation, his own sufferings and death. Mowinckel remarked that in the last Song the difficulty is to draw the line between what has already happened and what is still future, and argued that if the exaltation is still in the future, so also may the death be, even though, at the time of writing, it was as yet no more than a certainty.

'If the Servant is identical with the Prophet and author of the poem, his death is naturally still to come; but it is inescapable. There is no difficulty in this; from the standpoint of the speaker the whole, even the exaltation, is thought of as having already taken place. The line between what has actually taken place and what is only hoped for may therefore be drawn anywhere. Where—depends upon our whole conception'.[1]

This might pass if the verbs in chap. liii were either all in the perfect or all in the imperfect. As it is, they are mixed, mainly perfects for the death, and imperfects for the exaltation. Mowinckel, therefore, seems to be taking liberties both with

[1] Op. cit., p. 38 n.

grammar and with the realities of the psychological situation, and it is not surprising that he was obliged to give up his own theory in its original form because further reflection convinced him that the death of the Servant had already taken place before the last Song was written.[1]

Eissfeldt followed up his judgement about the 'outstanding importance' of Mowinckel's brochure by recording that 'a whole series of scholars promptly accepted' the new theory. Gunkel at once abandoned his earlier view[2] with reference to Mowinckel.[3] He did not add anything to what Mowinckel had said, but contented himself with a description of the character and calling of the Prophet in the light of the 'discovery' that he was the Servant. 'This explanation of the Servant of Yahweh as the Prophet himself gives a picture so uniform, historically intelligible, and impressive, that we may well take it for granted that, after some lapse of time, it will be widely accepted'.

In 1923 two essays endorsing the theory appeared in *Eucharisterion*, a volume of studies edited by Hans Schmidt, and presented to Gunkel on his sixtieth birthday. They were 'Das Problem des Leides in der israelitisch-jüdischen Religion',[4] by Emil Balla, and 'Die Kyros-Lieder Deuterojesajas'[5] by Max Haller.[6] In 1926 Hans Schmidt[7] intimated his acceptance of Mowinckel's thesis as 'the only one that really solves the enigma.' None of these scholars brought forward any further arguments in support of the theory. They simply accepted it as it stood, and Balla was unfortunate enough to explain chap. liii with the remark that the Prophet 'in his feverish dreams' let his imagination dwell upon the fate that awaited him, even to the description of the dishonoured grave. This was to expose the weakness of the theory with a vengeance. Haller, however, without directly discussing Mowinckel's thesis that the Servant was the Prophet, gave a new turn to the discussion by expanding certain observations the latter had made about the relation between the Servant and Cyrus in Deutero-Isaiah. Were it not that Cyrus did not suffer, Mowinckel had suggested, we might be tempted

[1] *ZAW* 49, p. 253.

[2] See *supra*, p. 70.

[3] In a short monograph *Ein Vorläufer Jesu*, 1921, followed in 1929 by a complete revision of his article, in the 2nd ed. of *RGG*, iii, cols. 1100–3.

[4] Op. cit., pp. 214–61.

[5] Op. cit., pp. 261–77.

[6] See also *Das Judentum*, 2. Aufl., 1925.

[7] *Gott und das Leid im Alten Testament*, pp. 29–32, 45 f.

to identify the Servant with him.[1] Of both it is said that they are called to free the prisoners (xlii. 7, xlix. 6; cf. xlv. 13); Yahweh takes both of them by the hand (xlii. 6; cf. xlv. 1); both are called in *ṣeḏeq* (xlii. 6; cf. xlv. 13), and by name (xlix. 1; cf. xlv. 3 f.). 'Cyrus it is, according to Deutero-Isaiah, who shall bring about the realization of Yahweh's purpose upon the plane of world-history; he is the political instrument of Yahweh'.[2] As such a Messiah (xlv. 1) he is not, however, king of the *Endreich*, but only the instrument by which it is to be established. The Prophet assigns the task of bringing in the kingdom to two persons: the outward and political to Cyrus; the spiritual and religious he took upon himself.

Haller followed this up by a study of the 'Cyrus-Songs'. These he defined as xliv. 24–8 and xlv. 1–8, in which Cyrus is actually named; and xli. 1–13, xli. 21–8, xliii. 1–7, xlv. 9–13, xlvi. 1–13, xlviii. 12–16, 'the so-to-speak indirect Cyrus-Songs', which contain clear references to him. To these he would even reckon xlii. 5–9[3]—which by many is regarded as a Servant-Song—and defends the expressions *bᵉrîṯ 'ām* and *'ôr gôyîm* (ver. 6*b*) as referring to Cyrus, on the ground that these epithets are not less remarkable than the title Messiah, which is given him in xlv. 1. He takes xlv. 4 as implying that the Prophet expected Cyrus to be converted to Yahwism. In xliv. 28 the raising up of Cyrus is the climax of an ascending series of mighty acts of Yahweh in the world of nature and of men. Notice also the tremendous impression made on the Prophet by the victories of Cyrus (xli. 2 f., 25).

As Mowinckel saw it, Cyrus and the Servant operate simultaneously in different spheres, the temporal and the spiritual. Haller's view of their relationship is somewhat different. At first the Prophet fixed his hopes on Cyrus. But as time went by he had reason to be disappointed in him, and thereafter came to the conviction that he himself was the destined instrument. It has long been observed that the Cyrus-Songs cease with chap. xlviii, and Haller follows this up by pointing out that the Servant-Songs increase in proportion as the Cyrus-Songs dimi-

[1] *KJ*, p. 7 f. [2] Ibid., p. 33.

[3] See also *Das Judentum*,[2] p. 33. Hans Schmidt (op. cit., p. 45) and Mowinckel in a later publication (*ZAW* 1931, pp. 94–6) agreed with Haller on this point. This involved a different delimitation, on Mowinckel's part, of the Songs from that earlier adopted, and the abandonment of what he had earlier regarded as a decisive consideration.

nish, all but one of them being in the second half of the prophecy. This, he maintains, is not because chaps. xl–xlviii are to be dated before and xlix–lv after the fall of Babylon, since lii. 11 f. still contains an exhortation to depart from Babylon. And since there appears to be sufficient plan in the book to rule out the supposition that it is a random collection of oracles without any chronological order at all, we can only conclude that the Prophet's disappointment in Cyrus was occasioned before Babylon fell. This could only be if Cyrus knew of the expectations that were entertained of him. One of the oracles (xlv. 1–7) is actually addressed to him, and the assumption that it was meant for his eye best explains the deliberate use in it of language modelled on the Babylonian court-style, such expressions as that Yahweh 'holds the right hand' of the monarch being paralleled in the Cyrus-cylinder. Haller, therefore, feels free to conjecture that 'the ground of the Prophet's disappointment lay in this, that Cyrus, already before the conquest of Babylon, gave a clear and decided refusal' to such suggestions as that he should rebuild Jerusalem and himself become a convert to Yahwism.

Some of the items in this construction of the circumstances, such as that the Prophet may have been in the actual entourage of Cyrus, are obviously highly conjectural and uncertain. Yet it must be admitted that Haller has made out a good case for seeing in the Servant—whoever he may have been—a figure deliberately contrasted with that of the Persian conqueror.

The contrast between Cyrus and the Servant was further underlined by Hempel.[1] The liberation-edict of Cyrus, as it has been preserved to us, fell far short of the Prophet's expectations.[2] He had been confident that Cyrus would be the first of the Gentiles to turn to the God who had called him by name and given him the victory. He is 'converted' indeed, but to Bel-Marduk! No Babylonian temple sinks into the dust; none of the gods is destroyed. Instead, the conqueror exerts himself to figure as their patron. Out of this crisis of terrible disillusionment the Servant-Songs were born. Hempel, however, does not subscribe to the belief that the Servant was the Prophet, though he agrees that the Prophet put his own experiences into the

[1] In an article entitled 'Vom irrenden Glauben', *ZST* 7, 1929, pp. 631–60.

[2] The reference is, of course, to the 'Cyrus-cylinder', not to the, probably, idealized form of the edict in 2 Chron. xxxvi. 23, Ezra i. 2 ff.

mouth of the Servant. All that he is prepared to say further is that the figure of the Servant remains an enigma unless, like Kittel and Rudolph,[1] we think of some definite figure in the circle of the Prophet, to whom the latter turned in faith and longing after he had been disillusioned about Cyrus.[2]

As already indicated, the obvious objection to Mowinckel's theory, in the form in which he originally stated it, is that it supposes the Prophet to have written about his own death and burial. If only we could detach the last Song from the series, it would be natural enough to think of the others as autobiographical. This was done by Volz,[3] though it is only fair to say that he has always[4] maintained that the last Song is a separate entity, so that this is not a late expedient to enable him to fall in with what is attractive in Mowinckel's hypothesis. His main reason for thinking that chap. liii is quite distinct from the other Songs is that the central thought in these is of an *active mission* of the Servant among the Gentiles, together with, if we will, the leading home and reorganizing of the tribes of Israel, and that such considerations are entirely absent from chap. liii. What is there described, according to Volz, is an act of divine grace, carried through with the help of a specially chosen instrument, the Servant. This act of grace is executed once for all, and seems to have no relation to the patient toil of the Servant in the earlier Songs. The section lii. 13–liii. 12 is, therefore, to be interpreted eschatologically, and comes, probably, from the fourth or third century B.C. What strikes us immediately is that on this principle the death of Christ can have no relation to the ministry of teaching and healing that preceded it. Is not the truth rather that the unwearied persistence of the Servant in the earlier Songs, and his death and burial in the last, are related in exactly the same way as their parallels in the Gospels? But let us, for the moment, take Volz's theory as it stands, and see to what extent it confirms the observations already made by Mowinckel, Haller, and Hempel. According to Volz, the Second Isaiah, like any other prophet, is in the first instance an *Eschatologiker*.[5] It is quite clear that for him the coming of Yahweh in a redemptive act in contemporary history will be

[1] See *infra*, pp. 85–8.

[2] Hempel, op. cit., p. 657 f.

[3] *Jes. II*, 1932.

[4] Ibid., p. 192, and cf. his article 'Jes. 53' in the *Budde-Festschrift*, *BZAW* 34, pp. 180–90.

[5] *Jes. II*, pp. xix–xxi.

the final advent of God into the world. With the redemption of Israel from the Babylonian captivity God's purpose in the world will have reached its end, and the restoration of Zion will pass over into the establishment of the kingdom of God. Yahweh's instrument for the attainment of this purpose is Cyrus. But Cyrus, instead of turning to Yahweh, turned to Marduk. Thus, like many another in the course of history, the Prophet had to learn that God's will is not the *eschatological* marvel that he had expected. Yet he was not the man to be defeated by disappointments. 'So did there break in upon him suddenly the recognition that the establishment of God's sovereignty upon earth would not come about eschatologically, but through human toil, and that he, Deutero-Isaiah, was called to this end. Not Cyrus, but he himself, would be the world-conqueror; not Israel, but he himself, would become God's witness'.[1] It was with this conviction that he composed the Songs—not, of course, the last—as a 'piece of autobiography', and, leaving his work among his own people, journeyed forth to the islands. Volz does not stress the contrast between Cyrus and the Servant as energetically as Mowinckel, Haller, and Hempel have done. But, apart from his treatment of the last Song, his position is similar to theirs, and he must be reckoned among those who see in the Servant a figure deliberately contrasted with Cyrus.

In 1930 Sellin once more entered the lists with two articles[2] in which he argued for the unity of Trito-Isaiah, whose work he dates from 530 to 515 B.C.[3] Trito- was a disciple of Deutero-Isaiah, whose prophecies he preserved for the most part intact, though with some additions. The martyred Servant is Deutero-Isaiah. To prove this, Sellin, like Mowinckel earlier, makes much of xli. 27, xlviii. 16, and li. 14 ff.[4]—with characteristic modifications of the text. The difficulty, he confesses, is that in the last Song the Servant is already dead; and to suppose that it could have been autobiographical is therefore unnatural.[5] It has some resemblance to the specific diction and ideas of Deutero-,[6] but more with those of Trito-Isaiah.[7] All things considered, therefore, it must be conceded that there is great probability

[1] Ibid., p. 167.
[2] 'Tritojesaja, Deuterojesaja und das Gottesknechtsproblem', *NKZ* 41, pp. 73–93, 145–73. See also the 7th ed. of his *Einleitung in das AT*, 1935.
[3] Ibid., pp. 74–91.
[4] Ibid., pp. 156 ff.
[5] Ibid., p. 159 f.
[6] Ibid., p. 161.
[7] Ibid., pp. 167 ff.

that the piece is from Trito-Isaiah, who composed it as an epilogue to the career of his martyred master.

In 1931 Mowinckel returned to the subject in two articles[1] in which he endeavoured to show that Deutero-Isaiah was not the author of his own 'book'. Instead, his oracles were gathered together by a disciple who moved in the circles that we commonly know as 'Trito-Isaianic'.[2] The principle on which the editor did his work was mainly external and stylistic: some more or less prominent idea, or, more usually, 'catchword' (e.g. *qôl*, in xl. 3, 6, 9), would form the link of connexion between two or more oracles; or it might be that oracles containing similar introductory or concluding formulae would be grouped together (e.g. the double imperatives in lii. 1, 11). Thus, the whole complex of oracles was put together in domino fashion. Another, though less important, principle of association was similarity of subject-matter, poems like those dealing with Cyrus, for example, being grouped together.

It is not necessary, at the moment, to discuss the validity of Mowinckel's principle. What we are immediately concerned with is his conception of the relation of the Songs to the rest of the prophecy. Mowinckel cannot find that, on the catchword principle, they are related to it at all. None of them affords a catchword by which it can be related to the oracle that precedes it. On the other hand, they sometimes contain catchwords relating them to what *follows*. His conclusion is that they are not contemporary with the other pieces in the prophecy, but were later interpolated into it. And since the editor of the main prophecy was not Deutero-Isaiah, but someone from among his disciples, it follows that the Songs cannot have been composed by the Prophet, nor yet by the author of the first edition of the book. Their origin is nevertheless to be sought in the general circle of 'Trito-Isaiah',[3] and it is especially noteworthy that expressions and expectations which in Deutero-Isaiah refer to Cyrus are in the Songs transferred to the Servant.[4]

If, now, Mowinckel has shattered his own original theory, has he any new suggestion to make as to who the Servant was? Not very positively. But he still inclines to the view that the

[1] 'Die Komposition des dj-ischen Buches', *ZAW* 49, pp. 87–112, 242–60.

[2] Ibid., p. 244 f.

[3] Ibid., p. 252.

[4] Ibid., p. 250.

original of the figure was an historical person. 'And so my earlier interpretation—that the Servant is the Deutero-Isaiah—may once more be considered as a *possibility*, though no longer in its "autobiographical" form, nor yet in the modified form of Sellin; but in the sense that the prophet Deutero-Isaiah might be he whom his disciples later in faith extolled as cult-hero and delineated with mythological colouring'.[1] We should then have to suppose that the Prophet had later suffered martyrdom, and that in the circle of his disciples the sufferings of the master were believed to have atoning value and significance.[2]

Sellin's theory that the last Song was the work of Trito-Isaiah, and that the Servant was Deutero-Isaiah, was expanded at length by Karl Elliger.[3] Elliger had already written a book attempting to prove the unity of Isa. lvi–lxvi,[4] and it would seem that Sellin had been indebted to this for his own latest theory. According to Elliger, the main body of Isa. xl–lv consists of materials left behind by Deutero-Isaiah, who had been put to death by the Babylonian authorities. These materials were for the most part unarranged, having been circulated as pamphlets during the time not long preceding the march of Cyrus on Babylon.[5] Trito-Isaiah collected and arranged them, adding materials of his own, which amounted to a quarter of the whole, and included the last Song. He continued to prophesy after the return, and died *c.* 500 B.C. His Palestinian oracles are contained in chaps. lvi–lxvi, which were assembled —of course with some additions—by an editor who finally joined them to the already extant chaps. xl–lv.[6]

In 1937 Sellin concluded his labours with what seemed intended as a *Vale* to the subject.[7] For forty years he had impelled the discussion this way and that, always in a tone of complete finality, owing and owning little in the way of suggestion to any of his contemporaries, brilliantly original, and highly polemical. He still breaks a lance with Volz and Mowinckel with something of the old vigour, but he has little to add to Elliger,

[1] In 'Til uttrykket "Jahvaes tjener": Streiflys fra Ugarit II' (*Norsk teologisk tidsskrift*, 1942, pp. 24–6) he has called attention to a possible parallel between the Servant and Keret, who is called by the dignified title *'bd 'el* in a Ras Shamra text.

[2] *ZAW* 49, p. 257.

[3] *DJ in seinem Verhältnis zu TJ*, *BZWANT* 63, 1933.

[4] *Die Einheit des TJ*, ibid. 45, 1928.

[5] *DJ in . . . Verhältnis zu TJ*, p. 268 f.

[6] Ibid., pp. 269 ff.

[7] 'Die Lösung des dj-ischen Gottesknechtsrätsels', *ZAW* 55, pp. 177–217.

and it is with a tinge of sadness that we see him at last sitting contentedly at the feet of a *Privatdozent*.

Elliger's proof of the Trito-Isaianic authorship of the last Song consists of a comparison, in the minutest statistical detail, of the language and ideas of the passage with those of Deutero- and Trito-Isaiah respectively. A full examination of this highly technical question must be deferred to a later stage in the discussion.[1] Meanwhile it will be convenient to offer at this point some preliminary observations on Elliger's general position and method. If it could be proved that the last Song was by an intimate and clearly recognizable disciple of Deutero-Isaiah, the Sellin–Elliger modification of the autobiographical theory would be very strong indeed. But the unity of Isa. lvi–lxvi—a condition precedent to our being able to speak of an individual prophet to be called Trito-Isaiah—is not the general view of scholars, despite Elliger's pleadings.[2] The personality of 'Trito-Isaiah' is even more elusive than that of his master. We never get to grips with him. Our only means of knowing him—on Elliger's own showing—is as the editor of Deutero-Isaiah, and then through his own editor. How, then, can Elliger know him so well as to say[3] that his exilic style, in chaps. xl–lv, is more dependent upon that of Deutero-Isaiah than his post-exilic style in chaps. lvi–lxvi? Does not such a statement throw doubt upon the usefulness of the attempt to separate out passages from xl–lv and ascribe them to the author of lvi–lxvi? Elliger says,[4] as against Volz, who does not accept the unity of Trito-Isaiah, that the difference between them is one of method: Volz examines the contents of the chapters and finds differences of historical situation and religious standpoint which, he feels, are inconsistent with unity of authorship; Elliger finds linguistic and stylistic similarities which, in his view, point to their unity. Even if we prefer Elliger's method—and everyone agrees that there are linguistic similarities between the various parts of Trito-Isaiah—we shall hardly be able to conclude otherwise[5] than that his handling of it is over-statistical. On his principle we might reasonably argue that all 'Deuteronomic' writings are from one pen. Further, as between writers so similar in style as Deutero- and 'Trito-'

[1] See *infra*, pp. 170–7.
[2] See Eissfeldt, *Einleitung in das AT*, 1934, pp. 383–8.
[3] Op. cit., p. 270. [4] Ibid., pp. 301 ff. [5] See *infra*, p. 177.

Isaiah, it is antecedently improbable that we can ever be so sure as Elliger is which chapter, or which half-verse, comes from the one and which from the other.

At the close of 1938 Joachim Begrich[1] brought the discussion back to much the same point as that from which Mowinckel had started it in 1921. His argument, of course, is no mere repetition of Mowinckel's, but he does maintain—what Mowinckel had meanwhile abandoned—that Deutero-Isaiah composed the last Song in anticipation of his own death. Begrich starts from the premiss that the Prophet was not the editor of any book, and that we must therefore distinguish between the several oracles and their arrangement in the collection as we now have it. There is no necessity to suppose that their present order is the correct chronological order. So far from the Prophet having exercised a ministry as late as the fall of Babylon, he was martyred not long after 546. His call came to him in 553/2, when the success of Cyrus against the Medes gave rise to widespread eschatological expectations, not only among the exiles, but throughout the world. This is the 'eschatological' period in his ministry, and to it the larger part of his oracles is to be referred. The 'eschatological' texts have nothing in common with the (later) Cyrus texts. After some years the general commotion died down, and, since events had not taken the course anticipated by the eschatological hope, the result was grievous perplexity and disappointment, alike for the Prophet and his auditors. Then, in 547/6, came the attack of Cyrus on Lydia, and the Prophet saw in the Persian conqueror the instrument by which Yahweh would execute judgement on Babylon and free His people. During this period the eschatological expectation disappears almost completely from the Prophet's message, and its place is taken by the thought of Yahweh as Creator. The end came shortly after the conclusion of the Lydian campaign, apparently at the hand of the Prophet's fellow exiles—though Begrich is not very explicit about this. The Servant-Songs, in the order of their composition, are xlii. 1–4, xlix. 8–13, xlix. 1–6, 7, xlii. 5–9, l. 4–9, and lii. 13–liii. 12. They accompanied the work of the Prophet from its beginning to its end, xlix. 8–13 being assigned to the eschatological period, l. 4–9 and lii. 13–liii. 12 to the end, when he had to reckon with the probability that he would be martyred.

[1] *Studien zu DJ*, *BZWANT* 77.

It is unnecessary to stress the point that Begrich's interpretation of the last Song labours under the same difficulty as that which had led Mowinckel to abandon his own first hypothesis, a difficulty, moreover, which had driven Sellin and Elliger to resort to the expedient of claiming that the last Song was composed by 'Trito-Isaiah'. We may grant that the several sections of the prophecy are not in exact chronological order. But that is not to say that they have suffered such a *bouleversement* as is necessitated by Begrich's theory. As he sees it, nearly everything in the second half of the prophecy comes from the earlier eschatological period, while the (later) Cyrus texts are all to be found in the first part. This, of course, is not absolutely impossible, when we remember that to read the Qur'ān in its chronological order is, roughly, to begin at the end and read backwards to the beginning.[1] But in Deutero-Isaiah the problem is not quite so simple, since the Cyrus texts are mixed up with eschatological materials with which, according to Begrich, they have no connexion. Further, it is remarkable that oracles which, had they been arranged in chronological order, would have been, to a large extent, in the reverse order from that in which we have them, should, despite the confusion into which they were suffered to get, nevertheless present an order which on the whole bears the stamp of verisimilitude. We are entitled to speak of the present 'confusion' of the prophecy, on Begrich's reading of it, because he nowhere accounts for what must surely, in his view, be the muddle in which it now stands. How was it that all this assortment of gold went into the furnace, and then came out in the semblance of such a shapely calf? The main points of this shapeliness have long been remarked: Jacob–Israel in chaps. xl–xlviii, never in xlix–lv; Zion–Jerusalem in xlix–lv, not (except xl. 9, xli. 27) in xl–xlviii; Cyrus and Babylon in xl–xlviii, never in xlix–lv; similarly the polemic against the idol-gods, and the appeal to prophecy, in xl–xlviii, never in xlix–lv. All this looks anything but accidental; some Aaron must have fashioned the calf. To this Begrich would in all probability agree, but then he would presumably have to suppose that the editor was ignorant of any true principle of arrangement, and was therefore obliged to devise one. What he devised has such an appearance of reasonableness about it that it has up to now deceived everybody. Had

[1] Cf. Rodwell's translation.

Begrich even accepted Mowinckel's 'catchword' theory his case might have been stronger, but he does not[1] seem to do that. We can only conclude that the arrangement of the prophecy is related to the historical circumstances in which it originated, that it is approximately chronological, and that taken as a whole chaps. xlix–lv are later than xl–xlviii. Also, it is not at all clear why Begrich should insist[2] that the eschatological texts have nothing in common with the Cyrus texts, and cannot be contemporary with them, nor why he should assign to the period 547/6 no texts except those which clearly refer to Cyrus. Is it not much more likely that the Prophet depicted the exploits of Cyrus, present and expected, with eschatological colouring?

The most recent advocate of the autobiographical theory is the British scholar, Dr. Sidney Smith,[3] who thinks the Prophet was the Servant of xlix. 1–6 and l. 4–9, and also, 'most probably',[4] of lii. 13–liii. 12. The Servant of xlii. 1–4, 5–9, on the other hand, was Cyrus. Although Smith does not say so in so many words—the lectures were delivered early in 1941—the Prophet, with his enthusiasm for Cyrus, was very much in the position of leader of an underground movement in the as yet unbroken Babylonian Empire. He was put to death by his compatriots, because he outraged them by announcing that Cyrus was the promised Messiah.

2. HISTORICO-MESSIANIC INTERPRETATION

Kittel's theory that the Servant was an anonymous historical and at the same time a Messianic figure was further developed by W. Rudolph.[5] According to Rudolph the Songs are xlii. 1–7, xlix. 1–9*a*, l. 4–9, and lii. 13–liii. 12. They are the work of Deutero-Isaiah, but were composed later than the main body of the prophecy. Had they been earlier, the influence of their distinctive ideas would have been more evident in the other chapters. They are not expansions of the main text, but were composed independently of it. They were inserted, in more or less appropriate contexts, by disciples of the Prophet.

[1] Op. cit., p. 132.

[2] Op. cit., p. 69.

[3] *Isaiah Chaps. XL–LV: Literary Criticism and History*, 1944.

[4] Ibid., p. 20.

[5] 'Der exilische Messias', *ZAW* 43, 1925, pp. 90–114; 'Die EJL als geschichtliche Wirklichkeit', ibid. 46, 1928, pp. 156–66.

In answer to the question, Who is the Servant?, Rudolph makes two preliminary observations. (1) The Songs do not make up a connected poem, nor can they be explained out of one and the same situation. Whereas in xlii. 4 the thought of death seems to be excluded, in the last Song the Servant is dead and buried. Even within the first three the circumstances change. The first says nothing of any activity of the Servant in the past; that is first mentioned in the second. The third is the first to speak of ridicule and ill-treatment, though there is still no hint of death. All four Songs come from the same hand and speak of the same person, and the constantly changing situation shows that they were composed at intervals, and reflect successive stages in the career of the Servant. (2) The tasks of the Servant are manifold—to Israel and to the heathen world. As regards the Israelites, he is not only to free them and lead them back to the homeland (xlii. 7, xlix. 6*a*, 9*a*), but to reorganize them there ('to make them inherit the desolate places', xlix. 8), which seems to contemplate the restoration of the old Northern Kingdom ('to raise up the tribes of Jacob', xlix. 6). But not only will he restore Israel outwardly; he is to lead them back to God (cf. *šôḇēḇ*, xlix. 5), and this work of conversion will reach out to the whole world (xlii. 1–4, 6, 7*a*, xlix. 6*b*, liii. 10, 12*a*). The task to Israel is thus, on the one hand, that of a military leader, statesman, and ruler, and, on the other, that of a teacher and prophet (xlix. 2, l. 4 f.). Interpretations which see in the Servant *only* a ruler, *or* teacher of the law, *or* an ideal prophetic figure, *or* the world-missioner, seize upon only one element, and are therefore incomplete. The Servant is all equally. We know only one figure in the Old Testament who answers to this description, and that is the Messiah. The only thing not otherwise predicated of the Messiah in the Old Testament is the mission to the heathen.

Combining (1) and (2) above, Rudolph submits the thesis that the author of the Songs saw one of his contemporaries as the Messiah, and, in the Songs, accompanied the successive stages of his fortune. He then endeavours, 'as well as may be' from the fragmentary nature of the Songs, to trace the history of this 'exilic Messiah'.

It was only after the Prophet had delivered the major part of his oracles that he came into association with the Servant. How the certainty came to him that this particular person, whom he never names, was the bringer of salvation, we do not know. We can hardly assume that the Unknown came forward with the Messianic claim and found acceptance with the Prophet. The analogy of Zerubbabel suggests, rather, that the initiative came from the side of the Prophet. We may, with due caution, hazard a conjecture as to how the idea came to him. The thought of a world-mission, as we have it in the Songs, is foreign to the rest of the prophecy. Outside the Songs the attitude to the Gentiles is either hostile, or, if they are to be converted, it is to be entirely Yahweh's doing, and Israel is completely passive in the matter. May it not be that the idea of Israel's world-mission came from the Unknown himself, that the Prophet hailed its author as Yahweh's ambassador, and then proceeded to ascribe to him the preliminary tasks of freeing and converting Israel? The autobiographical character of the second and third Songs is accounted for, Rudolph suggests, by the fact that the Prophet became so united in spirit with the Servant that he could, in poetic speech, identify himself with him.

The first part of his task that the Servant attempted was probably that of the moral and religious reformation of his own people (xlix. 5*a*). In it he met with no success, but what struck the Prophet as great about him was that he refused to be dismayed. The third Song ends on a note of confidence in the nearness of Yahweh. It came about otherwise, and before the composition of the last Song the Servant had died. His death was violent, at the hands of the Babylonian authorities (liii. 8), which means that his political aims must have come to their ears. Had he made some attempt to free his people? Or made overtures to the Persians? Or been denounced to the government? The text gives no answer. But it may with some certainty be affirmed that he was tortured as an agitator, and buried in a dishonoured grave. This was a fearful blow to the Prophet; yet he persisted in his belief that the Servant was guiltless, that he suffered, not for his own sins, but vicariously, and that he would rise again. This conviction of the Prophet was born out of a concrete situation, the quite personal achievement of a despairing soul which otherwise could not have been assured of Yahweh's truth and justice.

The Servant, then, is both an historical and an eschatological figure. Rudolph claims that this solves the problem as the conception of a purely future Messiah does not, since it is difficult to see how, in a purely future view, the hitherto unheard-of idea of a suffering Messiah could have been developed. The altogether unique thought of a suffering, dying, and rising Messiah could never have been born of theoretical considerations, but only out of concrete experiences, brutal facts, on which faith would have gone to pieces, if it had not found a solution. Or, if we suppose that the Prophet was wrestling with the general problem of suffering, why should he not have pictured the glorification of the Servant as already accomplished? In similar didactic stories, like Job, or Jonah, or the parables of Jesus, everything is represented as occurring in the past.

A similar theory, though less elaborately worked out, has been offered by W. O. E. Oesterley.[1] Who the Servant was, he is not prepared to say, other than that he was a real, not an idealized, man. There are, however, reasons for holding that the writer of the Songs believed him to be the expected Messiah. One of the functions of the Messiah was to lead Israel back from captivity and rule over them, if not as king, at least as prince. There are obvious similarities between the Servant and Zerubbabel, who was undoubtedly a Messianic figure. Thus the spirit of God is said to rest upon Zerubbabel (Zech. iv. 6, 14, Hag. ii. 4 f.; cf. Isa. xlii. 1). Also the title 'My Servant' is conferred upon Zerubbabel (Hag. ii. 23, cf. Isa. xlii. 1, &c.). Kings are to see and arise (xlix. 7), and many nations shall be startled (lii. 15). 'There would not be much point in these words if the "Servant" were thought of as an ordinary ruler; but they are very significant if he was intended to be thought of as the Messiah'.[2] The conclusion is, therefore, that the Servant was

'an actual person who, on account of his pre-eminent righteousness, was believed by the prophet to be the Messiah. He suffered in a "naughty" world because of his righteousness; but his suffering was to the prophet of comparatively small moment, because he was convinced that the "Servant" would rise from death to complete his work; and it was the "Servant's" close relationship with God, and the prophet's profound belief in the righteousness and eternity of God, that compelled this conviction'.[3]

[1] In Oesterley and Robinson, *Hebrew Religion: Its Origin and Development*, 2nd ed., 1937, pp. 303–9. [2] Ibid., p. 307. [3] Ibid., p. 309.

3. OTHER HISTORICAL-INDIVIDUAL INTERPRETATIONS

(a) *Uzziah*

In 1929 Karl Dietze[1] revived the theory of Augusti[2] that the Servant was King Uzziah. Not only does he find a 'clear testimony' to the validity of this identification in the words *wēlôhay hāyâ 'uzzî* ('and my God is become my strength', xlix. 5; Uzziah = Heb. *'uzziyâhû* = 'Yahweh is my strength'), but he discovers references to Uzziah in more than sixty psalms, and in the Book of Job. Job, indeed, appears to be none other than Uzziah! There is no need to multiply examples of Dietze's astonishing exegesis: his theory goes to pieces on the simple fact that he is obliged to attribute the Servant-passages to Isaiah of Jerusalem. He argues that the 'Book of Isaiah' was so called because it contained Isaianic matter in chaps. xl–lxvi, just as it contained non-Isaianic matter in chaps. i–xxxix, much as we find Pauline words in the Pastoral Epistles. But this is to ignore the obvious fact[3] that the literary affinities of the Songs are such that they cannot be disengaged by two whole centuries from their definitely exilic context. It is one thing to say that the whole of 'Isaiah' is by the prophet of that name; it is quite another to pick out some passages from the second half of the book and ascribe them to Isaiah, while leaving the main portions to the Prophet of the exile.

(b) *'Meshullam'*

In 1934 J. L. Palache, of Amsterdam,[4] put forward a suggestion very similar in its essentials to the Zerubbabel and Jehoiachin theories of Sellin. It is based upon the obscure word *mᵉšullām* in xlii. 19, which the RV translates as 'he that is at peace *with me*'. 'Meshullam' occurs as a proper name, referring to various persons, some twenty-five times in the Old Testament, and also in the Elephantine Papyri. Palache accordingly proposes to take it as a proper name here, and further to identify this Meshullam with the elder son of Zerubbabel, of whom nothing is known apart from the bare mention of his name in the genealogical table in 1 Chron. iii. 19. Certain other obscure texts, namely, xliv. 26, xlix. 7, and lii. 5, are emended to give the name Meshullam.

[1] *Ussia der KG.*

[2] See *supra*, p. 41.

[3] See *infra*, pp. 161–9.

[4] *The Ebed-Jahveh Enigma in Pseudo-Isaiah.*

To make such an obscure passage as xlii. 19 the corner-stone of any theory is hazardous enough. A further difficulty is that Meshullam, so far as our complete ignorance of him allows us to surmise, did not suffer martyrdom. Nor, indeed, does Palache assert that he did, but interprets the verses referring to the death and burial of the Servant in liii. 8 f. not literally, but figuratively, as in the parallel theory of Jehoiachin. Further, if one reason why Sellin abandoned his Zerubbabel theory was that it required too late a date for the composition of Deutero-Isaiah, the Meshullam theory is in a still greater difficulty in that regard. Palache, however, taking his cue from Caspari,[1] thinks that 'Pseudo-Isaiah' is not one organic whole, but 'a series of prophetical pronouncements, which have been preserved as fragments, dating from the sixth and perhaps even from the fifth century'.

4. MESSIANIC INTERPRETATION

In recent presentations of the Messianic interpretation it almost seems as if extremes have met. On the one side there are scholars, both Catholic and Protestant, who have proceeded along traditional lines; on the other, Gressmann, who had earlier[2] propounded a mythological interpretation, abandoned this for a highly speculative form of Messianic theory, which still retained some mythological colouring.

(*a*) It is difficult, within a reasonably short compass, to summarize Gressmann's ingenious and complicated theory in his posthumous work on the Messiah.[3] He believed that what we have in the Songs refers not to the past, but to the future. This is true even of the sufferings of the Servant in chap. liii. It is Messianic prophecy, though not in the traditional sense of pre-figuring the historical Christ.

There are seven Songs: xlii. 1–4, xlii. 5–9, xlix. 1–6, xlix. 7, xlix. 8–13, l. 4–10, and lii. 13–liii. 12. Their author was Deutero-Isaiah, and their fragmentariness precludes the supposition that they were ever an entity separate from the rest of the prophecy. For even though lii. 13–liii. 12 is the conclusion, xlii. 1–4 is not the beginning, but, rather, immediately precedes the end. The most suitable beginning is xlix. 1–6.

[1] *Lieder und Gottessprüche der Rückwanderer*, 1934, see *infra*, p. 158 f.
[2] See *supra*, p. 69 f.
[3] *Der Messias*, 1929, pp. 287–339.

The statement that xlii. 1–4 refers to a time shortly before the death of the Servant is made to depend upon a simple but drastic textual emendation in ver. 3. The verse, said Gressmann, is, in its present form and connexion, quite unintelligible. How shall a world-missionary succeed if he does not cry aloud? Not that he does. But this is not because he would not; it is because, for the moment, he cannot; he is ill. He himself is the bruised reed, the dimly burning wick. People stand outside his palace, waiting in vain for his judgements. But Yahweh comforts them with the assurance: 'I will not break the bruised reed, nor quench the dimly-burning wick'.[1] The Servant will, despite all present appearances, carry through his task. The figures used in the first Song, then, do not apply to a prophet, but to a king, whose task is to spread *mišpāṭ* (judgement) and *tôrâh* (law). 'These are originally juridical-priestly terms denoting civil and religious law' respectively. Here they stand together for true religion. The Servant's task is twofold: as the highest judge he announces *mišpāṭ*, and, as *summus episcopus*, *tôrâh*.

Other political traits in the figure of the Servant, though few in number, are clearly discernible. The Servant is to free the prisoners from the dungeon (xlii. 7, xlix. 9), to lead back the tribes of Jacob (xlix. 6), and to reapportion the waste lands of Palestine (xlix. 8). He is the future political ruler, in effect—though the expression is avoided—the Israelitish king. He is placed over against, and even raised above, other political figures (xlix. 7, lii. 15, liii. 12). He is, therefore, more than an ordinary ruler; he is the ideal king, the Messiah. All these hopes are summed up in the expression *b^e^rîṯ 'ām* ('covenant of the people', xlii. 6, xlix. 8).

Nevertheless, the prophetic traits in the character of the Servant are more important than the political. 'The Servant, who sits upon the royal throne, is at the same time adorned with the mantle of the prophet'.[2] This is so generally recognized that there is no need to repeat the details of Gressmann's exposition. What is important is that he tries to avoid letting the prophetic elements be swallowed up in the political. If the

[1] Reading *'ᵃḵabbɛnnâh . . . 'ɛšbōr* for *yᵉḵabbɛnnâh . . . yišbōr*. A similar meaning may be obtained, without emendation, by translating 'The crushed reed one shall not break: the smouldering wick one shall not quench' (indefinite subject), as in E. Burrows, *The Gospel of the Infancy*, p. 65.

[2] Op. cit., p. 310.

Servant is the Messiah, he is the prophetic, not the political, Messiah. His work is both kingly and prophetic. He is, we may say, the born King-Prophet.

Gressmann was emphatic that the Servant is neither the empirical Israel nor an historical person. Referring to the earlier Songs, he granted that 'if we take their words as they stand, they seem to say that the Servant lives and works already, though as yet he has no success, but is, rather, in great difficulty. . . . Accordingly, the Servant appears to be a particular contemporary of the Second Isaiah. But this appearance is deceptive'.[1] For we cannot, on this view, conceive how the Prophet should recognize in his contemporary the Messiah, the judge of the peoples, and missionary to the heathen. Could he really have prophesied of one of his friends or acquaintances, who like a flickering wick was nigh unto death, that he should not die until he had judged the nations and spread the law of Yahweh among all peoples? And so on. And he concludes: 'The motives which could have moved a Second Isaiah to proclaim as Messiah an unknown contemporary, who appeared to be the very antithesis of the Messiah, remain unintelligible'.[2] All this, though it seems *a priori* and even a violence of grammar, is not to be lightly dismissed. It is a weakness of Rudolph's theory that he is obliged to offer some explanation of the relationship between Servant and Prophet, and that he does not succeed very well.[3] Moreover, so Gressmann insists, 'the figure of the Servant is much too shadowy to belong to a real contemporary of the Prophet. The real conditions under which he lives are nowhere clearly recognizable. . . . The Servant must, therefore, be a figure projected by faith, who, indeed, is seen and described by the Second Isaiah as present, but is in reality raised above time and space'.[4] We get the same impression from the description of the Servant's sufferings in chap. liii. How did he die? Of sickness, as a leper? Or through ill usage? Or was he executed? Nowhere is the cause of death clearly indicated. This is manifestly intentional. 'All statements are therefore to be understood as figurative. . . . What the author describes is not reality, occurrence, what is past; but phantasy, faith, what is future'.[5] There is nothing to indicate that the Prophet lived

[1] *Der Messias*, p. 311 f.
[2] Ibid., p. 312.
[3] See *infra*, p. 194 f.
[4] Op. cit., p. 312.
[5] Ibid., p. 315.

between the death and exaltation of the Servant. The whole must therefore refer to the future.

If, now, the Prophet was not thinking of the empirical Israel, nor yet of a 'real man of flesh and blood', whence did he derive the conception? No doubt something of the fate of Israel is reflected in the picture. There is something, too, of the fate of the prophets. Perhaps individual prophets have contributed to the picture. There may be elements in it of the Second Isaiah himself. But the true original of the figure is Josiah. Of all the kings, it was Josiah who most appealed to the prophets. Of him it might truly be said that he was *b^e^rîṯ 'ām* (cf. 2 Kings xxiii. 3). We know also that in the time of the Chronicler his untimely and tragic death was still mourned, no doubt at its anniversary (cf. 2 Chron. xxxv. 24 f.). The custom, says Gressmann, was kept up as late as the time of Josephus,[1] though Josephus—mistakenly!—related it to Jehoiachin. Further, according to the Chronicler, Jeremiah composed an elegy on Josiah. This elegy is extant in Jer. xxx. 18–21, which, though not by Jeremiah, was in the book as the Chronicler knew it, and might therefore be quoted as Jeremiah's. The last verse of it reads: 'For who has ventured his life in my service?' (a questionable translation!). This, said Gressmann, is *in nuce* the same thought as in Isa. liii, and is evidence for a conception of a Messianic figure who must first pass through death before he can be glorified. 'Is it too bold a conjecture that the people, who up to that time had believed in the return of David, now hoped for a return of Josiah as the Messiah?'[2] Gressmann then refers to the mysterious passage Zech. xii. 9–14 (it should be said that his various analogies, parallels, and equations are sometimes very difficult to follow, and it may be impossible, in a brief summary, not to misrepresent him) which speaks of the mourning for a 'pierced one', like the mourning for Hadad-Rimmon in the valley of Megiddon. The parallel with Isa. liii comes immediately to mind. The name of the pierced one is not given, but he is doubtless a king, and, since the whole land is to mourn, he must be the Messianic king. We may well imagine that he is Josiah, who fell at Megiddo, and the purpose of the mourning would be to restore him to life, after the fashion of the Hadad-Rimmon (= Adonis) cult. Similarly, the

[1] *Ant.* x. 7. 1; 11. 2; *Bell. Jud.* vi. 2. 1.
[2] Op. cit., p. 329.

elegy in Isa. liii. 1–9 was intended to restore the Servant to life, and to raise him to the full Messianic dignity. Gressmann did not claim that the Servant is Josiah, but only that the figure of Josiah is the starting-point for a conception which reaches its highest expression in Deutero-Isaiah. With the exile there grew up, beside the old (purely political) conceptions of the Messiah, which gradually faded though they never entirely disappeared, the new idea that the Messiah must first suffer death in the service of Yahweh. Thoughts of sacrifice and martyrdom are henceforth inseparable from the Messiah.

What the Second Isaiah did, then, was to create a new Messianic ideal, the Messiah of the exile. Such a Messiah, the Prophet believed, would not long delay his coming. 'The prophets always announce what is in the immediate future', and in this respect Gressmann's theory differs from the traditional Messianic theories which would refer the Servant to the long-awaited Jesus. In conclusion, Gressmann asserted that although the Servant is an ideal figure, a supernatural being, raised, like all such conceptions of faith, above space and time, yet the Prophet can hardly have doubted his real existence.

(*b*) The work of the Catholic Johann Fischer is, on the whole, the most comprehensive, and even, in some ways, the most objective that the subject has ever received. This is so despite the fact that he has to keep within the terms of the Biblical Commission of 1908, which ruled that it cannot be proved that Isa. xl. ff. is *not* by Isaiah of Jerusalem. His first work[1] belongs properly to the Duhm to Mowinckel period, and in it he discusses in the minutest detail the relationship between the main prophecy and the Servant-passages. Isa. xl–lv, excluding the Servant-passages and some odds and ends of verses, is a unity, and none of it is later than the fall of Babylon. The Servant-passages are xlii. 1–7, xlix. 1–9*a*, l. 4–9, and lii. 13–liii. 12. They form a cycle of progressive prophecies, each wider in scope and more profound than that which precedes it.[2] They do not make up a connected poem, since they have no formal links with one another, and they never existed as a separate book. The character of the Servant in the pericopes is so different from that of the Servant-Israel of the main prophecy that, if he is Israel, we can only conclude with Roy[3] that he is

[1] *Isa. 40–55 und die Perikopen vom GK*, 1916.
[2] Ibid., p. 134. [3] See *supra*, p. 61 f.

the Israel of a later time than that of the main prophecy.[1] But the literary characteristics of the first three pericopes are so similar to those of Deutero-Isaiah that difference of authorship is excluded. Although this is not equally obvious for lii. 13–liii. 12, we cannot conclude that it is of different authorship from the others. 'What would the first three pericopes be without lii. 13–liii. 12? Mere fragments. In particular, l. 4–9 would be a process without decision, a battle in God's name without victory, a drama without any resolution of the plot'.[2] The pericopes must, therefore, be expansions of the original prophecy, and the conception of the Servant in them represents a later and higher stage in the development of the Prophet's thought.[3] They were inserted into the prophecy by the Prophet himself.[4]

This literary-critical study was followed by a further monograph on the identity of the Servant.[5] In it Fischer maintains that the principal, indeed the only, argument for the collective interpretation is that drawn from the context. But that the collective interpretation has its difficulties is clear from the fact that all collectivists, with the single exception of Roy, have had to qualify it in one way or another. Most of them are forced to say that liii. 1–7 already describes the sufferings of the exile. What, then, is meant by the death? And the burial?

'But the sufferings of the exile cannot be described now as sufferings, now as death, and now again as burial. That may be so of any one of them taken by itself; but in a progressive, culminating narrative like chap. liii it is impossible. If in chap. liii sufferings, death, and burial are all one and the same, the passage is emptied of all beauty and poetry, and has no rational meaning at all. We should then have in liii. 1–9 a meaningless playing with metaphors, a constant repetition of what is old. How can we believe the Prophet capable of such a thing? A theory which is forced to eliminate all progress of thought from chap. liii. 1–9 has passed sentence upon itself'.[6]

And if it be said that what we have is a personification, then to 'personify' still means to describe *as a person*!

[1] *Isa. 40–55 und die Perikopen vom GK*, p. 176.
[2] Ibid., p. 131 f.
[3] Ibid., p. 181.
[4] Ibid., p. 240.
[5] *Wer ist der Ebed in den Perikopen Is. 42, 1–7; 49, 1–9a; 50, 4–9; 52, 13–53, 12?* (Münster i. W., 1922). See also *Das Buch Isaias übersetzt u. erklärt*, II. Teil, Bonn, 1939; 'Das Problem des neuen Exodus in Isaias c. 40–55', *Theol. Quartalschrift*, 110, 1929, pp. 111–30.
[6] Op. cit., p. 41.

Nor is the Servant a contemporary of the Prophet. The theory that he is is based upon two principal arguments: (1) that he is to lead Israel out of exile, and, since the author of Isa. xl–lv expected a speedy return, he must have had in mind an actual contemporary; (2) the sufferings of the Servant are past; only his exaltation lies in the future. To the first of these arguments Fischer grants that, supposing there was a Deutero-Isaiah, we cannot take refuge in the assertion that his view of the future was void of perspective. If he lived towards the end of the exile it must be conceded that he expected the Servant to come in his own lifetime. The Servant is to be a second Moses and *Führer*; to deny this is to abandon any solution of the literary problem.

'But even though the Prophet may have looked round upon his contemporaries to see whether his figure of the Messiah was realized in one or another of them, it is nevertheless quite certain that he did not describe a *particular* actual contemporary. If he had done so, we should have been much more clearly informed about the person and sufferings of this man of sorrows. The Servant-pericopes are not at all like historical descriptions; they are rather a cycle of progressive prophecies, each wider in scope and more profound than that which precedes it'[1]

—thus returning to the position maintained in the former monograph.

To the second argument of the individual-historical theorists, namely, that the sufferings of the Servant are already past, and that only his exaltation lies in the future, Fischer replies that the distinction between the perfect and imperfect of the Hebrew verb does not always correspond exactly to past and future respectively. Moreover, in liii. 10 the sufferings already described are still conditional, 'If he gives up his soul as a guilt-offering. . . !'[2] And what are we to make of the 'and their iniquities he shall bear' (*yisbōl*, impf.) of ver. 11, when ver. 4 has already stated 'and our griefs he bore' (*s^eḇālām*, perf.)? Must we not conclude that the death, as well as the exaltation of the Servant, is still in the future?

I have ventured to characterize Fischer's work as in some

[1] Op. cit., p. 57.

[2] Duhm, by the way, had perceived this—'Why this conditional particle, after it has already happened?'—and therefore drastically altered the text; see Commentary, in loc.

ways the most objective that the subject has ever received. This is certainly true of his first monograph. The reader of the foregoing summary may feel that it is too generous an estimate of the second, that what Fischer gives is mainly a criticism of the theories of others, rather than a positive statement of his own. And yet I feel that my judgement of his work is justified. If anyone sets out, like Sellin or Mowinckel, to stake out a claim for a novel theory, his work may have the appearance of being altogether positive, whereas in fact he may be turning a blind eye to whole aspects of the problem. This Fischer does not do. He surveys the work of all who had written on the subject during the preceding generation, submits it to searching criticism, and, as he would claim, finds it inadequate. This gives his work a preponderantly negative and critical appearance. But he may be entitled to argue, on his premisses, that for eighteen centuries the Church stood by the Messianic interpretation, that this traditional interpretation has been assailed from many sides, that the newer theories are unproven, and that therefore we may return to something like the *status quo ante*. This, substantially, is his position. In the last fifth of his second monograph[1] he argues that the Servant-prophecy has been fulfilled in Christ. This he does in traditionally orthodox fashion, taking the Servant-passages one by one and pointing out correspondences between them and what is said about Christ in the New Testament. His conclusion is:

'I believe I have shown that by the side of the Messianic interpretation of the Servant the other explanations are impossible. The striking agreement between the fortunes of the Servant and the fortunes of Jesus Christ *cannot possibly be due to chance*. This agreement is so wonderful that even exegetes who believe that the Servant is "Israel", nevertheless confess that the figure was first completely realized in Christ'.[2]

The most recent Catholic monograph is by J. S. van der Ploeg, of Zwolle.[3] His position is substantially that of Feldmann and Fischer, whom he quotes more frequently than any other authors. His object is 'to review the whole problem from the Catholic standpoint, in accordance with the present position of exegesis, while treating at greater length questions which need to be studied more thoroughly than Feldmann and

[1] Op. cit., chap. iv, pp. 81–95. [2] Op. cit., p. 94.

[3] *Les Chants du Serviteur de Jahvé dans la seconde partie du livre d'Isaïe*, Paris, 1936.

Fischer have done or were able to do'.[1] This entailed a review of all the literature since Mowinckel, and the book is valuable for its full bibliography.[2]

Other works advocating the Messianic interpretation may be briefly mentioned. That of J. Schelhaas,[3] a pastor of the Dutch Reformed Church, is on strictly fundamentalist lines. He will have nothing of a 'Deutero-Isaiah'; the whole of Isaiah is from the prophet of the eighth century. A. H. Edelkoort,[4] also of the Dutch Reformed Church, deals with the Servant at some length, with full references to modern literature. His position is conservative, but he regards Deutero-Isaiah as a prophet of the exile. The Servant-Songs point to Christ. Edelkoort deliberately employs the term *Christusverwachting* ('the hope of Christ') rather than *Messiasverwachting* ('the Messianic hope') in his title, because, he believes, the Old Testament hope—including that in the Songs—was soteriological rather than Messianic in the narrower sense. According to Otto Procksch[5] the Servant-passages, among which Isa. lxi. 1–3 should be reckoned, are 'a prophecy, which has only once been fulfilled, namely in Jesus Christ'.[6]

A fresh approach to a Messianic interpretation has recently been suggested by Ivan Engnell.[7] He refers[8] to A. R. Johnson, who has noted[9] that in certain Psalms, particularly lxxxix, xviii,

[1] Op. cit., p. ix.

[2] Though he lists Kraetschmar [*sic!* for Kraetzschmar], *Der leidende GK Jes. 52, 13–53, 12*, 1899, which seems never to have been published. Kraetzschmar, to be sure, refers to it on p. 46 of his *Das Buch Ezechiel*, Göttingen, 1900, as if it had already appeared. But in the Introduction (p. xv) he has a note that the date of *Der leidende GK* should be altered to 1900. Presumably he wrote it, and its publication was delayed. When, soon afterwards, he died, it still had not appeared, and never has done.

[3] *De lijdende Knecht des Heeren*, Groningen, 1933.

[4] In *De Christusverwachting in het Oude Testament*, Wageningen, 1941, pp. 372–436.

[5] 'Jesus der Gottesknecht', in *In Piam Memoriam Alexander von Bulmerincq*, Riga, 1938, pp. 146–65.

[6] Ibid., p. 155. See also A. Guillaume, 'The Servant Poems in the Deutero-Isaiah', *Theology*, vols. 11 and 12; and M. Hoepers, *Der neue Bund bei den Propheten*, Freiburg i. B., 1933, and R. Koch, 'Der Gottesgeist und der Messias (11)', *Biblica*, 27, 1946, pp. 376–403.

[7] 'Till frågan om Ebed Yahve-sångerna och den lidande Messias hos "Deuterojesaja" ', *Svensk Exegetisk Årsbok*, 10, 1945, pp. 31–65. See Postscript, pp. 228–32.

[8] Ibid., p. 32, n. 4.

[9] 'The Rôle of the King in the Jerusalem Cultus', in *The Labyrinth*, ed. S. H. Hooke, 1935, pp. 71–111.

and cxviii, the Davidic king is represented as humiliated and suffering. Johnson, to be sure, does not draw any parallels between the suffering king and either the Suffering Servant or Tammuz. Engnell, however, would designate as 'Psalms of the Ebed-Yahweh type' not only those mentioned by Johnson, but a number of others also, and he sees a direct line of connexion between the Tammuz figure and the Servant of Yahweh, with the king as the bridge between the two. Not that the Servant *is* the suffering king and divine representative in the cult. He is rather the Messiah, depicted in these categories.[1] There is also a connexion between the Servant-Songs and the royal psalm of suffering, Isa. xxxviii. 9–20 (Hezekiah's Prayer), in that both have a place in the great complex of 'Isaianic' prophecies.

5. IDEAL INTERPRETATION

Closely related to, and yet to be distinguished from, the Messianic interpretation is a type of interpretation which, for want of a better word, may be called 'Ideal'. Not 'Ideal' in the sense of purely imaginary, for those who think of the Servant as an 'ideal' figure generally insist that the portrait is based upon, or at least reminiscent of, the experiences of an actual individual or individuals. They *may* also, with varying degrees of emphasis, insist that the ideal was expected to be realized in an actual Servant who should come. Pure ideals, without either precedent or concrete realization in history, had little in common with the Hebrew genius. These Ideal theories are usually eclectic, and, if only for that reason, are difficult to define precisely.

The general type of Ideal theory has been summarized by S. A. Cook[2] in these words:

'It has, therefore, been held that there has been some idealization, perhaps a fusion of types, or the personification of a conception: ideals have been welded together, they have been incarnated in a personality; the Servant is an abstract conception, a permanent type, an ideal to be realized—like the relatively modern conception of "humanity". All this, it will be observed, seems to cut the knots, and to remove the problem of the Servant's identity from the sphere

[1] Op. cit., p. 34. For some brief hints of his meaning in English, see his *Studies in Divine Kingship in the Ancient Near East*, Uppsala, 1943, especially pp. 152, n. 1, and 176, n. 4.

[2] In *Cambridge Ancient History*, iii, p. 492.

of strictly historical inquiry. Thus, the language, as it stands, will not be wholly applicable to individuals or groups, it will be a very early and supremely interesting example of the idealization of the real, and the problem must be approached by other avenues'.

Cook's own view is that it is reasonable to regard the conception of the Servant as 'neither necessarily limited in its application (sc. to collective or individual), nor confined in its reference solely to past events or to ideals in the future'.[1] It is generally agreed that actual individuals were in the minds of the writers and helped to shape the conception. Among them Jeremiah has *a priori* claims; but since Jeremiah did not suffer martyrdom 'the Servant is certainly not Jeremiah himself, but "Jeremian"'. Nor is he a contemporary of Jeremiah:

'he is a greater than Jeremiah. . . . His identity remains unknown. . . . Not a Messianic figure, whether conquering (Jer. xxii. 4), or conspicuous for his humility (Zech. ix. 9). Indeed, he is more than that; he is at once prophet and priest, missionary and intercessor; and his attributes make him almost more than human. He is mysterious; "spectral", he has been called. It has been suggested that we have behind Isa. liii some cult-hero, or some myth of the piacular death of the gods. Such views at least testify to the profound impression which the chapters leave, and, in common with the age-long Messianic interpretation of the Servant, indicate that there is much more than ordinary idealization. He is a semi-divine being'.[2]

A similar view is expressed by W. F. Lofthouse,[3] who says 'there is something unsatisfactory about the whole discussion' as it has centred round the opposite poles of historical individual and collective community. His solution is, therefore, that

'Jeremiah, or some less known figure, may have given the author the first suggestion for his portrait; all the unmerited suffering of the time (Jer. xxxi. 29, Ezek. xviii. 2) would intensify the conception; and in the new features which reveal themselves in each consecutive study we can see the poet-thinker concentrating on his mighty subject, and carried out of himself in so doing till he has left all

[1] *Cambridge Ancient History*, iii, p. 493.

[2] Ibid., p. 494 f. See also 'The Servant of the Lord', *ET* 34, pp. 440 ff., in which Dr. Cook speaks as though we must recognize behind Isa. liii an historical individual, 'a distinctive religious personality, an outstanding spiritual genius'. According to R. S. Cripps, in *The Atonement in History and Life*, ed. L. W. Grensted, 1929, p. 77, 'this approach would seem . . . to offer the most satisfactory solution of the historical problem'.

[3] *Israel after the Exile*, Clarendon Bible, O.T., vol. iv, 1928.

possible experience behind, and has produced the classic picture of representative or vicarious suffering and death'.[1]

It is as if the poet 'beheld with anointed eyes the unique sufferer, the ideal Servant and Saviour of mankind'.[2]

W. Caspari,[3] conformably with his theory[4] that Isa. xl. ff. is made up of isolated fragments from a variety of authors, thinks of a 'Servant-to-come' (*Zukunftsknecht*) who is the product of a poetic blending of several empirical individuals—xlii. 1–4, 5–9 has in mind a political figure, specifically Cyrus—all of whom have contributed something, and above whom he rises as an ideal.[5] The figures to whom the Servant-Songs were dedicated all differ somewhat from one another; the Servant-to-come is one.[6]

6. MYTHOLOGICAL INTERPRETATION

During the most recent phase of the discussion, the purely mythological interpretation has tended to recede into the background. As we have seen, neither Gressmann[7] nor Gunkel[8] was uncompromising in his advocacy of it, and, even so, both of them subsequently modified their views. Gressmann partially,[9] and Gunkel wholly,[10] abandoned the idea that the Servant was an importation from Babylonian mythology. Indeed, a thoroughgoing mythological interpretation could hardly survive the criticism that Tammuz was a nature-god pure and simple, and that his death had no atoning significance at all.[11] This had already been conceded in principle by Gressmann.[12] As a consequence, recent writers have not gone farther than to suggest that the Servant, whoever he may have been, was delineated with some mythological colouring. Such a view is consistent with the collective interpretation, as in Haller,[13] or

[1] Ibid., p. 103 f.
[2] Ibid., p. 38.
[3] *Lieder und Gottessprüche der Rückwanderer*, Giessen, 1934.
[4] See *infra*, p. 158 f.
[5] Cf. the 'An imaginative fusion of many individuals' of Cheyne, *Jewish Religious Life after the Exile*, p. 90, to whom Caspari refers with approval.
[6] Op. cit., p. 202.
[7] *Supra*, p. 69.
[8] *Supra*, p. 70.
[9] *Supra*, pp. 90–4.
[10] *Supra*, p. 75.
[11] Cf. Baudissin, *Adonis und Esmun*, 1911, pp. 184, n. 1, and 424, n. 1. For this and other reasons for rejecting the dependence of Isa. liii on the Mystery-cults see also H. Jahnow, *Das hebräische Leichenlied im Rahmen der Völkerdichtung*, *BZAW* 36, pp. 256–65.
[12] *Supra*, p. 69.
[13] In the 1st ed. of *Das Judentum*, see *supra*, p. 61, but later abandoned, see *supra*, p. 75.

with the Messianic, as in the Catholic, Martin Brückner.[1] According to F. M. Th. Böhl,[2] who seems to have been influenced by Haller, the Prophet saw, in one great vision, a composite ideal figure made up of elements from the nation Israel, the Davidic dynasty, and the *David redivivus* of the future.[3] He is the shadow of the coming Messiah,[4] and has features in common with Tammuz.[5]

The other suggestion, that of Zimmern,[6] that the Servant is to be understood in the light of the Babylonian cultus, has been developed by Lorenz Dürr,[7] with special reference to the ritual of the New-Year festival.[8] The part of the ritual to which Dürr gives prominence is that for the fifth day of the festival, which was definitely expiatory in its intention. On that day the king, who is called the 'servant' (*ardu*)[9] of the god, was publicly humiliated before the god, being smitten on the 'cheek'[10] by the high-priest. It is far from Dürr's intention to suggest that the Servant was a purely Babylonian conception. As a Catholic, indeed, he holds that the Servant is the Messiah. Nor does he believe that the figure of the Servant is drawn in imitation of a Babylonian original; instead, the Servant was intended as a contrast to the Babylonian king. 'We Israelites also', the Prophet would seem to say, 'as well as the Babylonians,

[1] *Der sterbende und auferstehende Gottheiland*, 1920, p. 41 f. See also G. H. Dix, 'The Influence of Babylonian Ideas on Jewish Messianism', *JTS*, 26, pp. 241–56, who concludes 'that the Babylonian Tammuz-songs influenced the Jewish prophet's description of the Suffering Servant, the Messianic Angel, and that the Songs indicate an individual and not the nation or any part of it'. This interpretation is based on an identification of the Servant with ' "the Arm of Yahweh", the Messianic Angel'. According to J. P. Hyatt ('The Sources of the Suffering Servant Idea', *Journal of Near Eastern Studies*, 1944, pp. 79–86) the ideas which the prophet presents in the Servant-passages are more important than the identification of the Servant. One of the sources of these ideas was the myth of the dying-rising god: 'the myth and its accompanying ritual have furnished the prophet with imagery and terminology which he used in his own original way'.

[2] *De 'Knecht des Heeren' in Jez. 53*, 1923.

[3] Ibid., p. 28.

[4] Ibid., p. 29.

[5] Ibid., p. 25.

[6] See *supra*, p. 70 f.

[7] *Ursprung und Ausbau der israel.-jüd. Heilandserwartung*, 1925, pp. 134–50.

[8] For the text see F. Thureau-Dangin, *Rituels accadiens*, 1921, pp. 127–48; Gressmann, *Altorientalische Texte und Bilder zum AT*, i, 1926, pp. 295–303; see also the description of the festival by C. J. Gadd, in *Myth and Ritual*, ed. S. H. Hooke, 1933, Essay 3.

[9] See Thureau-Dangin, p. 135, lines 263, 268; *Texte u. Bilder*, p. 298.

[10] There is now general agreement that the word *lêtu* means 'cheek', 'jaw', or the like, not 'back' (G. R. Driver in a private communication).

have our saviour and expiator, who shall deliver us out of our distress'. Hitherto the Hebrew saviour had always been the expected victorious son of David. Now he takes on also the character of mediator and penitentiary. 'Thus was the figure of Isa. liii shaped. It is simply the antitype of the Babylonian–Assyrian king, viewed against the splendour of the future . . . Israel has no need of foreign gods, or of foreign kings, the "servants of the gods", to make atonement for it. Its own "Servant of God" will come, and undertake this role for it'.[1] He will complete his task more gloriously than any king now in the world can do.[2]

7. COLLECTIVE INTERPRETATION

During the last two decades H. Wheeler Robinson in this country, and Otto Eissfeldt in Germany, have presented a modified form of the collective theory, based upon the Hebrew conception of corporate personality.[3]

There are, of course, differences in the way the two scholars present their case; but the similarities, both in the order and method of treatment, are remarkable. This is the more so since Eissfeldt had not seen Wheeler Robinson's book until after he had read his own paper. Their combined testimony is, therefore, entitled to more than the ordinary sympathetic consideration. It will make for clarity if we summarize their arguments separately before venturing to comment on either of them.

Wheeler Robinson assumes the boundaries of the Songs as originally defined by Duhm. He does not commit himself as to their authorship, but remarks, 'if we could assert with confidence identity of authorship'—that is, with the rest of the prophecy—'then we should have a very powerful argument for

[1] Op. cit., p. 143 f.

[2] Op. cit., p. 145.

[3] Wheeler Robinson's statement of it will be found in *The Cross of the Servant*, 1926, followed in 1936 by some further remarks in an essay on 'The Hebrew Conception of Corporate Personality', in *Werden und Wesen des ATs*, *BZAW* 66, pp. 49–62. Eissfeldt's was embodied in a paper entitled 'The Ebed-Jahwe in Isa. xl.–lv. in the Light of the Israelite Conceptions of the Community and the Individual, the Ideal and the Real', *ET* 44. A German version, with the addition of footnotes and references, was simultaneously published as a brochure, *Der GK bei DJ im Lichte der israel. Anschauung von Gemeinschaft und Individuum*, Halle, 1933. References here are to the English edition.

maintaining that the picture of the Servant in the Songs is really a picture of Israel'.[1] He maintains that 'no obscure and private person could have been the Servant intended by the prophet, and those who seek an individual reference have not yet discovered with any unanimity any prominent and public personage of this age adequate to the effect on the world described in the Songs'.[2] He then sets out to meet the two great objections to the collective interpretation. These are: (1) 'that the portrait is too special and elaborate in its details to represent any group', and (2) 'that . . . a real distinction seems to be made between the work of the Servant and the national life as its sphere of operation'.[3]

In reply to the first, he reminds us 'that we are reading a Semitic and Oriental book, written . . . by people to whom our abstract methods of thought and presentation were impossible. . . . To utter a general truth at all, they had to use the particular image' (cf. the Rabbis and the Parables of Jesus). The writers of the Old Testament had 'the Semitic genius for detail, and the Semitic weakness in generalization'. Examples of vivid individualization of a group are to be seen in Isaiah's description of Israel (Isa. i. 5 f.), in Ps. cxxix, and especially in Deutero-Isaiah's portrait of Zion (liv. 1–8), which is so detailed that 'if we did not know that the prophet is thinking of Jerusalem . . . we might have had monographs on this unknown female of the exile'. All these are examples of 'descriptive, though not ultimate, individualism'.[4]

The second objection is more difficult to meet, and 'even those who believe that in both cases Israel is intended must find it hard to think that the *definition* of Israel, the radius of the circle drawn round "the Servant" figure, can be the same. . . . The discerning and obedient Servant could be a picture at most only of those pious and devout Israelites who were always in a minority'.[5] Robinson is content to delete 'Israel' from xlix. 3, and, referring to xlix. 5 f., which seems to suggest a mission of the Servant to the nation, he points out that the Hebrew is ambiguous. But instead of taking refuge in Budde's translation,[6] he is prepared to grant that the Servant *has* a mission to Israel, and asks 'whether there is not *some category of earlier thought which*

[1] *The Cross of the Servant*, p. 22.
[2] Ibid., p. 24.
[3] Ibid., p. 25.
[4] Ibid., p. 28.
[5] Ibid., p. 30.
[6] See *supra*, p. 58 f.

enables us to transcend' this antithesis.[1] Such a category he finds in 'the ancient idea of corporate personality', and by way of illustration he refers to two writers of the French sociological school, Lévy-Bruhl and Durkheim.[2] According to Lévy-Bruhl, in a totemistic society 'Each individual *is* at one and the same time such and such a man, or such and such a woman, actually alive, such an ancestral individual (human or semi-human) who lived in the mythical times of the Alcheringa, and at the same time he *is* his totem, i.e. he participates mystically in the essence of the vegetable or animal species of which he bears the name'.[3] Hence 'there is a fluidity of conception, a possibility of swift transition from the one to the many, and vice versa, to which our thought and language have no real parallel'.[4] When, therefore, we set the individual and collective views over against one another as contraries, are we not arguing 'on an antithesis true to modern, but false to ancient modes of thought'?[5] There is, in some sort, 'truth in each of the rival views', even in Mowinckel's. 'We are to think of the prophet's consciousness as capable of a systole and diastole, an ebb and a flow, so that though he utters his own experience in the service of Yahweh, it is always with the sense implicit or explicit that these things are true of all the devout disciples of Yahweh, and that *they* are Israel'. At its widest extent we cannot rest content with anything less than the equation the Servant *is* Israel, for only so can we 'do justice to the imposing scale of the treatment'.[6] At the same time what we have in the Songs 'is essentially an individual experience', and 'in fact if not in form' the prophet 'must be thinking of the experiences of those to whom religion was a reality . . . ; probably in his deepest thoughts the prophet stood alone . . . and was projecting his own consciousness into that of men of lower spirituality'.[7]

Eissfeldt, for his part, would make the first Song consist of vv. 1–7 of chap. xlii. Like Wheeler Robinson, he does not insist that the Songs are from Deutero-Isaiah, though he goes so far as to say that 'style and phraseology form an argument *for* rather than *against* the view that Deutero-Isaiah was

[1] Op. cit., p. 32.
[2] In *Werden u. Wesen*, p. 53.
[3] Quoting from *Les Fonctions mentales dans les sociétés inférieures*, p. 94.
[4] *The Cross of the Servant*, p. 33 f.
[5] *Werden u. Wesen*, p. 58.
[6] *The Cross of the Servant*, p. 36.
[7] Ibid., p. 37.

the author'.[1] This, he claims, lessens the force of the argument advanced by some protagonists of individual interpretations, viz. that the Songs are not an original part of the main prophecy, and that therefore we are perfectly free to see in the Servant an individual. 'As matters now stand, the assumption that the Servant Songs were the work of Deutero-Isaiah, and that the figure of the Ebed therein is to be understood as elsewhere in Deutero-Isaiah, has the right of precedence on its side'.

Eissfeldt then proceeds to meet exactly the same objections to the collective theory as Wheeler Robinson had done. These, as he states them, are: (1) 'the "personification" of the people Israel . . . is supposed to be so exaggerated in the Servant Songs as to transcend the bounds of possibility', and (2) 'in one of the Servant Songs, xlix. 5, 6, the Ebed is assigned a commission to Israel; hence he cannot be Israel, because he is contrasted with the latter. Moreover, the view that possibly the ideal Israel is intended cannot be considered seriously, for in Hebrew such a conception is quite impossible'.

Dealing with the first objection, Eissfeldt takes exception to the word 'personification' as not doing justice to the facts. The Hebrews were Semites, and they did not, as we do, think of a community as the sum-total of the individuals comprising it, thus creating 'an abstract unity' out of a 'mass of individuals'. To them 'unity is prior to diversity, the community prior to the individual; the real entity is the community, and the individuals belonging to it have their origin therein'.[1] In support of this contention Eissfeldt refers to exactly the same writers as Wheeler Robinson had done, namely, Lévy-Bruhl and Durkheim, and to Wheeler Robinson's examples of 'descriptive individualism' he adds Ezekiel's minute descriptions of Oholah and Oholibah (Ezek. xvi, xxiii), symbolical of Samaria and Jerusalem respectively, and claims that this picture is painted in far greater detail than that of the Servant. His conclusion on this count is that 'it is impossible to maintain the objection against connecting the Ebed of the Servant Songs with the people Israel on the ground that the individualization or personification is exaggerated far beyond the bounds conceivable and admissible for such cases'.[2]

Turning now to the second objection, that the Servant is

[1] Op. cit., *ET*, p. 264.
[2] Op. cit., p. 266.

assigned a commission to Israel, Eissfeldt notes the ambiguity of xlix. 5 f., and allows that Budde's interpretation of the passage is 'grammatically possible'. On the other hand, like Wheeler Robinson, he thinks it is 'really quite improbable'. 'Hence it cannot be disputed that we have here a reference to a commission which the Ebed has to Israel-Jacob, and this would seem to imply that the Ebed . . . is bound to be regarded as an individual; for to think of an ideal Israel or the like is to-day tabu as far as most scholars are concerned'.[1] On this point he joins issue with those who will have nothing of an ideal Israel. He quotes Pedersen[2] to the effect that 'A people is not a collection of human beings. . . . It is a psychical whole, and in so far an ideal entity. . . . It is lived wholly in every generation, and yet is raised above it, is something which is given to it and makes claims upon it'. Hence, continues Eissfeldt, 'although his language knows so little of the conception of the "ideal" of a people or some other social group, the thing itself was familiar enough to the Hebrew'. Thus, an ancestor, or ancestress, 'by no means simply belongs to the past but lives on with the social group and is present in it'.[3] Israel is distinguishable from Israelites, Zion from her children. When Jeremiah (xxxi. 15 f.) describes Rachel weeping for her children, he is not merely indulging in a rhetorical figure. 'The distinction between the corporate individual and the particular members of the social group is thus quite a customary thing, and the contrast may also be of such a kind that the corporate individual is thought of as a model and a tutor', in effect, as an 'ideal' which makes demands upon succeeding generations. In the light of this conception it is surely not without significance, concludes Eissfeldt, that in xlix. 5 f. the object of the Servant's activity is 'not the corporate figure in the singular but the individual tribes or persons in the plural'.[4] The Servant in the passage, therefore, may be thought of as an 'ideal entity' at once identical with, and yet, in a sense, different from, 'the particular social group' contemporary with the prophet.

It will be noted that, in their treatment of the first objection, viz. that the portrait of the Servant is too minutely detailed to be

[1] Op. cit., p. 266.

[2] *Israel: Its Life and Culture, I–II*, p. 475.

[3] Op. cit., p. 266.

[4] Op. cit., p. 267; cf. Johansson, *Parakletoi*, p. 62, who substantially agrees with this position.

that of a nation, both Wheeler Robinson and Eissfeldt advance exactly the same arguments, and it must be admitted that they have made out a very strong case. Their illustrations of descriptive individualism admirably supplement and support one another, and compel the conclusion that the objection as such is *a priori*, and, taken by itself, cannot be sustained. Their replies to the second objection are similar, but worked out somewhat differently. Eissfeldt, despite all that has been advanced to the contrary, does not shrink from employing the category of an 'ideal' Israel. Robinson[1] is at pains to affirm that his interpretation of the problem 'is not to be confused with that which refers it to an ideal Israel', and quotes with approval Bertholet's remark that 'the thought of an ideal Israel is so little a Semitic one, that no interpretation raises greater difficulties'.[2] For Robinson the 'real Israel' to which the figure of the Servant contracts is the Prophet and those who were like-minded with him, and the object of his mission is first of all the nation as a whole, and, finally, the Gentiles. In this respect his interpretation approximates to that of Mowinckel. The *effective* Servant consists at the moment of a few individuals, perhaps of not more than one; it is only in an ideal sense that the nation as a whole is the Servant. Eissfeldt, while remarking in one place that the Prophet 'undoubtedly modelled the figure after himself; and to that extent it is right to identify the Ebed with Deutero-Isaiah', lays the major part of his emphasis upon the 'ideal' Israel, whose mission is to be to the individual tribes or persons comprising Israel, and finally, of course, to the Gentiles. Robinson is careful to emphasize that the sufferings of the Prophet-Servant and his like are 'real sufferings'. This is not so obviously true of Eissfeldt's 'ideal' Israel, for, when all is said, there is a high degree of the rhetorical and imaginative in such a description as that of Rachel weeping for her children. In this respect, Eissfeldt's way of putting things is more open to criticism than Robinson's.

Budde, reviewing Eissfeldt's work,[3] took exception to his appeal to Pedersen, on the ground that by 'an ideal entity' Pedersen meant only something existing in idea, imaginary (German *ideell*), not perfect and 'ideal' (German *ideal*) in the sense that the word normally has in English—English having

[1] *The Cross of the Servant*, p. 37.

[2] *Zu Jes. 53*, p. 7.

[3] *Theol. Litteraturzeitung*, 1933, No. 18, cols. 323–6.

only the one word, 'ideal', where German is able to make a distinction. Even if that were so, it would not, of course, invalidate Eissfeldt's attempt to make out a case independently. But a reading of the context in Pedersen makes it doubtful whether Budde's objection can be sustained. For Pedersen[1] goes on to say: 'Thus there rises out of the history of the people an invisible figure of grand proportions, bearing the impress of definite features, the features left by experiences. And this figure is identical with the ancestor. When the Israelites speak of their ancestor, then it is not as a remote figure which has disappeared long ago. He constantly shares in what happens, the history of the people is his'. This is, in effect, very much the line of thought which Eissfeldt develops, whichever be the proper sense of 'ideal' to apply to it. The conception may be remote from our ways of thinking, but there is no reason to doubt that it was real enough to the ancient Israelite. On the other hand, it is questionable whether the ideal ancestor is so clearly differentiated from the nation as to have a mission to it. The 'features' of the ancestor, so Pedersen seems to say, are not those of the original ancestor unchanged; they have been constantly modified by 'experiences', by what the ancestor has shared of the fortunes of his descendants. Until at any given moment the one is but the *alter ego* or counterpart of the other. Jacob is the typical Hebrew of the time when the sagas about him were written, and neither better nor worse than his descendants. Were it otherwise, the ideal ancestor would be an *ideell*, an imaginary entity. But even supposing that Eissfeldt's 'ideal' could be so distinguished from the 'real' as to have a mission to it, we are left wondering whether the conception had much relevance to the circumstances in which the Prophet and his fellow-exiles found themselves. In view of his approving admission[2] that 'there is justification for Hempel when he asserts with some satisfaction that "a fixed point here seems to have been reached in the matter of interpretation—namely, the conception of the Servant Songs as a correction of the Cyrus poems" ',[3] we expect him to say that the Servant is an individual, one greater than Cyrus, consciously intended to be a foil to him. What he offers seems too academic, the Songs as an allegorical interpretation of the sufferings of 'ideal' Israel. What xlix. 5 f.

[1] Op. cit., p. 475 f.
[2] Op. cit., p. 263.
[3] In *ZAW* 50, 1932, p. 209.

demands is one whose first and urgent task shall be to deliver Israel out of his afflictions.

We turn back now to Wheeler Robinson's handling of xlix. 5 f. According to him[1] 'the prophet is conscious of no contrast during the expansion' from the smaller to the larger mission of the Servant. 'He *is* Israel created to be the Servant; he is Israel, though working alone to make Israel what she ought to be; he is Israel finally become a light of nations to the end of the earth'. But is not this to think of the Prophet-Servant too much after the fashion of a modern pastor of souls? Part of the Servant's task is 'to raise up the tribes of Jacob', and that—note the word tribes—not only admits of a political reference, it even seems to require one. The message of Deutero-Isaiah is largely concerned with the expectation of a return to the homeland, and the Servant is to be the instrument for the accomplishment of this. That being so, it is difficult to see how the Prophet-Servant could be conscious of no contrast between himself and the nation, since, on any *historical* theory, someone—and who but himself?—was really committed to leading the nation back from exile. If we admit that, we are either back at the full autobiographical theory, with the problem of the fifty-third chapter still on our hands, or we must look for some other individual Servant. Moreover, if the Prophet was not conscious of any distinction between the Servant and Israel, why should he, as it would seem, so studiously avoid equating the Servant with Jacob-Israel *in*, and as studiously equate them *outside*, the Songs?[2] This lack of definition of the word 'Servant' in the Songs, contrasted with the explicit definition of it elsewhere, brings us to the fact that the character and calling of the Servant in the Songs are markedly different from what they are in the main prophecy.[3] This contrast is so marked that the argument for identifying the Servant with Israel is really weakened, instead of strengthened, if we suppose that Deutero-Isaiah was the author of the Songs. The identification, as Roy and Fischer insisted, is only natural if we assume that the Songs are of independent authorship, composed by someone who approached the subject in his own way, undeterred by Deutero-Isaiah's unflattering descriptions of the Servant Israel.

[1] *Werden u. Wesen*, p. 59.

[2] For a detailed discussion of this point, see *infra*, pp. 178 ff.

[3] See *infra*, pp. 181–4.

A still more composite theory is advanced by Wilhelm Vischer.[1] Indeed, it is difficult to know just where to place Vischer in the classification of interpretations. He insists upon the relative truth of nearly all the theories that have been put forward, using[2] the same phrase 'systole and diastole' as Wheeler Robinson, though he quotes it from Franz Delitzsch.[3] The variety of mutually exclusive interpretations reminds him of the Indian story of four blind men who tried to describe an elephant. The first felt a leg, and said it was a tree; the second an ear, and said it was a basket; the third its tusks, and said it was a plough; the fourth its trunk, and was sure it was a snake. Even so, thinks Vischer, the different theories of the Servant are due to the fact that scholars have treated as abstractions elements that ought to be combined into a unity. Scripture is a unity and so, for that matter, is the Book of Isaiah. And the only way to solve the problem of the Songs is to discover their meaning in their present context.

This might seem to commit him without further ado to advocacy of the thoroughgoing collective theory. But no! He says plainly that the Songs disturb their context, which, without them, presents an ordered sequence of ideas. If they were omitted they would not be missed, and it *may* even be that they are not from Deutero-Isaiah. They therefore call for consideration in themselves, as well as in their context. Looking at them so, Vischer is inclined to think, with Mowinckel, that they embody experiences of the Prophet himself; he even supposes that in the last Song he describes in anticipation his own sufferings and death. But that is not the whole of the matter. The Servant is not only a living individual, the Prophet; he is a witness to a greater who shall come, even as the moon may witness to the sun whose light it reflects while the primary luminary is still below the horizon.[4] In that sense the Songs are Messianic prophecy, and may be said to prefigure Christ. Nor is the Prophet the only such witness in the Old Testament. He is representative of many others, prophets, priests, and kings, and it is not without significance that his name is unknown. He

[1] 'Der GK. Ein Beitrag zur Auslegung von Jes. 40–55', in *Jahrbuch der theol. Schule Bethel*, 1930, pp. 59–115.

[2] Ibid., p. 87.

[3] *Biblischer Commentar über den Propheten Jesaja*, 3. Ausg., 1897, p. 448. Is the reference correct? The ET 1890 was from the 4th German ed.

[4] Op. cit., p. 107.

is, as it were, the 'unknown warrior'. And since the office of the Servant, as described in the Songs, has elements in it of the prophetic, priestly, and kingly, there is a measure of truth in all the theories that have identified him with individuals like Isaiah, Jeremiah, Josiah, Jehoiachin, Zerubbabel, and Moses.[1]

Outside the Songs the Servant is, of course, the empirical Israel. There is also a certain parallelism between this Servant and the individual Servant of the Songs. For example, Israel is the priestly community (cf. lii. 11 f.) because the Servant, fully accepting joint liability with it, the community of sinners, brings into the midst of it the offering of his own pure, sinless life. 'The Servant is an individual, but in his life and death he is so completely a substitute for the people that he must be actually identified with them. He is throughout distinguished from the people as a whole; he is the active, the people the passive Servant. . . . But the mystery of his life is that he will not as an individual be distinguished from the sinful people . . . but lives and suffers and dies in mutual participation with them'.[2] In their present context the Songs have therefore a *double meaning*. 'The Servant so completely unites himself with the people that it is true to say that he is the people and the people is the Servant. We must recognise both, that he is throughout not the people, and yet nevertheless is the people'.[2] It is the 'paradox' of the *unio mystica capitis et corporis*.[3]

We thus get a composite theory in which the Servant is and is not the Prophet, is and is not an historical person, is and is not Israel. Such a reconciling of contraries may be homiletically suggestive, but it is highly paradoxical, as indeed Vischer recognizes. We may grant that there is a certain parallelism between the Servant within the nation, and the Servant as the nation. But have we any right to make the parallels meet in the way Vischer does? No doubt, on the principle that any passage of Scripture 'means what it has come to mean' during the history of its interpretation, the Servant may be all sorts of things. But the primary question is, whom did the writer of the Songs intend by the Servant? This question is obscured by Vischer,

[1] Op. cit., p. 107 f. In *Das Christuszeugnis des ATs*, 2. Teil, Erste Hälfte, 1942, p. 556, he lays some stress upon Jehoiachin: 'Jojachin . . . hat dennoch und gerade durch sein Schicksal in der Verbannung wesentlich die Prägung der messianischen Hoffnung im Sinne des leidenden Gottes Knechtes bestimmt'.

[2] *Jahrbuch der theol. Schule Bethel*, 1930, p. 102.

[3] Ibid., p. 103.

who starts from the theological concept of the 'unity' of Scripture, and, even so, does not succeed in synthesizing the antitheses, except in a rather external way. While, therefore, there is a superficial resemblance between Wheeler Robinson's 'corporate personality' and Vischer's 'mystical union', the latter is a theological construction imposed upon the Songs from without, rather than something derived from them, or supposed to be discovered within them.

A theory similar to that of Vischer, though much less elaborately worked out, is offered by Theodor Brandt.[1] Brandt's view so far approximates to that of Volz[2] as that he regards only xlii. 1–4, 5–9, xlix. 1–6, and l. 4–9 as embodying actual personal experiences of the Prophet, though lii. 13–liii. 12 is similar to them in that the Prophet saw the despised and rejected Servant as one very like to himself. But none of the Songs can be understood as referring to the Prophet alone. History and eschatology meet together in them. By means of the present, light is thrown on the future. 'To this suffering and expectant man of the sixth century it was given to see Him upon whom God lays all the sin of the whole world'.[3] Isa. liii is thus a testimony to Christ.

Another highly composite theory is that of C. C. Torrey.[4] Torrey argues for the unity of Isa. xl–lxvi, which he would date, not from the time of Cyrus, but *circa* 400 B.C. He will not allow that the 'Servant Songs' may be considered apart from their context in the prophecy as a whole. His general view is that the Servant 'is in effect always the same; namely, the personified nation Israel, or Israel's personal representative'.[5] The phrase 'Israel's personal representative' has a very wide reference. 'Now it is an undefined personification, as in xlii. 1 ff. and l. 4 ff. Again it is Abraham'.[6] Other applications are to 'Jacob' . . . 'the primitive children of Israel' . . . 'the chosen race in its whole history' . . . 'the Jewish people of the prophet's own day' . . . 'the restored Israel' . . . 'Israel's better self, the

[1] *Der Prophet der Geschichte: Jes. 40–55*, 1933.

[2] See *supra*, p. 78 f.

[3] Ibid., p. 82.

[4] *The Second Isaiah: A New Interpretation*, 1928.

[5] Ibid., p. 135.

[6] Ibid., p. 141. Here Torrey, conformably with his theory that the prophecy has nothing whatever to do with Cyrus, applies to Abraham passages which are generally referred to Cyrus, e.g. xli. 25; xlvi. 11, reading *'abdî*, 'my servant', for *'ayiṭ*, 'bird of prey'; xlviii. 14, emended.

repentant nation as it should be and might be'. . . . 'Finally out of this personification of the ideal Israel of the future there emerges the figure of a great leader, the Anointed One'.[1] Again, some of the passages said to refer to the future Messiah are such as are generally referred to Cyrus.[2] It is noteworthy, too, that Torrey gives a *collective* interpretation to chap. liii.,[3] but an individual Messianic interpretation to xlii. 1 ff. and xlix. 1 ff.,[4] so that it is difficult to discover any principle that determines his choice of individual and collective. This, however, is quite consistent with his judgement that 'nothing could be more natural than that the poet should give his many-colored figure of speech these kaleidoscopic turns; nothing is more certain than that he did so'.[5]

This sketch of the history of the discussion, already quite long enough, may fittingly be brought to a close with some reference to the finally matured conclusions of the late Dr. A. S. Peake.[6] We have already noted[7] that Peake in 1904 associated himself with the collective interpretation, very much in the form that Giesebrecht had given to it. He maintained it stoutly to the last, and with little modification. After a searching review of all the theories from Duhm to Mowinckel, he came finally to that of his own allegiance. Arguing that there is a 'strong presumption that the term (Servant) will mean the same thing throughout'[8] the prophecy, he nevertheless agreed that too much stress should not be laid on unity of authorship. 'The fact is that the poems according to their present text present apparently irreconcilable phenomena. The right method is to start from more general features to gain an impression of the poems as a whole, to let the broad facts of the situation determine our provisional conclusions and then to enquire whether individual data can be harmonised with them, or, if not, how the refractory elements can most fairly be dealt with'.[9] There are several such obviously refractory elements. One is the alleged mission of the Servant to Israel in xlix. 5 f. The Hitzig–Budde expedient of making Yahweh the subject of the

[1] Op. cit., p. 141.

[2] xlv. 1–4, 13; xlviii. 14, p. 147, a passage already referred on p. 136 to Abraham.

[3] Op. cit., pp. 138, 140.

[4] Op. cit., p. 142.

[5] Op. cit., p. 143.

[6] These are embodied in *The Servant of Yahweh and other Essays*, published posthumously in 1931.

[7] See *supra*, p. 61.

[8] Ibid., p. 49.

[9] Ibid., p. 51.

infinitive clauses has already been mentioned.[1] Peake remarked that Duhm himself, individualist though he was, argued that it is Yahweh, not the Servant, who restores Israel from exile. (This, I suspect, was not because Duhm was willing to make concessions to the collectivists. Nor was it in deference to grammar. He was quite capable of making the Servant the political saviour of Israel, and no doubt would have done so had his 'obscure and leprous rabbi', as Peake[2] dubbed him, been equal to such a task.) However, Peake did not join the insecure alliance of Duhm and Budde on this point. The suggestion he made was that even if the Servant is the restorer, 'the tribes of Jacob and the preserved of Israel may quite possibly refer not to the Jews but to the Northern tribes which had gone into exile after the destruction of Samaria'.[3] This expectation of a reunion of Israel and Judah was a prominent feature of the prophecy of the period. Another 'refractory element' is the 'barely credible' supposition—on the almost invariable collectivist argument that the speakers in liii. 1 ff. are the Gentiles—'that the poet should have represented the heathen while still in heathen darkness as having expressed thoughts so deep that they find no parallel in the Old Testament'.[4] Here, Peake admitted the force of the difficulty 'if . . . the standpoint of the speakers is after the death, but before the resurrection, of the Servant'.[5] But it did not seem to him that this was the situation in which the words were spoken. 'The vital thing to observe is that this poem opens with the prediction of the Servant's exaltation and the amazement it will cause to the nations. . . . It is perfectly natural, then, that in what follows the emotions aroused in the nations should find expression'.[5] Yet another 'refractory element', the discrepancy between the character of Israel and that of the Servant, 'may be somewhat reduced if we remember that it is just in the confession of the heathen that this estimate of the Servant and this interpretation of his sufferings are to be found. We must not accordingly judge them as if they had been uttered by the prophet himself. . . . We must be prepared accordingly for a measure of exaggera-

[1] *Supra*, p. 58 f.

[2] Op. cit., p. 15.

[3] Op. cit., p. 53. Cf. L. E. Browne, *Early Judaism*, 1920, p. 19 f., who thinks of this wider Israel as including 'half-caste' Jews in various lands, who, 'by their Hebrew blood . . . were bound already in covenant to Yahweh, even if they were ignorant of it'.

[4] Op. cit., p. 59 f.

[5] Op. cit., p. 60.

tion; the contrast between Israel and the heathen is made somewhat more absolute than the prophet himself might have made it'.[1] After all, Israel had suffered 'double' (xl. 2), and a relative righteousness might justly be claimed for her. In the light of the nation's vocation the rather unlovely reality is transfigured.[2] Thus, while the ideal theory is 'extremely artificial', the description of the Servant has an ideal element in it. 'The Servant is not an ideal Israel, distinct from the empirical Israel, he is the empirical Israel regarded from an ideal point of view'.[3]

[1] Op. cit., p. 61 f.

[2] Op. cit., p. 63.

[3] Op. cit., p. 67. The full collective theory is also advocated by A. Lods, *Les Prophètes d'Israël et les débuts du judaïsme*, 1935, ET by S. H. Hooke, *The Prophets and the Rise of Judaism*, 1937, pp. 244–9.

PART II
CRITICAL

VII
THE SONGS: TEXT AND TRANSLATION

FIRST SONG: xlii. 1–4

1. Behold! My Servant whom I uphold,
My chosen in whom I delight!
I have endowed him with My spirit,
He shall announce judgement to the nations.

2. He shall not cry nor make any clamour,
Nor let his voice be heard in the street;
3. A reed that is bruised he shall not break,
And the wick that burns dimly he shall not quench.

Faithfully shall he announce judgement,
4. Not burning dimly nor himself being bruised,
Until he have established judgement in the earth,
And for his instruction the far coasts wait eagerly.

ver. 1. The LXX has 'Jacob my Servant . . . Israel my chosen. . . .' This would give a 4:4 line in a 3:3 context, and is clearly a gloss from passages like xli. 8.

ver. 2. *yiśśā'*, 'lift up' (sc. the voice), the object being postponed to the end of the line, with another verb intervening. This may be justified from Num. xiv. 1 (cf. Volz, in loc.), though we expect a parallel, without object, to *yiṣ'aq*. Targ. has יכלי 'make a noise', with which it renders *yiš'āg* ('roar') in Amos i. 2, Joel iv. 16. Beer (*BZAW* 33, p. 30) remarks on the reading *κραυγάσει* ('cry out', 'clamour') of Matt. xii. 19. Alliteration is in favour of *yiš'āg*.

ver. 3. *lɛ'ɛmɛṯ*: Giesebrecht, Peake (*Prob. Suffering*, p. 45), read *lᵉ'ummôṯ* (cf. Kittel's text 'prps' *lā'ummôṯ*), 'to the peoples'. But the word is rare, and never in DI, who only uses *lᵉ'ummîm*, a different word, in parallelism with some such word as *'iyyîm*. LXX *εἰς ἀλήθειαν*. The suggested emendation would leave us with a weak repetition of what has already been said (ver. 1).

ver. 4. *yārûṣ*: read *yērôṣ*, Niph. of *rṣṣ*.

SECOND SONG: xlix. 1–6

1. Hearken, ye far coasts, unto me,
And give attention, ye distant peoples!
Yahweh hath called me from the womb,
From my birth He made mention of my name:

2. And He made my mouth like a sharp sword,
In the shadow of His hand did He hide me;
And He made me a polished arrow,
In His quiver He concealed me;

3. And said to me, My Servant art thou,
Thou Israel by whom I will get Myself glory.
5*b*. So was I honoured in the eyes of Yahweh,
And my God became my strength.

4. But I said, In vain have I toiled,
For nought and vanity my strength have I spent;
Yet surely my cause is with Yahweh,
And my recompense with my God.

5*a*. And now, thus saith Yahweh,
Who formed me from the womb to be His Servant,
To restore Jacob unto Him,
And that Israel to Him should be gathered:

6. Too trifling is it that thou shouldst be My Servant
To raise up the tribes of Jacob,
And bring back the survivors of Israel;
So I make thee a light to the nations,
That My salvation may reach
To the end of the earth.

ver. 3. 'Israel': The genuineness of the word here was first questioned by J. D. Michaelis (op. cit., p. 249). Since then it has commonly been deleted by those who favoured an individual, and retained by those who supported a collective, interpretation, though there are exceptions on both sides; e.g. Praetorius, an individualist, retains it, and H. W. Robinson, Köhler, Moffatt (*The O.T.: A New Translation*, 1st ed.), among collectivists, delete it. Metrical grounds have been urged both for and against its retention. It is clearly a case where the scholar's judgement is liable to be determined by his attitude to the problem as a whole. Manuscript evidence is not sufficient to compel deletion. Yet the retention of the word, even on the collective interpretation, is difficult if the Servant is called Israel in ver. 3, and then given a mission to Israel in ver. 5 f., unless the infinitives there are to be taken as gerundives, with Yahweh as subject, which is very doubtful. Apart from this one passage the Servant of the Songs is anonymous. Outside the Songs, wherever Israel is called Servant it is always parallel with Jacob in the other stichos. An exception might be claimed in xlviii. 20*b* ('Jacob' without || 'Israel'). But there the metre is *Qīnah* (3:2), and although parallelism within the *Qīnah* line is possible, it is not constant; the second part of the line may complete the idea begun in the first. Both types of line are seen in xlviii. 20 f. Since xlix. 3 is trimeter, we should expect 'Jacob' in the one stichos if Israel had been in the other. It may well be, therefore, that the word should be deleted as a gloss in imitation of xliv. 23. On the other hand, to delete 'Israel' would result in a 3:2 line in a 3:3 context. It would greatly simplify the whole problem if we could with a good conscience delete 'Israel'. For that very reason I hesitate to do so, since I have a suspicion that it would be on theoretical rather than on manuscript or metrical grounds. I therefore retain it, but with what I feel, in all the circumstances, is justifiable hesitation. It cannot be said that the stichos is very euphonious, and there may be deep-seated corruption. For example, is there some dittography in *yiśrā'ēl 'ᵃšɛr*? Finally, it may be remarked that the case for the retention of 'Israel' is not so strong that the collective interpretation may without more ado be assumed.

ver. 5*aα*. Read 'and now thus (*kô*) saith Yahweh', with a number of manuscripts, LXX, Syr.; cf. xliii. 1.

ver. 5*a*. The translation is that of the Qere (לוֹ), Aq., Targ. The Keth. 'and that Israel be not (לֹא) swept away', gives a perfectly good sense (cf. lvii. 1, where *nɛ'ᵋsāp̱îm*, 'taken away' is || 'perishes'). For a similar negative following a positive see xlv. 1*b*. There is no material difference of meaning as between the two readings.

ver. 5*b*. Many point the verb as a *waw consec.* (וָאֶכָּבֵד), and transfer the whole sentence to the end of ver. 3. In its present position it is an awkward parenthesis, bracketed in the RV.

ver. 6. *Wayyômɛr*: Should be deleted. The *'āmar* of ver. 5 is sufficient introduction, and the insertion here may have been occasioned by the intrusion of the misplaced 5*b*.

mihyôṯᵉḵâ lî 'eḇɛḏ: There seems no compelling reason for deleting these words; there is an almost exact parallel in Ezek. viii. 17. Duhm calls it a 'barbarous sentence', but it looks as if his theory has influenced his textual criticism. Obviously, his teacher of the Law is not the kind of person to 'raise up the tribes of Jacob'. Nor is the collective Israel. And it is easier to make Yahweh, and not the Servant, the subject of the following infinitives if the clause is deleted.

THIRD SONG: l. 4–9

4. The Lord Yahweh Himself has given me
   The tongue of the taught,
That I should know how to answer
   The weary with a word.
In the morning He wakens my ear
   To hear as those that are taught.

5. (The Lord Yahweh Himself has opened my ear
   . . . .),
And I have not rebelled,
   Nor turned away backward.

6. My back I gave to the smiters,
   And my cheeks to them that pluck out (the beard);
My face I hid not
   From insult and spitting.

7. But the Lord Yahweh Himself will help me;
Therefore am I not dishonoured:
Therefore have I set my face like flint,
And I know that I shall not be ashamed.

8. Near is my Vindicator,
   Who will take proceedings against me?
   Let us stand up together!
Who is my adversary?
   Let him approach unto me!

9. Behold!
The Lord Yahweh Himself will help me!
Who then can secure a verdict against me?
Behold!
They all shall wear out as a garment,
      Moth shall consume them!

vv. 4–5. The text of these verses is clearly not in order, and there is no agreement about either the wording, or the arrangement, of the original. The translation above involves the substitution of *la'ᵃnôṯ*, 'answer' (cf. LXX εἰπεῖν) for the obscure *lā'ûṯ*, and the deletion of one or both words *yā'îr babbōqer* as a dittograph. In ver. 5 we must either suppose that something no longer recoverable has been lost, or that the opening sentence is itself to be deleted as a partial dittograph. None of the textual suggestions that have been made has any bearing on the main problem, unless it be that based upon the Targum 'teach' (for *lā'ûṯ*), from which an original *lir'ôṯ* ('feed', 'shepherd') has been supposed. This in its turn has been held (by Kittel, Sellin (*Mose*)) to indicate that the Servant is a ruler, since the verb 'shepherd', when used figuratively, is always, except in the corrupt Jer. xvii. 16, so used. But the emendation is too uncertain to contribute any answer to the main problem.

FOURTH SONG: lii. 13–liii. 12

lii. 13. Behold! My Servant shall prosper,
He shall be lifted up and greatly exalted.
lii. 14*aα*. As many were appalled at him,
. . . .
lii. 15. So shall many look upon him with amazement,
Kings shall shut their mouths;
For that which had not been told them shall they have seen,
And of that which they had not heard shall they discern the meaning.
liii. 1. Who could have believed what we have heard?
And the arm of Yahweh—over whom hath it been revealed?
liii. 2. For he grew up as a sapling,
And as a root from an arid soil;

No form had he nor stateliness,
Nor yet appearance nor attractiveness;
lii. 14*aβb*. So disfigured his appearance that he scarce seemed human,
Nor his form like that of the sons of men.

liii. 3. Despised and forsaken of men,
A man of sorrows and familiar with sickness;
And as one from whom men avert their gaze,
He was despised, and we regarded him not.

liii. 4. Yet ours were the sicknesses that *he* carried,
And ours the pains that *he* bore;
While *we* regarded him stricken,
Smitten of God, and afflicted.

liii. 5. But he was pierced through by reason of our rebellions,
Crushed by reason of our iniquities;
The chastisement leading to our welfare was upon him,
And by means of his stripes there is healing for us.

liii. 6. All we like sheep have gone astray,
Each to his own way we have turned;
And Yahweh caused to light upon him
The iniquity of us all.

liii. 7. He was harshly treated, though he humbled himself,
And opened not his mouth.
As a sheep borne along to the slaughter,
And as a ewe before her shearers,
He was dumb,
And opened not his mouth.

liii. 8. After arrest and sentence he was taken off,
And on his fate who reflected?
For he was cut off from the land of the living,
For our rebellions was he stricken to death.

liii. 9. And his grave was made with the wicked,
And with evil-doers his sepulchre;
Although he had done no violence,
Nor was any deceit in his mouth.

liii. 10. Yet Yahweh was pleased to crush him with sickness;
Truly he gave himself as a guilt-offering.
He shall see seed that prolongs days,
And the purpose of Yahweh shall prosper in his hand.

liii. 11. After his travail of soul he shall see light;
He shall be satisfied with his knowledge.
My Servant shall bring justification to many,
And their iniquities he shall bear.

liii. 12. Therefore will I assign him the many for his portion,
And numberless shall be his spoil;
Because he laid bare his soul unto death,
And with the rebellious he was numbered;
But he bore the sin of many,
And for the rebellious he interposed.

lii. 13. All the Greek versions, together with the Old Latin, appear not to have read *yārûm*. It seems metrically superfluous, unless we take the initial 'Behold!' as anacrusis.

lii. 14*aα*. Reading *'alaw* for *'alĕḵā*, with Syr., Targ., and (so Volz) MS. K. 224 pr. 576. The second stichos seems to have been lost. Attempts to restore it, such as Marti's 'And princes shuddered at him' (cf. xlix. 7, Ezek. xxxii. 10) must be regarded as approximate only. It is usual now to transfer 14*aβb* to the end of liii. 2.

lii. 15*a*. *yazzĕh*: The rendering 'sprinkle', though supported by the minor Greek versions, is now generally abandoned. The RV mg. 'startle' is based on an Arabic root meaning 'leap', hence 'cause to leap (in startled surprise)'. The LXX, followed by Old Lat., has θαυμάσονται, with 'many nations' as subject. This is recommended by the parallelism, both of 14*a* and of what follows in 15*aβ*. In xli. 23 θαυμασόμεθα is the LXX rendering of *ništa'â*, whence some would restore *yištā'û* or *yiš'û* here. But LXX employs θαυμάζειν for quite a number of Hebrew words. Hence others (following G. F. Moore in *JBL*, 1890, pp. 216 ff.) prefer to restore *yirgezû* for the two words *yazzĕh gôyîm*, which has the merit of approximating more nearly to MT, or *yištaḥawû* ('prostrate themselves'—Cheyne). In favour of retaining *rabbîm* only (without *gôyîm*) is the fact that, as Volz points out, it is the catchword of the Song (cf. lii. 14, liii. 11 f.). The translation above is based on the LXX, without attempting to decide what may have stood in the original. *'ālāw* should be taken with what precedes, following the LXX, and also on metrical grounds.

lii. 15*b*. *rā'û* and *hiṯbônānû* have the force of future perfects.

liii. 2. *lepānāw*: The suffix here is difficult. The EVV take it as referring to Yahweh in the previous verse. Although the versions presuppose the MT, it is usual to resort to emendation. The most common is *lepānēnû*, 'before us', following Ewald. Of suggestions designed to provide a parallel with what follows the most attractive is that of Volz, *lô' yāp̄ĕh* ('uncomely'). The translation above follows a suggestion by G. R. Driver (in *JTS* 38, p. 48), who takes the suffix as referring back to the subject of the verb 'he grew up', and quotes 1 Sam. v. 3 f., where it is said that Dagon was *nôp̄ēl lepānāw*, 'fallen straight forward'. So here, 'he grew (straight) up'. The picture then will be that of an immature and sickly plant, much in the sense of Volz's emendation.

wenir'ēhû: If this word be kept it seems necessary to transfer the *athnaḥ* to it, so making it parallel with *wenεḥmedēhû*. But this would make the stichos too long, and almost demands that *welô' hādār* should be displaced. It seems better to delete *wenir'ēhû*, which may well be a dittograph of the following *mar'ĕh*, and to read *weḥεmdâh* (cf. LXX κάλλος) for *wenεḥmedēhû*.

We then get a distich which in its piling up of epithets is similar to 3*a*, 4*b*, and quite in the manner of DI (cf. xli. 19, xliii. 20, li. 19).

lii. 14*aβb*. There is much to be said for reading this distich here. Where it stands in the MT it is in awkward parenthesis. If we read it after liii. 2 we have a fine example of inversion (in liii. 2 *tō'ar . . . mar'ĕh*; here *mar'ēhû . . . tō'ᵃrô*), similar to xlix. 24 f., li. 6, 8 (cf. Köhler, *DJ stilkritisch untersucht*, pp. 78 f., 95). For *mišḥaṯ* read *mošḥāṯ* (Hoph. Ptc.).

liii. 4. After *ûmaḵ'ôḇēnû* insert *hû'*, with some 20 manuscripts, Syr., Vulg.

liii. 5. *mᵉḥôlāl*: Aq. βεβηλωμένος = *mᵉḥullāl*, 'profaned'. This is preferred by some, but parallelism favours the Massoretic pointing.

liii. 7. Many would delete the last line as a dittograph. But repetition of the kind is characteristic of DI (cf. Köhler, op. cit., p. 94 f., who says of this example that 'it is the most beautiful and expressive repetition in the whole writing'). Some (e.g. Köhler) delete *nε'ᵋlāmâh*. To take the word with what precedes is attended by metrical difficulties. Hence others (e.g. Fischer, Elliger) would emend to the masc., with the Servant as subject. Rowley (*Israel's Mission to the World*, 1939, p. 22 n.) remarks on the 'rhythmical incompleteness of the line', and suggests that this is 'deliberate and impressive', similar to *ya'ᵃmōḏ* in Job iv. 16.

liii. 8. *mē'ōṣεr ûmimmišpāṭ luqqāḥ*: Difficulties here are occasioned by the uncertain meaning of *'ōṣεr*, and the triple sense ('away from', 'by reason of', 'without') of *min*. There are three possible translations: (1) 'From imprisonment (custody, arrest) and from judgement he was taken'; (2) 'By reason of an oppressive judgement (lit. 'oppression and judgement'—an example of hendiadys) he was taken'; (3) 'Without hindrance and without judgement he was taken', i.e. no one attempted to secure him a fair trial. The literal meaning of *'ōṣεr* is 'restraint', 'coercion', and it has been questioned whether it can be used in the more concrete sense of 'prison', or even 'imprisonment'. I do not think emendation is necessary, and have adopted the sense of rendering (1), with 'arrest' for the semi-abstract *'ōṣεr*. It is difficult to be positive about the meaning of a noun that is only used four times. But the verb *'āṣar* is used of putting in prison in 2 Kings xvii. 4, 'And the king of Assyria shut him up (*wayya'aṣᵉrēhû*) and bound him in prison' (*bêṯ kεlε'*), and in Jer. xxxiii. 1, xxxix. 15, the prophet is said to have been 'shut up' (*'āṣûr*) in the court of the guard. For *mišpāṭ* = 'judicial sentence', cf. Deut. xvii. 9, 11, xix. 6, xxi. 22, 1 Kings xx. 40, Jer. xxvi. 11,

16. For *luqqāḥ*, 'taken off (to death)', cf. Prov. xxiv. 11. Duhm understood it as 'removed', 'taken away (to God)', cf. Gen. v. 24 (Enoch), 2 Kings ii. 3, 5, 10 (Elijah), Ps. xlix. 16, lxxiii. 24. But the context here speaks clearly of the Servant's grave. It looks as if Duhm read the text in the light of his theory that the Servant died of disease, and not as the result of a judicial sentence. *we'ɛṯ-dôrô mî yeśôḥēaḥ*: It is grammatically possible to take this with what follows, as in the RV, *'ɛṯ* being occasionally used, chiefly in later style, with a new subject to give it definiteness (*G-K* § 117 *i–m*; *BDB*, p. 85*a*, 3). An objection to this is that in Hebrew poetry lines are usually end-stopped. The translation above is in the sense suggested by G. R. Driver (*JTS* 36, 1935, p. 403)—'and who doth consider his state?' He refers to Akk. *dûrum*, 'lasting state', 'permanent condition', and to Arab. *daurun*, 'turn', 'change of fortune', and quotes Ps. xxiv. 6, which he would render 'this is the state of them that seek him'. A similar sense is obtained by the frequently proposed *darkô* (lit. 'his way') for *dôrô*.

mippɛša' 'ammî: Although all the versions presuppose the MT, the suffix 'my' is difficult. Of those who retain it, some refer it to the Prophet, others to God. Usually, though not always (e.g. Skinner), they think of the Servant as an individual. But not all individualists retain it. The issue, therefore, need not be a partisan one, even though the commonest emendation, *mippešā'ēnû*, 'for our rebellions', is nearly always (Kittel is an exception) associated with the collective interpretation. The difficulty about the MT is that the suffix is unrelated. The same might be said of ver. 11, where hardly anyone queries it. It is generally agreed that at the beginning and end of the Song Yahweh is speaking. Here in the middle the context favours 'our' (cf. 'for our rebellions', ver. 5). Other emendations suggested are 'their rebellions', 'rebellions of the people(s)', 'rebellion of his people', 'rebellions' (LXX ἀπὸ τῶν ἀνομιῶν), 'rebellious ones'.

nɛga' lāmô: *lāmô* = 'for him' is difficult (cf. *G-K* § 103 f., N.3). Read (*ye*)*nugga' lammāwɛṯ* (LXX ἤχθη εἰς θάνατον).

liii. 9. *we'ɛṯ 'āšîr* is hardly suitable in this context. The LXX has the plural (πλουσίους); so Old Lat., Targ. Most read *'ôśê ra'*, 'evil-doers', or words of similar meaning. Praetorius' *śe'îrîm*, 'wilderness demons' (*ZAW* 36, p. 20), has attracted some; but it gives no proper parallel, and has since (*Nachtr. u. Verbess. zu DJ*, p. 45) been abandoned by Praetorius himself.

bemôṯāw: Lit. 'in his deaths' is meaningless. Some (e.g. Haller, 1914, Elliger) read the sing. *bemôṯô* (LXX ἀντὶ τοῦ θανάτου).

The several other suggestions all carry the sense of 'sepulchre', as a parallel to 'grave'. They are *bêṯô* ('his house', cf. Isa. xiv. 18, and 1 Kings ii. 34, where LXX^{L} and Syr. have 'his grave'), *bêṯ môṯô* ('his house of death', for which Haupt refers to Akk. *bît mûti*), *bāmāṯô* ('his mound', cf. Ezek. xliii. 7, though the word is dubious there), *bôrô* ('his pit', cf. Isa. xiv. 19), *'ᵃrēmāṯô* ('his heap', i.e. tumulus).

liii. 10. The text of this verse is very uncertain. *dakkᵉ'ô* as it stands means 'to crush him'. It may mean 'to cleanse him' (so LXX καθαρίσαι αὐτὸν) if it is an Aramaism. *hɛḥᵉlî* as vocalized is explained as the Hiph. Perf. of חלה, formed after the analogy of verbs *lamedh-aleph*, the quiescent *aleph* being dropped (*G-K* §§ 74*k*, 75*ii*). The consonants as they stand mean 'the sickness' simply. Both the major versions read 'sickness', though with different prepositions: LXX 'The Lord was pleased to cleanse him from sickness'; Vulg. 'The Lord was pleased to crush him with sickness'. Some moderns follow the one, and some the other. The LXX is difficult because, even if we allow the Aramaism, it takes the same verb in two different senses (cf. *mᵉḏukkā'*, ver. 5) in the same passage. The objection to the Vulgate is that it still speaks of the sufferings of the Servant, whereas we expect from this point on—especially after *ḥāpēṣ*—a description of his change of fortune. Another difficulty is that the distich (to *nap̄šô*) is open, not end-stopped. We hardly expect the protasis of a conditional sentence in a second stichos, unrelated to the first, with apodosis in the following distich. There is a presumption in favour of the two halves of the distich being parallel. Of the many readings that have been suggested I have adopted that of Rowley (op. cit., p. 22), who combines suggestions by Torrey (*The Second Isaiah*, p. 421, *hɛḥᵒlî*, adv. acc., 'with sickness') and Levy (*Deutero-Isaiah*, p. 266 f., *'ɛmɛṯ śām* for *'im tāśîm*)—'But Yahweh was pleased to crush him with sickness, Truly he gave himself as a guilt-offering'. There is no certainty that this is the original reading; but it only involves the deletion of a *yodh*, and has the merit of not importing anything into a text which is perhaps corrupt beyond repair.

liii. 11. Here also the text is very uncertain. For the temporal sense of *min* see *G-K* § 119*y*, N.3. After *yir'ɛh* LXX has 'light' (*'ôr*); similarly both the Qumran scrolls. *bᵉḏa'tô* is then to be taken with what precedes (so LXX). The metrically superfluous and grammatically impossible *ṣaddîq* is to be deleted as a dittograph of *yaṣdîq* preceding. It is wanting in three manuscripts.

liii. 12. Consistency recommends that *rabbîm* in ver. 12*a* should be rendered 'many' rather than 'great' (RV), if we do so in lii.

14 f. and liii. 12*b*. Volz remarks that *rabbîm* was a technical term in language relating to the idea of substitution (cf. Dan. xi. 33, xii. 3, Mark x. 45, Rom. v. 19). The one—whether collective or individual—stands over against the 'many'. For *rabbîm* || *'ᵃṣûmîm* with the meaning 'many' || 'numerous', see Prov. vii. 26. The translation above takes *rabbîm* as acc. object of *'ᵃḥallēq*, governed by *beth* (cf. *G-K* § 119*k*) with a certain emphasis (cf. *rā'āh b̲ᵉ* 'look upon', *mālak̲ bᵉ*, 'rule over'). It brings out the 'incomparable grandeur' (Van d. Ploeg) of the Servant better than a translation that would make him even the greatest of contending 'mighty' ones. Nor need *šālāl* ('spoil') point to a military victor. It is used in ix. 2 as a parallel to harvest rejoicing (cf. Prov. xxxi. 11), and is the kind of expression that could easily become detached from its primary meaning.

ARE ANY OTHER PASSAGES TO BE RECKONED AS 'SONGS'?

The 'Songs' as originally defined by Duhm were four in number, viz. xlii. 1–4, xlix. 1–6, l. 4–9, lii. 13–liii. 12. Since his time there has never been any doubt about the first two and the last, though for a while there was some hesitation about the third. Long before there was any thought of treating the Songs as distinct from the rest of Deutero-Isaiah, it had, not unnaturally, been common to interpret l.4–9 as an autobiographical fragment.[1] The last of these exegetes was Ley, whose *Historische Erklärung*, dated 1893, was apparently written without any knowledge of Duhm's work published in the preceding year. Laue[2] still held that l. 4–9 had originally to do with the Prophet, and that it was later transformed into a Song by the addition of vv. 10 f. But he agreed that the passage is a necessary link between chaps. xlix and liii, and proceeded to treat it as such. This was, in effect, to concede the point in dispute, and since Laue only Levy[3] has excluded it from the Servant-cycle. Though it is written in a different metre (*Qînah*) from the other Songs, and the word 'Servant' does not occur in it, the experiences of the speaker are in general similar to those of the Servant, and without it we are quite unprepared for the final tragedy.

[1] So, among others, Chrysostom, Grotius, Vogel, Dathe, Koppe, Hensler, Braun, Rosenmüller, Hitzig, Matthew Arnold, Knobel.

[2] *Die EJL*, 1898, pp. 7–11.

[3] *Deutero-Isaiah*, p. 16 f. Volz (*Jes. II*, p. 160) says it is not certain that it belongs to the Songs.

We have now to ask whether there are any other 'Songs' than those proposed by Duhm, and whether, perhaps, some of the Songs should include more than he assigned to them. The passages in question are xlix. 7–13, xlii. 5–9, l. 10 f., xlii. 19–21, xlviii. 14–16, li. 4–(6) 8, li. 9 (12)–16, and lxi. 1 ff. We proceed to examine them in that order.[1]

xlix. 7–13

ver. 7. Thus saith Yahweh,
The Redeemer of Israel, his Holy One,
To him who is deeply despised,
Abhorred by all,
A slave of tyrant rulers:
Kings shall see, and arise;
Princes, and they shall prostrate themselves,
On account of Yahweh, who is faithful,
The Holy One of Israel, who has chosen thee.

ver. 8. Thus saith Yahweh,
In a time of favour have I answered thee,
And in a day of salvation have I helped thee,
(And I form thee, and make thee to be
A covenant-bond of the people)
To resettle a land that is desert,
To re-people inheritances that are desolate;

ver. 9. Saying to those that are bound, Come forth!
To those that are in darkness, Come to the light!
By all pathways shall they feed,
And upon all bare heights shall be their pasture.

ver. 10. They shall not hunger nor thirst,
Neither shall scorching heat nor sun strike upon them:
For He that hath compassion upon them shall lead them,
And by springs of water shall He guide them.

ver. 11. And I will make all mountains into a pathway,
And My highways shall be exalted.

ver. 13. Cry aloud, ye heavens, and exult, O earth!
And break forth, ye mountains, into a ringing cry!
For Yahweh hath comforted His people,
And had compassion upon His afflicted ones.

(Ver. 12 should probably come after ver. 18, cf. lx. 4.)

[1] xlix. 7–13 is dealt with before xlii. 5–9 for reasons of convenience that will become clear during the discussion.

ver. 7. *lib̲^{e}zôh-nɛp̲ɛš*: Lit. 'to a despising of soul', abstract for concrete —'despised of soul'. Most would read either *lib̲^{e}zûj* (Qal Pass.), or *l^{e}nib̲zêh* (Niph.), without any difference of meaning. The phrase is best interpreted in the light of Ps. xvii. 9, where 'my deadly enemies' (RV) is literally 'my enemies against the soul'. Hence 'him who is deeply despised'. Another interpretation is 'self-despised' (G. R. Driver, Praetorius), based on LXX and Syr.

lim^{e}t̲āʿēb̲ gôy: Read *lim^{e}t̲ôʿab̲* (Pual). *Gôy*, lit. 'nation', in the general sense of 'people', as in lv. 5 (so Duhm). The word, generally with some emphasis on non-Hebrews, is used of the locust-swarm in Joel i. 6.

ver. 8. *w^{e}ʾɛṣṣor^{e}k̲ā w^{e}ʾɛttɛn^{e}k̲ā lib̲^{e}rît̲ ʿām*: The line seems defective. Syr. and the first hand of LXXא complete it with 'for a light to the nations'. But this is insufficient testimony that the words are original, especially since they might easily have been filled in from xlii. 6. After *ʾɛrɛṣ* some such word as *ṣiyyâh* should be inserted (cf. xli. 18, liii. 2), unless, with Volz, we suppose that something has fallen out before *l^{e}hāqîm*.

ver. 9. Before *d^{e}rāk̲îm* insert *kol-*, with LXX.

ver. 11. For *hāray* read *hārîm* (LXX πᾶν ὄρος).

The question whether these verses, or any part of them, refer to the Servant has been much disputed. Of those who answer the question in the affirmative Gressmann[1] would divide the passage into two Songs, ver. 7 and vv. 8–13.[2] Others[3] think there should be a break at the end of 9*a*.

Let us first examine vv. 8–13. It is not obvious that we have a fresh beginning at 9*b*. If we remove ver. 12 to follow ver. 18 there is no pause until the end of ver. 13, or at least of ver. 11. The supposition of a break at the end of 9*a* looks like an expedient to claim 7 (8)–9*a* as referring to the Servant, since what follows in 9*b*–13 reads exactly like a typical Deutero-Isaianic oracle on the deliverance of Israel.[4] If, then, vv. 8–(11)13 are a unity, to whom do they refer, to Israel or to the Servant? Were it not for 8*b*α, 'and I form thee, and make thee a covenant-bond of the people', this question would admit of only one answer, namely, that the reference is to Israel. This alone is

[1] *Messias*, pp. 299 ff.

[2] Similarly H. Schmidt (*Gott u. das Leid im AT*, p. 45) supposes two Songs, viz. ver. 7 and vv. 8–11.

[3] e.g. Rudolph, Fischer.

[4] For the language, which is even more markedly that of DI than that of the recognized Songs, see *infra*, p. 190 f.

sufficient to raise the question whether 8*bα* is original. When we look more closely at the words, we find them exactly repeated in xlii. 6. It may be of significance, too, that the order of the verbs in ver. 8 as now constituted is 'answer', 'help', 'form'.[1] The natural order, if the words were original, would be for 'form' to come earlier in the series (cf. xliii. 1), and before 'help' (cf. xliv. 2). Since vv. 8 ff. follow closely upon a Song it is probable that 8*bα* has been inserted for the purpose of making what was originally an Israel-Song into a Song about the Servant.[2]

The interpretation of ver. 7, and its relation to ver. 8, are obscure. The introductory formula (*aα*) is as Deutero-Isaianic as anything can well be, and we expect that what follows after 'the Redeemer of Israel, his Holy One', will have to do with Israel. Unfortunately, text and interpretation of *aβ* are alike uncertain, and what we have might apply equally well to Israel or to the Servant. The section *aγ* sounds reminiscent of the closing verses of chap. lii. With ver. 8 we have a new beginning, 'Thus saith Yahweh', but it lacks the expansive epithets which are usual in Deutero-Isaiah (cf. xliii. 1, 14, &c.). It is tempting to suppose that the whole of ver. 7, apart from the introductory formula, and of ver. 8 the introductory formula and *bα*, are later insertions in an Israel-Song which originally ran:

> Thus saith Yahweh, the Redeemer of Israel, his Holy One:
> In a time of favour have I answered thee,
> And in a day of salvation have I helped thee,
> To resettle a land that is desert,
> . . . .
> . . . .

In any case, ver. 7 is only a fragment which, for that reason, and because of the uncertainty of its reference, adds nothing to the description of the Servant. Together with 8*bα* it may point to a very early 'individual' interpretation of the person of the Servant, so early, indeed, that it may even go back to the time when the prophecy was edited. But it is not of equal authority with the unquestioned Servant-Songs, and an individual interpretation of them cannot be based upon it.

[1] If, as is fairly certain, *'ɛṣṣorᵉḵā* is from *yāṣar*.

[2] So Elliger, op. cit., p. 53 f.; Mowinckel, *ZAW* 49, p. 106; Sellin, *ZAW* 55, p. 200. Volz also omits.

xlii. 5–9

ver. 5. Thus saith the true God, Yahweh,
That created the heavens, and stretched them out;
That spread out the earth and its teeming life;
That giveth breath to the people upon it,
And spirit to them that walk therein:

ver. 6. I, Yahweh, have called thee in righteousness,
And will hold thee by the hand,
And form thee, and make thee to be
A covenant-bond of the people,
(A light to the nations);

ver. 7. To open blind eyes,
To bring out from the dungeon him that is bound,
From the prison-house them that sit in darkness.

ver. 8. I am Yahweh, that is My name;
And My glory will I not give to another,
Nor My praise to the graven images.

ver. 9. The former things, Behold! they are come to pass,
And new things do I declare:
Ere they spring forth
I make you to hear them.

ver. 6. The jussive of the 1st pers. is rare, and most scholars would point the verbs as imperfects with *Waw consec.* Even if we alter the Massoretic pointing the full effects of the initial call lie still in the future. We may therefore let it stand.

w^{e}*'ɛṣṣor*^{e}*ḵā*: May come either from *nāṣar* ('keep') or *yāṣar* ('form'). The latter is more pregnant with meaning, and is used by DI eight times as against two from *nāṣar*. Also there seems clear dependence on Jer. i. 5 in DI's use of the phrase *yāṣar mibbɛṭɛn* (xliv. 2, 24, xlix. 5).

l^{e}*'ôr gôyîm* is of doubtful genuineness. It is omitted by some manuscripts of the LXX, notably by the first hand of B.

More scholars have taken these verses, or part of them, as referring to the Servant than has been the case with xlix. 7 ff. Some think that ver. 5 begins a new Song, extending to the end of ver. 7, or to the end of ver. 9. Others regard either vv. 1–7 or vv. 1–9 as a unity. Those who divide the passage at the end of ver. 7 have usually claimed that vv. 8–9 were originally a continuation of xli. 29, now separated by xlii. 1–7.[1]

[1] Duhm and Schian regarded vv. 5–7 as a kind of secondary Song, a later addition by the editor who inserted vv. 1–4 into the prophecy.

There is sufficient continuity of subject-matter to make this plausible, though xli. 29 has the appearance of being the end of an oracle. Verses 8–9 are an equally good continuation of ver. 7, which, if nothing followed, would end abruptly. The problem whether a break should come after ver. 7 is similar to that whether the break in chap. xlix should come at 9*a*. Those who make it with ver. 7 are in the difficulty that if they admit vv. 8–9 as a continuation they are dealing with a typical Deutero-Isaianic oracle, with references to 'former' and 'new' things which elsewhere in the prophecy have no immediate connexion with the Servant. It is therefore best to treat vv. 5–9 as a unity. Further, the introductory formula marks it off as originally separate from vv. 1–4, and the 'address' of the passage is different. As in xlix. 7–13 the language is even more characteristic of Deutero-Isaiah than is that of the recognized Songs.[1]

The answer to the question, To whom do vv. 5–9 refer? is bound up with the interpretation of the difficult expression *b^e^rîṯ 'ām* (ver. 6, RV 'a covenant of the people'). Four renderings have been proposed: (1) 'Covenant-people', (2) 'Covenant (-bond) of the people' (i.e. of Israel), (3) 'Covenant (-bond) of the peoples' (i.e. of the nations), (4) 'Splendour of the people(s)'.

The rendering 'covenant-people' was common among the earlier advocates of the collective theory.[2] Although Hebrew would most naturally express this idea by *'am b^e^rîṯ*, it has been argued that *b^e^rîṯ 'ām* is grammatically possible.[3] The objection is that the expression, so understood, would give no parallel to *'ôr gôyîm* ('light of the nations') following. If 'nations' can only be a genitive of object, we expect the same of 'people', in the sense of suggestions (2) and (3). If we accept suggestion (2) it is natural to interpret the expression of an individual Servant, who is the medium through whom Yahweh is to make a covenant with Israel, and suppose that *b^e^rîṯ 'ām* has reference to his mission to Israel (cf. xlix. 5) and *'ôr gôyîm* to his mission to the Gentiles (cf. xlix. 6). This, the most natural interpretation, is open to the objection that it limits the scope of *'ām* to Israel, whereas in the verse immediately preceding it must

[1] See *infra*, p. 189 f.

[2] e.g. Hitzig.

[3] Cf. Prov. xv. 20, xxi. 20, *k^e^sîl 'āḏām*, 'fool of a man' = 'foolish man'; Gen. xvi. 12, *pɛrɛ' 'āḏām*, 'wild-ass of a man'; Isa. ix. 5, *pɛlɛ' yô'ēṣ*, 'wonder of a counsellor' = 'wonderful counsellor'.

comprise all mankind. If, then, in the sense of rendering (3) we think of one, whether collective or individual, who is to be the medium of a covenant with all mankind, we have indeed a perfect parallel to 'light of the nations'; but we are then faced with the difficulty that the idea of a covenant with all mankind, mediated through a person or group, is without analogy in the Old Testament. The rainbow-covenant of Gen. ix. 8–17 is not a proper parallel, though in the light of it we cannot exclude the possibility that *b^{e}rîṯ 'ām* means 'covenant (-bond) of humanity'.

The fourth suggestion, 'splendour of the people', was made by Torczyner,[1] and has been mentioned favourably by D. W. Thomas.[2] It would relate *b^{e}rîṯ* not to the Akkadian *barû*, 'bind', *birîtu*, 'covenant', but to *barāru*, 'shine'—hence 'splendour of the people', parallel with 'light of the nations'. The attractiveness of the suggestion is obvious; but on second thoughts it looks like a cutting of the Gordian knot. The *shewa* under the *beth* looks dubious from a root *double-'ayin*, though the word may originally have been differently vocalized, and later assimilated to the more familiar *b^{e}rîṯ*. There is, however, the possibility that in the *Nunc Dimittis* (Luke ii. 32) 'the glory (*δόξα*) of thy people Israel', following as it does upon 'a light for revelation to the Gentiles' (*φῶς εἰς ἀποκάλυψιν ἐθνῶν*), may be reminiscent of *b^{e}rîṯ 'ām* in the sense proposed by Torczyner.

We are now in a position to ask, To whom does xlii. 5–(7) 9 refer? The possibilities are three: (1) Cyrus, (2) Israel, (3) The Servant as distinct from Israel. According to Haller,[3] Mowinckel,[4] Hans Schmidt,[5] and W. E. Barnes,[6] the subject is Cyrus. Of Cyrus it is indeed said that he has been 'called' (xlv. 3 f., xlvi. 11, xlviii. 15) 'in righteousness' (xlv. 13), that Yahweh has taken him by the right hand (xlv. 1), that he is to release the exiles (xlv. 13). But it is hardly possible to think of Cyrus as *b^{e}rîṯ 'ām*—except on the dubious fourth interpretation of the words—or as a 'light to the nations'. The claim of Israel to be the subject of the passage is supported by more parallels than is that of Cyrus. Israel is 'called' (xli. 9, xliii. 1, 7, xlviii. 12,

1 *Journal of the Palestine Oriental Society*, 16, 1936, pp. 1–8.

2 In *Record and Revelation*, ed. H. W. Robinson, p. 395.

3 *Das Judentum*^{2}, p. 33, 'Die Kyros-Lieder DJas', pp. 262–5.

4 *ZAW* 49, pp. 94 ff.

5 *Gott u. das Leid im AT*, p. 45.

6 *JTS* 32, pp. 32–9.

liv. 6), 'taken by the hand' (xli. 9, 13), and 'formed' by Yahweh (xliii. 1, 21, xliv. 2, 21, 24, xlv. 11). But again we are in difficulty with *b^erîṯ 'ām*, which can only be applied to Israel if it means 'covenant-people' or a 'covenant-bond of mankind', both of which are improbable.

We are left with the third possibility, that the passage refers to the Servant, as distinct from Israel. Then our trouble is that 'people' in ver. 6 must be Israel, just after it has appeared in ver. 5 for all mankind. Further, while 'light of the nations' as applied to the Servant is attested by xlix. 6, it hardly seems in place at this point. If it were, we should have to suppose that ver. 7, 'to open blind eyes, to bring out from the dungeon him that is bound, from the prison-house them that sit in darkness', refers to the Gentiles. No doubt the Gentiles are spiritually blind, but we cannot take 'those that sit in darkness' as referring to spiritually blind, since they are in the prison-house (*bêṯ kɛlɛ'*), and the words are parallel with 'him that is bound'. There is no warrant in the prophecy for referring them to the Gentiles. Hence ver. 7 would seem to describe the captive Israelites, not the Gentiles. And if that is so, can 'light of the nations' be original? Surely not, unless we take the infinitives in ver. 7 as gerundives, with Yahweh as subject. This is grammatically possible (cf. xlv. 1), but is very unnatural after phrases that indicate the direction of the Servant's mission. And even supposing that, though unnatural, it is possible, we shall have to say that the whole passage (xlii. 5–9), including 6*bα*, refers to Israel, not to the Servant, unless, of course, the Servant is Israel. In which case, how is it that the advocates of the collective interpretation never regard it as a Song? Surely because, if it were, the odds would be heavily on the side of an individual, and against the collective interpretation. The suspicion that 'for a light to the nations' is secondary is confirmed by the fact that it is wanting in the first hand of LXX^{B}. We are then left with a defective line exactly as in xlix. 8, and must go on to ask whether it is any more genuine here than we found it to be there? Once 'for a light of the nations' goes the situation in both passages is exactly the same, and the same reasons that led us to delete xlix. 8*bα* justify us in regarding the same words as not original here.[1] Once more we have an oracle originally

[1] This has been done by Elliger and Sellin (*ZAW* 55, p. 200 f.), though on rather different lines from those advanced here.

relating to Israel, and subsequently transformed into a secondary Servant-Song. This would explain the dual reference of the word 'people' in vv. 5 and 6.

l. 10–11

ver. 10. Whoever among you fears Yahweh,
  Let him hearken to the voice of His servant!
He that walks in darkness,
  And has no ray of light,
Let him trust in the name of Yahweh,
  And lean upon his God!

ver. 11. Behold, all you that strike fire,
  That kindle sparks!
Walk in the light of your fire,
  And among the sparks you have burned!
From My hand has this come to you;
  In a place of torment shall you lie down!

ver. 10. For *šômēaʿ* read *yišmaʿ*, with LXX, Syr.

ver. 11. *meʾazzerê zîqôṯ*: lit. 'that gird sparks', is difficult. Read either *miṯʾazzerê* (Hithpa., cf. Ps. xciii. 1), 'Gird yourselves (with) sparks', or, as most, *meʾîrê*, cf. Isa. xxvii. 11, Mal. i. 10, where the Hiph. of *ʾôr* is used of kindling fire.

The view that these verses are an original part of the third Song has never found much support.[1] In vv. 4–9 the speaker is the Servant, ver. 10 is a fragment of exhortation in which both Yahweh and the Servant are referred to in the third person, and in ver. 11 the speaker is presumably Yahweh. True, in the last Song there is more than one speaker, but the cases are not really parallel. There is an inner unity there that is entirely wanting here. The verses have scarcely any literary affinity either with the Songs or with the main prophecy.

xlii. 19–21

In his *Ṣerubbabel*[2] and *Studien*[3] Sellin argued that this passage was a fragment of a Servant-Song, but he later[4] abandoned this view. More recently Hans Schmidt[5] supposed that the passage contains the Prophet-Servant's estimate of his own

[1] Gressmann (*Messias*, pp. 301 ff.) includes ver. 10 as part of the preceding Song.
[2] pp. 107 f., 216.
[3] pp. 207–17.
[4] *Rätsel*, pp. 122, 125 f.
[5] *Gott u. das Leid im AT*, p. 45.

condition as blind and deaf. He has just described the people thus (ver. 18), and he is too modest not to acknowledge his own share in their disability. He resumes his description of the people in ver. 22, the first word of which, says Schmidt, should be emended from the singular *wᵉhû'*, 'and he', to the plural *wᵉhēmmâh*, 'and they'. But there is not the slightest justification for this textual change. The singular pronoun refers to the people collectively, and the subject of vv. 18–22 is Israel throughout.

xlviii. 14–16

Schmidt[1] likewise holds that the Prophet-Servant is the speaker in xlviii. 14–16. But to take the repeated 'I' of ver. 15 as the Prophet is almost grotesque in view of the fact that elsewhere in the prophecy the calling and commissioning of Cyrus is Yahweh's sole purpose and act (cf. xli. 2, 4, 25 f., xlv. 1–4). It may be otherwise with xlviii. 16*b*, 'And now the Lord Yahweh hath sent me, and his spirit', which van Hoonacker[2] would insert between chap. xlix. 2 and 3. Here the speaker, as the verse now stands, can only be the Prophet, and advocates of the autobiographical theory have quoted it in their endeavours to prove that the person of the Servant in the Songs is consistent with what little we are able to glean of the Prophet elsewhere.[3] But if the sentence does refer to the Prophet-Servant it stands in no relation either to what precedes or to what follows. In form it is metrically impossible. Many would delete it as a gloss in a heavily interpolated chapter, based upon lxi. 1. Mowinckel[4] now regards it as corrupt, though he does not venture to reconstruct it.

li. 4–(6) 8

van Hoonacker[5] would take li. 4–8, introduced by l. 10, as a separate Servant-poem. W. B. Stevenson[6] reckons the Servant passages to be five in number, including li. 4–6. These are hazardous suggestions. No doubt there are strong resemblances to xlii. 1–4, but whose can the 'arm', and 'righteousness', and 'salvation' be but Yahweh's? This is sufficient proof

[1] *Gott u. das Leid im AT*, p. 45. [2] *Het Boek Isaias*, p. 236.
[3] So Mowinckel, *Knecht*, p. 11; Sellin, *NKZ* 41, pp. 156 ff., *ZAW* 55, p. 204.
[4] *ZAW* 49, p. 259.
[5] *Expositor*, 1916, p. 192; *Het Boek Isaias*, p. 245 f.
[6] *Expositor*, Sept., 1913: 'Werden u. Wesen des ATs', *BZAW* 66, p. 89, n. 2.

that the speaker is not the Servant, but Yahweh. It is widely held that the passage is an intrusive variant of the first Song,[1] or a patchwork largely composed of glosses.[2] Begrich[3] omits ver. 4 f. from his study as 'very probably not genuine'.

li. 9 (12)–16

Begrich[4] thinks that li. 9–16 reflects the experience of the Prophet-Servant between the period of his eschatological expectations and the advance of Cyrus against Lydia, though he would not reckon it among the Servant of Yahweh texts proper. Sellin, in his Jehoiachin period,[5] took li. 16 as referring to the Servant, and again in his first advocacy of the autobiographical theory[6] reckoned li. 12–16 as a Song, but he later[7] abandoned that view. van Hoonacker[8] would place li. 16 between xlix. 3 and 4, without any convincing reason. There is no case for transposing fugitive pieces of this kind unless they fit perfectly into an obvious gap. This particular fragment is probably a later insertion, in part reminiscent of xlix. 2.[9]

lxi. 1 ff.

A number of scholars have held that the words read by our Lord in the synagogue at Nazareth—'The spirit of the Lord Yahweh is upon me', &c. (Isa. lxi. 1 ff.; Luke iv. 18 f.)—were originally intended as an utterance of the Servant. This view was not uncommon so long as Isa. xl–lxvi was thought to be a unity, and before Duhm proposed to treat the four 'Songs' as distinct from the rest of the prophecy. Since Duhm it has generally fallen into abeyance. It has, however, been maintained by von Orelli;[10] by the group of Catholic exegetes who, following Condamin, reckon Isa. lx–lxii as a part of Deutero-Isaiah, now separated from the main work;[11] by Procksch,[12]

[1] Staerk, *EJL*, p. 43; Rudolph, *ZAW* 43, p. 114, n. 2; Mowinckel, *ZAW* 49, p. 108, n. 2.

[2] Fischer, *Isa. 40–55 u. die Perikopen vom GK*, pp. 54–8; van d. Ploeg, op. cit., p. 207.

[3] *Studien*, p. 5.

[4] Ibid., pp. 73, 114, 141.

[5] *Rätsel*, pp. 127 ff.

[6] *NKZ* 41, 1930, p. 157 f.

[7] *ZAW* 55, 1937, p. 199.

[8] *RB*, 1909, p. 518; *Expositor*, 1916, p. 190; *Het Boek Isaias*, pp. 237, 248 f.

[9] Fischer, op. cit., p. 58 f.; Volz, *Jes. II*, p. 126 f.

[10] *Knecht*, p. 16 f.; *Jesaja*, 3rd ed., p. 212.

[11] van Hoonacker, *Expositor*, 1916, p. 197 f.; *Het Boek Isaias*, pp. 266 ff.; Crampon, *La Sainte Bible*, p. 1084.

[12] See *supra*, p. 98.

Cannon,[1] and Torrey.[2] These writers are not agreed as to the number of verses in chap. lxi that relate to the Servant. Cannon would limit the fragment to vv. 1–3; but it is quite impossible to separate vv. 4 ff. from what precedes.[3] van Hoonacker would extend the section to include vv. 1–6, while von Orelli would apparently make it comprise the whole chapter. But as soon as we include anything more than the first three verses of the chapter in a Servant-poem, the likeness of the passage as a whole to the recognized Songs practically disappears. Even in ver. 10, which is in the first person, the speaker is not the Servant, but Zion, who rejoices in the garments of salvation promised in ver. 3. We can only regard lxi. 1 ff. as a Servant-poem if we lengthen the other Songs beyond the limits usually assigned to them—as, indeed, Condamin and his followers do. The undoubted similarities between lxi. 1 ff. and the Songs are sufficiently accounted for in the same way as are those between Trito- and Deutero-Isaiah, and until a more convincing case has been made out for regarding chaps. lx–lxii as an integral part of Deutero-Isaiah we are not warranted in treating lxi. 1 ff. as a Song.

[1] *ZAW* 47, pp. 284–9. Cannon's theory was that Isa. lxi. 1–3 belonged to the same poem-cycle as the Songs, and that it was inserted with them into the text of DI, which originally included chaps. lx–lxii.

[2] *The Second Isaiah*, p. 142.

[3] Note the *waw consec.* at the beginning of ver. 4.

VIII

THE SERVANT AS DEPICTED IN THE SONGS

FIRST SONG: xlii. 1–4

THE crucial question in this passage is, Is the Servant depicted as a prophetic or as a kingly figure? This is intimately bound up with the meaning of the expression *yôṣî' mišpāṭ* (EVV 'he shall bring forth judgement'). At the one extreme stands Volz,[1] who thinks of the Servant as a peripatetic missionary; at the other Sellin in his Zerubbabel-Jehoiachin period.

The title *'ɛḇɛḏ*, 'servant', is used of kings (e.g. 2 Sam. iii. 18+, David; Ezek. xxxiv. 23 f.+, the Messianic David; Hag. ii. 23, Zerubbabel; Jer. xxvii. 6, Nebuchadrezzar) and of prophets (Amos iii. 7+): *bāḥûr*, 'chosen', is used in the singular of Moses (Ps. cvi. 23) and David (Ps. lxxxix. 4 || *'aḇdî*), but not of any prophet; in the plural of Israelites (1 Chron. xvi. 13, Ps. cv. 43, cvi. 5, Isa. lxv. 9, 15, 22). But since both words are used by Deutero-Isaiah in parallelism with Jacob-Israel, it is probable that the choice of them in the Song is determined by that fact, and that we ought not to argue from them that either prophetic or kingly attributes are expressly implied of the Servant.

The expression 'I have endowed him with my spirit' is indecisive, since it might equally well apply to a prophet (Hos. ix. 7) or to a king (Isa. xi. 2). The ambiguity is only emphasized by Isa. lxi. 1, 'The spirit of the Lord Yahweh is upon me, because Yahweh anointed me', where the speaker is clearly a prophet, but is nevertheless 'anointed'.[2]

Nor is ver. 2, 'He shall not cry, &c.', any more decisive. Those who see in the Servant a prophet stress the contrasts between him and the vulgar ecstatics, or it may be a fiery spirit like Amos. But the contrast may equally well be with the conqueror Cyrus. Again, as an illustration of the difficulty of drawing sharp distinctions, Volz thinks that the Servant was

[1] *Jes. II*, p. 167.

[2] The only other passage which speaks of the anointing of a prophet is 1 Kings xix. 16 (Elisha), but there is nothing in the sequel to indicate that Elisha was anointed.

none other than the prophet Deutero-Isaiah, who set out on his mission with the conviction that he himself, and not Cyrus, was to be the world-conqueror.

We come now to the expression *yôṣî' mišpāṭ*. The fact that it is twice used in the Song, together with *yāśîm mišpāṭ* (ver. 4), shows that it is the central idea in the passage. *mišpāṭ* is properly a legal decision, or judgement, pronounced by a *šôp̄ēṭ*, or judge. Instances of 'judgement' pronounced by kings, priests, and local justices are so numerous as not to need citation. Whether a like authority was vested in the prophets is not so clear. The noun *mišpāṭ* is only twice used in connexion with prophets. Judges iv. 5 speaks of 'Deborah, a prophetess . . . and the children of Israel came up to her for judgement'. It is not indicated whether it was as a prophetess that Deborah pronounced judgement, or as a predecessor of judges like Gideon, Jephthah, and Samson, of whom it is said that they judged, but never that they prophesied. A similar ambiguity is apparent in the case of Samuel, who was both prophet (1 Sam. iii. 20) and judge (1 Sam. vii. 6, 15). Was his judging part of his functions as a prophet, or something that he exercised independently, as the successor of men like Gideon? He was not a warrior, despite the story in 1 Sam. vii. 7–13, and the qualities that gave him his pre-eminence were hardly military. Perhaps they were of the psychic kind that we associate with prophecy, or it may be that his 'judgeship' was due entirely to his personality and prestige, not to any particular office that he held. The whole matter is exceedingly obscure, but the total impression we get is that it was as Yahweh's vicegerent that Samuel exercised judgement. After the establishment of the monarchy the only passage in which *mišpāṭ* is associated with a prophet is Mic. iii. 8: 'I am full of power . . . and of judgement'; but there the prophet's function is not to pronounce legal decisions, but 'to declare unto Jacob his transgression, and to Israel his sin'. On the whole, therefore, the balance of probability thus far is that the exercise of *mišpāṭ* is a regal, or governmental, rather than a prophetic function.

On the other hand, without placing undue stress on the absence of the article, which in poetry may be of no significance, the word *mišpāṭ* in the Song seems to be used absolutely, in a widely inclusive sense. It is usual to interpret it in the light of 2 Kings xvii. 26 f. (EVV 'manner' = Heb. *mišpāṭ*) and Jer. v. 4 f., as the sum-total of the judgements of the Yahweh religion, and, therefore, as announced to the heathen nations, practically equivalent to 'religion'. Thus Hertzberg[1] concludes that '*mišpāṭ* is here more than the law; it is the right, the true law, in which Yahweh's spirit has found complete expression. It is the expression of Yahweh's will . . . as the true religion'. Many commentators have pointed out the parallel with the Arab. *dîn*, which has the same wide latitude of meaning (cf. ὁδός 'way', in the New Testament). 'Religion', of course, has associations that can hardly be carried back to the Old Testament. Hence Volz prefers to translate by the more general term 'truth' (*Wahrheit*). Whichever word best expresses the sense of *mišpāṭ*, if either of them does, the exercise of such *mišpāṭ* seems to exceed the functions of any king or prophet known to us.

Tôrâh ('direction', 'instruction', 'law'), which is parallel with *mišpāṭ* in ver. 4 (cf. Hab. i. 4, Ps. lxxxix. 31), is given, amongst others, by prophets (Isa. viii. 16, xxx. 9 f., Zech. vii. 12) and priests (Jer. ii. 8, xviii. 18, Ezek. vii. 26, Hag. ii. 11, Mal. ii. 6 ff.), but never, apparently, by the king. Sellin at one stage[2] argued that it was, and quoted Lam. ii. 9, which he interpreted as 'Her king and her princes are among the heathen, *so that there is* no tôrâh' (Heb. *'ên tôrâh*); but he gave way on this point[3] in deference to Giesebrecht's contention[4] that the reason why there is no longer any *tôrâh* is that the priests have gone into exile. This is confirmed by the continuation of the verse: 'Also her prophets find no vision from Yahweh'.[5]

In what sense is the verb *yôṣî'* used? Its literal meaning is 'cause to go out', 'bring out'. With the object *mišpāṭ* this should almost certainly be understood as 'bring forth' (from the mouth), that is, 'speak'. This is the true sense of Jer. xv. 19: 'If thou speak what is precious unmixed with what is worthless, thou shalt be as my mouth' (cf. Job viii. 10, Prov. x. 18). Whether the Servant is to exercise the ministry of a travelling preacher, or to publish *mišpāṭ* after the fashion of a ruler issuing edicts, is not said. The concluding verse of the Song suggests the former, a task that will require unwearied patience; but taken by itself the phrase suggests decisions uttered by someone vested with executive authority. His authority may be exercised

[1] *ZAW* 40, p. 41.
[2] *Studien*, p. 89.
[3] *Rätsel*, p. 69.
[4] *KJ*, p. 16.
[5] See Peake, *Century Bible*, in loc.

mildly—'A bruised reed he shall not break'—but the implication is that he could be severe if he wished.

Begrich[1] has suggested a highly original interpretation of xlii. 1–4. He sees in the Servant 'the servant of the king' (*'ɛḇɛḏ hammɛlɛk*), an official whose business was to make public the judicial sentences of the sovereign. It was customary, so he says, for such sentences to be proclaimed in the open street, and to be confirmed by the breaking of the staff and extinguishing of the lamp of the person condemned. The particular judgement which the Servant is to announce is Yahweh's pardon of Israel, and the audience to which it is addressed is the heathen peoples. This interpretation is attractive and may be largely conjectural, as indeed Begrich admits; but it does not tell us what the Servant *is* to do, only what he is *not to do*. This, perhaps, is equally true on any interpretation of the passage; it is a fine example of litotes, and as such introduces us to one whose task is without precedent, and can, therefore, only be described in negative terms. Once this is recognized it seems unimaginative to insist on emending the text of ver. 3, as Gressmann[2] and Sellin[3] do, to make the Servant himself the bruised reed. Nor does it follow that, because the later Songs describe the sufferings of the Servant, his sufferings must be foreshadowed here. We are not at liberty to assume that the picture of the Servant is homogeneous throughout the Songs. That is a question for further examination. Here in the first Song it is distinctly said that 'he shall not burn dimly nor himself be bruised, until he have established judgement in the earth'. No cloud is yet on the horizon,[4] and the thought of violent death seems definitely excluded.

The Servant is introduced as already present, and endowed with Yahweh's spirit. The audience to which he is presented is presumably wide, though unspecified. It can hardly be the Gentiles, since they are throughout referred to in the third person. It may consist of supra-mundane beings (cf. xl. 3 f.).[5] The mission of the Servant probably, and its fulfilment certainly, lie still in the future.

[1] *Studien*, pp. 135 ff., 161 ff.

[2] See *supra*, p. 91.

[3] *NKZ* 41, p. 154; *ZAW* 55, p. 187.

[4] None can be inferred from *'ɛṯmoḵ-bô* of ver. 1; cf. Prov. iv. 4, v. 5.

[5] Cf. Johansson (*Parakletoi*, p. 52): 'The poem begins with a monologue of Yahweh in heaven'.

SECOND SONG: xlix. 1–6

In this Song the Servant, having been introduced by Yahweh, now speaks in his own name. His words are addressed to the far coasts and distant peoples, to whom he had at the outset been commissioned. Presumably the time is somewhat later than that of his call, since meanwhile he has laboured, and laboured in vain. It is, of course, barely possible that this labour, which appears to be in a narrower sphere than that ultimately intended for him, was anterior to his introduction in xlii. 1–4; but such an assumption is unnatural. There is nothing in the first Song to support it, and if the surmise is right, that the audience there is supra-mundane, it is natural to assume that the Servant had not previously laboured publicly on earth. He had been called and endowed from birth (ver. 1*b*), and then, for a period not specified, kept in quiet and instant readiness for his task (ver. 2); a sword, sharp indeed, but sheathed in the scabbard, with the hand of the divine Warrior clasping its hilt; an arrow, polished indeed, but as yet concealed in the quiver. It must suffice him thus far that he is Yahweh's Servant by means of whom his divine Master will get Himself glory (ver. 3). That, for the present, is honour enough (ver. 5*b*). Next he speaks of fruitless toil which has exhausted his strength (ver. 4*a*). Is this only the natural impatience of the youth who is eager to be at the task which has fired his imagination, like a theological student who finds paradigms irksome? Surely not. The Servant has spoken in terms of full appreciation of the period of probation in which his powers have come to maturity. The 'But I said' of ver. 4 is not a protest against divine procrastination; it marks a fresh development, not only in his psychological reaction to his call, but in the call itself as it becomes clearer to him. In imaginative pieces like the Songs we must expect swift transitions to new situations. The Servant has *toiled* in vain, and *spent his strength* for nought and vanity. For the moment his 'just right' (for *mišpāṭ* in this sense see xl. 27) and his 'recompense of reward' (*pᵉʿullâh*, cf. xl. 10) seem denied him; but he is quite sure that they are safe with Yahweh. The labour which has been fruitless appears to be indicated in vv. 5–6. It has been to Israel. And Yahweh, instead of being deflected from His purpose for His Servant, and permitting him to engage in something less exacting (cf. Jer. xv. 19), widens the scope of his mission to embrace all mankind.

No contradiction is involved in the fact that the mission to the heathen, and that alone, has already been announced in the first Song, while here in the second it is only gradually unfolded to the Servant himself, and that through his apparent want of success in a lesser task. It is not obvious, nor is it necessary to assume, that the Servant has overheard the divine address in xlii. 1–4. His situation is similar to that of Job, who to the end was ignorant of the preliminary parleying that went on about him in heaven. The Servant, too, must come to the recognition of his full task naturally, through frustration and disappointment in a lesser task, if need be. He must begin with what lies near to hand, among his own people. And having thereby come to the knowledge of his calling in its widest extent, he addresses himself to the nations, and briefly recounts the stages by which his conviction has dawned upon him. The primary calling in the first Song, then, and the ultimate calling in the second, is to the heathen. The ministry to Israel is subsidiary, and, as it were, by the way.

Even so, an obvious difficulty presents itself. How, if the Servant is called Israel (ver. 3), can even a preliminary ministry to Israel be assigned to him? One remedy, from which even some collectivists do not shrink, is to delete 'Israel'. But the manuscript evidence is insufficient.[1] Nor, on the collective interpretation, if it were sufficient, would the difficulty be disposed of. How can Israel have a mission to Israel? The textual surgery of Giesebrecht[2] has met with no acceptance; nor has the Hitzig–Budde[3] expedient of making Yahweh the subject of the infinitives in vv. 5–6 fared much better. Even if it is Yahweh who is to restore Israel, we are still faced with the difficulty that, in words addressed to the Servant=Israel, Jacob-Israel is referred to by name in the third person. If, then, the deletion of 'Israel' does not solve the problem for the collectivist, and the manuscript evidence is not such that the individualist can delete it with absolute confidence, is there any way out of the impasse?

Those commentators of a century ago who related the poem to the Servant-cycle, and who clung to an individual interpretation while still retaining the word Israel, were accustomed to understand it in the sense of 'the true (embodiment of) Israel'. This expedient has latterly been rare, though it has been revived

[1] See *supra*, p. 118 f.
[2] See *supra*, p. 60.
[3] See *supra*, p. 58 f.

by Praetorius,[1] who says the idea is similar to *l'état c'est moi*.[2] This solution of what is in any case a stubborn difficulty is not to be dismissed out of hand. The second stichos of ver. 3, 'Israel by whom I will get myself glory', is a unity, and the comma after Israel in the English RV is hardly justified. 'Israel', a determinate proper noun, is qualified by a relative clause with *'ᵃšer*, similarly to a *ṣila* relative clause in Arabic with *allaḏî*.[3] Hebrew poetry in general, and Deutero-Isaiah in particular,[4] is so sparing of the relative particle, that its presence here may be taken as having not merely an attributive, but a qualifying signification. I cannot point to an exactly parallel case in which the content of a collective proper noun is *limited* by a relative clause.[5] Examples must, in the nature of things, be rare; but in view of all the difficulties here, such a thing is not to be ruled out as absolutely impossible. Moreover, the second person suffix in *bᵉḵā* reads very much as if the Servant were addressed as 'Thou Israel by whom I will get myself glory'. The writer would seem to say that here in the Servant is the true Israel found.[6] In any case, if we are not free to delete 'Israel' in ver. 3, and if that Israel has a mission to Israel in ver. 5, the Israel of ver. 3 must in some way be qualified.

Another problem raised by the second Song is whether the mission of the Servant to Israel is political, or spiritual only. In ver. 5 it is said that the Servant is to 'restore (*šôḇēḇ*, Poʿlel) Jacob unto him, and that Israel to him shall be gathered'; in ver. 6 the Servant is to 'raise up the tribes of Jacob, and to bring back (*hāšîḇ*, Hiph.) the survivors of Israel'. The words of Ps. xxiii. 3, 'he restoreth (*yᵉšôḇēḇ*) my soul', come immediately to mind, and we may be tempted to take the Poʿlel as indicating spiritual, and the Hiphʿil political, restoration. Even so, ver. 6 would still imply a political activity on the part of the Servant.

[1] *Nachträge und Verbesserungen zu DJ*, 1927, p. 32.

[2] 'Du, Knecht, bist der theologische Mittelpunkt, die treibende religiöse Kraft in Israel. . . . Du bist mir soviel wert wie das gesamte Israel.'

[3] Cf. Wright, *A Grammar of the Arabic Language*, ii, pp. 317 ff.; *G-K*, § 155*d*.

[4] Köhler, op. cit., p. 58.

[5] There does not appear to be limitation in xli. 8.

[6] For an interpretation similar to that of Praetorius see E. Burrows, *The Gospel of the Infancy and other Biblical Essays*, p. 63: 'It is to be observed that "Israel" is not a term of address (vocative), and not merely an apposition to "my Servant", but a name which is predicated. It need not therefore be an indication of the Servant's proper name. It can be understood as a name of honour applied to him for the reason indicated in the last clause . . . it is here honorific.'

But such a distinction between the Po'lel and the Hiph'il cannot be sustained; for the Hiph'il is used with the object *nεpεš* of spiritual restoration in Lam. i. 11, 16, 19, Ps. xix. 8, Prov. xxv. 13, Ruth iv. 15; and the Po'lel, which is only found eleven times in all, can have no other than a political reference in Isa. lviii. 12, Jer. l. 19, Ezek. xxxix. 27. Further, the expression 'to raise up the tribes of Jacob' (ver. 6) can only refer to political restoration, since a tribe is a political entity. Moreover, it is difficult to see how any prophet, especially in the conditions of the exile, could conceive of a spiritual restoration apart from the political rehabilitation of his nation. Even Jeremiah, who believed that nation and temple must come to an end in the interest of a higher and more spiritual religion, looked forward to what can only be interpreted as a measure of political restoration.[1] The distinction which the modern pastor is capable of making between the spiritual and temporal spheres of the Church's activity would hardly have been comprehensible to an Old Testament prophet. We must, therefore, conclude that in this second Song the Servant's mission to Israel involved, in its initial stages, some measure of concern for the political restoration of the nation.

THIRD SONG: l. 4–9

In this passage we witness, as it were, the Gethsemane of the Servant. So far as any human sympathy and companionship are concerned, he seems utterly forsaken. No clear political background is discernible. We see a lonely man, who has already suffered bitter persecution, and borne it bravely and patiently. The thwarted purposes, the stubbornness of will, and the latent opposition of which he had previously complained, have since given place to open hostility and brutal physical violence. The danger for the moment appears to be past, and the Servant is at liberty to reflect upon his condition and prospects. But the respite is only temporary; he speaks as if in instant expectation of further trial. Who the adversaries are we are left to conjecture, though it is natural to assume that they are encountered in the course of his main task, namely, the mission to the Gentiles. The mission to Israel was, in the

[1] Cf. Skinner, *Prophecy and Religion*, chaps. xvi, xvii; A. C. Welch, *Jeremiah: His Time and His Work*, chaps. xi, xii.

purpose of Yahweh, in any case preparatory, and ancillary to the mission to the Gentiles, and it is probable that xlix. 6 should be interpreted as indicating, not that the Servant was to carry on both parts of his mission simultaneously, but that he was to leave the first part unfulfilled, and, like Paul and Barnabas, 'turn to the Gentiles' (Acts xiii. 46). That need not, of course, carry with it the assumption that the physical violence came from the Gentiles. His most virulent opponents, like those of St. Paul, may still have been his fellow Israelites. The text does not say. We get the impression that the crisis cannot be long delayed. The passage ends on a note of perfect trust in Yahweh, and of complete confidence in the ultimate issue, and, near as the end may be, the Servant still has no expectation of untimely or violent death.

FOURTH SONG: lii. 13–liii. 12

The text of this passage is in places seriously corrupt, though it does not follow that if it had been preserved unimpaired, the answer to the main question would have been appreciably simplified. It may even be that the corruptions have in part been occasioned by an original obscurity of meaning, and that a well-intentioned copyist made matters worse by trying to straighten out what he already found perplexing. The most baffling, as well as, probably, the most corrupt, passage occurs at the point which apparently relates the turn in the Servant's fortunes (liii. 10). We look for a description of his rising from the dead, or at least a clear statement that he has so risen, or will rise. But it is quite possible that nothing so definite was ever there. The passage—*pace* Volz[1]—is earlier than the general acceptance of the doctrine of a future life, and the writer may not have been in a position to enter into details about something which he could only dimly apprehend. It is not compromising the question of the relation of the Servant to Tammuz conceptions, to remark that the Tammuz liturgies 'do not describe the ascent to the upper world, but pass at once to a crescendo movement, announcing that the lord is risen'.[2] This is very similar to the situation in the concluding verses of Isa. liii. No devotee ever doubted that Tammuz lived again. The Servant likewise died (liii. 8), and was buried (ver. 9), and lives

[1] Cf. *supra*, p. 78.

[2] Langdon, *Tammuz and Ishtar*, p. 22; cf. Baudissin, *Adonis und Esmun*, p. 426.

again (vv. 10*b*, 11),[1] and it may be that when the piece was written no fuller description of the transition from death to life was possible.

Does the passage even describe the death of the Servant? This has been disputed by Sellin[2] and Staerk,[3] as was inevitable on their theory that the Servant was Jehoiachin.[4] The fact that both of them subsequently abandoned the identification with Jehoiachin, while it renders their contention improbable, does not altogether absolve us from the necessity of considering the question on its merits. The chief points in Sellin's argument were that liii. 7, 'As a sheep borne along to the slaughter, &c.', describes no more than the dumb and patient bearing of the Servant, and that in the closely parallel Jer. xi. 19 the Prophet is not actually killed. The 'land of the living' from which the Servant is 'cut off' (ver. 8) is his homeland Canaan. Exile is as good as death. The 'grave' (ver. 9) is his Babylonian prison. There are no positive signs of real death, but only of 'expulsion, exile and imprisonment among the Babylonians'.[5] Staerk supplemented this by remarking that in Psalms descriptive of acute suffering there are characteristic hyperbolical expressions: the sufferer '*is* already arrived at the gates of death, *is* already cut off from the land of the living and laid in the grave; cf. only Ps. lxxxviii!'[6] An even better illustration than Ps. lxxxviii, where the sufferer says he is '*reckoned* with those who go down to the pit, and *like* a man without help', would be Jonah ii, where the drowning man cries for help from the womb of Sheol (ver. 3), the land of no-return, to which he has 'gone down' (ver. 7). But while a man may describe *himself* as, or as if, already dead, there is in the Psalms no analogy for a sufferer not yet dead being described *by someone else* as though he were. Further, it is a perilous procedure to take such descriptions as the physical maltreatment in l. 6 literally—Sellin[7] took the plucking out of the hair as referring to the captive Jehoiachin having his beard cut off!—and then to take the equally vivid descriptions of death and burial figuratively. Where, in that case, are we to draw the line, otherwise than as individual fancy or theory may dictate? No one would dream of taking

[1] For the expression 'see light' as a figure of life cf. Ps. xlix. 20 (Heb.).
[2] *Studien*, pp. 258 ff.; cf. *supra*, p. 51.
[3] *EJL*, p. 132, cf. *supra*, p. 52.
[4] Similarly Burrows, *The Gospel of the Infancy*, p. 70 f.
[5] Op. cit., p. 265. [6] Op. cit., p. 132. [7] Op. cit., p. 274.

the descriptions of death in liii. 7 ff. otherwise than literally, unless he were first determined to identify the Servant with some historical individual of whom he could not claim that he died a violent death. Of course, on the collective theory the death is allegory. There is no inconsistency in this, since the whole is allegory. But as soon as we begin to pick and choose, taking part literally and part figuratively, we are out of touch with reality. The Song describes an actual death and burial of the Servant. The whole may be allegory, or it may be ideal; but within the framework of the whole the details must first be understood literally, very much as in the *Pilgrim's Progress*.

The next question must be, How did the Servant die? Duhm, as we have seen,[1] argued that he was not judicially executed, but that he died a natural death, from leprosy. It is, perhaps, just possible to understand liii. 8 in this sense, and Duhm was able to point to Old Testament analogies for most of the details in his interpretation. At the same time, they can equally well, some of them better and more naturally, be understood of a death by violence; and certainly death by violence is a more natural sequel to l. 4–9 than death by leprosy. Duhm was concerned to show the absurdity of the collective theory, which is not seriously embarrassed even if there is a mixing of figures in the description of the death. But his own theory, that the Servant was an historical individual, did not easily harmonize with differences of representation of the manner of his death. A leper may conceivably be executed for felony; but it would be strange if Duhm's 'leprous rabbi' should contrive to get himself into such a situation that he was executed on a capital charge. Duhm had, therefore, to choose, and he chose leprosy as the cause of death. He may have been wrong in interpreting the *nāgûaʿ* ('stricken') of liii. 4 of leprosy, though he was able to refer to Lev. xiii. 22, 32, 2 Kings xv. 6, and the interpretation is as old as the Vulgate ('leprosus') and the early rabbis. Whether actual leprosy was intended or not, it remains that the Servant suffered pains and sickness sufficient in themselves to be mortal. Yet he was finally executed as a malefactor. It would seem as if the writer, without regard for consistency, pictures a man upon whom every conceivable indignity was heaped. He was unattractive even from birth (cf. 'sapling' and 'root', ver. 2). More positively, he was 'so disfigured that he

[1] *Supra*, p. 48.

scarce seemed human' (lii. 14), so physically repulsive that men averted their gaze from him (ver. 3). He was 'a man of pains'[1] and an habitual sufferer (ver. 3 f.). Those who saw him regarded him as 'stricken, smitten of God, and afflicted' (ver. 4). If chap. liii stood alone, we might suppose that the description thus far relates to the earlier life and ministry of the Servant. But there is nothing in the first three Songs to confirm this—rather, indeed, the contrary. The 'stripes', and perhaps the 'piercing through' and 'crushing', of ver. 5, together with the figure of the dumb sheep in ver. 7, agree well with the maltreatment of l. 6. That passes over into the arrest, the sentence, and the death and burial of ver. 8 f. Although from first to last there is a certain progression, culminating in a final climax, the whole reads like a general impression of the Servant's manifold sufferings rather than an enumeration of them in ordered sequence. Either, then, his sufferings, if related as they occurred, contain elements not entirely consistent with what we read in the earlier Songs; in which case we shall have to ask whether the Songs are *uno tenore* with one another. Or, if the account of the Servant's many trials was only intended to convey an overruling impression of their exceeding severity, we are compelled to ask whether such a description is possible in the case of any particular historical individual. Should the collective interpretation be adopted it is doubtless possible; but, should that interpretation prove untenable, it is pertinent to ask whether the historical individual theories are in any better case. Of course, we may say with T. H. Robinson[2] that 'no one individual sat for the ideal portrait, but that the writer draws on the experiences of at least two different men', a speculation which raises difficulties of its own.[3]

The most vigorously debated question arising from the last Song is, Who are the speakers in liii. 1 ff.? Collectivists, at

[1] *maḵ'ôḇôṯ*: the word is used of both physical and mental pain.

[2] *Hebrew Religion; Its Origin and Development*, 2nd ed., p. 345 f.

[3] J. Monteith, 'A New View of Isaiah liii', *ET* 36, pp. 498–502, proposes to divide the fourth Song into two originally distinct documents: (1) The Song of the Captive Nation, lii. 13 (reading 'Israel' for *yaśkîl*, with Budde), lii. 15, liii. 1, 5–8, 9*b*, 12*ab*, and (2) The Song of the Leper, lii. 13 (omitting *yaśkîl*), lii. 14, liii. 2–4, 9*a*, 10, 11, 12*c*. Both are later than Deutero-Isaiah, and their relationship to the other Songs is uncertain. This dichotomy only serves to aggravate unevennesses of another kind in the passage. The changes of speakers, which are understandable in the Song as we have it, become intolerable when reproduced in both the shorter parts.

least for many years, have been unanimous that the speakers are the Gentiles. On their theory this is almost necessary, since if the speakers are Jews, or the Prophet speaking on behalf of his co-religionists, the natural conclusion is that the salvation wrought is for the Jews, and that the Servant is one of their number, or at most a minority among them. On the other side, individualists have usually insisted that the speakers are the Jews, or the Prophet acting as their spokesman. But while, if the Servant is Israel, the speakers *must* be the Gentiles, it does not follow that if the speakers are the Gentiles, the Servant *must* be Israel. Accordingly, since Mowinckel[1] one or two individualists have admitted that the speakers are the Gentiles. There is much to be said for this, once we get off partisan lines, and recognize that the conclusion that the speakers are the Gentiles does not carry with it the corollary that the Servant must be Israel. The division between chaps. 52 and 53 is artificial, and may, of course, be disregarded. At the end of chap. 52 the amazement of the Gentiles is foretold. It is entirely natural, then, that what immediately follows should embody their judgement upon the Servant. Any other supposition disturbs the sequence of the passage, and destroys its artistic symmetry. True, in lii. 15 it is said that the Gentiles will be dumb with amazement. But it is usual for dumb astonishment to give place to voluble speech, once understanding has dawned, and that is what is promised. It has been argued that the heathen still in darkness, or only just waking from it, could not possibly give expression to thoughts so deep that they find no parallel in the Old Testament. The same is equally true of the Jews at any period. The essential thoughts of the passage must, therefore, be those of the Prophet. But it is not in his own name that he utters them. And if he is putting them into the mouths of others, they are as appropriate on the lips of the Gentiles as they are on those of the Jews. Indeed, more so, since from the beginning the Servant's primary commission was to the Gentiles, and it was to be successful (xlii. 4, xlix. 6). We expect that the last word from the human side will be that of the Gentiles, as the final word of all is from Yahweh Himself (liii. 11 f.). It would be strange if the Gentiles had nothing to say, and they have not, unless they are the speakers here.

[1] *Knecht*, pp. 37 n., 45.

The judgement of the Gentiles, as is fitting, is set in a framework of pronouncements by Yahweh.[1] In the introductory words of Yahweh the standpoint appears to be between the death and exaltation of the Servant. It is commonly assumed that this applies also to the confession of the Gentiles and Yahweh's final pronouncement. But since the text, at least in the form in which we have it, neither predicts nor describes an actual resurrection, but only presupposes that the Servant is once more alive, it may be that his exaltation has already begun. Such an actual manifestation of the Servant in glory would better explain the faith of the Gentiles than any verbal assurance, even though it were Yahweh who had given it. The sufferings are, in general, described as past, though the text is not quite consistent on this point. Several scholars have drawn attention to the conditional sentence 'If thou make his soul a guilt-offering' in the received text of ver. 10, and, as we have seen,[2] Duhm gave this as a major reason for emending it. Nevertheless, the text is anything but certain, and Feldmann[3] and Fischer[4] are not on very safe ground when they argue from it that the sufferings are still in the future. Nor can anything be based upon the fact that the final word of the Song (*yapgîaʿ*, 'he interposed') is imperfect. No one proposes to translate it as a future. The preterite-imperfect is quite common in narrative poetry,[5] and in this instance it is parallel with the perfect *nāśāʾ*, 'he bore'. Nor does anyone propose to take the twice-repeated *yiptaḥ* ('he opened') of ver. 7, or the *yᵉśôḥēaḥ* ('reflected') of ver. 8, as futures. On the other hand, neither does anyone propose to translate the *yisbōl* ('he shall bear') at the end of ver. 11 as a preterite. It occurs in a sequence of imperfects which can only have a future reference, and yet it is practically a repetition of *sᵉbālām* ('he bore them') in ver. 4. If the word and its parallel *yaṣdîq* ('he shall justify') refer to the Servant's sufferings, these are already in the past. And yet if we are to take it *au pied de la lettre* they are still future. The question, therefore, arises whether the whole passage is not written from an ideal point of view rather than as an account

[1] There are no cogent reasons for reading 'The Servant of Yahweh' for 'My Servant' in lii. 13, liii. 11, and 'He shall divide' for 'I will divide' in liii. 12, with Köhler, op. cit., p. 49; cf. Duhm, in loc. [2] *Supra*, p. 96, n. 2.

[3] *KJ*, p. 188 f. [4] *Wer ist der Ebed?* p. 61 f.; *Isaias II*, p. 137.

[5] For examples see S. R. Driver, *Hebrew Tenses*, pp. 31 ff., and for the probable explanation G. R. Driver, *Problems of the Hebrew Verbal System*, passim.

of something that has actually happened. In that case, the suspicions already aroused by the manifoldness of the Servant's sufferings would be confirmed.

What is meant by the 'seed' of the Servant (ver. 10) it is impossible to say with certainty. The expression may have been intentionally, or, perhaps, by reason of a limitation of the Prophet's horizon on the subject of an after-life, unconsciously vague. Consequently, the opinions of individual exegetes tend to be decided according to their views as to who the Servant was. We must go farther back and ask whether the Servant is to live again in the body upon this earth, or whether he is to live on beyond the boundary of things seen? Here again, the text gives no clear indication. Of course, when a scholar has examined the Songs as a whole, and come to the conclusion, all things considered, that the Servant is such-and-such, or so-and-so, he naturally feels justified in deciding these details in the light of his major conclusion. The collectivist thinks of the survival and world-mission of the historical Israel, and of the 'seed' as individual Israelites, or even Gentile proselytes. The orthodox Messianist (e.g. Fischer) shrinks from the idea of a physical seed, and thinks rather of spiritual posterity. The historical-individualist (Duhm) and the historico-messianist (Kittel, Rudolph) think of a return to life on this earth. At this point opinions may again diverge, and the seed be physical (Duhm) or spiritual (Kittel, Rudolph). The text is consistent with any of these views. It may be translated either 'He shall see seed, he shall prolong days', or, taking the second clause as a relative,[1] 'He shall see seed that prolongs days'. The closest parallel is Job xlii. 16: 'And after this Job lived 140 years, and saw his sons, and his sons' sons, four generations', and in the light of this Duhm interpreted it. But it does not follow that the words of the Song are to be taken as literally as those in Job. The parallel may be only verbal. If my suggestion[2] is right, that the glory of the Servant is already manifest to the Gentiles, it is natural to think of him as returned from the grave to this earth. Then, if Yahweh is to 'assign him the many for his portion'—for so we have translated ver. 12—it is most in keeping with the spiritual perception of the whole passage to think of 'the many' as his spiritual posterity. Farther than this we cannot go with any confidence. What is said about the seed

[1] So Volz, *Jes. II*, p. 171.

[2] See *supra*, p. 152.

and the prolonging of days must be determined by, rather than help to determine, the answer to the major question. And that is the procedure which most interpreters, consciously or unconsciously, have followed. Perhaps the ambiguity is only one more indication of the ideal character of the portrait.

It remains to ask whether the portrait of the Servant is consistent throughout the Songs? This is not quite the same question as that which asks whether the Songs are of common authorship. They might conceivably be from more than one author, and yet be intended to refer to the same Servant. Under this head there are two possibilities. The last Song might be from a later author, and intended to supplement the other three.[1] Or it might even be earlier than the others,[2] and edited with the object of contributing to one portrait with them. Again, the Songs might be from more than one author, and about different Servants.[3] Still another possibility is that the Songs are all from one author, and about one Servant, but that the portrait is nevertheless not altogether homogeneous.[4]

We are not at present considering whether the Songs are of common authorship, but only whether, as we have them, they present a consistent portrait. According to Staerk[5] 'the Servant of the first three Songs is a spiritual *hero-figure*, endowed with power from God to *act*, ready, indeed, to suffer for the cause of God, but by no means a silent sufferer. . . . On the other hand, the Servant of Isa. liii is a true *martyr-figure*, filled with power from God to *suffer*, consumed for others not in that he labours for them or strives with them, but in willing, silent, vicarious suffering'. Volz[6] likewise stresses the contrast between the active mission of the Servant in the first three Songs, and the 'act of divine grace' accomplished in the fourth. If this means that there must be two distinct Servant figures, exactly the same might be argued from the contrast between the Galilean ministry of Jesus and His death upon the Cross. Besides, the Gospels are, in the main at least, objective historical narratives. This cannot be assumed for the Songs, but remains to be proved, if it can be. What strikes the reader more and more is

[1] So Elliger, *supra*, p. 81, and, latterly, Sellin, *supra*, p. 79 f.

[2] So Schenkel, *supra*, p. 38.

[3] So Bertholet, *Zu Jes. 53*, cf. *supra*, p. 49; Staerk, *EJL*, pp. 118–21, cf. *supra*, p. 52; Volz, *Jes. II*, p. 192 f., cf. *supra*, p. 78.

[4] So Gressmann, *Ursprung*, p. 317.

[5] *EJL*, p. 121.

[6] *Jes. II*, pp. 189–93.

the essentially dramatic character of these Songs: the abruptness with which they open, the world-wide, even supra-mundane, setting, and the variety of speakers introduced, all serve to indicate this. Not that we can speak of drama in the modern sense, but that the four Songs could be worked up into a drama in four acts, a drama of surpassing magnificence. Indeed, they are that already. Now when a dramatist makes a beginning he may not know to the last detail whither he is going. Shakespeare clearly did not in *A Midsummer Night's Dream*. That may be due to careless or hurried workmanship. Even where the workmanship is perfect a character may appear to be almost a different person at the end from what he is at the beginning; Macbeth, for example. In the first Song there appears to be no anticipation of death, which even seems to be definitely excluded. The only hint we get of any untoward possibility is that the Servant's task will not be easy—'not burning dimly nor himself being bruised, until. . . .' The attempts of Gressmann[1] and Sellin[2] to make the Servant himself the bruised reed are dictated by a desire to remove the apparent contradiction between the first Song and the last. The third Song still ends on a note of high confidence, though that is not to say that the Prophet did not envisage what the end would be. There is, therefore, no necessary incongruity between the third and fourth Songs. There may be between the fourth and the first, since the assurance that the Servant 'shall not burn dimly nor himself be bruised, until he have established judgement in the earth', is Yahweh's own. A possible parallel to this is that Jesus, at the beginning of His ministry, may not yet have seen the Cross as a necessity. There are, besides, the difficulties, already indicated, of reconciling the manifold sufferings of the last Song with one another and with the healthy vigour of the Servant which seems natural from xlix. 1 ff. The former of these has no bearing on the question of authorship, but only on whether this is imaginative or historical writing; the latter might be lessened if we thought of the first two Songs as describing the relation of the Servant to God, while the last describes him as he appeared to men late in his career.[3] It must be admitted, however, that sufficient incongruities remain to leave open the question whether the Songs are from more than one writer.

[1] *Supra*, p. 91. [2] *ZAW* 55, p. 187 f. [3] Cf. van d. Ploeg, op. cit., p. 69.

IX

AUTHORSHIP OF THE SONGS

I. THEIR FORMAL RELATION TO THEIR CONTEXTS

WHEN Duhm asserted that the Songs were composed by an author who lived a century later than Deutero-Isaiah, and that they had been inserted at random into their present contexts, he challenged the collective interpretation at what had always been regarded as its strongest point. The collective interpretation had been based upon the assumption that Isa. xl–lv (lxvi) was a literary unity, and that the Servant must be Israel throughout, because in a number of passages Israel is explicitly called the Servant. Even disciples of Duhm, like Schian,[1] felt that he had treated the subject somewhat cavalierly, and were careful to base their conclusion that the Songs were not from Deutero-Isaiah upon grounds less fortuitous. On the other side, collectivists rallied to prove that the Songs were integrally woven into their contexts. It is not necessary now to go into all the details of the discussion in the two decades following Duhm,[2] since, as we shall see, the presuppositions underlying it have radically changed. It must be admitted that the collectivists were only moderately successful in their pleadings. König[3] might argue that all the Songs are related even to their preceding contexts. The most that Giesebrecht felt confident in asserting was that 'no Servant-passage stands altogether unrelated to its context. To be sure, the relations are not equally clear for all the passages: they are clearest for xlii. 1–4 and l. 4–9, in what follows; in lii. 13–liii. 12 clearer with what precedes; while in xlix. 1–6 they are shown principally in what immediately follows, which merges imperceptibly into an oracle of Deutero-Isaiah'.[4] He admitted that so far as the argument from the formal relation of the Songs to their contexts was concerned, they might conceivably be from another hand, and he could only base a somewhat hesitating conviction that they were actually from Deutero-Isaiah upon the ground of their close lexical and stylistic similarities to the rest of the

[1] *Supra*, p. 48.

[2] For the details see Fischer, *Isa. 40–55 u. d. Perikopen vom GK*, pp. 203–27.

[3] 'Deuterojesajanisches', *NKZ* 1898, pp. 899 ff.

[4] *KJ*, p. 203.

Prophet's work. Budde's assertion[1] that Duhm, by extruding the Songs, had 'put out the Prophet's eyes', appeared to be as drastically exaggerated as Duhm's own surgery.

Condamin and van Hoonacker,[2] in the interests of a Messianic interpretation, but still assuming the unity of the prophecy, argued that the chapters as we now have them are not in their original order. But they were not in full agreement about the transpositions proposed,[3] and van Hoonacker could not accept the strophic theory which was the basis of Condamin's reconstruction. Moreover, Lagrange, who belonged to the same school of Catholic interpreters, did not believe that the main transference—that of xlii. 1 ff. after xlix. 1 ff.—was necessary. It was becoming evident that the attempt to buttress the collective theory by appeal to the immediate contexts of the Songs had broken down, while the effort to establish, in a different interest, a more convincing unity of structure in the prophecy, was hardly more successful.

In 1914 Gressmann[4] challenged the whole conception of Deutero-Isaiah as a *book* written according to a definite plan. He was not primarily concerned with the Servant-Songs, nor did he question that they were from Deutero-Isaiah. It was already generally recognized that the pre-exilic prophets, at least, were speakers rather than authors. But the conception of Deutero-Isaiah as primarily a 'writing prophet' still held the field, partly because of the general tendency for spoken prophecy to give place to written, and Deutero-Isaiah, it was supposed, occupied an intermediate position between the two, and partly because, so it was assumed, he would have little opportunity in the conditions of the exile to 'let his voice be heard in the street'. Gressmann argued that the spoken word was 'simply inseparable' from prophecy, even so late as John the Baptist and Jesus. Were we to think of Deutero-Isaiah as an exception? He might, in the circumstances of the exile, have had to be careful, but neither he nor Ezekiel could have been satisfied simply with writing. A prophet who only writes is a 'contradiction in himself'. Gressmann went on to argue that Budde's conception of the book as a unity contains an

[1] *Das Buch Jes. 40–66, HSAT*, p. 612.

[2] *Supra*, p. 68.

[3] Cf. Condamin, *Isaïe*, passim; van Hoonacker, *Het Boek Isaias*, passim.

[4] 'Die literarische Analyse DJas', *ZAW* 34, pp. 254–97.

inner contradiction. Budde had laid it down[1] that the prophecy contains four main sections (xlii. 1–xliv. 23, xliv. 24–xlviii, xlix–li. 8, li. 9–liii), together with an introduction (xl–xli) and conclusion (liv–lv). These several sections were circulated anonymously, and secretly, very much as fly-sheets. This involved, as Budde had recognized, some overlapping and repetition, and the whole could hardly be a unity each part of which was connected with the preceding. It is characteristic of fly-sheets, continued Gressmann, that each is a unity in itself; but none of them necessarily presupposes another, and there can, therefore, be no question of one large composition. A unity of 16 chapters would be unique in the prophetical literature of Israel. Nor are we to think of Deutero-Isaiah thus, because a writer who sets out to compose an artistic whole does not repeat himself, except for special reasons. Hitherto literary criticism had been too much concerned with the idea of book-unity (*Bucheinheit*), an idea based essentially upon modern literature, but which does not apply to Hebrew writings. The prophets contain mostly only quite short oracles (*Sprüche*).

Gressmann then proceeded, largely on the basis of introductory and concluding formulae, such as 'Thus saith Yahweh' and 'Saith Yahweh of Hosts', to divide the 16 chapters into 49 independent *Sprüche*, varying in length from 1 to 20 verses apiece, with an average of 6 or 7 verses each. These have nothing to do with one another, except that they are from the same author. This position has been largely accepted by subsequent writers. Thus Köhler[2] proposes 70 units, including the Songs, which are from Deutero-Isaiah; Mowinckel[3] 41, not reckoning the Songs, which are not from Deutero-Isaiah; Volz[4] 50, excluding the Songs, of which xlii. 1–4, xlii. 5–9, xlix. 1–6, l. 4–9 are from Deutero-Isaiah, and lii. 13–liii. 12 is not; Oesterley and Robinson[5] 54, including the Songs, which are from Deutero-Isaiah; Eissfeldt[6] 'some 50', the Songs from Deutero-Isaiah; while Caspari,[7] on similar premisses, thinks that the several units are from a variety of authors,[8] and that

[1] Op. cit., p. 612.
[2] *DJ stilkritisch untersucht*, 1923.
[3] *ZAW* 49, 1931, pp. 87–112, 242–60.
[4] *Jes. II.*
[5] *An Introduction to the Books of the O.T.*
[6] *Einleitung in das AT*, 1934, p. 379.
[7] *Lieder u. Gottessprüche der Rückwanderer*, 1934.
[8] Ibid., p. 95.

'the personal Deutero-Isaiah was an indoor plant grown on the study-table'.[1]

This view of the composition of Isa. xl–lv (lxvi) has not gone unchallenged. The most recent protest against it is that of E. J. Kissane,[2] who insists that Isa. xl–lxvi is a literary unity, and consists of ten poems, each with a conclusion, or 'tail-piece'. Each of these longish poems is further subdivided into three, and the whole is made up of ten triads on a logically developing theme. The 'Songs' of the Servant never had an independent existence, and each is to be interpreted in accordance with the context in which it stands. Incidentally, it follows from this that in chaps. xlii. and xlix the Servant is Israel, in lii. 13–liii the Messiah, while in l. 4–9 the speaker is the Prophet himself.

The general principle underlying Dr. Kissane's treatment of Isa. xl–lxvi is very similar to that of Torrey,[3] notwithstanding that the latter would assign these chapters to the period *circa* 400 B.C. This similarity extends even to details: for example, Torrey thinks that chaps. xxxiv–xxxv should go with xl–lxvi, and that the whole consists of 27 poems; both think that xli. 1–4, 25–6 refers to Abraham, not Cyrus; and both, having related the beginning of chap. lvi to what precedes, have to regard the following vv. 2–6 (Torrey), or 3–8 (Kissane), as secondary. Both think of the author as a poet rather than as a prophet, and according to Kissane his purpose was to expound the teaching of the eighth-century Isaiah to his fellow exiles.[4] This seems an extremely academic view to take of the vivacious, not to say eschatological, Prophet of the exile. Both Kissane and Torrey seek to end the apparent confusion in contemporary criticism of Isa. xl–lxvi by brushing aside the work of the past thirty years, and proposing, rather dogmatically, constructions of their own. But neither of them really attempts to answer Gressmann's important 1914 article on the literary analysis of Deutero-Isaiah.

Notwithstanding the protests of Torrey and Kissane, there-

[1] Ibid., p. 244.

[2] *The Book of Isaiah, vol. II* (*XL–LXVI*), Dublin, 1943.

[3] *The Second Isaiah*, 1928.

[4] This view differs fundamentally from that of Glahn, *Der Prophet der Heimkehr*, 1934, who does indeed regard Isa. xl–lxvi as a unity, but as the work of a prophet who exercised a genuine prophetic ministry between 540 B.C. and the time of Haggai and Zechariah. Glahn has worked in close co-operation with Köhler, and has no objection to the latter's division of xl–lxvi into a large number of relatively short pieces.

fore, it remains that most critics now regard Isa. xl–lv(lxvi) as a collection of short oracles, without prejudice to the question whether the Songs are, or are not, from Deutero-Isaiah. It is from this standpoint that we must proceed with our inquiry. Some think that the Songs are from Deutero-Isaiah, others that they are not. The opinion of the majority at the moment is that they are. The only writer who thinks that the present arrangement proves that they are not is Mowinckel.[1] There is undoubtedly a measure of truth in his 'catchword' theory of the association of the oracles with one another, but the thoroughgoing form in which he applies it has met with only qualified acceptance. Volz[2] remarks that if pressed too hard it becomes 'an artificial and external scheme', and Eissfeldt[3] that 'it is hardly right, at least not everywhere . . . rather would it appear that, at all events here and there, a grouping according to subject-matter is to be recognized'. Sellin[4] maintains that there are some catchwords connecting the Songs with their preceding contexts which Mowinckel has overlooked, and it is at least arguable that the vocabulary of Deutero-Isaiah is so distinctive that we might put his oracles in any order we please, and still find catchwords of the kind that Mowinckel postulates. It is to be noticed, too, that Mowinckel himself admits similarity of subject-matter as a secondary principle of association. He can hardly have it both ways, and it looks as if he is putting the cart before the horse, and that community of subject-matter is the primary principle of association.[5] This raises the question whether Gressmann did not go too far when he denied the *Bucheinheit* of the prophecy. All the same, his contention that the prophecy is made up of a series of short oracles probably stands. That being so, we can no longer argue, either on the basis of a formal connexion of the Songs with their contexts, or on the lack of such formal connexion, that the Songs are, or are not, from Deutero-Isaiah. For want of any surer criterion we are forced to a consideration of the vocabulary, style, metrical forms, and ideas of the Songs in relation to those of the main prophecy. If this should seem like reducing the whole question to one of statistics, there appears to be no alternative.

[1] *ZAW* 49; cf. *supra*, p. 80.
[2] *Jes. II*, p. xxxv.
[3] *Der GK bei DJ*, p. 10.
[4] *ZAW* 55, p. 180 f.
[5] Cf. *supra*, p. 84 f., in the criticism of Begrich.

2. LANGUAGE OF THE SONGS

In what follows, passages of doubtful genuineness are indicated by a query (in brackets)—e.g. li. 4 (?)—and references to other passages in the Songs are italicized.

xlii. 1–4

ver. 1. *'abdî*, 'my servant': cf. *xlix. 3, lii. 13, liii. 11*. Elsewhere in DI, and equated with Jacob-Israel, xli. 8, 9, xliv. 1, 2, 21 (also *'ebed lî*), xlv. 4. In xlii. 19, xliii. 10, the context requires us to understand Israel, though in both cases the plural 'my servants' should perhaps be read. *'abdô*, 'his servant', equated with Jacob, is found in xlviii. 20. The same form in l. 10 (?) refers to the Servant; but in xliv. 26 the parallelism, supported by LXX^A, Targ., seems to require the plural 'his servants'. *'ebed*, without suffix, occurs in *xlix. 5, 6*, and elsewhere in the prophecy xlii. 19, xlix. 7. The plural 'servants of Yahweh' appears in liv. 17. In TI *'ebed* is never found in the singular, while in the plural it is found 10 times (lvi. 6, lxiii. 17, lxv. 8, 9, 13 (*ter*), 14, 15, lxvi. 14).

'etmok-bô, 'whom I uphold': cf. xli. 10, of Israel.

beḥîrî, 'my chosen': cf. xliii. 20, xlv. 4, both times of Israel, and in the latter case || 'my servant', as here. The plural 'my chosen ones' is found in TI (lxv. 9, 15, 22). Note also the verb *bḥr*, 'to choose', in xli. 8, 9, xliii. 10, xliv. 1, 2, with Israel as object. (*beḥartîkâ*, xlviii. 10, should probably be read *beḥantîkâ*, 'I have tested thee'.)

râṣetâ, 'delighteth': cf. xl. 2 (Niph.) in a different sense from here.

nâtattî rûḥî 'âlâw, 'I have put my spirit upon him': cf. the similar expression 'I will pour out (*'eṣṣōq*) my spirit', in xliv. 3, with reference to Israel's seed; also *nôtēn nešâmâh . . . werûaḥ* (xlii. 5) with reference to mankind in general. But note that the (to us) peculiar sense of *ntn* as 'put', 'set', is not uncommon in O.T.

mišpâṭ, 'judgement': cf. *vv. 3, 4*. Outside this Song only in li. 4 (?) in the same sense as here.

yôṣî', 'he shall announce': cf. *ver. 3*. Hiph'il in sense of uttering tidings, only xlviii. 20, and rare and mostly late elsewhere (see *BDB*, 425*a*). The Qal is used with the subject *tôrâh* || *mišpâṭ* in li. 4 (?), cf. xlv. 23, xlviii. 3, lv. 11. Such use of the Qal is both early and late (cf. *BDB*, 423*b*).

ver. 2. *yašmîa'*, 'he shall make heard': Hiph'il altogether 62 times in O.T., 13 of them in DI outside this passage (xli. 22, 26, xlii. 9, xliii. 9, 12, xliv. 8, xlv. 21, xlviii. 3, 5, 6, 20, lii. 7 (*bis*)), and two in TI (lviii. 4, lxii. 11).

ver. 3. *qânēh*, 'reed': cf. xliii. 24, xlvi. 6.

yišbōr, 'he shall break': Qal only here, but Pi'el in xlv. 2.

ûpištâh kēhâh lô' yekabbennâh, 'and the dimly-burning wick he shall not quench': cf. xliii. 17. Outside these two passages *pištâh* is only found in Exod. ix. 31, of flax in growth. The figure of extinguishing a wick in the two DI passages is therefore the more striking. The somewhat rare *kēhâh* and *yikhēh* (ver. 4) do not appear elsewhere in DI, but note TI lxi. 3.

ver. 4. *mišpāṭ* || *tôrâh*: cf. li. 4 (?).

'iyyîm, 'coastlands': cf. *xlix. 1.* Thirty-eight times in O.T., 7 of them in DI (xl. 15, xli. 1, 5, xlii. 10, 12, 15, li. 5 (?)), outside the Songs, and 3 in TI (lix. 18, lx. 9, lxvi. 19). For a striking parallel to *'iyyîm yeyaḥēlû* see li. 5 (?).

Summary. The only words found in this passage and not elsewhere in DI are *rāṣûṣ, yērôṣ* (vv. 3, 4), and *kēhâh, yikhēh* (vv. 3, 4). To these we may perhaps add the peculiar sense of *mišpāṭ*. Almost every other expression has close and even frequent parallels elsewhere in the prophecy, especially in chaps. xl–xlviii. It is impossible on the ground of vocabulary to deny authorship by Deutero-Isaiah.

xlix. 1–6

ver. 1. *šimeʿû 'iyyîm 'ēlay*, 'Hearken, ye far coasts, unto me': cf. *haḥarîšû 'ēlay 'iyyîm*, xli. 1. The phrase *šimeʿû 'ēlay* is found in xlvi. 3, 12, li. 1, 7, lv. 2; elsewhere in the O.T. only Judges ix. 7. For *'iyyîm* see on xlii. 4.

wehaqšîbû, 'and give attention': cf. xlii. 23, xlviii. 18, li. 4 (?).

le'ummîm, 'peoples': cf. xli. 1 (|| *'iyyîm* as here, this parallelism nowhere else in O.T.), xliii. 4, 9, li. 4 (?), lv. 4; elsewhere in the plural only 24 times, 14 of them in Pss.

mērāḥôq, 'from afar': cf. xliii. 6, xlix. 12 (? reading). TI 4 times.

ver. 2. *wayyāśem pî ke*, 'and he made my mouth like': for *śîm* with acc. and *ke* (about 24 times in O.T.) cf. *l.* 7, li. 3, 23.

ḥereb ḥaddâh, 'sharp sword': *hap. leg.* in DI, but only 4 times in all.

beṣēl yādô, 'in the shadow of his hand': cf. li. 16 (?); phrase not found elsewhere.

wayeśîmēnî le, 'and he made me into': for *śîm* with acc. and *le*, cf. xli. 15, 18, xlii. 15, 16, xlix. 11, liv. 12. This idiom in the sense of to make or transform something into is found about 45 times in O.T.

ḥēṣ bārûr, 'polished arrow': both words *hap. leg.* in DI, though see lii. 11 for Niph. *hibbārû*.

'ašpāṯô, 'his quiver': *hap. leg.* in DI, and only 6 times in all.

ver. 3. *wayyômer lî 'abdî 'āttâh*, 'and he said to me, Thou art my servant': cf. the striking parallel in xli. 9, of Israel, and see also xliv. 21*ab*.

'ɛṯpā'ār, 'I will get myself glory': cf. xliv. 23, lv. 5 (Pi'el), xlvi. 13 (*tip̄'artî*), of Israel. Forms from the root *p'r* are more frequent in DI and TI than anywhere else in O.T.

ver. 4. *lᵉrîq yāḡa'tî*, 'in vain have I toiled': phrase, and word *rîq*, not elsewhere in DI; but TI (lxv. 23) has something very similar. Of the 26 occurrences of the verb *yg'* in the O.T., 9 are in DI (xl. 28, 30 f., xliii. 22 ff., xlvii. 12, 15, and here) and 2 in TI.

tôhû, 'nought': 20 times only in O.T., 7 of them in DI (xl. 17, 23, xli. 29, xliv. 9, xlv. 18 f.) apart from this passage.

hɛḇɛl, 'vanity': *hap.leg.* in DI.

kōaḥ, 'strength': cf. xl. 9, 26, 29, 31, xli. 1 (? reading), xliv. 12(*bis*) (?), l. 2.

killêṯî, 'I have spent': √ not otherwise in DI.

'āḵēn, 'surely': cf. xl. 7 (? reading), xlv. 15, *liii. 4*; only 18 times in all.

mišpāṭî, 'my just right': cf. xl. 27 for this sense of the word.

ûp̄ᵉ'ullāṯî, 'and my recompense': cf. xl. 10, and TI lxi. 8, lxii. 11, lxv. 7. The word occurs only 14 times in O.T., 10 of them in the same sense as here.

ver. 5. *wᵉ'attâh*, 'and now': cf. xliii. 1, xliv. 1, xlvii. 8, xlviii. 16*c* (?), lii. 5 (?). The phrase *wᵉ'attâh kô* (so read) *'āmar Yahwɛh*, only xliii. 1, Jer. xliv. 7, Hag. i. 5, and here, with slight variation in Jer. xxxii. 36.

yôṣᵉrî mibbɛṭɛn, 'who formed me from the womb': cf. xliv. 2, 24, of Israel, and preceded, as here, by *kô 'āmar Yahwɛh*; similarly xlvi. 3, xlviii. 8. *mibbɛṭɛn* only 18 times in O.T.

lᵉšôḇēḇ, 'to restore': cf. xlvii. 10, but in sense of 'seduce'. The Po'lel of *šûḇ* only a dozen times in O.T.

Ya'ᵃqōḇ || *Yiśrā'ēl*: frequent in DI.

wā'ɛkkāḇēḏ bᵉ'ênê Yahwɛh, 'and so I was honoured in the eyes of Yahweh': cf. xliii. 4, of Israel.

ver. 6. *nāqēl*: √ not elsewhere in DI.

lᵉ'ôr gôyîm, 'for a light to the nations': cf. xlii. 6, and *lᵉ'ôr 'ammîm*, li. 4 (?).

yᵉšû'āṯî, 'my salvation': cf. xlix. 8, li. 6, 8, lii. 7, 10. The word is infrequent except in Pss. (45 times).

'aḏ-qᵉṣê hā'ārɛṣ, 'to the end of the earth': cf. xl. 28, xli. 5, 9, xlii. 10, xliii. 6, xlviii. 20. The same, or similar, phrase, is found about 24 times elsewhere, and is practically confined to Deut., Jer., and Pss.

Once more, the parallels with Deutero-Isaiah are so close that it is impossible, on grounds of vocabulary alone, to deny identity of authorship. Again, too, the parallels are mostly with chaps. xl–xlviii, though correspondences with the distinctively Servant-Israel passages are not so striking as in xlii. 1–4.

l. 4–9

ver. 4. *'ᵃḏônāy Yahweh*, 'the Lord Yahweh': 4 times in this passage; cf. xl. 10, xlviii. 16*c* (?), xlix. 22, li. 22, lii. 4 (?). The phrase is not very common, except in Ezek.

limmûḏîm, 'disciples': cf. liv. 13. Only 3 times outside DI.

lā'ûṯ: hap.leg., but reading doubtful.

yā'ēp̱, 'weary': cf. xl. 29. Only twice outside DI. The corresponding verb only 9 times, 4 of them in DI.

yā'îr, 'he wakens': cf. xlii. 13; also xli. 2, 25, xlv. 13, of Cyrus. The Hiph'il is found 32 times, a large proportion of them in definitely exilic contexts. In DI the Qal is found in li. 9 (*ter*), and in lii. 1 (*bis*), and the Hithpo'lel in li. 17 (*bis*), quite a fair proportion of the total number of uses.

ver. 5. *pāṯaḥ lî 'ōzen*, 'he has opened my ear': cf. xlviii. 8.

mārîṯî, 'rebelled': *hap.leg.* in DI.

'āḥôr lô' nᵉsûḡôṯî, 'I did not turn backward': cf. xlii. 17. Only 15 examples of the verb are found.

ver. 6. *gēwî*, 'my back': cf. li. 23. *gēw*, as distinct from *gaw*, is always, except in Isa. xxxviii. 17, found in contexts describing beating or other humiliation, and only 6 times in all.

ûlᵉḥāyay lammôrᵉṭîm, 'and my cheeks to them that pluck out': both words *hap.leg.* in DI.

pānay lô' histartî, 'my face I hid not': cf. liv. 8, and similarly *liii. 3*.

mikkᵉlimmôṯ, 'from insults': cf. xlv. 16. Word 30 times in all, 13 of them in Ezek. Verb *klm* xli. 11, xlv. 16 f., liv. 4.

rōq, 'spitting': *hap.leg.* in DI, but only 3 times in all.

ver. 7. *ya'ᵃzor-lî*, 'he will help me': cf. xli. 10, 13 f., xliv. 2, of Israel.

lô' niḵlāmtî || *lô' 'ēḇôš*, 'I am not dishonoured || I shall not be ashamed': cf. xlv. 17, liv. 4, of Israel, also xli. 11, xlv. 16, where the humiliation of others than Israel is stressed by way of contrast. In all these passages *klm* is parallel with *bôš*, as here. The Niph'al of *klm* is found 26 times in all, and in conjunction with *bôš*, outside DI, only 9 times. *bôš* by itself is also used in xlii. 17, xliv. 9, 11 (?), xlv. 24, xlix. 23. Only in Jer. and Pss. is it used more often than in DI.

śamtî pānay kaḥallāmîš, 'I have set my face like flint': for *śîm* with acc. and *kᵉ*, see on xlix. 2. *ḥallāmîš*, only 5 times in all, is *hap.leg.* in DI.

ver. 8. *qārôḇ maṣdîqî*, 'near is he that justifies me': cf. *qārôḇ ṣiḏqî*, li. 5 (?).

mî yārîḇ 'ittî, 'who will contend with me?': for *rîḇ 'ēṯ*, cf. xlv. 9, xlix. 25.

yāḥaḏ, 'together': typically DI. Of the 45 uses of *yaḥaḏ* DI has xlii. 14, xliii. 26, xliv. 11 (?), xlv. 8, and of the 92 of *yaḥdaw* xl. 5, xli. 1, 19, 20, 23, xliii. 9, 17, xlv. 20 f., xlvi. 2, xlviii. 13, lii. 8 f.

yiggaš 'ēlay, 'let him approach unto me': in sense of entering on a legal process cf. xli. 1, 22 (reading Qal with Verss.), Hiph'il xli. 21, xlv. 21, Hithpa'el xlv. 20. Of the 125 uses of the verb only 8 at the most, outside DI, have this forensic reference.

ver. 9. *yaršî'ēnî*, 'he will condemn me': cf. liv. 17.

kabbɛgɛd yiḇlû, 'as a garment they shall wear out': cf. li. 6, 8.

'āš yôḵelēm, 'moth shall consume them': cf. li. 8. *'āš* only half a dozen times in O.T.

The proportion of peculiar words in this passage is higher than in those previously examined. At the same time there are sufficient correspondences with DI to make it hazardous, on grounds of vocabulary alone, to deny his authorship. They extend over chaps. xlix–lv as well as xl–xlviii.

lii. 13–liii. 12

lii. 13. *hinnēh*, 'behold': cf. xl. 9, 10, xli. 15, xlii. 9, &c.

yaśkîl, 'shall prosper': not otherwise in DI in sense of either RV or RV mg.

(*yārûm*) *weniśśā' wegāḇah*, 'he shall be (high and) lifted up and exalted': cf. *rām weniśśā'*, lvii. 15 (though *yārûm* lii. 13 should most likely be deleted), *gāḇôah weniśśā'*, lvii. 7. For *gḇh* alone cf. lv. 9.

ka'ašɛr . . . kēn (ver. 15), 'as . . . so': cf. liv. 9 (where certainly read *ka'ašɛr*), lv. 10, 11, though there is nothing singular about the construction.

lii. 14. *šāmemû*, 'were appalled': only here in DI in this sense.

rabbîm, 'many': cf. liv. 1.

mošḥāṯ (so point?), 'disfigured': Hoph'al ptc., only twice in O.T. The form *mišḥaṯ* is *hap.leg.*

mar'ēhû wetō'arô, 'his appearance and his form': cf. *liii. 2.* Not elsewhere in DI (*tō'ar* only 15 times in O.T.).

lii. 15. *gôyîm . . . melāḵîm*, 'nations . . . kings': cf. xli. 2, xlv. 1, for the same parallelism. But the reading *gôyîm* is doubtful (see *supra*, p. 123). Similarly TI lx. 3, 11, 16, lxii. 2. Only three other examples of this parallelism are found in the O.T., viz. Pss. lxxii. 11, cii. 16, cxxxv. 10.

yiqpeṣû, 'shall shut': *hap.leg.* in DI; √ only 7 times in all.

suppar, 'was related': Pi'el in xliii. 21, 26; not of any significance.
rā'û, 'have seen': for this verb in sense of 'see (and wonder)' cf. xl. 5, xli. 5, xlix. 18, lii. 8, 10.
hiṯbônānû, 'have discerned': cf. xliii. 18. Hithpo'lel 22 times in all.

liii. 1. *hɛ'ᵉmîn*, 'believed': cf. xliii. 10, but of no significance.
šᵉmû'āṯēnû, 'what we have heard': *hap.leg.* in DI and TI.
zᵉrôa' Yahwɛh, 'the arm of Yahweh': the only other occurrence in O.T. of the expression in exactly this form is in li. 9. The 'arm' of Yahweh is spoken of 41 times in all, most commonly in Deut. and Pss. Apart from li. 9, liii. 1, DI has 6 examples (xl. 10, 11, xlviii. 14 (? read *zɛra'* LXX), li. 5 (*bis*, but ? *aβ*), lii. 10)), and TI 4 (lix. 16, lxii. 8, lxiii. 5, 12).
niglāṯâh, 'been revealed': cf. xl. 5. The other examples of the Niph'al in DI are of no significance.

liii. 2. *wayya'al*, 'for he grew up': cf. lv. 13 (*bis*). Verb only 16 times in O.T. of the growth of vegetation.
yônēq, 'sapling': *hap.leg.*
šōrɛš, 'root': *hap.leg.* in DI.
'ɛrɛṣ ṣiyyâh, 'arid ground': cf. xli. 18. Phrase only 7 times elsewhere (Ps. cvii. 35 a quotation from xli. 18), and no other writer uses it twice.
hāḏār, 'stateliness': ? cf. xl. 6, *hᵃḏārô* for *haṣdô* (LXX, 1 Pet. i. 24 δόξα, which is the LXX reading here).
wᵉnɛḥmᵉḏēhû (or *wᵉḥɛmdâh*?), 'that we should desire him': in either case *hap.leg.* in DI.

liii. 3. *nibzɛh*, 'despised': cf. xlix. 7 (?), where perhaps read Niph'al Ptc. The Niph. of *bzh* (always ptc.) only 9 times in all.
ḥᵃḏal, 'forsaken': *hap.leg.* in DI; only 3 times in all.
'îšîm, 'men': this form only 3 times, and *hap.leg.* in DI.
'îš maḵ'ōḇôṯ, 'a man of pains': Fischer (*Pɛrikopen*, p. 143) refers to xl. 13, xli. 11 f., xlii. 13, xlvi. 11 for similar construction. But there seems nothing peculiar in this. *maḵ'ōḇôṯ* not in DI outside chap. liii; only 16 times in all.
wîḏûa', 'and familiar with': Qal ptc. only here and Dan. i. 13, 15.
ḥōlî, 'sickness': not in DI outside this chapter. Only 23 times.
mastēr, 'hiding': only here in DI, but note *l. 6*.
ḥᵃšaḇnûhû, 'we regarded him': Qal not in DI outside this chapter. Niph'al in xl. 15, 17.

liii. 4. *'āḵēn*, 'surely': cf. xlix. 4, q.v.
nāśā' || *sᵉḇālām*, 'carried || bore': for the same parallelism see xlvi. 4, 7. Outside DI *sbl* is only used 4 times (twice in Qal), and never parallel with *nś'*.
nāgûa', 'stricken': form elsewhere only Ps. lxxiii. 14. √ elsewhere in DI only in lii. 11, in different sense from here.

mukkêh, 'smitten': Hoph'al not elsewhere in DI. Hiph'il only xlix. 10.

*m*e'*unnēh*, 'afflicted': not in DI outside this chapter.

liii. 5. *w*e*hû'*, 'but he': cf. ver. 12, so also xlii. 22 to emphasize a contrast.

*m*e*ḥôlāl*, 'pierced through': this is the only example of the Po'al of the verb. The Po'el is found in li. 9, otherwise only Job xxvi. 13. Of other forms of the verb there are only 4, and of these Ps. lxxvii. 11 is doubtful. (If we read *m*e*ḥullāl* the only other example is Ezek. xxxvi. 23.)

*p*e*šā'ēnû* || *'*a*wônôṯēnû*, 'our rebellions || our iniquities': cf. l. 1 for the same parallelism, which occurs about 20 times in O.T.

*m*e*ḏukkā'*, 'crushed': rare (not more than 18 times in all) and not in DI outside this chapter.

mûsar, 'chastisement': *hap.leg.* in DI; rare except in Proverbs.

*ḥ*a*ḇûrāṯô*, 'his stripes': *hap.leg.* in DI. Only 6 times in all.

nirpā', 'it is healed': √ *hap.leg.* in DI.

liii. 6. *ṣō'n*, 'sheep': *hap.leg.* in DI.

tā'înû, 'we went astray': cf. xlvii. 15.

pānînû, 'we turned': cf. xlv. 22 and xl. 3 (Pi'el).

hip̄gîa', 'caused to alight': cf. xlvii. 3 (?) Qal.

liii. 7. *niggaś*, 'he was harshly treated': *hap.leg.* in DI. Niph'al only 4 times, and Qal, apart from substantive ptc., only 4 times.

*na'*a*nēh*, 'humbled himself': see *m*e'*unnēh*, ver. 4.

tεḇaḥ, 'slaughter': *hap.leg.* in DI. Only 12 times in all.

yûḇāl, 'he was borne along': cf. lv. 12. Hoph'al of root only 11 times.

rāḥēl, 'ewe': *hap.leg.* in DI; only 4 times.

*gôz*e*zêhâ*, 'her shearers': *hap.leg.* in DI. Verb *gzz* only 15 times.

*nε'*ε*lām(âh)*, 'dumb': *hap.leg.* in DI. Verb *'lm* only 9 times.

liii. 8. *'ōṣεr*, 'arrest': *hap.leg.* in DI. Only 3 times in all.

luqqāḥ, 'he was taken': cf. xlix. 24, 25, lii. 5 (?). Qal pass. of *lqḥ* only 15 times.

dôrô, 'his fate (?)': cf. xli. 4, li. 8, 9. But question whether of any significance.

*y*e*śôḥēaḥ*, 'reflected': *hap.leg.* in DI. Po'lel only twice, Qal 18 times.

nigzar, 'he was cut off': *hap.leg.* in DI. Verb only 13 times in all.

liii. 9. *qiḇrô*, 'his grave': *hap.leg.* in DI. Similarly *ḥāmās*, 'violence', and *mirmâh*, 'deceit'.

liii. 10. *Yahwεh ḥāp̄ēṣ*, 'Yahweh was pleased': the only other example of the phrase in exactly this form, with Yahweh first for emphasis, is in xlii. 21. The verb is also found with Yahweh as subject in lv. 11. For *ḥēpεṣ Yahwεh*, 'the purpose of Yahweh', cf.

xliv. 28, xlvi. 10, xlviii. 14. This sense of 'will', 'purpose', 'business' for *ḥēp̄ɛṣ* is peculiar to DI and TI (lviii. 3, 13) except in Prov. xxxi. 13. The even later sense of 'matter', 'affair', is peculiar to Eccl.

'āšām, 'guilt-offering': *hap.leg.* in DI.

ya'ᵃrîḵ, 'prolongs': cf. xlviii. 9, liv. 2. The verb is used 34 times, mostly in the Deuteronomic phrase 'prolong days'.

yiṣlāḥ, 'shall prosper': cf. liv. 17. Qal only 15 times in all. For the Hiph'il (about 40 times) see xlviii. 15, lv. 11.

liii. 11. *'ᵃmal*, 'travail': *hap.leg.* in DI. Fifty-four times (Job. 8, Eccles. 21, Ps. 13).

yiśbā', 'he shall be satisfied': only xliv. 16 (?).

yaṣdîq, 'he shall justify': cf. *l. 8.* The Hiph'il of the root only 12 times. For the Qal (22 times, 14 in Job) see xliii. 9, 26, xlv. 25.

liii. 11 f. The language of these verses is almost entirely peculiar to the Song, except *pôšᵉ'îm*, 'rebellious', for which see xlvi. 8.

There are, omitting seriously doubtful readings, some forty-six words or expressions in the Song which are not otherwise found in Deutero-Isaiah. Some are common words like *ṣō'n*, *šālāl*, and *māwɛṯ*. Their use in the Song and not otherwise in Deutero-Isaiah signifies nothing, since all writers must have been equally familiar with them, and ready to use them if the subject-matter required it. Others are very little used at all, and concerning them it seems fair to assert that if they are used by Deutero-Isaiah outside the Song it is significant, but that it is not necessarily significant if they are not so used. Every writer employs some rare words, and what is rare we cannot expect to find uniformly distributed, or to be other than *hap.leg.* in any one writer. Also, a word may be rare in the literature without having been rare in common speech. For example, the word 'shearer' (liii. 7) must have been common enough, both in early and in late times. Yet the word 'to shear' is used only fifteen times (Qal ptc. seven times); four times in the story of Nabal (1 Sam. xxv), twice of Judah (Gen. xxxviii. 12 f.), twice of Absalom (2 Sam. xiii. 23 f.), and once each of Laban (Gen. xxxi. 19) and Job (i. 20). Deduct another for Deut. xv. 19, and that leaves but four for the prophets. The inference is that uncommon words are not of themselves decisive evidence on questions of authorship. Given two passages sufficiently alike in vocabulary, we may perhaps affirm identity of authorship. But as between two passages of widely different vocabulary, we are not free to assert the contrary. It depends upon the subject-matter, and the subject-matter of Isa. liii is unique. Moreover, there are in Isa. xl between fifty and sixty words not found elsewhere in Deutero-Isaiah, and, as if the Prophet would show his virtuosity, he employs eight of them in a single verse (12). In chap. xlvii, which contains only fifteen verses, there are close on forty. In chap. liv there are thirty-two. Agreement of vocabulary, or, better still, similarity of phraseology, is a better criterion than difference of vocabulary. Nor is it a question of quantity only. The phrases 'the arm of Yahweh', 'arid ground', 'Yahweh was pleased', and 'the purpose of Yahweh', and the parallels 'carried || bore' and 'nations || kings' (though the text here is doubtful), though not decisive, are strong evidence of Deutero-Isaianic authorship. It is not permissible, on grounds of vocabulary, to assert that the passage *is* by Deutero-Isaiah; but neither is it permissible to deny it.

The Problem of the Last Song

It is clear from the preceding that Deutero-Isaianic authorship cannot, on linguistic grounds, be asserted with the same confidence as for the other Songs. The suspicion that it comes from a different source has been voiced, with varying degrees of emphasis, by Martini,[1] Schenkel,[2] Ewald,[3] Cheyne,[4] Bredenkamp,[5] Dillmann,[6] Duhm,[7] Schian,[8] Kosters,[9] Bertholet,[10] and Staerk.[11] At first the suggestion arose more from a feeling that the general tone and subject-matter of the piece were different, than from any minute examination of its contents, though Ewald did say in a footnote that the language has much that is otherwise quite unusual in Deutero-Isaiah. More recently Sellin,[12] Elliger,[13] and Volz[14] have argued the matter in more detail. Sellin and Elliger, indeed, have undertaken to prove conclusively that lii. 13–liii. 12 was written by 'Trito-Isaiah'. This contention we must now proceed to examine, and it will

[1] *Commentatio . . . in loc. Es. LII, 13–LIII, 12*, p. 6.
[2] Cf. *supra*, p. 38.
[3] *Die Propheten des Alten Bundes*[1], ii, p. 407 f.
[4] *Prophecies of Isaiah*, 1st ed., ii, p. 39; *Introduction to the Book of Isaiah*, p. 304 f.
[5] Cf. *supra*, p. 43.
[6] *Jesaia*, p. 453.
[7] Cf. *supra*, p. 47.
[8] Cf. *supra*, p. 48.
[9] Cf. *supra*, p. 63.
[10] Cf. *supra*, p. 49.
[11] Cf. *supra*, p. 52.
[12] Cf. *supra*, p. 79 f.
[13] Cf. *supra*, p. 81.
[14] Cf. *supra*, p. 78.

be sufficient to do so in the form in which Elliger has put it, since he has treated the subject at considerable length.[1]

Elliger sets forth fifty-seven words or phrases in the Song, and claims that of twenty-five of them Trito-Isaiah has more than one example, 'while the whole or almost the whole of the rest of the Old Testament, or at any rate Deutero-Isaiah, has no example, so that we must speak of *specifically* Trito-Isaianic choice and arrangement of words'.[2] Such a statement is not to be refuted by a generalization. The examples adduced by Elliger must be examined seriatim. But before we do this it is only reasonable to point out that thirteen of the twenty-five have parallels in Deutero-Isaiah, albeit in passages which Elliger[3] regards as from Trito-Isaiah, and that, instead of letting them at least be neutral, he lists them *against* Deutero-Isaiah. In what follows these passages will be put into italics, following Elliger's example.[4]

(1) *yārûm wᵉniśśā' wᵉgāḇah* (lii. 13): cf. *rām wᵉniśśā'* (lvii. 15), *gāḇôah wᵉniśśā'* (lvii. 5). Here it must be said that lvii. 15 is so obviously reminiscent of vi. 1 that it can hardly be called specifically Trito-Isaianic. That *yārûm* should stand in the text of lii. 13 is by no means certain.[5] One parallel, therefore, is all that can be confidently quoted for TI, and that a phrase in the reverse order. Why should not TI have borrowed it from the Song?

(3) *ka'ᵃšɛr . . . kēn* (lii. 14): cf. *liv. 9, lv. 10f.*, lxv. 8.

(5) *šāmᵉmû* (lii. 14): cf. lix. 16, lxiii. 5 (both Hithpo'el). Is there any significance in this?

(7) *rā'û . . . šāmᵉ'û* (lii. 15): cf. lxiv. 3, lxvi. 8. There is no real correspondence here. In lxvi. 8 the words are in parallelism, but in the reverse order; so also in lxiv. 3, and with another verb in between; in lii. 15 they are not strictly parallel at all. What remains is the general association of seeing and hearing, about which there is nothing remarkable.

(14) *kᵉmastēr pānîm* (liii. 3): cf. *liv. 8*, lvii. 11, 17, lix. 2, lxiv. 6. Elliger's contention here is that *pānîm* ('face') without the suffix refers to God. The use of the bare word in such a hypostatic sense is doubtful so early as the sixth century, especially

[1] *DJ in seinem Verhältnis zu TI*, pp. 6–27.
[2] Ibid., p. 14.
[3] Cf. *supra*, p. 81.
[4] The numbers in brackets are those of Elliger's own examples, and together they make up his total of twenty-five.
[5] Cf., *supra* p. 122.

since lix. 2, the only passage to which Elliger can appeal, is textually uncertain. (LXX[ℵ], [A], [Q], Syr., Targ., appear to have read a suffix, and the final *mem* may well be a dittograph.) Why, too, should TI not have used *pānîm* absolutely in *liv. 8*, lxiv. 6? In lvii. 17 the verb is used without *pānîm* at all, and lvii. 11 does not seem relevant, even when *mēʿôlām* ('for ever') has been emended to *maʿlîm* ('concealing'). Moreover, the nearer parallel in liii. 3*a* supports the interpretation that the Servant was an abhorrence to men. 'Stricken, smitten of God', follows in the next verse.

(17) *hû'*, emphasized subject (liii. 4): cf. *xlvii. 10*, lix. 16, lxiii. 5, 9. In the Song we have a simple case of emphatic pronominal subject, which, in view of the solemn contrast and the order of the words—object, subject, verb—is not singular. In *xlvii. 10*, lix. 16, and lxiii. 5 the pronoun picks up and emphasizes a *preceding* subject with suffix, a suffix which is in the same person as the object of the verb following—'my fury, it upheld me'. Without it the sentence would be intolerably bald or metrically deficient. The cases are not really parallel.

(18) *mukkêh*, Hiphʿil [*sic!*] with God as subject (liii. 4): cf. lvii. 17, lx. 10 (both Hiphʿil).

(19) *meʿunnêh* (liii. 4): cf. lviii. 3, 5, 10, lx. 14, lxiv. 11. The first two of these examples are Piʿel, in the technical phrase 'afflict the soul' = 'fast' (cf. Lev. xvi. 29). Similarly in lviii. 10 (Niphʿal), which in this context must mean 'the soul afflicted by fasting', not, as Elliger says, 'afflicted by God'. Piʿel also in lx. 14, in the phrase 'the sons of them that afflicted thee'. In lxiv. 11 God, indeed, is subject, but again the form is Piʿel. None of the passages quoted by Elliger presents a real parallel to the word in the Song, and if he is going to quote against DI forms of the root in other themes than the Puʿal, it should be noted that the root is fairly common (some eighty times in all), and evenly distributed. Elliger's further remark that TI twice uses the substantive forms *ʿānāw*, *ʿānî* does not seem very relevant. Why should he not?

(20) *wehû'* (liii. 5): cf. *xlii. 22*, lvi. 11, lxiii. 10, lxvi. 5. Here it may be remarked that xlii. 22 is perhaps not by DI, though whether it is by 'Trito-Isaiah' is another matter. In lvi. 11 *wehēmmâh rôʿîm* is probably corrupt. Also Elliger quotes against DI two further passages from the Song (vv. 7, 12), which is to assume the conclusion he is engaged to prove.

(21) *pɛšaʿ* || *ʿāwôn* (liii. 5): cf. *l. 1*, lix. 12.

(25) *ṣō'n* (liii. 6): cf. lx. 7, lxi. 5, lxiii. 11, lxv. 10. Elliger remarks that DI never uses *ṣō'n*, whereas he uses *ʿēḏɛr* ('flock'), *ṭelā'îm*

('lambs'), and *'ālôṯ* ('milch-ewes') all in one verse (xl. 11). That he does so only shows what resources of vocabulary he has (see *supra*, p. 169), not any reluctance to use the word *ṣō'n*. What poet would say *ṣō'nô* when such a superbly alliterative phrase as *kᵉrô'ĕh 'ɛḏrô yir'ĕh bizᵉrô'ô yᵉqabbēṣ* came to his lips? On the other hand, in liii. 6 the commoner, and monosyllabic, *ṣō'n* is natural, while either 'lambs' or 'milch-ewes' would be pedantic and absurd.

(26) *tā'înû* (liii. 6): cf. *xlvii. 15*, lxiii. 17 (Hiph.).

(27–8) *'îš lᵉḏarkô pānînû* (liii. 6): cf. *lv.* 7, lvi. 11, lvii. 17, 18, lxv. 2, lxvi. 3. Here Elliger says that DI, apart from the doubtful *lv.* 7, never uses *dɛrɛḵ* of man's (evil) way, and that the phraseology of lvi. 11, lvii. 17 closely resembles that of the Song.

(29) *niggaś*, Niph'al (liii. 7): cf. lviii. 3 (Qal), lx. 17 (Qal ptc.). There is no parallel here beyond the use of words from the same root.

(33) *luqqāḥ* (liii. 8): cf. *xlix. 24f.*, lvii. 13. Is there any real similarity between either of these passages and the Song, and is either of them to be assigned to 'Trito-Isaiah'?

(35) *pɛša'* (liii. 8): cf. lvii. 4, lviii. 1, lix. 20. Elliger insists here that, however liii. 8 should be emended, the singular should be kept; that the singular form is a peculiarity of TI, and that DI only uses the word in the plural. The text of liii. 8 is not sufficiently certain to form the basis of any confident deduction, and in ver. 5 the plural 'our transgressions' seems assured; that, we take it, is contrary to TI's usage, and in accordance with DI's.

(36) *rᵉšā'îm* (liii. 9): cf. *lv.* 7, lxiii. 18 (where read, as most agree, *rᵉšā'îm*). Elliger further points to the use of the noun *rɛša'* ('wickedness') in lviii. 4, 6.

(37) *'ôśê ra'* (liii. 9): cf. lvi. 2, lxv. 12, lxvi. 4. The emendation in liii. 9 is commonly accepted, and likely enough; but the three parallels adduced by Elliger are of the most general kind, simply cases of the noun 'evil' as the object of the verb 'do'.

(41) *taḥaṯ 'ᵃšɛr* (Elliger's emendation of *hɛḥɛlî 'im-t"*, liii. 10): cf. *lv. 13*, lx. 15, 17, lxi. 3, 7. Although Elliger's emendation in ver. 10 is most improbable, the words do, of course, occur in ver. 12. His argument is that TI is fond of the word *taḥaṯ* to express future compensation in contrast to present circumstances. Be that as it may, the comparison is only approximate; in the five (?) TI passages adduced by Elliger, the expression is simply this *instead of* that; in liii. 12 the Servant is to be rewarded '*because* he poured out his soul . . . '.

(42) *ya'arîk* (liii. 10): cf. *xlviii. 9*, *liv. 2*, lvii. 4. The only valid comparison here is between lengthening days and sticking out the tongue. There is not a little doubt, too, whether lvii. 4 is from 'Trito-Isaiah'.

(45) *yiśbā'* (liii. 11): cf. lviii. 10 f. (Hiph.), lxvi. 11. Elliger further points to the noun *śob'âh* in *lv. 2*, lvi. 11.

(46) *hiṣdîq* (for *yaṣdîq*) *ṣaddîq* (liii. 11): here Elliger's contention is that the root *ṣdq* is used with a specifically Trito-Isaianic meaning, as a technical term for human righteousness = piety (cf. lvi. 1, lvii. 1, 12, lviii. 2, lx. 21, lxiv. 4 f.) as contrasted with the usual sense of *Sieg* and *Heil* in DI. But when *ṣaddîq* has been deleted, with most scholars, we are left with the verb in the Hiph'il, used, despite Elliger's protestations, in the forensic sense of l. 8. (The Hiph'il is used only a dozen times in O.T., and not at all by TI.)

(47) *yeḥallēq* (liii. 12): cf. the noun *ḥēleq*, 'portion', in lvii. 6, lxi. 7. Of what significance can this be?

(50) *yapgîa'* (liii. 12): cf. *xlvii. 3*, lix. 16, lxiv. 4 (Qal). The only close parallel is between the Song and lix. 16. In the former the Servant 'interposes'; in the latter Yahweh is 'amazed that there is none to interpose'. Why should not Trito-Isaiah have borrowed the idea from the Song?

None of the foregoing examples, unless it be nos. 27–8, nor all of them together, go to prove Elliger's case. The comparisons adduced are mostly with the commoner words and phrases used in the Song, not, as Elliger claims, with expressions of which 'the whole or almost the whole of the rest of the Old Testament . . . has no example'. If they were with the more distinctive expressions in the Song the case might be different. There are in the Song about fifteen words or forms which occur less than ten times in the Old Testament. None of them except *mastēr*—which is *hap.leg.*—come into Elliger's list. On the other hand, the few expressions and parallelisms noted above[1] as strong evidence of Deutero-Isaianic authorship are still evidence for Deutero- rather than for Trito-Isaiah; and, few as they are, they outnumber Elliger's effective parallels between the Song and Trito-Isaiah. This is certainly so for *'ereṣ ṣiyyâh* and *nāśā'* || *sebālām*, neither of which occurs in Trito-Isaiah. With regard to *zerôa' Yahweh*, the proportion is five to four in favour of Deutero-Isaiah. For *ḥāpēṣ* and *ḥēpeṣ* in reference to Yahweh,

[1] See *supra*, p. 169.

the balance is even (xlii. 21(?), xliv. 28, xlvi. 10, xlviii. 14, lv. 11 || lxii. 4 *bis*, lxv. 12, lxvi. 4). With regard to the parallelism *gôyîm . . . mᵉlāḵîm* (lii. 15), it may be that *gôyîm* is not original in the text, in which case it does not call for consideration. But let us suppose, with Elliger, that it was in the original text; the proportions are then four to two in favour of Trito-Isaiah. Yet that would be no indication that the passage in the Song was his. A disciple not infrequently borrows an expression from his master, and uses it more than his master did. It is not simply a matter of statistics. Outside Isa. xl–lxvi the parallelism is only found in three Psalms. Of them Ps. lxxii is probably pre- and Pss. cii and cxxxv post-exilic. Be that as it may, the parallelism acquires something of a new originality in the circumstances of the exile, and the originator is Deutero-Isaiah.

Elliger allows that a few words in lii. 13–liii. 12 are on the side of Deutero- rather than of Trito-Isaiah. These are *hiṯbônānû* (lii. 15, cf. xliii. 18, in Hiph'il xl. 14, 21, xliii. 10 || lvi. 11, lvii. 1), *mᵉḥôlāl* (cf. li. 9), *yip̱taḥ* (seven times to three), and one or two others. There is no need to lay stress on any of these, unless it be *hiṯbônānû*. But Elliger should have observed *'āḵēn* (liii. 4: cf. xlv. 15, xlix. 4—not in TI).

Another consideration urged by Elliger[1] in favour of the Trito-Isaianic authorship of the last Song is that it betrays the same 'poverty of language' (*Wortarmut*) as is characteristic of Trito-Isaiah. He notes fourteen examples of repetition, of which two, viz. *rabbîm* (lii. 14, 15) and *kullānû* (liii. 6*ab*) are 'best explained as due to artistic purpose'. The other cases are all due to 'deficiency in the power of expression'. They are *'îšîm . . . 'îš* (liii. 3*a*), *nibzêh* (3*ab*), *ḥōlî . . . ḥᵒlāyēnû* (3*a*/4*a*), *maḵ'ôḇôṯ . . . maḵ'ôḇēnû* (3*a*/4*a*—'this might be intentional if the change from the feminine to the masculine were not to be explained as a timid attempt to vary the expression'—can we really imagine any such thing?), *ḥᵃšaḇnûhû* (3*b*/4*b*), *'ᵃwônôṯ . . . 'ᵃwôn* (5*a*/6*b*), *mᵉ'unnêh . . . na'ᵃnêh* (4*b*/7*a*), *nāgûa' . . . nugga'* (4*b*/8*b*), *pîw* (7/9*b*), *Yahweh hāp̱ēṣ . . . hēp̱eṣ Yahweh* (10*a*/*b*), *rabbîm* (11*b*/12*a*/*b*), and *pôšᵉ'îm* (12*a*/*b*). Also 'in ver. 9 the colourless expression "when he died" must be a substitute for a parallel word which was not at the writer's disposal'.

To take this last point first. Most commentators believe the last word of 9*b* to be corrupt, and one reason why there is no

[1] Also Sellin, *NKZ* 41, p. 168 f.

convincing emendation is that Hebrew had no common parallel word to *qeḇer* ('grave'). What would Elliger have? *gāḏîš* seems to be Arabic, and is found only once, in Job (xxi. 32), a book whose Arabic affinities have often been remarked. *šaḥaṯ* ('pit') is a passable synonym for Sheol, but hardly does for an individual grave. The same applies to *bôr*, though some would read that here (cf. Isa. xiv. 19). The poverty of expression is the fault of the Hebrew language, not of the writer.

On the general question, this poverty of language has been alleged at some length by Köhler[1] as one of the peculiarities of *Deutero-Isaiah*, and he gives a number of examples from passages which even Elliger does not assign to Trito-Isaiah. He ascribes it to 'the rhetorical impetus in Deutero-Isaiah's style'. Duhm remarked something of the same kind in his note on xlii. 15 (twice repeated 'dry up'), and set it down to 'hasty composition'. Assuming that *both* Deutero- and Trito-Isaiah show poverty of language—whether the charge is justified or not is immaterial—that is no proof that lii. 13–liii. 12 is from Trito-Isaiah, since it only shares a characteristic common to both writers. If the poverty in lii. 13–liii. 12 is particularly marked, and if, further, such poverty is more marked in Trito- than it is in Deutero-Isaiah, there may be something to be said for Elliger's contention, though again the statistical argument may be so finely drawn as to be quite inconclusive. But, we are entitled to ask, are the verbal repetitions in the Song really due to poverty of language? Elliger himself volunteers the suggestion that two of them are intentional. May that not also be true of the others? Köhler[2] has called attention to what he terms Variation and Echo (*Nachklang*) in the style of Deutero-Isaiah. This may, he thinks, be partly intentional, and partly due to poverty of language. For our present purpose it does not matter which it is. It is sufficient to ask whether the resultant effect is similar to what we find in lii. 13–liii. 12? Of the nineteen passages cited by Köhler as examples, the first (li. 6, 8) may serve as an illustration. It reads:

> But my *deliverance shall be for ever,*
> And my *victory* shall not be abolished.
>
> . . . .
>
> But my *victory shall be for ever,*
> And my *deliverance* from generation to generation.

[1] *DJ stilkritisch untersucht*, p. 96 f.

[2] Ibid., pp. 93 ff.

Here we have the same words, repeated in the reverse order. Wherein does it differ from the style of the Song?

> *Despised* and forsaken of men,
> A man of *pains* and familiar with *sickness*;
> And as one from whom men avert their gaze,
> He was *despised*, and we *regarded* him not.
>
> Yet ours were the *sicknesses* that he carried,
> And ours the *pains* that he bore;
> While we *regarded* him *stricken* (cf. ver. 8),
> Smitten of God and *afflicted* (cf. ver. 7).

This is not *Wortarmut*, but consummate art. A wealth of words in such a context would ruin it all. And wherein do these verses differ from ver. 6, in which, according to Elliger, the repetition is intentional? Of the repeated 'he opened not his mouth' (ver. 7) Köhler says that it is 'the most beautiful and expressive *Nachklang* in the whole writing; and yet there are those who would strike it out!'[1] And he concludes, 'Altogether it must be said that, however the Songs may differ in content, in style they fit in perfectly with the other parts of Isa. xl–lv'.

Elliger also seeks to show that the matter of the last Song is in contrast with the thought-world of Deutero-Isaiah, but in harmony with that of Trito-Isaiah. He does not stress this as much as he does the argument from language and style, only insisting[2] 'that the ideology of the piece largely supports this assumption, if it does not exactly demand it'. Thus, in Deutero-Isaiah Yahweh has redeemed Israel, and wiped out its sins; how comes it, then, that a special atonement is necessary through the Servant? We cannot, he says, get over the difficulty by saying that the expiatory suffering of the Servant is for the heathen, since this interpretation goes to pieces on the simple fact that the speakers in liii. 1 ff. are not the heathen.[3] This is surely a *non sequitur*. Even if we give Elliger the benefit of the doubt on the question who the speakers are, it is not simply a matter of who is speaking in liii. 1 ff. In liii. 12 the Servant has borne the sin of 'many'. These 'many'—they are surely the same—are in lii. 15 parallel with 'kings'. The horizon of the Songs extends beyond Israel to the *heathen*.

The plain fact is that the last Song is unique. There is nothing quite like it in either Deutero- or Trito-Isaiah, nor, for

[1] *DJ stilkritisch untersucht*, p. 95. [2] Op. cit., p. 27. [3] Op. cit., p. 23.

that matter, in the whole of the Old Testament. If it belongs, as Elliger says, to the earliest work of Trito-Isaiah, it is strange that there is not more similarity between it and his later work than the very meagre correspondences that Elliger, with all his interest in establishing identity of authorship, is able to point to. If, on the other hand, it is perhaps the latest utterance of Deutero-Isaiah,[1] we need not be surprised that a disciple—or disciples?—should fail to grasp and reproduce the full import of it.

All things considered, the verdict must be that Elliger's theory that the last Song is the work of 'Trito-Isaiah' is unproven. It is based almost entirely upon literary statistics, and although the argument from statistics may have its uses—I have had to employ it myself in what precedes—it can easily be overdone. I do not insist that lii. 13–liii. 12 *must*, on grounds of language, be assigned to Deutero-Isaiah. All I claim is that there is nothing in the language that is inconsistent with his authorship, and that the passage has definite points of contact with his writing, indeed more in common with his work than with that of any other writer known to us. Elliger, on the other hand, sets out to prove positively that the Song is by 'Trito-Isaiah'. He marshals his proofs with relentless thoroughness, and with a complete lack of any sense of humour; and when we come to examine them closely they simply fall to pieces.[2]

3. STYLE AND METRE OF THE SONGS

According to Duhm[3] the Servant of Yahweh poems are distinctive by reason of 'their style, their quiet language, and the symmetry of their stichoi and strophes. . . . The author of these calm, deep, and not dazzling poems, cannot for temperamental reasons be identical with the swiftly moving, voluble Deutero-Isaiah'. Skinner[4] agreed that 'while neither in language nor in metrical structure are the Servant passages clearly distinguished from the rest of the book, there is yet a certain "temperamental" difference between the subdued concentration and artistic

[1] Cf. *infra*, p. 187 f.

[2] For a summary and criticism of Volz's reasons for separating the last Song from the others see *supra*, p. 78. His suggestion (*Jes. II*, p. 192) that the textual corruption of the passage points to separate provenance need not be taken too seriously, and, if not due to accident, may be otherwise explained (cf. *supra*, p. 147).

[3] *Jes.*, p. 284.

[4] *Isa. XL–LXVI*, p. 29.

completeness of thought in these twelve lines (sc. xlii. 1 ff.), and the more exuberant strains which predominate in the Deutero-Isaianic poetry. So much must be conceded to Duhm. . . .' On the other hand, who is to measure the range of Deutero-Isaiah's 'temperament'?[1] It is doubtless within the bounds of possibility that the difference in 'temperament' is due to a difference of authors; but it is equally possible and, in view of the similarities of vocabulary, more likely, that the Songs derive from a different mood, or a different period, in the life of one author.

As to the metrical forms of the Songs, he would be a bold man who should deny them to Deutero-Isaiah on the score that these are different from his. Neither Itkonen[2] nor Köhler,[3] who have dealt with the subject most fully, makes any such suggestion. The former, it is true, does refer the Songs to different authors,[4] but not on metrical grounds.

4. THEOLOGICAL STANDPOINT OF THE SONGS

Our finding so far is that the language, style, and metrical forms of the Songs are not only consistent with, but actually point to, common authorship with the main body of Deutero-Isaiah. If these were the only considerations, there could be but one conclusion, at least for the first three Songs. But there are other factors to be taken into account, factors which by many are thought to outweigh the evidence of language. No one, for example, supposes that everything in the Old Testament which bears strong marks of 'Deuteronomic' style is therefore by the author of Deuteronomy, nor even that Deuteronomy is all from one hand. Similarly, Schian,[5] who made an analysis of the language of the Songs, freely admitted how like it is to that of Deutero-Isaiah, and yet he was constrained to deny that he was their author. Others have taken the similarities of language for granted, and come to the same conclusion. It remains, therefore, to ask whether the ideas contained in the Songs are consistent with those of Deutero-Isaiah.

The following considerations have been urged against identity of authorship.

(*a*) *Outside the Songs the Servant is equated with Jacob-Israel; the Servant of the Songs is anonymous.* It is possible to take exception

[1] Cf. Skinner, op. cit., p. 259.
[2] *DJ metrisch untersucht.*
[3] *DJ stilkritisch untersucht.*
[4] Cf. *supra*, p. 56 f.
[5] Cf. *supra*, p. 48.

to both these statements: the Servant is called 'Israel' in xlix. 3, and in five passages outside the Songs (xlii. 19, xliii. 10, xliv. 26, xlix. 7, l. 10) he is not named. With regard to 'Israel' in xlix. 3, the reading is not certain, though, in order that this study may be as free from bias as possible, I have retained it.[1] That, however, is not to say that the Servant is equated with Israel in the explicit sense that he is in xli. 8 and elsewhere. If he were, those collectivists who delete the word would not be content to let it go on what is, from the purely manuscript point of view, quite flimsy evidence. The difficulty, even when 'Israel' is retained in xlix. 3, is to see how this Israel can be identical with the Israel of ver. 5 f. It would seem that if we retain it, it must be as an honorific title.[2] Either way, outside the Songs the Servant is regularly, and unambiguously, called Israel (xli. 8 f., xliv. 1, 2, 21, xlv. 4, xlviii. 20); in the Songs he is called Israel at the most only once, and then in a sense which plainly requires some qualification.

What of the five passages outside the Songs in which the Servant is not named? xlii. 19 speaks of 'my servant' and 'the servant of Yahweh'. The text of the verse is perhaps corrupt; LXX and Old Lat. read: 'Who is blind, but my servants (plur., and note the plurals in MT of the preceding verse), and deaf, but their rulers? And the servants (plur.) of God became blind'. Many scholars think that the verse is not genuine, and even Fischer[3] thinks it has been glossed. The verses that follow are full of grammatical solecisms, and the Aramaism 'and they were not willing in his ways to walk' (ver. 24) is suspicious in Deutero-Isaiah, as is also the expression about 'magnifying tôrâh' in ver. 21. One of the most recent expositors, Begrich,[4] leaves the whole passage xlii. 18–25 outside his study, because he can make nothing of it. The next passage, xliii. 10, is again beset with difficulties. Does it mean, 'Ye are my witnesses—'tis the oracle of Yahweh—and (so is) my servant whom I have chosen', taking 'my servant' as a second subject? Or does it mean, 'Ye are my witnesses—'tis the oracle of Yahweh—and (ye are also) my servant whom I have chosen', taking 'my servant' as a second predicate? If the former, the identity of 'my servant' is a matter of pure guesswork. He can hardly, without further indication, be the Servant of the Songs, and

[1] See *supra*, p. 118 f.
[2] See *supra*, p. 144 f.
[3] *Isa. II*, p. 58.
[4] *Studien zu DJ*, p. 5.

Fischer's identification[1] of him with Cyrus is equally unrelated to anything in the context. If the latter, we should expect the plural 'my servants' as a parallel to 'my witnesses', and this solution is favoured by commentators as diverse as Duhm and Feldmann.[2] In xliv. 26 the parallelism requires 'his servants', which is read by LXX^A^, Targ. In xlix. 7, 'a slave of tyrant rulers', even if it is original and refers to Israel, does not affect the present discussion. Finally, in l. 10, 'his servant' does not refer to the Servant Israel of the main prophecy, but to the Servant of the Song immediately preceding, to which the verse is secondary. It would therefore seem that not one of the apparent exceptions to the statement that outside the Songs the Servant is always explicitly equated with Israel can be relied upon, and the conclusion may be accepted with some confidence, namely, that outside the Songs the Servant is (always) equated with Jacob-Israel; while the Servant of the Songs is anonymous. It need not, however, follow from this that the Songs are of different authorship; the same author may be writing of two different Servants.

(*b*) *The Anonymity of the Servant in the Songs is accompanied by heightened individualization in the portrait of the Servant.* On this point there is substantial agreement. Zillessen, a collectivist, remarked in 1904[3] that outside the Songs the term Servant is 'nothing but one predicate of Israel by the side of others, and that expressions which accompany it, such as "chosen", apply not to the Servant but to Israel'. In the Jacob-Israel passages we can hardly speak of personification, but only of a rapidly changing series of figures. In them the term Servant is nothing but a name, one of many applied to Israel. For example, 'Thou, Israel, my servant, Jacob whom I have chosen, the seed of Abraham my friend; thou whom I have taken hold of from the ends of the earth, and called thee from the corners thereof, and said unto thee, "Thou art my servant" ' (xli. 8 f.). It shines clearly through such passages that the Servant is 'my people Israel'. Zillessen even went so far as to say that if the Songs are later insertions, the Servant in Deutero-Isaiah has no content and no root, but is altogether suspended in the air. The Songs are, therefore, he argued, an integral part of the whole prophecy, no matter where they may have come from,

[1] Op. cit., p. 63. [2] *Isa. II*, p. 71.
[3] 'Israel in Darstellung u. Beurteilung DJ', *ZAW* 24, pp. 251–95.

because without them Deutero-Isaiah is unintelligible. Be that as it may, it is certain that the personalization of the Servant is carried farther in the Songs than it is in the rest of the prophecy. It is clear, too, that the descriptions of the Servant as an individual become more minute and detailed as we proceed from the first Song to the last of the series. This explains why so many scholars have interpreted the first two of Israel, but have felt constrained to maintain an individual interpretation for the last. Again, the conclusion may be that there were two different Servants, not that there were two different authors.

(*c*) *The character of the Servant in the Songs is different from that of the Servant Israel in the rest of the prophecy.* There is no need to insist at length that the moral and spiritual stature of the Servant in the Songs is greater than that of any other character in the Old Testament. Like Jeremiah and Job he suffers undeservedly, but, unlike them, in patient and uncomplaining silence. Israel suffers, suffers, indeed, 'double', but the initial cause of the suffering is its own sins (xl. 2). The Servant suffers first and last for the sins of others (liii. 4 ff.). Israel complains, 'my just right (*mišpāṭ*) passes over unheeded by my God' (xl. 27); the Servant is confident that 'my just right is with Yahweh' (xlix. 4). The similarity of thought and language, and the contrast in outlook, are equally striking.

Since outside the Songs the Servant is unquestionably Israel, anything that is said of Israel may be predicated of Israel as the Servant. Sometimes the character of Israel, notably in xlii. 18–25 and xlviii. 1–19, is portrayed in colours so dark as almost to exclude the possibility that the two Servants are the same. If it could be established that such passages are not genuine, the contrast between the two Servants would to some extent be modified. We have already seen[1] that xlii. 18–25 is suspicious, and probably secondary. It is widely held, too, that while chap. xlviii contains a genuine nucleus, interpolations have been so extensively made, that the passage now consists of the original, together with, as it were, an 'interlinear commentary'[2] in which Israel is placed in a most unfavourable light.[3] It would be natural if this easing of their problem were welcomed and adopted by those who identify the Servant of

[1] *Supra*, p. 179.
[2] Marti, *Jes.*, p. 321.
[3] Moffatt's *The O.T.: A New Translation*, in loc., gives a clear view of the resultant patchwork.

the Songs with the empirical Israel, though it cannot be said that it always has been. It so happens that Marti, who, of all writers, presented the collective theory in a form necessitating no distinction between the ideal and the empirical Israel,[1] was decidedly of the opinion that chap. xlviii is composite; but he did not appeal to this interpretation of the chapter as evidence for his identification of the Servant with Israel as it was. Budde, who did draw some distinction between the ideal and empirical Israel,[2] did not think that chap. xlviii had been glossed. It should be noted, too, that the interlinear theory of chap. xlviii originated with Duhm, a strong individualist. It is not, therefore, the case that collectivists regard the chapter as composite, while individualists do not. Interpretation of it has not, as might have been expected, run on partisan lines. In recent years the tendency has been to abandon the interpolation theory,[3] and to regard the chapter once more as a unity.

A similar and somewhat related problem is raised by lii. 3–6. In this passage Israel has been 'sold for nought', and shall be 'redeemed without money', whereas in l. 1 it has been sold 'for your iniquities', and in xliii. 3 Yahweh has 'given Egypt for thy ransom, Ethiopia and Seba for thee'. But here again, lii. 3–6 is widely regarded as spurious,[4] if only because it is prose. Volz, however, with some minor adjustments, as confidently defends it. I do not think Volz is right, but at least his defence of the passage should put us on our guard against assuming that a prophet must always be consistent, or that, failing consistency, we must posit difference of authorship. Once more, the solution may be that the Servants, not the authors, are different.

(*d*) *The Servant of the Songs has an active mission, both to Israel and to the heathen; the Servant Israel outside the Songs is the passive recipient of salvation.* The first of these statements needs no further argument. The second has been much disputed, more especially by König.[5] Schian,[6] following Duhm's lead,[7] had called attention to the fact that the Songs 'speak very clearly of a *vocation* of the Servant. . . . Of such a vocation the other

[1] See *supra*, p. 60 f.
[2] See *supra*, p. 58.
[3] So not only the Catholics Feldmann and Fischer, but also Volz.
[4] So Duhm, Marti, Köhler, Mowinckel, Fischer.
[5] 'Deuterojesajanisches', *NKZ*, 1898, pp. 915–30.
[6] *EJL*, p. 13 f.
[7] *Jes.*, p. 341.

Servant passages know little or nothing.' Wherever outside the Songs there is mention of the Servant, it is always of 'his destiny, his sufferings, his preservation by God, his exaltation, consolation, and deliverance. Israel is throughout passive, or, at the most, active in its sinfulness (xliii. 22 ff.). In none of these passages is it said that Israel the Servant of God has been designated by Yahweh to carry out any sort of a mission.' This was further underlined by Laue,[1] who argued that the standpoint of the original Deutero-Isaiah is throughout theocentric, and that he knows of no intermediary who works as Yahweh's plenipotentiary toward Israel and the heathen. (Is this quite true, in view of the role of Cyrus in the prophecy?) The external and internal restoration of Israel is the work of Yahweh alone, so that no room is left for any anthropocentric activity of the Servant. This divinely wrought salvation is to be completed swiftly, almost magically. The Servant of the Songs, on the other hand, is to meet with opposition, and only through suffering and death will he accomplish his work. This involves a complete break with the theological standpoint of Deutero-Isaiah, and we can only suppose, said Laue, that the Songs are interpolations. König attempted to parry this by arguing that Israel is 'called' (xli. 9, xlviii. 12) to be Yahweh's 'witnesses' (xliii. 10, xliv. 8). 'Is not that to credit Israel with an *active* role?'[2] The difference of standpoint between the Songs and the main prophecy is, therefore, relative, not total. But in order to maintain his position König had to fall back upon the conception of an 'internal distinction' within Israel, whereby a minority has an active (xlix. 6) and passive (liii. 4 f., 8*b*) relation toward the rest of the nation. He also committed himself to the paradox that 'Israel's negative encounter (*negative Aktion*) against the heathen would have in the end a positive result'.[3] This was really to give his case away. There seems no escape from the conclusion that outside the Songs the Servant Israel is always passive, while in the Songs the title has an 'active' signification. In the Songs the exaltation of the Servant is due to the faithfulness with which he has accomplished his task; the exaltation of Israel is an act of divine grace, pure and simple, and has no relation to any task that Israel has performed. No case against this can be based upon xliv. 26, 'that confirmeth

[1] *EJL*, pp. 14–23.
[2] Op. cit., p. 916.
[3] Op. cit., p. 924.

the word of his servant', since the plural 'his servants' should be read.[1] Nor yet upon xlii. 5–7, which in its present form is secondary, and, even so, relates to the Servant *kat' exochén*.[2] The nearest that Israel comes to having an active vocation is in the summons to be Yahweh's 'witnesses' (xliii. 10, xliv. 8) in His judicial process against the idol-gods, a process in which His sole Godhead really needs no demonstration, but is manifest to all from what He has done for Israel. This, in its original context, is the point of xliv. 23, 'and by means of Israel he will get himself glory', which has such a close external resemblance to xlix. 3. Yahweh is not to get Himself glory by reason of what Israel has done for Him, but by reason of what He has done for Israel. Nevertheless, the conclusion on the question of authorship is as for *a*, *b*, and *c* above.

(*e*) *The attitude to the heathen is more sympathetic in the Songs than it is in the rest of the prophecy.* Here we may have a real difference of outlook, not patient of explanation by a theory of two Servants. Exception need not be taken to the polemics against idolatry (xl. 19 f., xli. 6 f., 29; xliv. 9–20 is secondary), nor to the scathing denunciations of Babylon (xlvi f.), which are natural enough in the circumstances. Oh the other hand, xlix. 22–6 is said to stand in 'dissonant contrast'[3] even to the main body of Deutero-Isaiah, and especially to the high idealism of the Servant-Songs, and there must be many who wish they were free to delete at least vv. 23, 26. Duhm regarded the whole section, with its references to the Diaspora rather than to the exiles, as from a later poet after the manner of Trito-Isaiah (cf. chap. lx). His successors, on the whole, have been more cautious. We are not to suppose that the passage would offend the conscience of Deutero-Isaiah's contemporaries to the extent that it offends us. The hyperbolical language of ver. 23 was as old as the Amarna letters;[4] any Oriental might protest that it would give him the greatest pleasure to fall down and lick the dust at the feet of his superior, or even of his friend. Even if we deny the passage to Deutero-Isaiah we are left with xlv. 14, the genuineness of which is disputed by none. In it Israel is assured of a primacy over the African peoples: 'thine shall they

[1] So LXX^{A}, Targ., and note the parallel 'his messengers'.

[2] See *supra*, pp. 131–4.

[3] Whitehouse, *Isa. XL–LXVI*, p. 165.

[4] Cf. Knudtzon, *Die el-Amarna Tafeln*, nos. 100, 253 f., and frequently.

be; behind thee shall they walk; in chains shall they pass over; and unto thee shall they prostrate themselves, unto thee shall they make supplication. . . .' Again, we may reflect that no Old Testament writer could very well free himself from such nationalist assumptions. At the same time, it is just here that the thought of a conversion of the heathen is adumbrated, thus providing a bridge between the main prophecy and the Songs (cf. xliv. 5, xlv. 22 f.). The substance of the nations' supplication is 'Surely God is in thee, and there is no God beside; verily with thee doth God hide himself; the God of Israel is a Saviour.' It would therefore seem that while in the Songs the thought of a mission to the heathen is more generously anticipated than in the prophecy as a whole, there is in this respect no gulf fixed between Songs and prophecy, nor anything to preclude the supposition that they are from the same hand.

(*f*) *There is, it is alleged, a radical difference between the conceptions of salvation and atonement in the Songs and those in the main prophecy.* Here, at length, is a theological difference, which, if it can be sustained, may point to difference of authorship. Speaking broadly, the salvation which Deutero-Isaiah envisages is a salvation which Yahweh is to accomplish for Israel by His overthrow of Babylon and the utter discrediting of its gods. It is to be 'deliverance by a supernatural operation of divine power'.[1] While this is an act of divine grace, there is nevertheless a sense in which it is due to Israel, since Israel has expiated its guilt by suffering 'double'. This manifestation of divine power and grace will excite the interest of the whole world, and will result in the universal recognition of Yahweh as the one only God. Compared with chap. liii, with its doctrine of the vicarious suffering of the Servant, this, it is argued, seems external, superficial.

Yet it is surely an over-simplification of the issue to suppose that even in the main prophecy the salvation of Israel is only external and political. The Prophet's conception of salvation is more complex than that, and provides for the inner purification and spiritual redemption of his people (xliv. 3, 22, lv. 6 f.). This aspect of the matter, to be sure, is not so pronounced as to form a well-balanced whole with the other. But what of that? The prophets were not *Systematiker*. The very fact that the emphasis in the main prophecy is apparently one-sided should

[1] Skinner, op. cit., p. xlvii.

lead us to expect that so great a prophet would have more to say by way of complement to it. The scope of his imagination is so vast that we should be surprised if he had had nothing more to deliver than the eschatological message with which he began. What we have in the Songs restores the balance. In the main prophecy the Prophet is speaking in the expectation of an imminent display of divine power which will set Israel free from its bondage. Why should he straightway enter into the deeper problems occasioned by its abiding spiritual needs? But what if his eschatological expectations remain largely unfulfilled, and Cyrus proves a disappointment, and he must descend into the valley of the shadow? Are we—since the Songs are bound up with his work, and there are, as we have seen, excellent prima-facie reasons for regarding them as his—to deny him the possibility of having emerged once more from the valley, and climbed to a point from which he can even look down upon the high mountain from which he first lifted up his voice to tell good tidings to Zion? I cannot see anything in the theological standpoint of the Songs that is *inconsistent* with the main prophecy. Many poets, not to mention prophets, have travelled as far as Deutero-Isaiah did between their first work and their last.

The conclusion, therefore, to which I feel compelled is that the Songs are by Deutero-Isaiah. Granted that he may have thought of two Servants, Israel and another, or, alternatively, that his conception of the one Servant may have developed with the maturing of his thought, any theological differences there may be between the Songs and the main prophecy are readily explained. The evidences of common authorship, admittedly, do not amount to positive proof, but the weight of probability seems to me to lie heavily on that side. However, if there are those who remain unconvinced, I am willing, for the sake of a measure of agreement that may enable us to proceed farther in our inquiry, to leave the question of authorship open, always provided that it is agreed that Songs and prophecy have the same general background, and that they must be nearly contemporary with one another. That background is the closing days of the exile.

There remain two further questions: (1) Are the Songs earlier, or later, than the main prophecy? (2) Were they composed together, or at intervals?

1. The question whether the Songs are earlier, or later, than the main prophecy must be asked, whether or not we think of Deutero-Isaiah as the author of both. My own conviction is that the Songs are somewhat later. If Deutero-Isaiah was their author, and if the Songs are early, it is difficult to understand why the conceptions that give them their distinctiveness should be absent from the rest of his work. That work certainly does not give the impression of coming from a man whose earlier, and higher, inspiration had failed him. It is original and creative work of sustained imagination, not in the least like that of a Wordsworth in his declining years, who may produce an occasional great poem, but whose vigour and inspiration have mostly departed. If Deutero-Isaiah composed the main prophecy after the Songs, we are faced with the inexplicable paradox that a prophet could keep his freshness, and yet apparently forget the most vital part of his earlier and more deeply inspired message. The case is much the same if we think of the Songs as from another, and earlier, prophet than Deutero-Isaiah. He then found in Deutero-Isaiah an imitator indeed, an imitator of creative originality, who nevertheless missed the vital heart of his message. If, on the other hand, the Songs are somewhat later than the main prophecy, whether by Deutero-Isaiah or another, we can account both for their similarity of language and general ideas, and the deeper and more mature conceptions of the Songs.

This conclusion is supported by two further considerations: (*a*) the place of the Songs in the present arrangement of the prophecy, and (*b*) the quieter tone of the Songs as compared with the rest of the prophecy. The fact that three of the Songs are in the second half of the prophecy ought to count for something, *pace* those who think that all collections of prophetic oracles have been put together at random. There is order in Deutero-Isaiah,[1] and the presence of the first Song in the first half of the prophecy may well have been dictated by the desire of the editor, whether Deutero-Isaiah himself or some other, to present a contrast with Cyrus. As to the quieter tone of the Songs as compared with the main prophecy, this is no indication, as Duhm would have it, that they are from another hand; but it may well be an indication of a somewhat later date. Between the style of the main prophecy and that of the Songs

[1] See *supra*, p. 84.

there is, indeed, a perceptible difference, similar to that between the vigorous and often tumultuous verse of Shakespeare's middle period, and the 'Our revels now are ended' of *The Tempest.*

2. Were the Songs composed *uno tempore*, or at intervals? We have already[1] found indications that the Songs are not entirely *uno tenore* with one another. This could be explained in either of two ways: (*a*) that the divergencies between them were intentional, revealing consummate art; or (*b*) that the prophet himself only gradually apprehended 'the burthen of the mystery', in which case the Songs must have been composed at intervals. The second alternative, based upon such considerations as that the first Song seems definitely to exclude the violent death of the last, seems to me the more likely. If the Songs as a whole are later than the main prophecy, itself composed over a period of time, it is antecedently probable that they too were composed at intervals. If the Prophet only gradually learned the truths embodied in the last Song, the first three register stages in his spiritual pilgrimage. The concept of progressive revelation can as well apply to a single prophet as to Scripture as a whole. The four Songs together do not make up a single poem. There are obvious gaps between them, so much so that some writers, Duhm among them, have supposed that they may once have formed part of a larger collection, some items in which have been lost. This is not impossible, though it hardly seems likely. The Songs, for all their individual fragmentariness, have the impressive unity of a great cathedral. At the same time, the unity is consistent with the individuality of the several parts. If Deutero-Isaiah was his own editor, the fact that he dispersed the pieces at intervals in his work would confirm the suspicion that he composed them at intervals. But whoever arranged them as they are, the fact that he did so dispose them suggests that they came into his hands as separate pieces, rather than as poems composed in one burst of inspiration. And it would be natural for separate pieces to have been composed at intervals.

To sum up: Songs and prophecy are nearly contemporary, the Songs being rather later than the prophecy, and almost certainly by the same author. It is probable that they were not all composed at the same time.

[1] See *supra*, pp. 150, 154 f.

APPENDIX TO CHAPTER IX

Note on the Linguistic Affinities of the Secondary Servant-Songs

xlii. 5–9

ver. 5. *hā'ēl*, 'the (true) God': with art. only here in DI, and without art., referring to the (true) God in xl. 18, xliii. 10, 12, xlv. 14, 15, 21, 22, xlvi. 9. Otherwise mostly Pss. and Job.

bôrē', 'Creator': this √ some 50 times in O.T., 16 of them in DI, and 4 in TI. DI uses the ptc. 7 times (xl. 28, xlii. 5, xliii. 1, 15, xlv. 7 *bis*, 18). *bôrē' haššāmayim* also in xlv. 18.

nôṭêhεm, 'stretched them out': cf. xl. 22, xliv. 24, xlv. 12, li. 13.

rôqa' hā'ārεṣ, 'that spread (lit. beat) out the earth': cf. xliv. 24, where also the expression is || *nôṭεh šāmayim*. Note also *yᵉraqqᵉ'εnnû* (xl. 19), and that the verb is only found 4 times of God's creative activity.

wᵉṣε'ᵉṣā'êhâ, 'and that which came out of it': only 11 times in all, twice, apart from this passage, in DI (xliv. 3, xlviii. 19), and twice in TI (lxi. 19, lxv. 23). Elsewhere only Job.

nᵉšāmâh, 'breath': *hap.leg.* in DI.

ver. 6. *'ᵃnî Yahwεh*, 'I am Yahweh': emphatic and very frequent in DI (xli. 4, 13, 17, xlii. 8, xliii. 3, 15, xlv. 3, 5, 6, 7, 8, 18, 19, 21, xlviii. 17, xlix. 23, 26).

qᵉrā'ṯîḵâ, 'I have called thee': cf. the same or similar expressions of Israel (xli. 9, xliii. 1, 7, xlviii. 12, liv. 6), of Abraham (li. 2), of Cyrus (xlv. 3, 4, xlvi. 11, xlviii. 15), of the generations of mankind (xli. 4). For the expression *qᵉrā'ṯîḵâ ḇᵉṣεḏεq* cf. *hᵃ'îrôṯîhû ḇᵉṣεḏεq* of Cyrus (xlv. 13).

wᵉ'aḥzēq bᵉyāḏêḵâ, 'and I will take thy hand': cf. xli. 9, 13 of Israel, the former || *qr'*, as here; and xlv. 1, of Cyrus.

wᵉ'εṣṣorᵉḵâ, 'and form thee' (from *yṣr*): cf. also xlix. 5, of the Servant; xliii. 1, 21, xliv. 2, 21, 24, xlv. 11, of Israel.

liḇᵉrîṯ 'ām, 'for a covenant of the people': otherwise only xlix. 8, where reading doubtful.

lᵉ'ôr gôyîm, 'for a light to the nations': cf. *lᵉ'ôr 'ammîm* li. 4 (?).

ver. 7. *lipqōaḥ*, 'to open': cf. xlii. 20.

'iwᵉrôṯ, 'blind': cf. xlii. 16, 18, 19.

masgēr, 'dungeon': *hap.leg.* in DI.

'assîr, 'bound': *hap.leg.* in DI, but *'ᵃsûrîm*, xlix. 9.

bêṯ kεlε', 'prison-house': cf. the plur. in xlii. 22. Outside DI the phrase only found 6 times, one of them in Chron. in a passage cited from Kings.

yôšᵉḇê ḥōšεḵ, 'dwellers in darkness': as figure of imprisonment cf. xlvii. 5, xlix. 9 (in the latter || *'ᵃsûrîm*, cf. *'assîr* in this verse).

vv. 8–9. The Deutero-Isaianic character of these verses needs no showing.

The language of this passage is even more obviously akin to that of DI than is that of xlii. 1–4. The parallels have a wider range than those of the Song preceding, though they are largely confined to chaps. xl–xlviii. Not only do we find them in the Servant-Israel sections, but also in those relating to Cyrus. It is impossible on grounds of vocabulary to deny authorship by DI.

xlix. 7–9*a* (13)

ver. 7. *gô'ēl yiśrā'ēl qᵉḏōšô*, 'the Redeemer of Israel, his Holy One': cf. xli. 14, xliii. 14, xlvii. 4, xlviii. 17, liv. 5. *gô'ēl* alone is found in xliv. 6, 24, xlix. 26, liv. 8. Outside DI and TI *gô'ēl* as a noun referring to God only 5 times. Of other verb forms from the root there are about 60 examples, rather less than half with God as subject. Of them 10 are in DI and TI. *qᵉḏôš yiśrā'ēl* alone is found in xli. 16, 20, xliii. 3, xlv. 11, lv. 5. Of the 31 examples of the phrase, only 6 are found outside Isaiah.

liḇᵉzōh nɛp̄ɛš: cf. liii. 3 (*bis*).

limᵉṯō'aḇ gôy (so point): *hap.leg.* in DI. Fischer (*Perikopen*, p. 141) notes *'ᵃṣûḇaṯ rûaḥ*, liv. 6, as an example of a similar pregnant construction. It cannot, however, be claimed that there is anything unusual in this type of genitive relation (cf. *G-K* § 128*xy*).

môšᵉlîm, 'rulers': cf. lii. 5 (?)

yir'û: for this verb in the sense of 'see (and wonder)', generally without object expressed, cf. xl. 5, xli. 5, xlix. 18, lii. 8, 10, *15*.

wᵉyištaḥᵃwû, 'and shall prostrate themselves': cf., with Israel as object, xlv. 14 (subject 'heathen'), xlix. 23 (subject 'kings'); also xlvi. 6.

lᵉma'an Yahweh . . . qᵉḏôš yiśrā'ēl, 'for the sake of Yahweh the Holy One of Israel': cf. the striking parallel in lv. 5.

nɛ'ᵉmān, 'faithful': cf. lv. 3. There is nothing special in this, but it may be worth remarking in view of its proximity to the parallel just noted above.

wayyiḇḥārɛkkā, 'and he has chosen thee': cf. the note on *bᵉḥîrî* (xlii. 1, *supra*, p. 161).

ver. 8. *rāṣôn*, 'favour': *hap.leg.* in DI.

yᵉšû'āh, 'salvation': see on xlix. 6 (*supra*, p. 163).

'ᵃzartîḵā, 'I have helped thee': exactly the same form in xli. 10, 13 f., of Israel; similarly xliv. 2. Also l. 7, 9 of the Servant.

lᵉhanḥîl, 'to cause to inherit': *hap.leg.* in DI.

šōmēmôṯ, 'desolate': cf. xlix. 19, liv. 1, imitated by TI (lxi. 4 *bis*).

Otherwise the ptc. is rare (12 times) and practically confined to Lam. and Dan.

ver. 9*a*. Note the general similarity to xlii. 7.

Here again the language, if not that of DI, has been very skilfully imitated from him. We have already (see *supra*, p. 130) found reason to think that parts of vv. 7, 8 are secondary to the passage. In vv. 9*b*–11, 13 the language and diction are so like that of DI that there is no need to analyse them in detail.

l. 10–11

These verses have hardly any literary affinity either with the Songs proper or with the main prophecy.

X

CRITICAL SUMMARY AND CONCLUSION

I. HISTORICAL INDIVIDUAL INTERPRETATIONS

(*a*) *Theories which identify the Servant with some individual named.* In addition to the historico-messianic and autobiographical interpretations, which will be considered separately, and that connected with Duhm's unknown teacher of the law, the names of some fifteen historical individuals have been suggested for the title of Servant. They are Isaiah, Uzziah, Hezekiah, Josiah, Jeremiah, Ezekiel, Job, Moses, Jehoiachin, Cyrus, Sheshbazzar, Zerubbabel, Meshullam, Nehemiah, and Eleazar. The claims of most of them have either been abandoned by, or have died with, those who have sponsored them, and it is improbable that any further names will ever be proposed.

If our conclusions about the authorship of the Songs are sound, we must rule out Isaiah, Uzziah, and Hezekiah, since the Songs date from the exile, not from the eighth century. Jeremiah has no advocate to-day,[1] and although his claims are in some respects attractive, it cannot be said that he suffered uncomplainingly. The most that can be said is that he contributed something to the portrait (liii. 7, cf. Jer. xi. 19). Josiah, apart from Gressmann's supposition that he was the historical original of the Messianic Servant, has received only one vote, that of Abarbanel.[2] Kraetzschmar's promised monograph on Ezekiel as the Servant never appeared, and even if it had it is difficult to imagine that it would have been very convincing. Had the claims of Job been strong, they would have deserved more attention; Luzzatto merely remarks that 'Rabbi Eliezer, the German . . . interprets it of Job'.[3] We can hardly take

[1] Beyond Sheldon H. Blank's suggestion that the Servant is '*Israel in the guise of a martyr prophet—of a prophet after the pattern of Jeremiah*' ('Studies in DI', *HUCA* 15, 1940, p. 29); cf. F. A. Farley, 'Jeremiah and "The Suffering Servant of Jehovah" in Deutero-Isaiah', *ET* 38, 1926–7, pp. 521–4, who thinks of the Servant as 'Idealized Prophecy', based on the fortunes of Jeremiah.

[2] Cf. *supra*, p. 21.

[3] *Supra*, p. 21. Volz's listing (*Jes. II*, p. 188) of Cheyne as at one time having regarded Job as the Servant does not seem justified. In his Commentary on Isaiah, vol. ii, Cheyne had an Essay (No. IX) on 'Job and the Second Isaiah: A Parallel' in which he spoke of the Servant as being 'like another Job'. He noted points of detail in the affinity, and equally strong points of contrast. He thought

seriously the claims of Cyrus.[1] Winckler's temporary advocacy of Sheshbazzar was a random guess about a man of whom we know almost nothing.[2] Nor have we any stronger case for Nehemiah than Weissmann's remark that the picture 'suits' him.[3] I am not aware that Bertholet has ever abandoned his Eleazar suggestion; but so far as I know he has never found a convert to it. Zerubbabel, Jehoiachin, and Moses are associated with the advocacy of Sellin, who abandoned them all in turn. The first two were *Jammerprinzen*, quite inadequate for the parts that Sellin called upon them to play. Zerubbabel *may* have died a violent death; we do not know. Jehoiachin did not, as Sellin admitted; and he had, therefore, against all the indications of the last Song, to insist that the Servant was not stricken to death. Moses was a man of gigantic moral and spiritual stature. But in order to make out a case for him Sellin was obliged to resort to conjectural textual surgery with passages far outside the Songs, passages which most scholars will feel are quite irrelevant to the subject. The only convert Sellin ever made was Freud,[4] who, for the purposes of his own psychoanalytical theories, adopted it years after Sellin himself had abandoned it. Uzziah, whose claims are presumably still advocated by Dietze, must be ruled out for the reason already given; so Palache's Meshullam theory[5] alone remains, a meagre survival of all the persistent attempts to discover in the Servant an historical individual.

The claims for some of the names proposed seem almost frivolous. Yet even allowing for the fact that some of them ought never to have been suggested, a sufficient number remain to compel us to ask whether this type of interpretation must not be based on wrong premisses. What are we to say of a principle of interpretation under which claims can in all seriousness be made for men so different as Jeremiah and Jehoiachin? Further, no one can fail to remark that the names suggested fall into two main, and almost opposite, categories; prophets on the one hand, and kings or rulers on the other. There is, of

Job was earlier than Isa. xl ff., but did not suppose that the former had anything more than a 'general and, if I may say so, atmospheric influence' on the latter. When Kissane (*The Book of Isaiah*, vol. ii, p. lxiv) says that Cheyne identified the Servant with Job he is probably uncritically following Volz.

[1] See *supra*, p. 57.
[2] See *supra*, p. 50.
[3] See *supra*, p. 21.
[4] *Moses and Monotheism*, 1939.
[5] See *supra*, p. 89 f.

course, reason for this, in that the texts themselves depict a man with a prophetic calling, and, at the same time, at least some of the functions of a ruler. Only one man of those proposed fulfils both these conditions, and that is Moses. If he fails us, it is vain to seek farther among the heroes whose names have been preserved. If we are to look for an historical individual, it must be for someone anonymous.

(*b*) *The Historico-Messianic Theory.* We come now to the theory, first proposed by Kittel, then elaborated by Rudolph, and supported by Oesterley, that the Servant was an anonymous contemporary of Deutero-Isaiah, to whom the Prophet looked as the promised Messiah.[1] Volz,[2] while recognizing that Rudolph has sought to do justice to the historical power of the poems, says that his suggestions are open to the same objections as the purely historical hypotheses, namely, that if the poet had been describing a contemporary he would have been more concrete and clear. Moreover, Volz asks; is it likely that there lived, at the same time as Deutero-Isaiah, a yet greater leader and prophet who has remained quite unknown to us? Further, does not Rudolph's interpretation altogether misplace the emphasis of the Songs? It lays stress upon the political elements in the person and work of the Servant, whereas these are throughout of only secondary importance.

To this we may add, does not the relation between Servant and Prophet present an insurmountable psychological difficulty? It is true that here Rudolph speaks with caution. But since some suggestion about the relation of his Boswell to his Johnson was necessary, what he offers, however tentatively, must run the gauntlet of criticism. That the Prophet could become so united in spirit with the Servant as to be able to put into his mouth the autobiographical Songs (xlix. 1–6, l. 4–9) is not, perhaps, psychologically inconceivable. The difficulty is that the Servant, as he makes his first appearance to the Prophet, looks the most unlikely person to be a political leader. He had, indeed, no such pretensions—here I am summarizing Rudolph's own argument—and his claim to the Prophet's admiration at first consisted solely in his conception of a world-mission. It needed the Prophet to point out to him what he really was. In this the Prophet appears to be greater than he. Unfortunately, the Prophet fired him with enthusiasm for less

[1] See *supra*, pp. 55 f., 85–8.

[2] *Jes. II*, p. 184.

spiritual objectives, in the pursuance of which he met his death. In other words, the Servant needed the encouragement of the Prophet to make him fully conscious of himself, and then fell a victim to the Prophet's enthusiasm for the political liberation of Israel. It is true that even those who were most intimate with Jesus looked to Him to further political projects which He entirely repudiated. It is thus conceivable that the Servant, like Jesus, was executed on political charges of which he was entirely innocent. But if we are to say, with Rudolph, that the motive force in the alliance of Servant and Prophet was the prophetic word, we should surely hesitate before implying that the Prophet, who so reverenced the Servant, was really his evil genius. The association of the two men, as Rudolph imagines it, was not altogether fortunate, and as a result neither of them is quite as great as we had thought him.

(*c*) *The Autobiographical Theory*. We have seen that Mowinckel has abandoned the autobiographical theory in the form in which he originally presented it, though he still thinks it possible that the portrait of the Servant, now 'delineated with mythological colouring', may be based upon the experiences of the (conjecturally) martyred Deutero-Isaiah himself.[1] For the rest, Sellin and Elliger have advanced the theory that the last Song was composed by Trito-Isaiah as a threnody upon his martyred master.[2] Volz would still further separate lii. 13–liii. 12 from the original Song-cycle, which he thinks was composed by the Prophet about himself, and consisted of xlii. 1–4, xlii. 5–9, xlix. 1–6, l. 4–9.[3] Meanwhile, Begrich has returned to a position similar to that originally sponsored by Mowinckel, but based upon a rather different theory of the composition of Isa. xl–lv.[4]

We have found reason to believe that none of these reconstructions of the original autobiographical theory can be sustained. This, however, is not to say that the view that the Servant was the Prophet may now forthwith be dismissed. The Servant may conceivably be the Prophet, no matter what may be the precise dates, or order, of the prophecies, and whether or not the Songs are all from one hand. But even when we have conceded this, we are still left with the fundamental difficulty presented by any form of the Servant-Prophet theory, namely, that of establishing any convincing and neces-

[1] See *supra*, p. 81.
[2] See *supra*, pp. 79 f., 81.
[3] See *supra*, p. 78.
[4] See *supra*, pp. 83 ff.

sary psychological connexion between the Songs and the rest of the prophecy.

If, let us suppose, we know something of the character, but are uninformed about the person of the Servant, and if we know the person—though not his name—but next to nothing of the history of the Prophet, it is tempting to assume that Servant and Prophet are the same person. But there are obvious difficulties in this assumption, for the simple reason that the two sets of data seem to be playing hide-and-seek with one another. For example, it is usual for those who hold the autobiographical theory to make much of the fact that two of the Songs (xlix. 1–6, l. 4–9) are in the first person.[1] Therefore, so the argument goes, since the speaker cannot be Yahweh, he can only be the Prophet. Elliger goes on to say that the fact that the first Song is in the third person is no objection, since 'the third person form is also possible in "autobiographical" style'. But Elliger offers neither proof nor illustration of his statement, notwithstanding that it really commits him to the hazardous proposition that the Prophet had the temerity to represent God as composing a part of His Servant's autobiography. Granted, therefore, that two of the Songs composed by the Servant are in the first person, it still remains that one of them, in Elliger's presentation of the case—(not counting the 'Trito-Isaianic' lii. 13–liii. 12)—and four of them in Begrich's (xlii. 1–4, xlix. 8–13, xlii. 5–9, lii. 13–liii. 12), are in the third. Concerning lii. 13–liii. 12 Begrich[2] says, as against Sellin and Elliger, that 'the form of the text is no hindrance to Deutero-Isaiah's authorship. How is he to speak of himself otherwise than in the third person, if he is to explain the result of his death and resurrection to those whom his direct word cannot reach?' The necessity for this postulate is not very convincing. An autobiography intended for posthumous publication does not need to switch over to the form of biography. And since the Prophet had already used the first person in two of the Songs, there would have been less ambiguity, if he had continued to use it in the last.

Another aspect of this fundamental psychological difficulty is that the autobiographical theory invariably and inevitably limits the horizon of the Songs. Mowinckel[3] did allow that in

[1] Mowinckel, *Knecht*, p. 9; Elliger, op. cit., p. 87; Begrich, op. cit., p. 132.
[2] Op. cit., p. 146.
[3] Op. cit., p. 45.

liii. 1 ff. the speakers are the Gentiles. But when we read Sellin, Elliger, and Begrich, we are left wondering why the Gentiles receive such prominence in the Songs as they unquestionably do (cf. xlii. 1–4, xlix. 6, lii. 15, liii. 12). In the Songs the Servant is destined to be 'a light to the Gentiles', not failing or being discouraged until he has accomplished his task. It needs no saying that, unless Volz's conjecture is right, the Prophet did not actually go to the Gentiles. That, it may be, is not a decisive objection to the Servant-Prophet theory, though it is a little disconcerting to find that realization fell so far short of anticipation. Unless the Prophet-Servant was a dreamer doomed to complete disillusionment, we do expect that he should go at least some way towards realizing the destiny ordained for him by God. Not only did he not do this, but Sellin, Elliger, and Begrich appear to say that nothing of the kind was ever seriously intended for him, nor even by him. Thus, Sellin[1] is at pains to show that Volz's conception of the Prophet as a peripatetic missionary to the heathen is wrong. Perhaps it is; but ought it to be, if the Servant is the Prophet, and if he is to be 'a light to the Gentiles'? Sellin[2] further describes xlii. 1–4, xlix. 1–6 as 'words of comfort' (*Trostworte*) to the Prophet-Servant. But xlii. 1–4 is an exordium which, to whomsoever addressed, is *about* the Servant, not addressed *to* him. Begrich describes xlix. 1–6 as a 'hymn of thanksgiving' (*Danklied*) by the Prophet. To those who are not completely under the spell of the now fashionable Psalm-types it reads much more like an address of the Servant to the Gentiles. Begrich goes on to say of xlix. 1–6 that

'we must not be misled by the introduction into assuming that we have here a proclamation which the prophet wished to make known to all the world. To explain it so is to treat poetry as prose. We must not understand the introduction in any way differently from that in which we understand similar introductions to other hymns of thanksgiving (e.g. Pss. xviii. 50, xxii. 28, 30, lvii. 10, lxvi. 8, ciii. 20–2—Heb.). In it the degree of overflowing thankfulness finds such expression that all the world must be apprised of the experience. But it is not, therefore, to be assumed that the *Danklied* is addressed to any beyond the limited circle presupposed by the Servant-texts.'[3]

To this it must be answered that the Psalm-passages to which

[1] *ZAW* 55, pp. 188–96. [2] Ibid., p. 191.
[3] Op. cit., p. 140.

Begrich refers are inadequate parallels to what we have in the Song. None of them is the introduction to the *Danklied* in which it is found. They are incidental to the main theme, and some of them are soliloquies not addressed to the world at large. To be sure, there are Psalms with introductions addressed to all the world (e.g. lvi, xcvi, c); but in them the heathen are bidden to 'make a joyful noise unto God', or the like, not, as in the Song, to hearken to the voice of a man. If, as the protagonists of the autobiographical theory appear to say,[1] the Songs are monologues, dialogues with God, words of comfort to the Prophet, thanksgivings of the Prophet to God, which the Prophet—for whatever reason—only communicated to a small circle of disciples, we are left wondering why they are so concerned about the Gentiles, since the Prophet was not destined, either in fact or, apparently, in intention, to exercise the ministry designed for him. It is no doubt possible that the Songs were only committed to a small circle of disciples, and such a possibility is quite consistent with most theories about the Servant. It is, however, difficult to reconcile it with the autobiographical theory, and yet the exponents of that theory, paradoxically, seem the most concerned to limit the scope of the Servant's opportunities. It is the price they have to pay for the necessity that is laid upon them of proving that the Songs do not break through the bounds of the rest of the prophecy. In effect, they are forcing the Songs, which are unique, into categories of their own framing. They do not, indeed they cannot, in view of the plain language of the Songs, deny that the Servant has a mission to the Gentiles; but they minimize that element in the Songs as much as possible, and they put the Prophet in a position which makes it impossible for him to exercise the wider ministry. The references to the Gentiles seem superfluous embroidery, since the Gentiles are hardly allowed even the role of a Chorus.

There is, no doubt, an element of truth in the autobiographical theory. Whoever the Servant may have been, if he was not an actual historical person, and even if he was, it was almost inevitable that the Prophet would, perhaps quite unconsciously, put something of himself into his portrait. That is true of the creative artist in any medium. Very much as Elgar in the *Enigma Variations* set out to picture his friends, and inevitably

[1] Sellin, op. cit., p. 182; Elliger, op. cit., p. 85; Begrich, op. cit., p. 140.

gave us a portrait of himself, so did Deutero-Isaiah unconsciously put himself into his portrait of the Servant. But that is a very different thing from saying that he intended a conscious self-portrait.

It is argued that the strength of these historical individual theories lies in the fact that the character and fortunes of the Servant are so vividly drawn that we can only think of a portrait from life. On that principle we should have to say that every convincing character in drama or in fiction is taken from actual life. That is very far from being true. On the human side the Songs are the work of a creative artist, and any artist is an artist in proportion as he makes his characters convincingly real. Who is there that reads *Hamlet* and does not involuntarily catch his breath as he recognizes something of himself in the title role? That is the reason why so many names have been proposed for the Servant. Many prophets, and even kings, have doubtless contributed something to the picture. Even so, there are features in it which transcend the bounds of any single human life. The strength of the collective interpretation lies in the fact that it insists that no single individual could have produced such consternation among the nations as the Servant is said to have done (lii. 14 f.). Who is this that is going, apparently single-handed, to establish judgement in all the earth (xlii. 4, xlix. 6)? Are we not dealing with a figure of superhuman proportions, one who is, in the last resort, *übermenschlich*? Again, we have already asked, How did the Servant die? Of sickness, or as a malefactor?[1] It is as though the Prophet heaped upon him every imaginable suffering. Dr. Theodore Robinson's suggestion, that 'it would seem that no one individual sat for the ideal portrait, but that the writer draws on the experiences of at least two different men', has already been noted.[2] It should be observed that he speaks of the 'ideal' portrait. A composite portrait must necessarily be ideal, and if we are to think of two or more sitters we are no longer thinking in terms of the historical individual theories as they are generally understood. Dr. Robinson, in a private communication, has explained his view to me more fully in these terms:

'I feel that the passage is too keen and poignant to have been written purely as a piece of imagination; it *feels* like a record of fact.

[1] *Supra*, p. 149 f.

[2] See *supra*, p. 150.

Its intention, I agree, is to present a general picture of what the service of God may involve, but it looks to me as if there were some historical figure(s) who served as models. I cannot agree with any of the proposals for the identification of this figure with an individual. . . . This is partly because, I feel, elements from the experience of at least two sufferers have been combined. The distinctive traits of leprosy are too obvious to be overlooked, and at the same time it is hardly likely that a leper would have taken so much part in common life as to incur the fate of the persecuted and executed saint. Consequently I am reduced to the suggestion that the poet had the experiences of two people known to him in mind; either alone might have served as an illustration of his general principle, but in order to make his point fully clear he put them together.'

Such a view of the case is both intelligible and reasonable. But the resultant portrait belongs to the category of the ideal rather than of the real. It is similar to forms of ideal theory which have already[1] been described, and this is perhaps the most convenient point at which to consider, briefly, the general principle underlying such theories. I find it difficult to believe that the writer of the Songs was discussing a 'general principle', or 'presenting a general picture of what the service of God may involve', or that he was constructing a theodicy. It was not the habit of the Hebrews to discuss moral problems in the abstract. Even of the Book of Job which comes nearest to such an attempt, it has been said that the supreme interest lies 'in the history of a soul, rather than the discussion of a problem',[2] and that 'The writer's purpose is never so directly formulated as Milton's—to

assert Eternal Providence
And justify the ways of God to men.'[3]

The Servant is a real person, whether he has already appeared, or is still to come. All the same, and with this qualification, there is much to be said for Skinner's view[4] that 'the most fundamental contrast between rival interpretations of the Servant idea is not between *collective* and *individual* theories, but between *historical* and *ideal*'. The historical individual theories

[1] See *supra*, pp. 99 ff.

[2] Peake, *Job*, *Cent. Bible*, p. 12. Job, it may be remarked, was a popular figure in Hebrew story (Ezek. xiv. 14), even though the book in its present form is largely fiction.

[3] Driver-Gray, *Job*, *I.C.C.*, p. li.

[4] *Isaiah XL–LXVI*, p. 265, cf. *supra*, p. 63.

must be ruled out one by one and, finally, all together. Those that remain, the mythological, the Messianic, and the collective, are severally forms of 'the ideal' theory, on Skinner's definition of the term, and it would seem as if we must turn to them, if we are to find a solution of the problem.

2. MYTHOLOGICAL INTERPRETATION

We have already seen that, in the most recent phases of the discussion, any enthusiasm there may once have been for the *purely* mythological and cultic interpretations of the Servant has perceptibly cooled. It is sufficient criticism of them to say that the Servant is a soteriological figure, while nature gods of the Tammuz variety are not. The most that can be pleaded is that the Servant is delineated with some mythological colouring, or, with Dürr,[1] that his sufferings may be *illustrated* from the part played by the king in the Babylonian cultus. Even so, it would seem that Dürr misplaces the emphasis of the Songs, when he thinks of the Servant as the antitype of the Babylonian *kings*.

Even if it could be proved that there are close verbal parallels between the Songs and the mythological texts, this would not mean that the Servant is a mythological figure. There are undoubted echoes of mythology in the Old Testament, but the Hebrews, whenever they were true to their religious tradition, did no more than take broken fragments from the general mythological pattern, with which to embellish descriptions of Yahweh's redeeming acts in history, particularly the Exodus (cf. Isa. li. 9 f., Ps. lxxiv. 12–17). Their emphasis was upon the concrete and historical, and purely mythological conceptions would have been abhorrent to them. They firmly believed in a divine purpose being wrought out in history, and consequently they developed an eschatology. The surrounding nations, on the other hand, had abundance of myth and drama, but no conception of God at work in history, and, consequently, no clearly attested eschatology.[2] There are even, it may be, some general resemblances between the myth of the dying and rising god and the story of Jesus. But that is not to say that the Gospels are mythology, or that the resemblances are anything

[1] See *supra*, p. 102 f.
[2] Cf. W. Eichrodt, *Theologie des ATs*, 1. Bd., p. 269.

more than superficial. It would seem to be true that 'whether it is thought to have been part of the deliberate divine purpose or not, there was undoubtedly in the pagan world a "Praeparatio Evangelii", nor could the gospel have won its way if it had not found an echo in the religious searchings and even the religious beliefs of the time'.[1] On the same principle we may account for any similarities there may be between Tammuz and the Suffering Servant.

3. COLLECTIVE INTERPRETATION

The history of the discussion has shown that the collective interpretation has assumed many forms, forms which have frequently been combined with one another 'by divers portions and in divers manners'. In our examination of the theory as a whole it is convenient to begin with those modifications of it which see in the Servant something other than Israel in its entirety, whether the Ideal Israel, or a Minority within Israel.

It seems clear that all these modifications of the full collective interpretation are by way of being what the Germans would call *Auskunftshilfe*, expedients to avoid the obvious difficulty of supposing that Israel, just as it was, blind and dumb, was the Servant depicted in the Songs. It is fairly certain that no one would have restricted the Servant to a Minority within Israel, or set the Ideal over against the Empirical Israel, if the claims of the Empirical Israel had been above question. Some even of the medieval Rabbis felt constrained to limit the circle of the true Israel.[2] The only modern writer to maintain that the Servant was Israel without any qualification or idealization is Roy.[3] This he could only do by suggesting that the Songs are considerably later than the main prophecy and, if our conclusion about the date of the Songs is right, his theory must be ruled out as inadmissible.

If, however, it is difficult to affirm that the whole of Israel was the Servant, it is attractive, on *a priori* grounds, to suppose that the Servant was the godly Minority within Israel. No theory appears so antecedently reasonable, and the beginner is apt to accept it at once. It seems to make the best of both worlds. But when we come to delimit or qualify, where are we

[1] Bailey, *Phases in the Religion of Ancient Rome*, 1932, p. 270, quoted by E. O. James in *The Labyrinth*, ed. S. H. Hooke, 1935, p. 237.

[2] See *supra*, p. 19 f.

[3] See *supra*, p. 61 f.

to stop? It would seem that we are at once on an inclined slope, and that there is no arresting the process of being carried down until we touch bottom with the admission that what we have in the Songs 'is essentially an individual experience'.[1] Hence attempts like that of Matthew Arnold[2] and, with a somewhat different emphasis, of Wheeler Robinson, to hold all degrees of collective theory together. Moreover, when we ask what is the positive evidence for the modified collective theories, we find none except that the Servant has a mission to Israel. That is just as consistent with an individual as with a minority-collective interpretation. No doubt there were degrees of spiritual responsiveness among Israelites, as there are in any religious community; and even though as early as the exile it is not possible to speak of a well-defined party of *ḥasîdîm*, such as we meet with in the later Psalms and in the time of the Maccabees, we may yet think in terms of the 'disciples' of a prophet like Isaiah (viii. 16; cf. l. 4). But what positive indication is there in the Songs, or indeed anywhere in Deutero-Isaiah, that that Prophet thought of these as the Servant, rather than of an individual, or Israel as a whole? The various 'Minority hypotheses' are more a recognition of the inherent difficulty of the collective theory than a convincing solution of the problem.

Moreover, they raise difficulties of their own. In the last Song the Servant has suffered what the 'many' deserved to suffer, but from which apparently they went free. We can hardly say that a pious minority in Israel suffered while the heedless majority did not. The suffering was shared by all. To say that the physical suffering of the remnant was accompanied by a deeper mental anguish than the majority could feel may be true enough, but such a distinction is over-subtle, and cannot be substantiated from the texts.

When we turn from the 'Minority' theories to the 'Ideal' theory, this difficulty is only accentuated. In what sense can it be maintained that the Ideal Israel suffered for the Empirical? That would only be possible as the Ideal Israel became embodied in an Empirical Minority; in which case we are back where we were. This, indeed, is the course which the Ideal theory has generally taken; it tends to become dissolved into some form of Minority theory, just as the Minority theories

[1] Wheeler Robinson, cf. *supra*, p. 105.
[2] See *supra*, p. 32.

tend to dissolve into one another. Where it has not done this, as with Beck and Kleinert,[1] it has been too abstract and metaphysical to accord with Hebrew conceptions, or indeed with any sort of convincing reality. An exception may be made for Eissfeldt's statement of the Ideal theory, which, however, raises difficulties of its own.[2]

It is, therefore, significant that in the most recent discussions the ordinary Minority theories have almost failed to enlist any supporters. In the period since Mowinckel their only advocates, so far as I have been able to discover, are Miss A. E. Skemp, who asks briefly whether the Servant may not be '*a personification of the faithful in Israel*',[3] A Loisy,[4] who thinks of 'the ideal Israel, the faithful *élite*', and Ed. Bruston,[5] who briefly revived the theory that the Servant was 'an *élite* within the *élite* of the nation', namely, the order of prophets.[6] Of recent advocates of the Ideal theory I have only, apart from Eissfeldt, met with Levy,[7] the only Jew[8]—again so far as I am aware—who has ever owned allegiance to it; and he does not make it clear whether he means ideal in the more abstract sense, or ideal as embodied in a righteous remnant.

It would seem, then, that if we are to adopt the collective interpretation, it must be either in the full sense, or in the 'corporate personality' form of it as advocated by Wheeler Robinson and Eissfeldt. The former, although he allows that a relative truth attaches to the various Minority theories, even to the theory that the Servant is the Prophet himself, neverthe-

[1] See *supra*, p. 32 f.

[2] See *supra*, pp. 105–9.

[3] '"Immanuel" and "The Suffering Servant of Jahweh": A Suggestion', *ET* 44, 1932–3, p. 94 f.

[4] *La Consolation d'Israël*, Paris, 1927, p. 65, and *La Religion d'Israël*, 3e éd., 1933, p. 190 f.

[5] Art. 'Serviteur de l'Éternel', in *Dictionnaire encyclopédique de la Bible*, 2e tome, 1932, pp. 664–7.

[6] The view of Sheldon H. Blank, already mentioned (*supra*, p. 192 n.), though similar, is to be distinguished from this. According to him (op. cit., pp. 20, 29) the Servant is 'the people of Israel, personified as a prophet. . . . *Israel in the guise of a martyr prophet—of a prophet after the pattern of Jeremiah*'.

[7] See *supra*, p. 20.

[8] Blank (see note 6) remarks that 'Deutero-Isaiah distinguishes between the ideal Israel, assigned the role of a prophetic people witnessing to Yahveh's divinity, and the real contemporary Israel, itself still recalcitrant', and quotes with approval Budde's 'Das Volk, wie es werden muss und wird'. If we may distinguish between the Ideal Israel and an idealized Israel, Blank's choice is for the latter, and we may therefore class him with the Empirical Israel theorists.

less insists that the full collective interpretation alone does full justice to the portrait. 'We cannot . . . be true to his (the Prophet's) conception as a whole without saying that for him the Servant *is* Israel. . . . Nothing less than the spectacle of Israel once humiliated, and now to be rehabilitated in the eyes of the nations of the world, will do justice to the imposing scale of the treatment in the fifty-third chapter.'[1] I have already ventured[2] upon some criticisms of the special differentia of the corporate personality exposition of the collective theory. It now remains to examine the collective theory as a whole. We may begin at the two points where Robinson and Eissfeldt anticipate objections to the theory, objections which they grant have a prima-facie reasonableness, and which they seek to remove. Those objections are (1) that the portrait of the Servant is too individual to apply to a community, and (2) that the Servant appears to have a mission to Israel. With regard to the first, it is conceded that the conception of corporate personality would provide a sufficient answer, if that were the only question in dispute. With regard to the second, we took exception to Robinson's suggestion that the Prophet, the effective Servant, was conscious of no contrast between himself and the nation as a whole. However that may be—we will not pursue the matter for the moment—it is significant that this most recent, as well as most attractive, exposition of the collective interpretation does grant that there must be an inner distinction within the Servant Israel. But there are other difficulties in the collective theory besides the two that Robinson and Eissfeldt recognize. Most of them have frequently been urged against the belief that the Songs are by Deutero-Isaiah. We did not feel that they are of sufficient cogency for that; they may, nevertheless, compel the conclusion that the Servant of the Songs is not identical with the Servant Israel of the main prophecy. If I may be permitted to repeat them, they are:

(*a*) *That the Servant in the Songs is anonymous; outside the Songs he is equated with Jacob-Israel.*[3] It is difficult to resist the conclusion that this difference is intentional. Even if it is not intentional, it is hardly less significant.

(*b*) *That the anonymity of the Servant in the Songs is accompanied by a heightened individualization in the portrait of the Servant.*[4] The

[1] *The Cross of the Servant*, p. 36.

[2] See *supra*, p. 110.

[3] See *supra*, pp. 178 ff.

[4] See *supra*, p. 180 f.

real difficulty, a difficulty which the corporate personality theory does not appear to recognize, is not that the portrait of the Servant is highly individualized, but that a markedly heightened individualization appears *pari passu* with anonymity. This also seems intentional. It is, therefore, not sufficient to quote parallels to the individualized conception in the Songs. What we have to account for is the heightened individualization of the Songs, accompanied as it is by anonymity, as contrasted with the Servant Israel of the main prophecy.

(*c*) *That the character of the Servant in the Songs is different from that of the Servant Israel in the rest of the prophecy.*[1] This has always been a stone of stumbling for the full collective theory. The corporate personality theory implicitly, though not explicitly, recognizes the difference. It is a difference that is capable of explanation on the corporate personality principle; but again, it is a question whether the difference is an unconscious one, as the corporate personality theory requires.

(*d*) *That the Servant of the Songs has an active mission; the Servant Israel outside the Songs is the passive recipient of salvation.*[2] Closely related to this is the fact that the attitude to the heathen is more sympathetic in passages relating to the Servant than it is in the rest of the prophecy.[3]

(*e*) Yet another, and, as it seems to me, decisive objection, is one which has been forcibly urged by Fischer,[4] namely, that on the collective theory all the disappointments, the uncomeliness, the sicknesses, sufferings, and death of the Servant are so many allegorical representations of the exile. There is no real progress from the situation depicted in one Song to that depicted in the next. Everything is, so to speak, presented on a flat surface. Instead of a drama moving steadily to a climax, we have a series of tableaux all representing the same situation. This is an obstinate difficulty, and I do not see how even the corporate personality theory is to deal with it.

Nevertheless, if the Songs are by Deutero-Isaiah, or, failing the absolute certainty of that,[5] by a very near contemporary who copied his style and entered deeply into his thought-world, it is clear that we must take as our starting-point the equation the Servant = Israel. But in view of the anonymity of the

[1] See *supra*, p. 181 f.
[2] See *supra*, pp. 182 ff.
[3] See *supra*, p. 184 f.
[4] See *supra*, p. 95.
[5] It will be remembered that we left the question open (*supra*, p. 186).

Servant in the Songs, accompanied as it is by a more distinct individualization, the mission of the Servant to Israel and the heathen, together with other theological differences, it would seem as if we must narrow down the definition of the Servant, as indeed most collectivists have been obliged to do. The higher the task of the Servant becomes, the less is any community capable of fulfilling it. There is expansion and contraction, as the corporate personality theory urges. But I do not think the case is fully met by the suggestion that the effective Servant is the unself-conscious and undifferentiated Prophet himself. I think Dr. H. H. Rowley is right when he says: 'I believe the writer himself would have found difficulty in defining with precision what was in his own mind.'[1] Rowley numbers himself among the collectivists, and in intention he follows Wheeler Robinson.[2] But he goes on to say: 'In general, I believe the author was personifying Israel, but in the fourth poem that personification is carried to a point where it is hard to escape the feeling that he really thought of an individual, so supremely the Servant of Yahweh that within the Servant community He stood out as its representative and leader, carrying its mission of service to a point no other could reach.'[3] Presumably the individual so thought of had not yet appeared, but was still to come. Is, then, the interpretation still collective, or are we not back once more at what is essentially the traditional Messianic interpretation?

4. MESSIANIC INTERPRETATION. CONCLUSION

The fundamental objection to the traditional Messianic interpretation is that it is wedded to a too mechanical doctrine of inspiration. This seems to put it out of court as unworthy of serious consideration. The Prophet is a mere amanuensis, and what he writes has no relevance to the circumstances of his own time. Moreover, if this implies that he 'sees' in advance One who was not to come for another five or six centuries, it raises the difficult philosophical problem whether there can be an actual prevision of history.

It must be admitted that the final appeal to the Messianic interpretation has frequently been based upon verbal similarities, sometimes obscure or even remote, between what is said

[1] *Israel's Mission to the World*, 1939, p. 12.
[2] Ibid., p. 11.
[3] Ibid., p. 13.

about the Servant in Isaiah and what is said about Christ in the New Testament. This objection might even be urged against the otherwise admirable work of Fischer.[1] At its worst it would almost seem as if the exegete approaches the Songs from a systematic theological standpoint of Christ as Prophet, Priest, and King, and reads them in that light.

This fundamentalist attitude to the problem, however, was abandoned by Ley, a contemporary of Duhm,[2] and his lead has since been followed by an increasing number of Messianic interpreters. No one would dream of labelling Gressmann theologically orthodox or conservative, yet he in his last phase came down decisively on the side of a Messianic interpretation.[3] That his exposition was highly speculative is unimportant; the essential point is that the traditional form of Messianic interpretation has given place to one more realistic, which fully recognizes that the conception of the Messiah-Servant arose out of the personal and historical circumstances in which the Prophet found himself, and that, therefore, there need not be entire congruence between the prophecy and its fulfilment in Christ. A few correspondences more or less between the Servant and Christ are not of vital significance. There are, of course, correspondences, but there are also differences; for example, there is no reason to suppose that Christ was so disfigured that He scarcely seemed human—this appears to be a permanent feature of the Servant in the last Song, not in consequence of maltreatment—nor was He buried in a dishonoured grave. The problem of exact and photographic prevision of the future does not, therefore, arise. The essential likeness between the Servant and Jesus lies in this: that whereas prophets like Jeremiah suffered in the course of, or as a result of, their witness, for both the Servant and Jesus suffering is the means whereby they fulfil their misssion and bring it to a triumphant conclusion. This conception is unique in the Old Testament. Hosea's suffering may have taught him his message, but it can hardly be said that he suffered in order to save Gomer or Israel. Jeremiah did not suffer uncomplainingly. Nor is the case of Job really parallel: Job suffers to vindicate God's faith in him in face of the cynical aspersions of the Satan; he does not suffer for others, and even his friends get no farther than the Gentiles

[1] See *supra*, p. 97.
[2] See *supra*, p. 64 f.
[3] See *supra*, pp. 90–4.

did in their first confessedly wrong estimate of the Servant, that he was 'smitten of God, and afflicted'.

To resume at the point to which we arrived in the preceding section, namely, that it is an individual Servant with whom we have at long last to deal: the objections to the newer type of Messianic interpretation are mainly two: (1) that the Servant is to lead Israel out of exile, and therefore, since the Prophet expected a speedy deliverance, he must have had in mind an actual contemporary, someone already born (cf. xlix. 1); (2) that the sufferings of the Servant are past; only his exaltation lies in the future.

These objections are stated by Fischer[1] as being advanced by individualists in favour of an historical as against a Messianic interpretation. Accordingly, they tempt a return to criticism of the historical-individual theories, which we have already found decisive reasons for rejecting. To go over the same ground again would only to be involve ourselves in a vicious circle. Every writer on the subject finds himself obliged to break the circle somewhere, since there is no theory that has been altogether immune from criticism. Moreover, it is only too easy to establish one conclusion by the negative precedure of disproving the others, and this method has far too often been followed. The objections adduced must therefore be met, if that is possible, positively, without once more engaging in recriminations against the historical-individual interpretations. They are:

1. *That the Servant is to lead Israel out of exile, and, since the Prophet expected a speedy deliverance, he must have had in mind an actual contemporary, someone already born.* There is, it is said, no time for the Servant to be born and grow to manhood in the ordinary course of nature. Therefore, since he is 'born of a woman' (cf. xlix. 1), he must be 'already there'.

We should, however, be careful not to exaggerate the definiteness of the political background. We must not be misled by xlii. 6 f., with its reference to one who is to be 'a covenant-bond of the people . . . to open blind eyes, to bring out from the dungeon him that is bound, and them that sit in darkness out of the prison-house'. In its present form the passage probably refers to the Servant, but we have found good reason to believe[2] that it originally referred to Israel, and that it was transformed by means of interpolations into a secondary Servant-Song.

[1] See *supra*, p. 96.

[2] See *supra*, p. 134 f.

Few, indeed, regard it as belonging to the original Song-cycle. Nevertheless, its proximity to the first Song, of which it now reads almost like a continuation, may mislead us, albeit unconsciously, into overweighting the balance in favour of a political activity of the Servant. Actually, the only definite political reference in the generally accepted Songs is in xlix. 5 f., the raising of the tribes of Jacob and the restoring of the survivors of Israel. Even that is ancillary to the conversion of the Gentiles, and it may well be, as we have surmised,[1] that Yahweh directs the Servant to abandon it for the more far-reaching task.[2] Moreover, the whole of the second Song, with its 'Yahweh called me from the womb, from my birth he made mention of my name', is set within the framework of Yahweh's pronouncement—which is mainly in future 'tenses'—in the first Song, an announcement addressed[3] to an audience of supramundane beings whose existence is outside the time-series. In the third Song the political background is so vague that we are left entirely to conjecture as to who the adversaries are. In the fourth, any definite political situation has disappeared. True, the captains and the kings are there, but the whole scene appears to be conceived *sub specie aeternitatis*.

2. *That the sufferings of the Servant are past; only his exaltation lies in the future.* On the vexed question of the tenses it is argued that if the Messianic interpretation were right the tenses would have been either all future, or all past, whereas they are partly past, and partly future. Why, if the Prophet was thinking of someone still to come, did he not, when he described the sufferings as past, also describe the resurrection and exaltation as already accomplished? That, it is claimed,[4] would have made the story really telling. But would it? Would it not rather have presented the whole on a flat surface, with consequent loss of perspective? Further, Isa. liii dates from a time before a belief in the resurrection became general. That may well be the reason why liii. 10 is so ambiguous.[5] The resurrection of

[1] See *supra*, pp. 143 f., 147.

[2] It may be said that I have no right to criticize Wheeler Robinson (*supra*, p. 110) for overlooking the political aspects of the Servant's task, and then myself try to explain them away. My answer is that since Robinson's theory so far approximates to the autobiographical that he thinks of the Prophet himself as the effective Servant, he is not at liberty to overlook the political implications. The position I am advocating is not under the same disability.

[3] See *supra*, p. 142.

[4] So Rudolph, *ZAW* 43, p. 107.

[5] See *supra*, p. 147 f.

the Servant was something which the Prophet must have had difficulty in apprehending clearly. There were a few precedents for it in the literature (1 Kings xvii. 21 ff., 2 Kings iv. 34 f., xiii. 21), but, even supposing that the Prophet was familiar with them, they were not such as to furnish the materials for a circumstantial description. Moreover, as Fischer has very cogently pointed out,[1] there are not wanting indications in chap. liii that the sufferings of the Servant, as well as his exaltation, are still in the future. Even if the Hebrew perfect and imperfect exactly corresponded to our past and future—which they do not—there is no need for us to make quite such a bogey of them as we often do in this connexion. The whole of the last Song is future to the first, which itself is already future.[2] Within it the sufferings of the Servant are described, though not consistently, in past 'tenses'. Moreover, the sufferings in the last Song are set within the framework of Yahweh's declaration concerning his future exaltation. They are described by Gentiles whose eyes are now opened. It is, therefore, in relation to the future that the death of the Servant is past, not in relation to the present of the writer.

In a Presidential Address to the Oxford Society of Historical Theology,[3] Dr. W. F. Lofthouse says of the Suffering Servant:

'To my mind, we can best find in the picture, using the phrase of Dr. J. A. Stewart,[4] the report of a moment of heightened consciousness, so tense and clear that we begin to see, as it were, into the heart of things. It is not a piece of history, biography, or autobiography. The author's experience may have been at work in his mind; and those who look back for a human prototype could not discover a better than Jeremiah himself. But there is no extended representation of the actual. It is not deduced. It comes as something seen: as surprising to the beholder as to those to whom he described it. The abysmal suffering, the contempt and loathing, worse than any agony of the flesh, the divination that it is for their sakes, and the triumph which is nothing but the reinstatement of the hostile mass of the nations in the grace of him who sent the servant on his unimaginable mission—was all this the fruit of long brooding over a martyr's fate? A Christian can hardly be expected to appreciate the dark splendour of it all. "Why", he says, "it is Jesus; if not in detail, yet in every essential". Our faith has made it current coin.

[1] See *supra*, p. 96. [2] See *supra*, p. 142.

[3] *Abstract of Proceedings for the Academic Year 1945–6*, p. 15.

[4] *The Myths of Plato*, 1905.

But that is precisely its glory. Five centuries before Calvary, the enigma of the cross was seen, and understood. It came, as such rare things will—Plato's myths, for example, if Stewart may be followed here—not with observation. Like the Kingdom of Heaven, it had to be waited for, received, seized. Details, repellent to us and inconsistent with each other, when viewed separately, now assume an unexpected fitness, aesthetic no less than religious. Without it the problem of the crucified Messiah itself might have been as perplexing to us as to the Messiah's first disciples'.

Accordingly, Lofthouse would call the Songs by what he intends, in this context, to be the dignified name of myth: they 'may be regarded as the summit of Old Testament Prophecy, where prophecy indeed rises to something else to which I would give the name of Myth'. Here it must be remarked that neither of us is now using the words myth and mythological quite in the sense in which they have previously been used in this study, of theories which regard the figure of the Servant simply as a development from or suggested by, Babylonian or other extra-Israelite mythologies. In what sense, then, are we using it? I imagine in the sense defined by Dr. C. C. J. Webb:[1]

'A philosophic myth, then, after the fashion of Plato, is a story told about individuals, where memory and history and prophecy (if such a thing there be) have failed us, so that we do not know from these, the only possible sources of information about individual facts in the past and future, what was or what will be the fate of the individuals about whom we are curious. It is a story thus which is quite likely to be untrue—nay, even quite unlikely to be true in detail, but which is in the Platonic phrase "like the truth", because it is controlled by our knowledge, obtained through Philosophy, of that fundamental nature of the universal system which any particular event falling within it must of necessity exemplify. It thus illustrates our philosophical knowledge without adding to it, and gives the outline of the historical fact, which is unknown in detail, because it belongs either to a forgotten past or to an unforeseen future (I do not here inquire whether the future can ever be foreseen) or again, to a present beyond our ken'.

If we substitute Prophecy/prophetic for Philosophy/philosophic, and Deutero-Isaiah for Plato in this paragraph, we have a striking commentary on the nature and purpose of the Servant-Songs. Webb is cautious as to 'whether the future can ever be foreseen', but that does not alter the fact that many

[1] *God and Personality*, 1918, p. 170.

myths do relate to the future: the *Phaedrus* Myth, for example, and the *Divina Commedia* of Dante;[1] and if Plato had developed Glaucon's prophecy of the fate of the just man,[2] we might have had a myth strikingly similar to Isa. liii. Another possible parallel is the fourth Eclogue of Virgil, on which R. S. Conway comments: 'Understood in the only way possible to the mind of the early centuries, that Eclogue made him a direct prophet, and therefore an interpreter of Christ; and it is not the deepest students of Virgil who have thought him unworthy of such a ministry'.[3]

Further, to quote Webb again: 'the philosophical myth may provisionally take the place of history which we have not at hand in memory or on record.'[4] 'Provisionally', since presumably the historian, as he pushes his researches back into the past, may recover tidings of some happening for which myth has had to serve in the meantime. Presumably also, a myth may subsequently become actualized in history, as Isa. liii was. For 'it is scarcely necessary to add that, if the interpretation put by the Christian Church on certain occurrences should be admitted, genuine history would then to a certain extent supersede myth'.[5]

It so happens that Webb's discussion of philosophic myth is extraordinarily relevant to the problem with which we are engaged. He has been arguing[6] that of metaphors which may be used to express the relation of the Divine Spirit to our spirits, that of *creation* emphasizes the *difference*, and those of *procreation* and *emanation* the *identity* between the two terms of the relation. The conception of a Mediator, who is the *Son* of God and so distinguished from *created* spirits, is an attempt to unite the advantages of the two metaphors of creation and procreation; and if it be objected that such a conception of a Mediator must be dismissed as mythological, the objection is inadmissible. Such is the gist of Webb's argument, though he is not, of course, dealing directly with the Servant.

Now the issue as between creation and emanation is not

[1] 'the greatest of all Myths', Stewart, op. cit., p. 339.

[2] *Republic*, ii. 362.

[3] *Ancient Italy and Modern Religion*, the last sentence in the book.

[4] Op. cit., p. 177.

[5] Op. cit., p. 179: 'to a certain extent' does not invalidate the application of the principle to the portrait of the Servant and its fulfilment in Christ; Webb explains it as meaning that for any description of the pre-existent and the ascended life of Christ we must still resort to myth.

[6] Op. cit., Lecture VII, 'The Problem of Creation'.

contemplated in the Old Testament. The Old Testament knows nothing of pantheism, though its emphasis upon the transcendence of God did in time raise problems of its own, and lead to conceptions of angelic and other mediators. The horizons of Old Testament thought are more restricted than those of either Greek philosophy or Christian theism. The problems it faces are practical and soteriological, not speculative and philosophical. For the Hebrews it is moral factors that complicate the relation of the Divine to the human spirit. Nor is the Servant yet the Son of God, but he is in a real sense a mediator. And very much as the Alexandrian doctrine of the Logos became actualized in the Word become flesh, so did the Deutero-Isaianic portrait of the Servant become actualized in Him who gave His life 'a ransom for many'. If there was to be any anticipation of Calvary in the Old Testament—as, on any showing, there is in Isa. liii—it is difficult to see what form it could take except one analogous to Platonic myth. No 'extended representation of the actual', to use Lofthouse's phrase, whether of Israel, or the Remnant, or Jeremiah, or Jehoiachin, or the Prophet himself, could produce the Servant-Songs. We may make any selection from them that we please—which is to say that we shall then be dealing with an ideal and not an historical figure—and we shall have the incongruities of the Songs. But even if we take all of them together we shall still be left with something more. As to where that something more came from it is not the purpose of this book to inquire. I only insist that there is something more, and that none of the historical interpretations does adequate justice to it.

We have, then, when we have done our best with the historical interpretations, to deal with a plus, a plus to any one of them taken singly, a plus to any selection of them, a plus even to all of them taken together. That plus is a unique individual who obviously has not yet appeared. By this I do not mean to impose a uniform interpretation on all the Songs. If, as we have seen, the Songs are the work of Deutero-Isaiah, there is reason in Snaith's contention[1] that 'we have in Isa. xl–lv a great number of separate pieces, in some of which there are references to the Servant, but with four of them at one end of the scale, similar enough in substance for Duhm to be led to notice them particularly and to isolate them from the rest'. Let it be granted,

[1] 'The So-called Servant Songs', *ET* 56, p. 80.

then, that we have a passage like xli. 8, with its explicit 'Israel my servant', at the one end, and lii. 13–liii. 12 at the other. Snaith's contention is 'that the whole case for insertion (i.e. of the "Songs" in the rest of the prophecy) breaks down. The so-called Servant Poems are no more insertions than any other sections in Isa. xl–lv'. This may readily be granted; there is now hardly any question of 'insertions' in the sense that Duhm asserted. At the same time, we have four passages 'at one end of the scale', passages which are 'similar enough in substance' to justify our treating them more or less separately from the rest. In them we seem to be dealing with a Servant *kat' exochén*. Whether the line between him and the Servant-Israel should be drawn exactly where Duhm drew it may be open to question, though most scholars since his time have drawn it approximately where he did. What if, perchance, a line, or even lines, should be drawn within the 'Songs' themselves, with (say) xlix. 1–6 on this side, and lii. 13–liii. 12 on the other? We have seen[1] that the four 'Songs' are not *uno tenore* with the prophecy, nor yet entirely so with one another. Nor are they *uno tempore* with the prophecy, nor again with one another.[2] I am prepared to grant that the Prophet's thought reaches its highest level in the last Song; at the same time the first Song does mark a distinct advance upon anything that is said about the Servant in the prophecy outside the Songs. But wherever we draw our line, on one side of it is a plus for which we cannot account by any of the historical interpretations.

This means that if we consider Deutero-Isaiah's thought as a whole, or even, it may be, within the confines of the four 'Songs', there is a certain fluidity in his conception of the Servant. Bentzen[3] rightly reflects the trend of current opinion when he says that we ought not to confine ourselves to 'either-or' categories—'The Servant of Yahweh is at once the Messiah, and Israel, and Deutero-Isaiah, and his circle'. By including the Messiah, he goes beyond Wheeler Robinson, who did so much to emphasize the expansion and contraction of the Servant-idea. Nowhere in his references to individual theories does Wheeler Robinson appear to have contemplated the possibility of an ultimate ideal or Messianic interpretation. As I understand him, the 'ebb and flow' of Deutero-Isaiah's

[1] *Supra*, pp. 150, 154 f. [2] *Supra*, p. 188.
[3] *Indledning til det Gamle Testamente*, p. 100.

thought was from Israel *to his own prophetic consciousness*, and back to Israel. As I see it, the direction was rather from collective Israel to an individual who was neither himself nor anyone else who had lived hitherto. This is substantially the position of Umbreit[1] and Delitzsch[2] a century ago. The figure is a pyramid, not a circle.

It remains to be asked whether, and in what sense, the interpretation to which we have been led is properly to be called 'Messianic'. It is agreed on all hands that the portrait of the Servant did ultimately find its actualization in Christ. But, did the Prophet expect anything of the kind? Did he look for a fulfilment of his vision in history? Or were the Songs only his Hebrew way of discussing the problem of suffering? A distinction must be made between Messianic and Ideal, and the mythological approach is consistent with either interpretation. Is the Prophet only saying, much as Glaucon said of the perfectly just man, 'In such a situation the just man will be scourged, racked, fettered, will have his eyes burnt out, and at last, after suffering every kind of torture, will be crucified,' which is only conditional prophecy, since there may be no perfectly just man? Is he saying, '*If* such a one as the Servant were to come, this is how he *would* be treated'? Or is he saying, 'The Servant will come, and this is how he *will* be treated'?

The answer is hardly in doubt; the Prophet expected the Servant to come. He may, perchance, have been so rapt in contemplation of the vision that he did not stay to ask if it would ever be actualized. But if he had been asked, 'Do you look for the Servant to come?' his answer must surely have been, 'Certainly'. The Songs are myth—provisional or anticipated history—not allegory.

'Myth thinking may be described as an imaginative picture of the world shaped in terms of the powers and feelings of man's own inner life. In creative mythological imagination these powers take on an independent life and character of their own; they become the actors in cosmogonies and theogonies, and are not thought of as mere personified abstractions. . . . Allegory is a mode of expression in which the author and reader are aware that the figures are fictions —personifications of forces, emotions, virtues, temptations—and the meaning can be translated back into conceptual terms'.[3]

[1] *Supra*, p. 38. [2] *Supra*, p. 44.

[3] Dorothy M. Emmet, *The Nature of Metaphysical Thinking*, 1945, p. 100.

On this definition the Servant is anything but an allegorical figure. Even though the vision may have appeared to the Prophet from heaven, it is on earth that the tragedy and its sequel are enacted. The chastisements of the Servant are to bring peace to the Gentiles. It was a real world, this world, in which he was to accomplish his mission.

Even so, is there—as the critics of the Messianic interpretation have a perfect right to demand—any relation between the Prophet's vision of the Servant and the circumstances in which he found himself at the close of the exile? Assuredly there is. The Songs are quite evidently born of an intense anguish of soul, anguish such as the Prophet must have experienced when Cyrus, whom he had expected to be a kind of first-fruits of Yahwism among the Gentiles, proclaimed instead his enthusiasm for Bel-Marduk. This point has been made by Eissfeldt, Hempel, and others;[1] the Servant is to be a complete contrast to Cyrus. It is clear, in any case, that the glowing expectations of the Prophet in his early ministry were very inadequately realized. The fall of Babylon did not usher in the golden age, but a time of disillusionment and hopes deferred.

Another point: the Prophet can hardly have been blind to the inadequacy of his own people to be the perfect Servant of Yahweh. Nor was he. This is quite clear from what he says about them, even if we regard as later insertions those passages in the book which depict them in the darkest colours. After all, no nation or, for that matter, no religious community ever has acted, or perhaps ever can act, as the Servant does in the last Song; and the Prophet was realist enough to know it. Cyrus failed. Israel failed. We may well believe that the Prophet suffered a martyrdom of soul, even though there is no evidence that he suffered the physical martyrdom conjectured by Mowinckel, Elliger, and Sidney Smith.

The Songs give little indication of the time when the Servant was expected to come, whether in the near or the distant future. If we are to look for any indication at all, it is in what is said of the raising of the tribes of Jacob and the restoring of the survivors of Israel in xlix. 5 f. This might seem to demand a speedy fulfilment. But compared with the ultimate mission of the Servant it is relatively unimportant, and the reference to it is almost disparaging: 'Too trifling (*nāqēl*) is it that thou shouldest

[1] See *supra*, pp. 77, 109.

be my servant to raise up the tribes of Jacob, and to restore the survivors of Israel; so I make thee a light to the nations. . . .' A political role—especially if Yahweh bids the Servant abandon his first attempts to undertake it—is as little relevant to the real mission of the Servant as it was to that of Jesus; indeed, if we may assume that Jesus at the beginning of His ministry had some thought of a dominion that would bring about the political emancipation of His own people (cf. Matt. iv. 8 f., Luke iv. 5 ff.), the correspondence between the Servant myth and its actualization in history is all the more striking. However that may be, the Songs themselves throw little light upon the question, how soon did the Prophet expect the Servant to come?

In conclusion, is the Servant the Messiah as the Messiah was conceived in Old Testament times, as the anointed King of the house of David? For my part, I do not think that anything is to be gained by attempts to prove that the Servant is the Davidic Messiah of Isa. ix and xi. Though there are undoubtedly kingly features in the Servant, there is nothing in the Songs to indicate that he was to be an anointed king. In what came to be the traditional Jewish sense of the word Messiah, the Servant is less a Messianic figure than Jesus was, since it can hardly be insisted that he was of the lineage of David. Indeed, it was precisely because the Messianic consciousness of Jesus was so dominated by the Servant conception that the Jews failed to recognize Him as the Messiah. The Servant is a soteriological rather than a political Messianic figure.

The Prophet, then, saw Reality in a few brief but vivid flashes, and he pictured what he saw, not indeed in a portrait photographically exact, but full and exact enough for Jesus to recognize it as pointing to Himself. Can we discern a divine purpose in this? I believe we can. It is almost universally admitted that Jesus saw His way by the light that Isa. liii shed upon His predestined path. His acceptance of the Cross, if we may say so reverently, would have been more difficult than it was if He had not 'served Himself heir' to the Servant. May we not, then, in the light of the principle of the unity of Scripture, believe that in the purpose of God the Servant-Songs were primarily intended to afford Him guidance? This, of course, could be true no matter who the original Servant was, whether he was the collective Israel, or even Jehoiachin. But since there appears to be no intermediate link between the Servant as the Prophet described him, and the Servant as Jesus fulfilled the description—no writer between the Exile and the Advent took it up and expanded it, and what fleeting references there are to it show that its true significance was not grasped at all—I find it hard to believe that the Prophet in his moments of deepest insight intended one thing and the Holy Spirit another. It seems more natural to conclude that both intended the same. Original and Fulfilment join hands across the centuries.

POSTSCRIPT

RECENT SCANDINAVIAN DISCUSSIONS[1]

THE debate in Scandinavia resolves itself into a triangular contest between Oslo, Uppsala, and Copenhagen, with, as we should expect, some differences of view within the Uppsala group itself.

We may begin with Oslo. As has already been said,[2] Mowinckel[3] in 1921 advanced the theory that the Servant was the Prophet, Deutero-Isaiah himself. The Prophet-Servant composed all the 'Songs', even the last (Isa. lii. 13–liii. 12), in which he anticipated his approaching death. By 1931 Mowinckel felt constrained to abandon this view of the provenance of the Songs.[4] Instead, we are to look for their origin in 'Trito-Isaianic' circles. He still adhered, though with somewhat less confidence, to his original thesis that the Servant was the Prophet. The Servant was *possibly*, indeed even probably Deutero-Isaiah, who, it is to be presumed, had been martyred and was now 'in faith extolled as cult-hero and delineated with mythological colouring'. On this last point he has since[5] called attention to a possible parallel between the Servant and *Krt*, who in a Ras Shamra text is called 'the servant of El' (*'bd 'el*).

Mowinckel's later and penultimate position is expounded in the third volume of the Norwegian Translation-Commentary on the Old Testament.[6] It does not differ materially from the modified 'autobiographical' theory which he adopted in 1931. On one or two points of exegesis he appears to have changed his mind. He no longer speaks of the Servant as having been martyred,[7] but as dying of leprosy.[8] The speakers ('we') in chapter liii are no longer the Gentiles,[9] but 'the poet himself and the circle of Jews who share his view of the Servant'.[10]

[1] For a summary of Swedish discussions, with full bibliography, see C. Lindhagen, 'Ebed Jahve-problemet i svensk exegetik. En översikt', *SEÅ* 18–19, pp. 32–71.

[2] See *supra*, pp. 72 ff.

[3] *Der Knecht Jahwäs.*

[4] See *supra*, p. 80 f.

[5] 'Til uttrykket "Jahvaes tjener": Streiflys fra Ugarit II', *Norsk teologisk tidsskrift* 43, pp. 24 ff.; cf. *supra*, p. 81.

[6] *Det Gamle Testamente, III: De Senere Profeter*, oversatt av Sigmund Mowinckel og N. Messel, Oslo, 1944, pp. 192–201 and notes on the several Songs.

[7] Cf. *supra*, p. 81.

[8] *GT III*, pp. 194, 248 f.

[9] As in *Der Knecht Jahwäs*, pp. 37 n, 45.

[10] *GT III*, p. 246.

Mowinckel insists that the Servant is depicted as a prophet, not as a king.[1] He still thinks that the most likely answer to the question, 'Who was the Servant?' is that he was 'an actual historical person, a prophet and missionary who lived among the Jews not long before the poet's own time; and who, the poet and others expected, would soon be raised again from the dead';[2] and since two of the Songs are in the first person, the most natural assumption is that he was the Second Isaiah, who was the founder and inspiration of the 'Trito-Isaianic' circle. But—and this is the significant difference between Mowinckel's position in 1944 as compared with 1921–31—'What is decisive, however, is not *who* the historical Servant was, but *what* he *is*.'[3] This leads him to say that 'the historical person who in the present instance stands behind the Servant-figure may, for that matter, have been more an occasion for the prophetic description of the future, perfect Servant of God and saviour, than an exact model'.[4] This, of course, raises anew 'the question whether the Servant belongs to the present (or immediate past) of the poet, or whether he belongs entirely to the future, perhaps as an eschatological great-figure (*størrelse*)?'[5] On this, says Mowinckel, no absolutely decisive answer is possible. But the tenses in the Songs 'do not exclude the possibility that the Servant is a purely future figure whom the Prophet had seen and heard in his inspired imagination. The thought is then: (not a political and military Messiah, but) such an one as he has described in this prophetic picture of "the Servant" must and shall one day come. . . .'[6] Finally, Mowinckel stresses that in any case the Servant is a 'soteriological' rather than a 'Messianic' or 'eschatological' figure—'The Servant is a "saviour-figure", behind whom there stands an historical person.'[7]

Mowinckel's emphasis upon the immediate historical background of the Servant-figure does not mean that he overlooks traces in it of more ancient conceptions. It is relevant to notice these here because they are in a measure parallel with those

[1] Ibid., pp. 192 *et passim*.
[2] Ibid., p. 196.
[3] Ibid. It may be remarked that Mowinckel seems to go out of his way to write a *Christian* commentary on the texts—a welcome precedent for future expositors.
[4] Ibid.
[5] Ibid., p. 195.
[6] Ibid.
[7] Ibid., p. 197.

adduced almost contemporaneously by H. S. Nyberg.[1] For one thing, since the Servant conception is the high-water mark of the prophetic revelation, it may be taken as certain that features from earlier prophets and men of God have been taken up into it. A second antecedent is the concept of what in English we are accustomed to call corporate personality. Mowinckel does not intend this as a concession to the collective interpretation, nor as any admission that there are collective features in the portrait. What he has in mind is only that 'the one can atone for all in such measure as they by their own will and consciousness identify themselves with the one, with his person and his work'.[2] For the same reason it is natural for the poet to express his thoughts about the death and saving work of the Servant in figures taken from the sacrificial ritual. A further not unimportant precursor of the poet's faith in the Servant's resurrection is to be seen in thoughts and style-forms derived from psalms of lamentation and thanksgiving. In these a sick man was wont to describe himself as if he were gone down to the grave and were already dead, or to give thanks because he had been raised from the dead. In the Psalms this is little more than a style-form, though the suppliant no doubt did believe that God could perform such a miracle as raising the dead. But what in the Psalms is only a figure, is, in the last Servant-Song, to become a reality. Finally, Mowinckel refers to the widespread myth of the dying and rising god as having contributed something both to the psalms of lamentation and to the last Song, and he calls attention once more to the title *'bd 'el* in the text from Ugarit.

Mowinckel's most recent word on the subject is contained in his book on the Messiah.[3] He is still prepared to concede that the Servant may be a purely future figure 'whom the prophet saw and heard in his inspired imagination'.[4] But he thinks it most probable that he was an actual historical in-

[1] Nyberg's article (see *infra*, p. 223, n. 7) was published two years before the Norwegian *GT III*. Once only, so far as I can discover, in a textual note on Isa. liii. 10 (op. cit., p. 793), does Mowinckel refer to it. What he writes about the origins of the Servant conception makes no reference to Nyberg, and it may be assumed that it was written before Nyberg's work was published.

[2] Op. cit., p. 197.

[3] *Han som kommer*, 1951. An English translation of this is in preparation by G. W. Anderson, under the title *He That Cometh*. References in what follows are to the Norwegian edition.

[4] Op. cit., p. 167.

dividual. 'This prophetic figure probably lived some time after Deutero-Isaiah, we know not where, but in all probability in Palestine.'[1] This is very like Duhm's 'leprous rabbi' theory over again, since Mowinckel thinks that the Servant died of leprosy, not as a malefactor. It also discounts the close linguistic affinities between the Songs and Deutero-Isaiah, which Mowinckel asserts can be sufficiently accounted for if we assume that their author 'adopted figures and phrases from Deutero-Isaiah'.[2]

Mowinckel has never wavered in his conviction that the Servant is a prophetic, not a royal figure, and he argues this strongly against Engnell's attempt to see in the Servant the future Messiah depicted in the categories of the pre-exilic kings.[3] He can find no proof that the Israelite king was 'Tammuz', nor that a representation of the king's suffering and death had any place in the cult-rituals.[4] 'Even if ideas about the tree of life which dies and blossoms again, and the king-god who dies and lives again, should be the ultimate ideological and stylistic background for the thought of the Servant's death and resurrection—and in a certain sense it is correct to say that that was the case—this does not in the least prove that the Servant was thought of as a king. For in both Babylonian and Israelite religion these figures became in the course of time "democratized"; that is to say, although they were first employed in the cultus to describe the relationship of the king to the god . . . they came later to be applied to ordinary men and their relationship to the god.'[5] He adds in a footnote,[6] 'This is admitted by both Widengren and Engnell, so that the question ceases to be relevant to the historical and exegetical interpretation of the Servant's identity, and becomes only a question of the ultimate background of this or that feature in the portrait'. We should see more clearly round all these problems if we could determine when the 'democratization' of the old rituals and concepts began.

I turn now to Uppsala. There is little doubt that Nyberg's article 'Man of Sorrows' in the *Swedish Exegetical Yearbook*[7] will take its place as one of the great contributions to the subject.

[1] Ibid., p. 168.
[2] Ibid., p. 170.
[3] See *infra*, pp. 228 ff.
[4] Op. cit., p. 62.
[5] Ibid., p. 152.
[6] 154, p. 345.
[7] 'Smärtornas man. En studie till Jes. 52.13-53.12', *SEÅ* 7, pp. 5–82.

He begins by observing that modern exegetes are accustomed to assume from the obscurities of Isa. lii. 13–liii. 12 that its text must be seriously corrupt, and that they then proceed to emend it on the basis of the versions, particularly the LXX, cheerfully resorting to conjecture where the versions fail. But, insists Nyberg, an obscure text is not necessarily a corrupted text, witness the Indian Sutras and the Persian Gathas. To resort to conjectural emendation is waste of time, because if a text really is corrupted no amount of guesswork can cure it, and we must be as content as we can with what we have. Nor are we free, without further ado, to emend on the basis of a version, even a version as old as the LXX. We must first carefully examine the version—in this case particularly the LXX—to see what are the ideas which dominate it. It may be that the differences between it and the MT are due not to its being translated from a different Hebrew recension, but to the translator's contriving to force the original into a thought-pattern of his own.

Nyberg then proceeds to analyse the LXX. He finds that the text as printed in Swete (Codex B) is not in all points the original LXX, that the oldest witness to the present LXX is Clement of Rome (A.D. 96), and that the New Testament citations point in places to something closer to the original. He maintains that the Hebrew text from which the LXX was first made differed very little from our MT, and that the differences between the LXX and Hebrew texts of Isa. liii are due to the translator's having handled his original so roughly as to come very near to doing violence to it. What he, an Egyptian Jew, had in mind, and proceeded to accommodate his translation to, was a triangular drama between God, the sinful world of men, and a righteous man, 'my παῖς'. This Hellenistic interpretation of the Servant was carried farther by the Wisdom of Solomon (iv. 20–v. 23).

Nyberg prefaces his examination of the MT with some observations on the question of metre. He denies that Hebrew metre was as regular as is commonly assumed, and he will allow no emendation *metri causa.* So far as I can see he defends the MT to the last consonant, and manages to extract a coherent translation from it, just as it stands. If this should seem impossible, we do well to remember that it is only what the Authorised and Revised Versions did without any serious reservations, though sometimes, of course, Nyberg has to treat as deliberate archaisms, expressions which most moderns assume to be textual corruptions. In a word, Nyberg would have us believe that the LXX and the MT go back to a common original which, almost to the last detail, was identical with the present MT.

What Nyberg has accomplished in his handling of the Greek and Hebrew texts may turn out to be a *tour de force*. But it is, to say the least, remarkable that he wrote what he did five years before the discovery of the Qumran scrolls. These scrolls are widely asserted to date from the pre-Christian era, and both the Isaiah texts reveal a text of Isa. liii more like the MT than the emended texts on which, since Duhm, expositions of the passage have frequently been based. If the scrolls are pre-Christian, and if Nyberg's explanation of the differences between the LXX and MT is the right one—and a pre-Christian date for the scrolls would go far to say that he is—then most commentaries on the passage will have to be rewritten.

The most striking detail in Nyberg's translation of the passage is his treatment of the word *šᵉmûʿāṯēnû* (RV 'our report', mg. 'that which we have heard') in liii. 1. This he understands as 'the myth preserved in the tradition', a rendering which has since occasioned lively discussion. Like Mowinckel, too, he thinks the Servant is depicted as a leper, and he takes the expression 'kings shall shut their mouths at him' as meaning that they take every precaution to avoid contamination from him.

Viewing the description as a whole, Nyberg says it is clear from the beginning that the Servant is a more-than-individual (*överindividuell*) figure, notwithstanding that the description moves throughout on the individual plane. He has been at work in the past and will continue to be active in the future. 'This oscillation in time is equally typical of the text with the oscillation between individual and that which is more than individual.'[1]

The roots of the Servant-idea, or *myth*, as it is proper to call it, are to be found in three motifs: (1) the shoot (EVV. 'tender plant', liii. 2) which springs up in the desert leads us to the Tammuz-mystery; (2) the man who, though guiltless, bears the wrong-doings of many, and endures woe and punishment for them so that it may be well with them, leads us to the

[1] Op. cit., p. 64.

kingship-ideology of the Ancient East and to the role of the king in the great cult-drama at the beginning of every new year; (3) the man who secures a long and happy existence for his descendants leads us to the ancestor-ideology which was so powerful a factor in the tribal organization of the desert.

There is no need to reproduce in any detail Nyberg's exposition of these three motifs. All of them are sufficiently familiar to English-speaking readers. Thus, it has long been suggested that there is some relation between the Servant-figure and Tammuz, whether it be that the Servant is Tammuz, or, as is more usual, that there are more or less conscious literary reminiscences of the Tammuz-mystery in the descriptions of him.[1] As to kingship-ideology, Britain is generally regarded abroad as the home of the 'Myth and Ritual' school,[2] rather to the embarrassment of British scholars, who find their suggestions carried farther by Uppsala than they ever anticipated or intended. As to ancestor-ideology, this is substantially Wheeler Robinson's 'corporate personality', though Nyberg's handling of it is more akin to that of Pedersen and Eissfeldt than to that of Wheeler Robinson.[3]

We are familiar, then, with each of Nyberg's motifs, taken singly. What is original about his presentation is that he appeals to all of them together, and since he does so, the expectation lies near to hand that he will attempt some sort of a synthesis of them. As, indeed, he does. Take the first two, the Tammuz-mystery and the kingship-ideology. The Hebrews learned their kingship from the Canaanites. They could hardly do otherwise. Now the divinized founders of Canaanite dynasties were supposed to be incarnations of the dying and rising god. 'We have therefore every reason to assume', says Nyberg, that among the Hebrews 'the usual Canaanitish Adonis-conceptions about death and rebirth were associated with the king's person and with the dynasty-founder David, and that the king's penance was an integral part of the New-year-festival ritual.'[4] In other words, the king was Tammuz.

Further, in accordance with the conception of corporate personality—to use again our familiar English term for it—

[1] Cf. *supra*, pp. 69 ff., 101 f., 201 f.

[2] Cf. *Myth and Ritual*, 1933, and *The Labyrinth*, 1935, both edited by S. H. Hooke.

[3] Cf. *supra*, pp. 105–9.

[4] Op. cit., p. 68.

the king represents the ancestor Jacob-Israel; indeed, he *is* Jacob-Israel.[1] This in its turn means that Jacob-Israel, the founder of the nation, is a kind of prototype of the king. From this there results a certain transformation of the ancestor-ideology which Israel had inherited from the desert. The ancestor comes to assume some of the features of Tammuz and to be involved in a Tammuz-drama.[2] Here the sufferings of Jacob at Bethel and the Jabbok acquire significance. Thus: 'In and with the New-year-festival conception of the king's vicarious suffering, the conditions are given for ideas about the vicarious suffering of an ancestor Jacob or Israel for the people who are his seed, because with him the king was actually identified.'[3]

According to Nyberg, then, what we have in the Hebrew original of Isa. liii is a figure of super-individual, superhuman proportions, very different from the somewhat conventional lay-figure of the LXX. He embraces the people as a whole, and the ancestor Jacob who still lives and suffers in his descendants. He is at once individual and collective. The disjunctive collective *or* individual is therefore false. The Servant is both or neither, whichever we please. He is Israel in the sense both of ancestor and people. The ancestor in him bears clear traces of the kingship-ideology, which in its turn has taken up into itself the Tammuz-Adonis drama. At the same time the text goes far beyond the kingship-ideology and the Tammuz-Adonis drama. It has completely broken through the thought-boundaries in which it was originally conceived. Indeed, we can almost speak of an allegorical use of the myth-material. The old myth has become little more than an outer vestment, a style-form.[4] The inner reality behind the drama of the Servant is of a completely different kind. This means that the Tammuz = king elements in the description should not be taken too literally. The individual features in the Servant must be derived from actual models, and they cannot be derived from the kingship-ideology, still less from any individual king. For the kingdom was fallen, dead and doomed. During the exile it stood condemned as the most shocking example of apostasy from Yahweh. Instead, the prophets themselves assumed the

[1] Ibid, p. 71.
[2] Ibid., p. 72; cf. H. Riesenfeld, *Jésus transfiguré*, pp. 86 ff. [3] Ibid., p. 74.
[4] Ibid., p. 78.

position of religious founders and leaders. They had long claimed the title 'servants of Yahweh'. They could, therefore, as well as the king, be said to represent the ancestor Israel and therewith also his descendants; they were the ideal, the true Israel. In this connexion we cannot forbear to think of Jeremiah and Isaiah, especially if, as is not impossible, there is truth in the tradition that the latter had suffered martyrdom under Manasseh.

So Nyberg comes to his final paragraph: 'The spiritual development among the Greeks describes a curve which can be expressed in the formula "from *mythos* to *logos*": the world of myth is succeeded by the world of reason, the thought-forms of myth by abstract thought-forms, and the mythical associations of ideas by systematized knowledge. The Semitic development presents a completely different curve, for which we may suitably employ the formula, "The Word became flesh": what was once conceived in the words and thought-forms of myth is taken up into a living man, in whom it takes manhood and becomes a reality in and through him.'[1]

This brings us to another Uppsala scholar, Ivan Engnell,[2] whose interpretation is avowedly Messianic. To understand his theory, one must know the views of the Uppsala 'School' about the place of the king in the thought and cultus of Israel.[3] On this Engnell may speak for himself. Briefly, all kings in the Ancient East were

. . . *sacral* kings, priest-kings, with all that that implies from the cultic and ideological standpoint. Their kingdoms were thus supposed to be of divine origin, instituted by the gods, and at the same time representations of conditions in the heavenly world. . . . The king himself was of divine origin, begotten in the womb of the mother-goddess by the god himself, born as his son, indeed, before birth

[1] Op. cit., pp. 81 f.

[2] 'Till frågan om Ebed Jahve-sångerna och den lidande Messias hos "Deutero-jesaja"', *SEÅ* 10, 1945, pp. 31–65, published in a revised English translation as 'The Ebed Yahweh Songs and the Suffering Messiah in Deutero-Isaiah', in *Bulletin of the John Rylands Library*, vol. 31, No. 1, Jan. 1948, pp. 1–42. See also article 'Herrens Tjänare' in *Svenskt Bibliskt Uppslagsverk*, Första Bandet, utgivet av Ivan Engnell och Anton Fridrichsen, 1948, cols. 844 ff. Engnell's position is shared by Geo Widengren, *Religionens Värld*, 1945, p. 6, n. 3; similarly H. Riesenfeld, *Jésus transfiguré*, Copenhagen, 1947, pp. 81–96, and F. F. Hvidberg, *Den Israelitiske Religions Historie*, Copenhagen, 1944, p. 169.

[3] See Engnell's article 'Konung' in the *Uppslagsverk*, i, cols. 1221–6; also *Gamla Testamentet: en traditionshistorisk inledning*, i, pp. 142 ff., and, in English, *Studies in Divine Kingship in the Ancient Near East*, 1943, *passim*.

pre-existent as a divine being. He is 'identical' with the god himself, both with the creator 'high-god' and especially with 'the young god', the dying and rising god of vegetation. For this reason all divine attributes are ascribed to him: he is eternal, almighty, all-wise, absolute judge, creator, and sustainer, embodying completely in himself, and therewith also responsible for, the cosmic order, 'righteousness', and the seasonal changes of nature, particularly the rain, upon which all fruitfulness depends.[1]

With this 'myth' there is associated an elaborate ritual. The ritual is primary to the myth, and the myth is an integral part of the ritual. The features of this 'pattern' are familiar enough to readers of *Myth and Ritual*.

The particular aspect of the kingship which Engnell emphasises in connexion with the Servant is that in which the king 'suffers' in the New-year ritual, when he is publicly humiliated before the god and smitten on the cheek by the high-priest.[2] This parallel was noted as long ago as 1925 by Lorenz Dürr,[3] though only in relation to the New-year festival in Babylonia, which the Prophet in exile, he thought, may actually have witnessed. Nyberg took it as 'certain' that something of the kind was an element in the corresponding pre-exilic Israelite ritual,[4] though he did not adduce any direct evidence for it in the Old Testament. Engnell, however, following a suggestion by A. R. Johnson[5] that in certain Psalms the Davidic king is represented as humiliated and suffering, proposes to treat Johnson's and a great many other Psalms as 'psalms of the Ebed-Yahweh type', and then to see in the Servant the future Messiah depicted in the categories of the pre-exilic kings.[6] Indeed, he goes so far as to assert that a large proportion of pre-exilic Psalms—and this for him means a large proportion of the Psalms as a whole—are Royal Psalms. The ground for this assumption is that the Temple was originally a royal chapel, with the king's person central in the cultus. The king was the incarnation of Yahweh and at the same time representative of the people over whom he ruled and in whose name he prayed. All Psalms entitled 'Of David' are Royal Psalms, the term *l^e^dāwîḏ* being a tech-

[1] *Uppslagsverk*, i, col. 1221.
[2] Cf. *supra*, p. 102.
[3] *Ursprung und Ausbau der israel.-jüd. Heilandserwartung*, pp. 134–50.
[4] Op. cit., p. 67.
[5] The Rôle of the King in the Jerusalem Cultus', in *The Labyrinth*, pp. 71–111.
[6] *Rylands Bull.*, p. 6.

nical term meaning 'for the king'.[1] The 'I' of such Psalms is the king, and wherever in them the psalmist is depicted as suffering, we have psalms of the Ebed-Yahweh type. Later on, so the theory goes, the 'pattern' became 'disintegrated' and 'democratized', so that what originally referred specifically to the king came to be appropriate on the lips of private individual worshippers.

With regard to the composition of Deutero-Isaiah, Engnell dissents from the now widely current view that it was a loose concatenation of independent short oracles. Instead, he maintains that Deutero-Isaiah, including the Servant-Songs, was '*a prophetic remodelling* (or imitation) of a liturgical composition belonging to the Annual Festival'.[2] This enables him to bring the last Song into fairly close proximity to Isa. lv. 3 f., the passage about 'the sure mercies of David', thus strengthening his argument that the Servant is a Davidic Messianic figure.

Naturally, Engnell has to interpret the language of the 'Songs' of the Servant in consistently royal categories. For example, in the first Song (xlii. 1 ff.) the endowment of the Servant with the spirit and his imparting of *mišpāṭ* and *tôrâh*, stamp him as king, not as prophet. In the second and third Songs the epithets 'my God' (xlix. 4) and 'my Lord' (l. 4) are proper only upon the lips of a king, since 'aboriginally it is the king alone who calls the god "my God", with the first personal suffix'.[3] The third Song 'may best be rubricated as *a royal psalm of confidence* (of course still in imitation of the original cultic pattern) in parallelism with the Accadian so-called innocence psalms'.[4] In the fourth Song the Tammuz-motif is as obvious as it can be, and the equation Tammuz = king is as clear to Engnell as it is to Nyberg. Where Engnell parts company from Nyberg—in addition to repudiating his theory that the Servant was a leper—is at the point where Nyberg goes far towards abandoning all he has had to say about the Tammuz-king motifs in the description, as though these were little more than literary reminiscences employed to embellish a portrait which was really conceived after the likeness of the prophets. Instead, Engnell adheres throughout to his interpretation of the Servant in

[1] *Studies in Divine Kingship*, p. 176 f.

[2] *Rylands Bull.*, pp. 5 f., 13: this suggestion was first made by Gyllenberg in *SEÅ* 5, 1940, p. 87 f.

[3] *Rylands Bull.*, p. 20, n. 2.

[4] Ibid., p. 19 f.

Messianic categories, saying that he is 'the [Davidic] Messiah *victorious and triumphant* through his vicarious suffering'.[1]

To sum up the differences between Engnell and Nyberg: Nyberg's theory is complicated, Engnell's is simplicity itself, granted its presuppositions; Nyberg makes a synthesis of the myth-motifs, Engnell fuses them into one, the oscillation between individual and collective being sufficiently accounted for by the fact that the king embodies in himself the whole people, whose guilt he takes upon himself and atones for.

It seems to me that we need to be a good deal clearer than as yet we have any right to be about the Tammuz-kingship ideology before we can venture to apply it rigorously to such texts as the Servant-Songs. For example, Cyrus H. Gordon has renounced what he now calls 'the erroneous view' that 'Tammuz is said to die and revive *annually*: a generally accepted idea for which I can find no support in the Mesopotamian mythological texts; annual celebrations prove nothing, for holidays tend to be annual affairs; no one would maintain that Columbus discovers America every year because Columbus day is celebrated every 12th October'.[2] The Ugaritic texts, too, he says, 'tell us nothing of any annual death and revival of Baal'.[3] Even Engnell volunteers to say that the complete 'cultic pattern' is a *Konstruktion*, that it naturally took different forms in a petty city kingdom in Canaan from what it did in the great centres of culture, and that 'the utmost caution must be exercised when we attempt to frame a reconstruction of it out of its varied forms'.[4] Yet when he reads in the first Servant-Song that the Servant is endowed with the spirit, he immediately takes that as one of 'the royal qualifications of the Servant', this, presumably, because 'the spirit plays a special role in the kingship-ideology'.[5] The idea appears to be that the king unites in himself the offices of both priest and prophet, so that when he delegates his priestly and prophetic functions to cultic specialists, they, the priest and the prophet, really derive the spirit from him.[6] This, of course, is pure *Konstruktion*. So far as I have been able to discover, the idea of the spirit of Yahweh is peculiarly Israelite, and no real parallels to it are forth-

[1] Ibid., p. 23.
[2] *Ugaritic Literature*, Rome, 1949, p. 3, n 2.
[3] Ibid., p. 4.
[4] *Uppslagsverk*, i, col. 1222.
[5] Article 'Ande', in *Uppslagsverk*, i, col. 66.
[6] Ibid., col. 67.

coming from outside Israel.[1] Moreover, in Israel the conception of the spirit is earlier than the monarchy, and Saul, the first king, only received the spirit when he came into contact with prophets who already had it. Considerations like this should make us hesitate to force the Servant into the pattern of kingship.

A moderate and attractive presentation of the Nyberg-Engnell-Widengren position is offered by yet another Uppsala scholar, Helmer Ringgren.[2] Ringgren is more cautious than his colleagues in that he admits that language derived from the kingship-ideology does not prove that the Servant is a king.[3] He begins by saying that the best sources for our knowledge of the Israelite kingship-ideology are the Royal Psalms, in which the pattern of kingship is definitely related to the Babylonian-Canaanite.[4] The monarchy proved a disappointment and to it there succeeded the expectation of a future Messiah who should embody in himself the ideals which the kings had failed to realize.[5] Features of the kingship-ideology are to be discerned in the Servant-Songs. In the first (xlii. 1–7) it is kingly features which predominate; in the second (xlix. 1–13) and third (l. 4–11) the portrait is more like that of a prophet, though kingly features are not entirely absent.[6] In the fourth Song (lii. 13–liii. 12) there are certain striking similarities to the Babylonian Tammuz-literature and the kingship-ideology, blended with elements from the ritual of the Day of Atonement, which, although in its fully-developed form post-exilic, nevertheless preserved some part of the pre-exilic New-Year festival.[7]

There is no doubt that elsewhere in Deutero-Isaiah the title 'Servant of Yahweh' denotes Israel. Can the Servant of the Songs also be Israel? To this Ringgren answers: 'This cannot be asserted without further ado. But we can assume that it was the Prophet's reflexions on the fate of Israel that moved him to compose the Songs. Why, he asked, had Israel to

[1] Cf. J. Hehn, 'Zum Problem des Geistes im alten Orient und im AT', *ZAW* 43, 1924, pp. 210–25.

[2] *Messias Konungen* (pp. 88), Uppsala, 1954. An English translation is in preparation. Meanwhile, those who read German but not Swedish may consult the same writer's article 'König und Messias', *ZAW* 64, pp. 120–48. References here are to *ZAW*.

[3] Op. cit., p. 146.

[4] Ibid., pp. 123–9.

[5] Ibid., p. 130.

[6] Ibid., p. 140 f.

[7] Ibid., pp. 143 ff.

experience such manifold sufferings? He found the answer to the enigma in the old idea of the king as the representative of his people. . . . But the conception of the king who makes atonement led to thoughts of a figure who should come, in whom these tasks should, so to speak, be concentrated, a coming Messiah, if we will, who should bear the sins of many. This figure is the Servant of God and it is from this that all the individual features in the Songs come, features which have occasioned such difficulty to those who have maintained the collective interpretation. That the Prophet in such words spoke of himself or of any other prophet, seems to me quite out of the question. In the Servant Songs there is such a blending of people, king, and Messiah that the separate features can hardly be disengaged from one another.'[1]

A study by the Lund scholar, Joh. Lindblom,[2] lies somewhat outside the field of the present discussion. Lindblom's conclusion is that the Servant-Songs proper are 'allegorical pictures, the connected passages giving the interpretation, or application, of them'.[3] The Servant of the first Song (xlii. 1–4) is a king. In the second (xlix. 1–6) and third (l. 4–9) we hear a prophet speaking about his own experiences. The Servant of the fourth Song (liii. 2–12) 'is a fictitious person, who (from the pyschological point of view) is conjured up in the prophet's imagination, and (from the religious point of view) is the subject of a divine revelation'.[4] The interpretative passages (xlii. 5–9; xlix. 7; l. 10 f.; lii. 13–liii. 1) 'in all cases deal with the people of Israel. Thus the servant signifies Israel. . . . The servant of the Songs is thought of as an individual . . . but he symbolizes allegorically a community, namely Israel'. This solution, of course, is not actually new: advocates of the collective theory have always admitted the individual features in the portrait of the Servant and have likewise treated the Songs as allegories.[5]

We come now to the third corner of the triangle, Copenhagen. Aage Bentzen was a prolific writer and his contributions to the debate were extensive.[6] He shared to a large extent the Uppsala theories on the sacral kingship. On general critical questions his affinities were usually with Mowinckel,

[1] Ibid., p. 147.

[2] *The Servant Songs in Deutero-Isaiah: A New Attempt to Solve an Old Problem*, Lund, 1951.

[3] Op. cit., p. 102. [4] Ibid., p. 46. [5] Cf. *supra*, pp. 29, 60, 206.

[6] See supplementary Bibliography, *infra*, p. 252.

though on the particular problem of the relation of the Servant-Songs to their contexts he stood nearer to Uppsala than to Oslo.

Bentzen prefaces his discussion[1] by referring to the new points of view which Nyberg and Engnell have brought into the debate. His most polemical passages are directed against Engnell's attempt to force the Songs into the strait-jacket of the Tammuz-kingship ideology. For example, when Engnell takes the first Song in close connexion with its preceding context—and Bentzen agrees with him that it is right to do this—the word *m*^e^*ḇaśśēr* in xli. 27 (EVV. 'one that bringeth good tidings') should make it clear that the subject of the Song is a prophet, not a king.[2] When Engnell says that 'the king was in principle the only oracle receiver', the expression 'in principle' suggests uncertainty, and in the Old Testament it is not true even 'in principle', but only in some few cases. Prophetic circles and their spiritual exercises illustrate the matter just as well.[3] To say that the expression 'my Lord' (l. 5) is only proper on the lips of a king is methodologically unjustifiable. 'It is too general a word in the Old Testament to be used in this manner here, unless other important evidence supports the suggestion'.[4] If we are to say, whenever we meet with language reminiscent of the kingship ideology, that we are dealing with a king, we shall have to say that Jeremiah was a king, because the account of his call could quite easily be made to bear that interpretation. Linguistic parallels with the Tammuz-ideology have an antiquarian interest, but for the understanding of the text as the Prophet intended it they are quite irrelevant. There is much that is 'typically royal' in the descriptions, 'but, in Deutero-Isaiah's day, the "democratization of the ritual" must have been so developed that this question cannot be answered unequivocally. Here, the context must decide whether the Servant of the Lord should be regarded as king or as prophet, and the example of Jeremiah's inaugural vision must be decisive.'[5]

In his Isaiah commentary Bentzen took exception to Nyberg's 'tradition' (liii. 1)—'How can an old myth be some-

[1] In *King and Messiah*. Quotations and references in what follows to ET.

[2] Op. cit., p. 49.

[3] Ibid., p. 53.

[4] Ibid.

[5] Ibid., p. 54. Cf. Mowinckel, *supra*, p. 223.

thing which no one has ever heard or seen before?'[1] To this Engnell retorts[2] that 'the mysterious message of the ancient cult-myth is, contemporaneously, always new, i.e. experienced over and over again'. But Bentzen sticks to his point: the rehabilitation of the Servant is something 'new', not merely in the meaning that we find in the 'new song' of the Accession Psalms, that the circle of the year is begun anew, that the world by means of the ritual is once more secured, 'new' created again, but something *absolutely* new. Deutero-Isaiah makes use of the old forms of the New-Year festival and of the conception of the 're-creation' of the world, but in a quite different, 'literal' way, so that the 'new' is something greater than that which was experienced in the 'old' festival over and over again.[3]

Bentzen further objects to Engnell that his interpretation denies *a priori* that the Servant is an historical figure with a basis in real life. If everything is dissolved into Messianic-mythology we may as well deny the historicity of Cyrus in Isa. xl–lv. Besides, if the Prophet was composing an imitation of a New-year liturgy, he must have had in mind some historic actualization of the myth. He must have thought of a particular Davidic prince, much as Haggai and Zechariah later saw in Zerubbabel the Messiah.[4]

In Bentzen's view, then, the kingship-ideology is not the only possibility for the interpretation of the texts. Many features in the portrait of the Servant are common to both king and prophet. When Engnell says that the king is in principle the 'primordial prophet' (*Urprofet*) he should go farther back. For the all-comprehensive 'primordial phenomenon' (*Urphänomenon*) is not the king but the 'First Man' (*Urmensch*), from whom chieftain, king, priest, prophet, and

[1] *Jesaja fortolket*, ii, p. 103.

[2] *Rylands Bulletin*, p. 30, n. 6.

[3] *King and Messiah*, p. 57.

[4] Ibid., p. 60 f. In a concluding note to the last paragraph of the English edition of his 'Ebed-Yahweh article Engnell says he has been criticized by Nyberg (he gives no reference and I have been unable to find one) on the ground that he has denied the foundations of the Servant-conception in real life. This charge he repudiates, and retorts with a *tu quoque* that 'on the contrary it would seem very questionable how Nyberg's own, newly-repeated interpretation of 'Ebed-Yahweh as a "prophetic collective" or "Isaiah as a collective figure" could imply a stronger and firmer "foundation in real life" than the interpretation of the 'Ebed as the Davidic Messiah'.

the rest, all derive their several functions. We can therefore equally well, and in the present case better, think with Nyberg in terms of prophet, ancestor, and cult-founder.[1]

The only thing with which Bentzen finds fault in Nyberg's final interpretation of the Servant-figure in prophetic categories is his failure to find any place for Moses as model for the Servant. This, for Bentzen, is a feature of cardinal importance. Deutero-Isaiah pictured the return from Babylon as a new and more wonderful Exodus, from which it is clear that the figure of Moses must have played for him an important role, a role which both Nyberg and Engnell quite ignore. The Deutero-Isaianic Messiah is the Moses *redivivus* of the 'new world-order' with a 'new' cult-myth. This raises the question of his relation to 'David' in lv. 3 ff. The 'I' of two of the Songs (xlix. 1 ff., l. 4–9) shows that the Prophet must have taken upon himself the task of the new Moses. The coming David must thus by the side of him be thought of as an independent leader of the return. When we consider how the Exodus traditions served as a model for Deutero-Isaiah, it is very probable that he thought of *two* leaders of the coming time, corresponding to Moses and Aaron, or better to Moses and Joshua. In this partnership the Servant = Moses *redivivus* is the Prophet himself. We thus reach the conclusion: 'The "Ebed Yahweh" is Deutero-Isaiah and Israel, the new Moses ("Messias" in radically changed form) and the congregation for which he is ready to die, in one single person.'[2]

What this means may not be immediately clear, so it may be well to set beside it Bentzen's conclusion as he expresses it in his *Introduction*.[3] After saying, 'I think it most probable that we have to uphold the autobiographical theory of the Servant Songs, as it was propounded by Mowinckel in 1921', he ends:

When all this is taken together, we come to the assumption that the Servant of Yahweh is not only an ideal figure of Messianic character, but also a concrete historical person, identical with the prophet. The prophet perceived in the Servant a model for his own life. Like Moses he has to identify himself with his people 'for better and for worse'. It may be expressed in the following way: The Servant Songs belong to the same circle as the rest of the Deutero-Isaianic poems, representing the profoundest thoughts uttered con-

[1] *King and Messiah*, p. 64. [2] Ibid., p. 67.
[3] Engl. ed., vol. ii, p. 112 f.

cerning the problem of suffering and concerning the task of Israel as the prophet of Yahweh to the world, expressed in one individual figure, in whom the prophet and his disciples have seen both a Messianic promise and a programme for their personal life. ʿEbed Yahweh is both the Messiah and Israel and Deutero-Isaiah and his band of disciples.

This seems to mean that the Servant was an ideal figure, Messianic after the pattern of Moses, who was to deliver Israel in the near-approaching new Exodus, and that the Prophet sought to actualize the figure in his own person and in the lives of his disciples. The Davidic Messiah—if we may call him so—of Isa. lv. 3 ff. is another person, a kind of Joshua to the Servant Moses.

What is difficult to grasp in this presentation is the identification of someone now living with an ideal figure still to come. As I see it, Bentzen has complicated the situation by assuming (1) that the autobiographical form of two of the Songs obliges us to conclude that the Servant was the Prophet, and (2) that the last Song must have some relation to the expected deliverance from Babylon. With regard to (1): the Songs, from first to last, are set in a framework of divine pronouncements, in 'tenses' which are timeless, if not actually future. Surely then, within the framework, the Servant may speak in the first person without our being obliged to conclude that he and the author of the poems are the same person.[1] In any case, the Servant's task of raising up the tribes of Jacob and restoring the survivors of Israel is ancillary to the conversion of the Gentiles (xlix. 5 f.), and it looks as if Yahweh directs the Servant to abandon it for the more far-reaching task.[2] In regard to (2): I can see no definite political background to the last Song,[3] nor any reason why Bentzen should, as it would seem, regard the *šᵉmûʿâh* of liii. 1 as the same thing as the *ḥᵃḏāšâh/ôṯ* ('new things') of xlii. 9, xliii. 18 f.[4] The *ḥᵃḏāšâh* refers to the new Exodus, the *šᵉmûʿâh* to the atoning death and rehabilitation of the Servant. It looks to me as if the consequences of regarding Deutero-Isaiah as a co-ordinated literary whole involve us in such complications, that it is much more likely that the chapters

[1] Cf. *supra*, p. 210. [2] Ibid., pp. 143 f., 147. [3] Ibid., p. 210.

[4] *Studia Theologica* i, p. 185; cf. my article 'The "Former Things" and the "New Things" in Deutero-Isaiah', in *Studies in Old Testament Prophecy*, ed. H. H. Rowley, p. 125 f.

are a collection of more or less separate oracles, even though, as I have tried to prove, the Songs are by the author of the main prophecy.[1]

I put these difficulties to Bentzen himself and he replied[2] in these terms:

> You say, you cannot combine someone who is to come with someone who is already there. But I would answer that you have to do that in the case of the fulfilment of the prophecy. Jesus is both the present Suffering Servant and the coming Christ in the Glory of the World to Come. He is so, whether you think of the Gospel narratives or in sacramental-ecclesiastical categories. I think it is theologically very interesting, methodically, that in this case we can use the fulfilment as a means of explaining the O.T. text. The Servant in Isaiah II is, in my conception, the personal centre of a religious *corpus Christi*, in his life and after his death living in his circle of disciples like Jacob in the *sod* (EVV. 'council') of his sons (Gen. xlix. 6), and he has believed in his own being the future saviour of Israel. In my opinion the answer to your remarks lies in the idea of 'corporate personality' applied to the prophet-founder and his disciples.

This, at last, I think, is reasonably clear. Bentzen's position, even to details, was very similar to that of Wheeler Robinson.[3]

Concerning the composition of Deutero-Isaiah, Bentzen told me that Mowinckel wrote a long criticism of his views some years ago,[4] on much the same lines as I have done, but that he had lately examined the question afresh and found his own views better grounded than before. As I see it, the solution of the isagogic problem is likely to be decisive for the problem of the identity of the Servant. If we take Isa. xl–lv as a whole, exactly as it stands, it would seem as if we must attempt some kind of synthesis of the seemingly disparate elements in it—as that the Servant *is* Israel (xli. 8 f., &c.), the Servant has a mission *to* Israel (xlix. 5 f.), the Servant is an individual still to come (lii. 13–liii. 12). The result will be what is really a theological interpretation, much on Bentzen's and Wheeler Robinson's lines, though I still do not find it necessary to conclude from the 'I' in two of the Songs that the Servant must be the Prophet

[1] Cf. *supra*, p. 186.

[2] In a personal letter dated 18 Oct. 1949.

[3] *The Cross of the Servant*, esp. III, The Messiah-Servant, pp. 64–87. This is the more striking because, although Bentzen was of course familiar with Wheeler Robinson's exposition of 'Corporate personality' in *Werden und Wesen des Alten Testaments*, ed. J. Hempel, 1936, he never read *The Cross of the Servant*.

[4] In *Dansk Teologisk Tidsskrift*.

himself. It seems to me that the last Song is *sui generis*, in a real sense distinct from the main body of Deutero-Isaiah, and that in it the Servant is an individual still to come. Bentzen's synthesis is devotionally, theologically, and religiously valuable, and ultimately we all come to it when we think of the Servant as Christ, the Head of the redeemed and redemptive society of the Church which is His body. That *is* the ultimate interpretation and fulfilment of the prophecy. The question is whether the sixth-century Prophet, in the moment of supreme inspiration when he composed the last Song, was thinking of the Servant in so many different (even if related) categories as Israel, Moses, the Messiah, and himself. Bentzen thought he did, and we must leave it at that.

LIST OF WORKS CONSULTED

ALEXANDER, J. A.: *The Later Prophecies of Isaiah*, New York, 1847.

AMMON, C. F. VON: *Entwurf einer Christologie des alten Testamentes*, Erlangen, 1794.

ANON.: *Ausführliche Erklärung der sämmtlichen messianischen Weissagungen des Alten Testaments*, Altenburg and Erfurt, 1801.

ARNOLD, MATTHEW: *Isaiah XL–LXVI, with the shorter Prophecies allied to it*, London, 1875.

AUGUSTI, J. C. W.: 'Ueber den König Usia, nebst einer Erläuterung Jesaia 53', in *Magazin für Religionsphilosophie, Exegese und Kirchengeschichte*, herausgegeben von H. P. C. Henke, 3. Bd., Helmstadt, 1795, pp. 282–99.

—— (with J. G. CH. HÖPFNER): *Exegetisches Handbuch des Alten Testaments für Prediger, Schullehrer und gebildete Leser*, Leipzig, 1797–1800. (Isa. 40 ff. is dealt with in the *Zweite Abtheilung*, 7 Stück, 1800.)

—— *Apologien und Parallelen theologischen Inhalt's*, pp. 1–40, Gera and Leipzig, 1800.

AYTOUN, R. A.: 'The Servant of the Lord in the Targum', *JTS* 23, 1922, pp. 172–80.

BADE, JOH.: *Christologie des Alten Testamentes*, 3 Theile in 4, Münster, 1850–2. (3. Bd., pp. 195–375, deals with the Servant.)

BAHRDT, K. F.: *Die Kleine Bibel, Erster Band; Geschichte von Erschaffung der Welt bis auf die Zerstörung Jerusalems durch die Römer*, Berlin, 1780. (Published anonymously.)

—— 'Von den Weissagungen, die in den Evangelien und apostolischen Briefen auf Jesu Person und Schicksale gezogen werden', in *Freymüthige Versuche über verschiedene in Theologie und biblische Kritik einschlagende Materien*, Berlin, 1783, pp. 99–144. (Published anonymously, ed. Heinrich Corrodi?)

BALLA, E.: 'Das Problem des Leides in der israelitisch-jüdischen Religion', in *Eucharisterion* Hermann Gunkel (ed. Hans Schmidt), Göttingen, 1923, pp. 214–61.

BARNES, W. E.: 'Cyrus the "Servant of Jehovah" Isa. xlii, 1–4(7)', *JTS* 32, 1931, pp. 32–9.

BAUDISSIN, W. W. GRAF: *Adonis und Esmun*, Leipzig, 1911.

—— 'Zur Entwicklung des Gebrauchs von ʿebed in religiösem Sinne', in *Budde Festschrift*, *BZAW* 34, 1920, pp. 1–9.

BAUER, BRUNO: *Die Religion des Alten Testamentes in der geschichtlichen Entwickelung ihrer Principien dargestellt*, 2. Bd., Berlin, 1838, pp. 414–34.

BAUER, G. L.: *Scholia in Vetus Testamentum*, vol. ix, Nürnberg, 1795.

BECK, FR.: *De capite quinquagesimo tertio libri Jesajani*, Hauniae, 1840, pp. 80 ff.

—— *Die cyro-jesajanischen Weissagungen, oder die Capitel 40–66 des Jesajah, kritisch und exegetisch bearbeitet*, Leipzig, 1844, pp. 151 ff.

BECK, JOSEPH: *Ueber die Entwicklung und Darstellung der messianischen Idee in den heiligen Schriften des alten Bundes*, Hannover, 1835, pp. 69–100.

BEER, G.: 'Die Gedichte vom Knechte Jahwes in Jes 40–55. Ein textkritischer und metrischer Wiederherstellungsversuch', in *Baudissin Festschrift*, *BZAW* 33, 1918, pp. 29–46.

BEGRICH, J.: *Studien zu Deuterojesaja*, *BZWANT*, 4. Folge, Heft 25, 1938.
BENTZEN, AAGE: *Indledning til det Gamle Testamente*, Copenhagen, 1941.
BERTHOLET, A.: *Zu Jesaja 53: Ein Erklärungsversuch*, Freiburg i. B., 1899.
BLANK, S. H.: 'Studies in Deutero-Isaiah', *Hebrew Union College Annual*, 15, Cincinnati, 1940, pp. 1–46.
BLEEK, F.: 'Erklärung von Jesaja 52, 13–53, 12', *TSK* 34, 1861, pp. 177–218.
BLEEKER, L. H. K.: 'Jojachin, der Ebed-Jahwe', *ZAW* 40, 1922, p. 156.
BÖHL, F. M. TH.: *De 'Knecht des Heeren' in Jezaja 53*, Haarlem, 1923.
BRANDT, T.: *Der Prophet der Geschichte Jesaja 40 bis 55*, Leipzig, 1933.
BRAUN, HEINRICH; *Die göttliche heilige Schrift des alten und neuen Testamentes in lateinischer und deutscher Sprache durchaus mit Erklärungen nach dem Sinne der heiligen römisch-katholischen Kirche u. s. w.*, Augsburg, 1789–97. (Isaiah is in 8. Bd., 1795.)
BREDENKAMP, C. J.: *Der Prophet Jesaia erläutert*, Erlangen, 1887.
BRIERRE-NARBONNE, J.-J.: *Le Messie souffrant dans la littérature rabbinique*, Paris, 1940.
BROWN, S. L.: 'Introduction to the Study of Isaiah 40–66', *The Interpreter*, 7, 1910/11, pp. 397–403.
BROWNE, L. E.: *Early Judaism*, Cambridge, 1920.
BRÜCKNER, M.: *Der sterbende und auferstehende Gottheiland*, *Religionsgeschichtliche Volksbücher*, 1. Reihe, 16. Heft, Tübingen, 1920.
BRUSTON, CHARLES: 'Le Serviteur de l'Éternel dans l'avenir', in *Marti Festschrift*, *BZAW* 41, 1915, pp. 37–44.
BRUSTON, ED.: 'Serviteur de l'Éternel', in *Dictionnaire encyclopédique de la Bible*, 2e tome, 1932, pp. 664–7.
BUDDE, K.: *Die sogenannten Ebed-Jahwe-Lieder und die Bedeutung des Knechtes Jahwes in Jes. 40–55: Ein Minoritätsvotum*, Giessen, 1900. Published in English under the title 'The so-called "Ebed-Jahweh-Songs" and the Meaning of the Term "Servant of Yahweh" in Isaiah Chaps. 40–55', *The American Journal of Theology*, July 1899, pp. 499–540.
—— *Das Buch Jesaia Kap. 40–66*, in *Die Heilige Schrift des Alten Testaments, übersetzt und herausgegeben von E. Kautzsch*, 3. Aufl., 1. Bd., Tübingen, 1909, pp. 609–71.
BUNSEN, C. C. J. (Baron): *Gott in der Geschichte*, 1. Theil, Leipzig, 1857.
—— *Vollständiges Bibelwerk für die Gemeinde*, 2. Bd., Leipzig, 1860.
BURNEY, C. F.: 'The Book of Isaiah: A New Theory, II', *Church Quarterly Review*, 75, 1912, pp. 99–139.
BURROWS, E.: 'The Servant of Yahweh in Isaiah: An Interpretation', in *The Gospel of the Infancy and other Biblical Essays*, London, 1941, pp. 59–80.
CANNON, W. W.: 'Isaiah 61 1–3 an Ebed-Jahweh Poem', *ZAW* 47, 1929, pp. 284–8.
CARPENTER, L. L.: *Primitive Christian Application of the Doctrine of the Servant*, Durham (North Carolina), 1929.
CASPARI, W.: *Lieder und Gottessprüche der Rückwanderer (Jesaja 40–55)*, *BZAW* 65, 1934.
CHEYNE, T. K.: *The Book of Isaiah Chronologically Arranged*, London, 1870.
—— *The Prophecies of Isaiah: A New Translation with Commentary and Appendices*, 2 vols., London, 1880–1, ²1882, ³1884, ⁴1886, ⁵1889.
—— *Introduction to the Book of Isaiah*, London, 1895.

CHEYNE, T. K.: *Jewish Religious Life after the Exile*, New York, 1898.
—— *The Book of the Prophet Isaiah: Critical Edition of the Hebrew Text*, S.B.O.T., Leipzig, 1899.
—— 'Servant of the Lord', *Ency. Bibl.*, cols. 4398–410.
CLARKE, ADAM: *A Concise View of the Succession of Sacred Literature*, 2 vols., London, 1830.
COBB, W. H.: 'The Servant of Jahveh', *JBL* 14, 1895, pp. 95–113.
COLLINS, ANT.: *The Scheme of Literal Prophecy considered*, London, 1727.
CÖLLN, D. G. C. VON: *Dr. Daniel Georg Conrad von Cölln's biblische Theologie, mit einer Nachricht über des Verfasser's Leben und Wirken, herausgegeben von Dr. David Schulz*, Erster Bd., AT., Leipzig, 1836.
CONDAMIN, A.: *Le Livre d'Isaïe: Traduction critique avec notes et commentaires*, *EB*, 1905.
—— 'Le Serviteur de Jahwé. Un nouvel argument pour le sens individuel messianique', *RB*, nouvelle série, 5e tome, 1908, pp. 162–81.
—— 'Les Prédictions Nouvelles du chapitre XLVIII d'Isaïe', *RB*, N.S., 7e tome, 1910, pp. 200–16.
COOK, S. A.: In *Cambridge Ancient History*, iii. 490–5.
—— 'The Servant of the Lord', *ET* 34, 1922–3, pp. 440 ff.
CORNILL, C. H.: 'Die neueste Litteratur über Jes 40–66', *Theologische Rundschau*, 3, 1900, pp. 409–20.
—— *Der israelitische Prophetismus*, 4. Aufl., Strassburg, 1903. ET *The Prophets of Israel*, by S. F. Corkran, 7th ed., Chicago, 1907.
—— *Introduction to the Canonical Books of the Old Testament*, ET by G. H. Box, London, 1907, p. 290 f.
CRAMPON, A.: *La Sainte Bible, Traduction d'après les textes originaux*, édition revisée, Paris, 1923.
CRIPPS, R. S.: 'The Contribution of the Prophets of Israel', in *The Atonement in History and in Life*, ed. L. W. Grensted, London, 1929, pp. 65–96.
DALMAN, G. H.: *Der leidende und der sterbende Messias der Synagoge im ersten nachchristlichen Jahrtausend*, Berlin, 1888.
—— *Jesaja 53 das Prophetenwort vom Sühneleiden des Gottesknechtes*, 2. Aufl., Leipzig, 1914.
DATHE, J. A.: *Prophetae majores ex recensione textus hebraei et versionum antiquarum latine versi notisque philologicis et criticis illustrati*, Halae, 1779.
DAVIDSON, A. B.: 'The Book of Isaiah.—Chapters XL–LXVI', *The Expositor*, 2nd ser., vol. 8, 1884, pp. 250–69, 350–69, 430–51.
—— *Old Testament Prophecy*, ed. J. A. Paterson, Edinburgh, 1903.
DAVIDSON, SAMUEL: *An Introduction to the Old Testament, Critical, Historical, and Theological*, vol. iii, London, 1863.
DELITZSCH, F.: *Biblical Commentary on the Prophecies of Isaiah*, ET from the 4th ed., by J. S. Banks and James Kennedy, Edinburgh, 1890.
DENIO, F. B.: 'The Servant of Jehovah', *The American Journal of Theology*, 5, 1901, pp. 322–7.
DIETZE, K.: *Ussia der Knecht Gottes: sein Leben und sein Leiden und seine Bedeutung für den Propheten Jesaja*, in *Schriften der Bremer Wissenschaftlichen Gesellschaft*, Heft 1/2, Jg. 4, Bremen, 1929.
DILLMANN, A.: *Der Prophet Jesaia, Kurzgefasstes exegetisches Handbuch zum Alten Testament*, 5th ed. of Knobel, Leipzig, 1890.

DIX, G. H.: 'The Influence of Babylonian Ideas on Jewish Messianism', *JTS* 26, 1925, pp. 241–56.

DÖDERLEIN, J. C.: *Esaias ex recensione textus hebraei . . . latine vertit notasque varii argumenti*, Altdorfi, 1775, ²1780, ³1789.

DODSON, M.: *A New Translation of Isaiah: with Notes supplementary to those of Dr. Lowth. . . .*, London, 1890.

DRECHSLER, M.: *Der Prophet Jesaja übersetzt und erklärt. Dritter Theil nach dem Tode Drechslers fortgesetzt und vollendet von F. Delitzsch und A. Hahn*, Berlin, 1857.

DRIVER, G. R., 'Linguistic and Textual Problems: Isaiah XL–LXVI', *JTS* 36, 1935, pp. 396–406.

DRIVER, S. R. *Isaiah: His Life and Times and the Writings which bear his Name*, London, 1888, ²1893.

—— *An Introduction to the Literature of the Old Testament*, 9th ed., Edinburgh, 1913.

—— and NEUBAUER, A.: *The Fifty-third Chapter of Isaiah according to the Jewish Interpreters*. I. Texts edited by Ad. Neubauer. II. Translations by S. R. Driver and Ad. Neubauer, Oxford and London, vol. i, 1876, vol. ii, 1877. (References are to vol. ii.)

DUHM, B.: *Die Theologie der Propheten*, Bonn, 1875, pp. 287 ff.

—— *Das Buch Jesaia übersetzt und erklärt*, Göttingen, 1892, ²1902, ³1914, ⁴1922.

DÜRR, L.: *Ursprung und Ausbau der israelitisch-jüdischen Heilandserwartung. Ein Beitrag zur Theologie des Alten Testamentes*, Berlin, 1925.

—— *Wollen und Wirken der alttestamentlichen Propheten*, Düsseldorf, 1926.

ECKERMANN, J. C. R.: *Theologische Beyträge*, Altona, 1790, ²1794, 1. Bd., Erstes Stück, pp. 209–40.

EDELKOORT, A. H.: *De Christusverwachting in het Oude Testament*, Wageningen, 1941.

EICHHORN, J. G.: *Allgemeine Bibliothek der biblischen Litteratur*, 6. Bd., Leipzig, 1794–5.

—— *Die hebräischen Propheten*, Dritter Band, Göttingen, 1819.

EISSFELDT, O.: *Der Gottesknecht bei Deuterojesaja (Jes. 40–55) im Lichte der israelitischen Anschauung von Gemeinschaft und Individuum*, Halle (Saale), 1933. In English: 'The Ebed-Jahwe in Isaiah xl.–lv. in the Light of the Israelite Conceptions of the Community and the Individual, the Ideal and the Real', *ET* 44, pp. 261–8.

ELLIGER, K.: *Deuterojesaja in seinem Verhältnis zu Tritojesaja*, *BZWANT*, Vierte Folge, Heft 11, 1933.

ENGNELL, I.: 'Till frågan om Ebed Jahve-sångerna och den lidande Messias hos "Deuterojesaja"', *Svensk Exegetisk Årsbok*, 10, 1945, pp. 31–65. ET in *Rylands Library Bulletin* 31, Jan., 1948.

EULER, K. F.: *Die Verkündigung vom leidenden Gottesknecht aus Jes. 53 in der griechischen Bibel*, *BZWANT*, Vierte Folge, Heft 14, 1934.

EWALD, H.: *Die Propheten des Alten Bundes*, 2 Bde., Stuttgart, 1840–1 (Relevant material in vol. ii, p. 407 f.), 2nd ed., 3 Bde., Göttingen, 1868. ET of 2nd ed., *Commentary on the Prophets of the Old Testament*, by J. Frederick Smith, 5 vols., London, 1875–81. (Relevant material in vol. iv.)

FARLEY, F. A.: 'Jeremiah and "The Suffering Servant of Jehovah" in Deutero-Isaiah', *ET* 38, 1926–7, pp. 521–4.

FEILCHENFELD, W.: *Das stellvertretende Sühneleiden und die Exegese der Jesaianischen Weissagung Kap. 52, 13–15 und Kap. 53*, Dessau, 1883.

FELDMANN, FR.: *Der Knecht Gottes in Isaias Kap. 40–55*, Freiburg i. B., 1907.

—— *Die Weissagungen über den Gottesknecht im Buche Jesaias*, 3. Aufl., Münster i. W., 1913.

—— 'Das Frühere und das Neue. Ein Beitrag zur Jesajakritik', in *Festschrift Sachau*, Berlin, 1915, pp. 162–9.

—— *Das Buch Isaias übersetzt und erklärt, Exegetisches Handbuch zum Alten Testament*, 14. Bd., Zweiter Teil, Münster i. W., 1925–6.

FINDEISEN, H.: 'Er ist begraben wie die Gottlosen, gestorben wie ein Reicher', *NKZ* 9, 1898, pp. 473–8.

FISCHEL, H. A.: 'Die deuterojesajanischen Gottesknechtlieder in der juedischen Auslegung', *Hebrew Union College Annual*, 18, 1943–4, pp. 53–76.

FISCHER, J.: *Isaias 40–55 und die Perikopen vom Gottesknecht*, Münster i. W., 1916.

—— *Wer ist der Ebed in den Perikopen Js 42, 1–7; 49, 1–9a; 50, 4–9; 52, 13–53, 12?* Münster i. W., 1922.

—— 'Das Problem des neuen Exodus in Isaias C. 40–55', *Theologische Quartalschrift*, 110, 1929, pp. 111–30.

—— *Das Buch Isaias übersetzt und erklärt, II. Teil: Kapitel 40–66*, Bonn, 1939.

FLIER, A. VAN DER: 'Drieërlei verklaring van den Ebed-Jahwe bij Deuterojezaja', *Theologische Studiën*, Utrecht, 1904, pp. 345–76.

FORBES, J.: *The Servant of the Lord in Isaiah XL–LXVI. Reclaimed to Isaiah as the Author from Argument, Structure, and Date*, Edinburgh, 1890.

FÜLLKRUG, G.: *Der Gottesknecht des Deuterojesaja. Eine kritisch-exegetische und biblisch-theologische Studie*, Göttingen, 1899.

GESENIUS, W.: *Der Prophet Jesaia. Uebersetzt und mit einem vollständigen philologisch-kritischen und historischen Commentar begleitet*, Dritter Theil, Leipzig, 1821.

—— *Thesaurus philologicus criticus linguae hebraeae et chaldaeae Veteris Testamenti*, vol. ii in 1840 ed., Leipzig, p. 979.

GIESEBRECHT, F.: *Beiträge zur Jesajakritik*, Göttingen, 1890. (Special section on 'Die Idee von Jes. 52^{13}–53^{12}', pp. 146–85.)

—— *Der Knecht Jahves des Deuterojesaia*, Königsberg i. Pr., 1902.

GLAHN, L., and KÖHLER, L.: *Der Prophet der Heimkehr*, Giessen, 1934.

GLAZEBROOK, M. G.: *Studies in the Book of Isaiah*, Oxford, 1910.

GRESSMANN, H.: *Der Ursprung der israelitisch-jüdischen Eschatologie*, Göttingen, 1905.

—— 'Die literarische Analyse Deuterojesajas', *ZAW* 34, 1914, pp. 254–97.

—— *Altorientalische Texte und Bilder*, 2. Aufl., Berlin, 1926.

—— *Der Messias*, Göttingen, 1929, pp. 287–339.

GROTIUS, H.: *Annotata ad Vetus Testamentum*, Tomus II, Paris, 1644.

GUILLAUME, A.: 'The Servant Poems in the Deutero-Isaiah', *Theology* 11, 1925, pp. 254–63, 309–19; 12, 1926, pp. 2–10, 63–72.

GUNKEL, H.: 'Der Knecht Jahwes', *RGG* iii, 1912, cols. 1540 ff., 2. Aufl., 1929, cols. 1100 ff.

—— *Ein Vorläufer Jesu*, Bern, 1921.

HALÉVY, J.: 'Le עֶבֶד יְהוָה d'Isaïe, LII, 13–LIII, 12', *Revue sémitique*, 7e Année, 1899, pp. 193–213, 289–312.

HALLER, M.: *Das Judentum: Geschichtsschreibung, Prophetie und Gesetzgebung nach dem Exil*, in *Die Schriften des Alten Testaments in Auswahl übersetzt und für die Gegenwart erklärt*, 2. Abt., 3. Bd., Göttingen, 1914, 2. Aufl., 1925.

—— 'Die Kyros-Lieder Deuterojesajas', in *Eucharisterion* Hermann Gunkel, Göttingen, 1923, pp. 261–77.

HANSI, J. I.: *Commentatio philologico-theologica in vaticinium Jesa. LII, 13–LIII, 12*, Lipsiae, 1791.

HAUPT, P.: 'Understandest thou what thou readest?' in *Marti Festschrift*, *BZAW* 41, 1915, pp. 118–27.

HEMPEL, J.: 'Vom irrenden Glauben', *ZST* 7, 1929, pp. 631–60.

HENDERSON, E.: *The Book of the Prophet Isaiah, translated from the Original Hebrew, with a Commentary*, London, 1840, 2nd ed., 1857.

HENDEWERK, C. L.: *Des Propheten Jesaja Weissagungen, chronologisch geordnet, übersetzt und erklärt, Zweiter Theil, Die deuterojesajanischen Weissagungen*, Königsberg, 1843.

HENGSTENBERG, E. W.: *Christologie des Alten Testaments*, Berlin, 1829–35, 2. Aufl., 3 Bde., 1854–6, ET by T. Meyer, *Christology of the Old Testament*, vol. ii, Edinburgh, 1858.

HENSLER, C. G.: *Jesaias, neu übersetzt, mit Anmerkungen*, Hamburg, 1788.

HERTZBERG, H. W.: 'Die Entwicklung des Begriffes משפט im Alten Testament', *ZAW* 40, 1922, pp. 256–87, 41, 1923, pp. 16–76.

HEZEL, W. F.: *Die Bibel des alten und neuen Testaments mit vollständig erklärenden Anmerkungen*, Fünfter Theil, Lemgo, 1784.

HITCHCOCK, F. R. M.: 'The "Servant" in Isaiah and the New Testament', *Expositor*, 8th ser., vol. 14, 1917, pp. 309–20.

HITZIG, F.: *Der Prophet Jesaja, übersetzt und ausgelegt*, Heidelberg, 1833.

HOEPERS, M.: *Der Neue Bund bei den Propheten*, Freiburg i. B., 1933.

HOFMANN, J. C. K.: *Weissagung und Erfüllung im alten und im neuen Testamente*, Erste Hälfte, Nördlingen, 1841, pp. 257–76.

—— *Der Schriftbeweis. Ein theologischer Versuch*, Zweite Hälfte, Erste Abt., Nördlingen, 1853, pp. 89–102, 124–39.

HÖLSCHER, G.: *Geschichte der israelitischen und jüdischen Religion*, Giessen, 1922.

HONTHEIM, J.: 'Bemerkungen zu Isaias 40, 41, 42', *Zeitschrift für Katholische Theologie*, Jg. 30, 1906, pp. 159–70, 361–75, 745–61.

HOOKE, S. H. (edited by): *Myth and Ritual. Essays on the Myth and Ritual of the Hebrews in relation to the Culture Pattern of the Ancient East*, Oxford, 1933.

HOONACKER, A. van: 'L'Ébed Jahvé et la composition littéraire des Chapitres XL ss. d'Isaïe', *RB*, N.S., 6e tome, 1909, pp. 497–528.

—— 'Questions de critique littéraire et d'exégèse touchant les chapitres XL ss. d'Isaïe', *RB*, N.S., 7e tome, 1910, pp. 557–72; 8e tome, 1911, pp. 107–14, 279–85.

—— 'The Servant of the Lord in Isaiah XL ff', *Expositor*, 8th ser., vol. 11, 1916, pp. 183–210.

—— *Het Boek Isaias*, Brugge, 1932.

HYATT, J. P.: 'The Sources of the Suffering Servant Idea', *Journal of Near Eastern Studies*, 3, 1944, pp. 79–86.

ITKONEN, L.: *Deuterojesaja (Jes. 40–55) metrisch untersucht*, Helsinki, 1916.

JAHNOW, H.: *Das hebräische Leichenlied im Rahmen der Völkerdichtung*, *BZAW* 36, 1923.

JEREMIAS, A.: *Das Alte Testament im Lichte des alten Orients*, Leipzig, 1906, 4. Aufl., 1930.

JOHANSSON, NILS: *Parakletoi. Vorstellungen von Fürsprechern für die Menschen vor Gott in der alttestamentlichen Religion, im Spätjudentum und Urchristentum*, Lund, 1940.

KELLY, W.: *Lectures on the Book of Isaiah*, London, 1871.

KENNETT, R. H.: *The Servant of the Lord*, London, 1911.

KISSANE, E. J.: *The Book of Isaiah: Translated from a Critically Revised Hebrew Text with Commentary, vol. ii (XL–LXVI)*, Dublin, 1943.

KITTEL, RUD.: *Der Prophet Jesaja erklärt von Dr. August Dillmann. Für die sechste Auflage herausgegeben und vielfach umgearbeitet*, Leipzig, 1898.

—— *Zur Theologie des Alten Testaments. II. Jesaja 53 und der leidende Messias im Alten Testament*, Leipzig, 1899.

—— *Gestalten und Gedanken in Israel*, Leipzig, 1925. ET by C. A. Knoch and C. D. Wright, *Great Men and Movements in Israel*, London, n.d., pp. 367–406.

—— *Geschichte des Volkes Israel*, 3. Bd., Stuttgart, 1927, pp. 203–57.

KLAUSNER, J.: *Die messianischen Vorstellungen des jüdischen Volkes im Zeitalter der Tannaiten*, Berlin, 1904.

KLEINERT, P.: 'Ueber das Subject der Weissagung Jes. 52, 13–53, 12', *TSK* 35, 1862, pp. 699–752.

KNABENBAUER, J.: *Erklärung des Propheten Isaias*, Freiburg i. B., 1881.

—— *Commentarius in Isaiam prophetam*, vol. ii, Paris, 1887.

KNOBEL, A.: *Der Prophet Jesaia*, Leipzig, 1843; 4th ed., edited by L. Diestel, 1872.

KOCH, R.: 'Der Gottesgeist und der Messias (II)', *Biblica*, 27, 1946, pp. 376–403.

KÖHLER, L.: *Deuterojesaja (Jesaja 40–55) stilkritisch untersucht*, *BZAW* 37, 1923.

KÖNIG, ED.: Deuterojesajanisches', *NKZ* 9, 1898, pp. 895–935, 937–97.

—— *The Exiles' Book of Consolation contained in Isaiah XL–LXVI. A Critical and Exegetical Study*, ET by J. A. Selbie, Edinburgh, 1899.

—— *Das Buch Jesaja eingeleitet, übersetzt und erklärt*, Gütersloh, 1926.

KONYNENBURG, J.: *Untersuchung über die Natur der alttestamentlichen Weissagungen auf den Messias, aus dem Holländischen übersetzt*, Lingen, 1795, pp. 301–4.

KOPPE, J. B.: *D. Robert Lowth's Jesaias neu übersetzt nebst einer Einleitung und critischen philologischen und erläuternden Anmerkungen mit Zusätzen und Anmerkungen*, 4 Bde., Leipzig, 1779–81.

KÖSTER, F.: *De servo Jehovae apud Jesaiam commentatio*, Kiel, 1838.

KOSTERS, W. H.: 'Deutero- en Trito-Jezaja', *Theologisch Tijdschrift*, 30, 1896, pp. 577–623.

KRAETZSCHMAR, R.: *Die Bundesvorstellung im Alten Testament in ihrer geschichtlichen Entwicklung*, Marburg, 1896.

—— *Das Buch Ezechiel übersetzt und erklärt*, Göttingen, 1900.

KRUIGER, J. D.: *De verisimillima oraculi Jes. LII, 13 seqq. et LIII interpretandi ratione*, Leipzig, 1809.

KUENEN, A.: *The Prophets and Prophecy in Israel. An Historical and Critical Inquiry*, ET by A. Milroy, London, 1877.

LAGRANGE, M.-J.: *Le Messianisme chez les Juifs*, *EB*, 1909.

—— *Le Judaïsme avant Jésus-Christ*, *EB*, 1931.

LAUE, L.: *Die Ebed-Jahwe Lieder im II Teil des Jesaia exegetisch-kritisch und biblisch-theologisch untersucht*, Wittenberg, 1898.

—— 'Nochmals die Ebed-Jahwe-Lieder im Deuterojesaja', *TSK* 77, 1904, pp. 319–79.

LEVY, R.: *Deutero-Isaiah: A Commentary*, Oxford, 1925.

LEY, J.: *Historische Erklärung des zweiten Teils des Jesaja nebst einer Abhandlung: Über die Bedeutung des 'Knecht Gottes'*, Marburg, 1893.

—— 'Die Bedeutung des "Ebed-Jahwe" im zweiten Teil des Propheten Jesaia mit Berücksichtigung neuerer Forschungen', *TSK* 72, 1899, pp. 163–206.

—— 'Zur Erklärung der Bedeutung des Knechtes Jahwe in den sogenannten Ebed-Jahwe-Liedern', *TSK* 74, 1901, pp. 659–69.

LODS, A.: *Les Prophètes d'Israël et les débuts du judaïsme*, Paris, 1935; ET by S. H. Hooke, *The Prophets and the Rise of Judaism*, London, 1937, pp. 244–9.

LOFTHOUSE, W. F.: *Israel after the Exile*, Clarendon Bible, O.T., vol. iv, Oxford, 1928.

—— 'Some Reflections on the Servant Songs', *JTS* 48, 1947, pp. 169–76.

LOISY, A.: *La Consolation d'Israël (Second Isaïe), traduction nouvelle avec introduction et notes*, Paris, 1927.

—— *La Religion d'Israël*, 3e éd., Paris, 1933.

LOWTH, R.: *Isaiah, a new Translation with a Preliminary Dissertation and Notes, Critical, Philological, and Explanatory*, London, 1778, 11th ed., 1835.

LUNDBORG, M.: *Begreppet Herrens Tjänare hos Andre-Esaias*, Lund, 1901.

MCCAUL, A.: *The Doctrine and Interpretation of the Fifty-third Chapter of Isaiah*, London, 1845.

MÄCKLENBURG, A.: 'Über die Auffassung der Berufsthätigkeit des Ebed-Jahwe nach den Ebed-Jahwestücken 42, 1–7, 49, 1–9', *ZWT* 48, 1905, pp. 313–43; 'Über die Auffassung des Berufsleidens des Ebed-Jahwe in Jes. 52, 13–53, 12', ibid., pp. 483–517.

MARGOLIOUTH, D. S.: 'Recent Exposition of Isaiah LIII', *Expositor*, 7th ser., vol. 6, 1908, pp. 59–68.

MARMORSTEIN, A.: 'Zur Erklärung von Jes 53', *ZAW* 44, 1926, pp. 260–5.

MARTI, K.: *Das Buch Jesaja erklärt, Kurzer Hand-Commentar zum Alten Testament*, Abt. X, Tübingen, 1900.

—— *Geschichte der israelitischen Religion*, 4th ed. of August Kayser's *Theologie des Alten Testaments*, Strassburg, 1903.

MARTINI, C. D. A.: *Commentatio philologico-critica in locum Esaiae LII, 13–LIII, 12*, Rostock, 1791.

MAURER, F. J. V. D.: *In Jesaiam Commentarius grammaticus criticus in usum academiarum adornatus*, Lipsaiae, 1836.

MICHAELIS, J. D.: *Deutsche Uebersetzung des Alten Testaments, mit Anmerkungen für Ungelehrte*, Der achte Theil, Göttingen, 1779.

MOFFAT, R. M.: 'The Servant of the Lord', *ET* 13, 1901–2, pp. 7–10, 67–9, 174–8.

MOLDENHAWER, J. H. D.: *Übersetzung und Erläuterung des Propheten Jesaia*, Quedlinburg, 1780.

MONTEITH, J.: 'A New View of Isaiah liii', *ET* 36, 1924–5, pp. 498–502.

MOWINCKEL, S.: *Der Knecht Jahwäs*, Giessen, 1921.

—— 'Die Komposition des deuterojesajanischen Buches', *ZAW* 49, 1931, pp. 87–112, 242–60.

—— 'Til uttrykket "Jahvaes tjener": Streiflys fra Ugarit II', *Norsk teologisk tidsskrift* 43, 1942, pp. 24–6.

NÄGELSBACH, C. W. E.: *The Prophet Isaiah*, ET by S. T. Lowrie and D. Moore, Edinburgh, 1878.

NETELER, B.: *Das Buch Isaias aus dem Urtext übersetzt und . . . erklärt*, Münster i. W., 1876.

NIKEL, J.: 'Die neuere Litteratur über Jes. 40–66, insbesondere über die Weissagungen vom Gottesknechte', *Theologische Revue*, Münster i. W., 1. Jg., 1902, cols. 73–7, 105–11.

NORTH, C. R.: 'Who was the Servant of the Lord in Isaiah LIII?' *ET* 52, 1940–1, pp. 181–4, 219–21.

NYBERG, H. S.: 'Smärtornas man. En studie till Jes. 52, 13–53, 12', *Svensk Exegetisk Årsbok*, 7, 1942, pp. 5–82.

OEHLER, V. F.: *Der Knecht Jehova's im Deuterojesaja*, 2. Theile, Stuttgart, 1865.

OESTERLEY, W. O. E., and ROBINSON, T. H.: *Hebrew Religion: its Origin and Development*, London, 1930, ²1937.

ORELLI, C. VON: *The Old Testament Prophecy of the Consummation of God's Kingdom*, ET by J. S. Banks, Edinburgh, 1885.

—— *The Prophecies of Isaiah*, ET by J. S. Banks, Edinburgh, 1889.

—— *Der Prophet Jesaja ausgelegt*, 3. Aufl., München, 1904.

—— *Der Knecht Jahve's im Jesajabuche*, Berlin, 1908.

PALACHE, J. L.: *The 'Ebed-Jahveh Enigma in Pseudo-Isaiah: A New Point of View*, Amsterdam, 1934.

PARVISH, S.: *An Inquiry into the Jewish and Christian Revelation*, London, 1739.

PAULUS, H. E. G.: 'Zur Erklärung von Jes. K. LIII', in *Memorabilien*, Drittes Stück, Leipzig, 1792, pp. 175–92.

—— *Philologischer Clavis über das Alte Testament für Schulen und Akademien. Jesaias*, Jena, 1793.

PEAKE, A. S.: *The Problem of Suffering in the Old Testament*, London, 1904.

—— *The Servant of Yahweh and other Lectures*, Manchester, 1931.

PETERS, N.: *Weltfriede und Propheten*, Paderborn, 1917.

—— *Das Trostbuch Israels: Isaias ausgewählt und übertragen*, Paderborn, 1923.

PLOEG, J. S. VAN DER: *Les Chants du Serviteur de Jahvé dans la seconde partie du livre d'Isaïe*, Paris, 1936.

PRAETORIUS, F.: 'Bemerkungen zu den Gedichten vom Knechte Jahwes', *ZAW* 36, 1916, pp. 8–20.

—— *Nachträge und Verbesserungen zu Deutero-Jesaias*, Halle (Saale), 1927.

PROCKSCH, O.: 'Jesus der Gottesknecht', in *In Piam Memoriam Alexander von Bulmerincq — Abhandlungen der Herder-Gesellschaft und des Herder-Instituts zu Riga*, 6. Bd., Nr. 3, Riga, 1938, pp. 146–65.

Reinke, L.: *Exegesis critica in Jesaiae cap.* 52^{13}–53^{12}, Monasterii, 1836.

—— *Die messianischen Weissagungen bei den grossen und kleinen Propheten des Alten Testaments*, 2. Theil, Giessen, 1860, pp. 1–197.

Reuss, Ed.: *Les Prophètes*, 2e tome, Paris, 1876.

—— *Die Geschichte der heiligen Schriften Alten Testaments*, 2. Aufl., Braunschweig, 1890.

Robinson, H. W.: *The Cross of the Servant: A Study in Deutero-Isaiah*, London, 1926.

—— 'The Hebrew Conception of Corporate Personality', in *Werden und Wesen des Alten Testaments*, *BZAW* 66, 1936.

Rohling, A.: *Der Prophet Jesaja übersetzt und erklärt*, Münster, 1872.

Rosenmüller, E. F. C.: *Scholia in Vetus Testamentum, Tomus tertius, Jesaiae vaticinia complectens*, Leipzig, 1783, Editio secunda, 1820.

—— 'Leiden und Hoffnungen der Propheten Jehova's, Jes. LII, 13, 14, 15, LIII', in Gabler's *Neues theologisches Journal*, 13. Band, 4. Stück, 1799, pp. 333–69.

Roth, O.: 'Die neuesten Deutungen vom leidenden Gottesknecht in Jesaja 53', *Protestantische Monatshefte*, 7. Jg., 1903, pp. 95–106, 141–57.

Rothstein, J. W.: Review of Sellin's *Studien I und II*, in *TSK* 75, 1902, pp. 282–336.

—— *Die Genealogie des Königs Jojachin und seiner Nachkommen (I. Chron. 3, 17–24) in geschichtlicher Beleuchtung, nebst einem Anhange: Ein übersehenes Zeugnis für die messianische Auffassung des 'Knechtes Jahwes'*, Berlin, 1902, pp. 121–62.

Roy, H.: *Israel und die Welt in Jesaja 40–55. Ein Beitrag zur Ebed-Jahwe-Frage*, Leipzig, 1903.

Rudolph, W.: 'Der exilische Messias', *ZAW* 43, 1925, pp. 90–114.

—— 'Die Ebed-Jahwe-Lieder als geschichtliche Wirklichkeit', *ZAW* 46, 1928, pp. 156–66.

Schegg, P.: *Der Prophet Isaias uebersetzt und erklärt*, 2 Theile, München, 1850.

Schelhaas, J.: *De lijdende Knecht des Herren (Het Ebed-Jahwe-Problem)*, Groningen, 1933.

Schenkel, D.: 'Kritischer Versuch über den Knecht Gottes (Jes. 40–66) mit Berücksichtigung der neuesten darüber aufgestellten Meinungen', *TSK* 9, 1836, pp. 982–1004.

Schian, M.: *Die Ebed-Jahwe-Lieder in Jes. 40–66. Ein litterarkritischer Versuch*, Halle, 1895.

Schiller-Szinessy, S. M.: הנה ישכיל עבדי *An Exposition of Isaiah LII 13. 14. 15 and LIII delivered before the Council of the Senate in the Law School on Friday April 28, 1882*, Cambridge, 1882.

Schmidt, Hans: *Gott und das Leid im Alten Testament*, Giessen, 1926, pp. 29–32 and *Anmerkungen*.

Schuster, C. G.: *Jesaiae orationem propheticam Cap LII, 7–LIII, 12 explicare studuit*, Gottingae, 1794.

Seidelin, P.: 'Der 'Ebed Jahwe und die Messiasgestalt im Jesajatargum', *ZNW* 35, 1936, pp. 194–231.

Sellin, E.: *Serubbabel. Ein Beitrag zur Geschichte der messianischen Erwartung und der Entstehung des Judentums*, Leipzig, 1898.

SELLIN, E.: *Studien zur Entstehungsgeschichte der jüdischen Gemeinde nach dem babylonischen Exil. I. Der Knecht Gottes bei Deuterojesaja*, Leipzig, 1901.

—— *Das Rätsel des deuterojesajanischen Buches*, Leipzig, 1908.

—— *Mose und seine Bedeutung für die israelitisch-jüdische Religionsgeschichte*, Leipzig, 1922.

—— 'Hosea und das Martyrium des Mose', *ZAW* 46, 1928, pp. 26–33.

—— 'Tritojesaja, Deuterojesaja und das Gottesknechtsproblem', *NKZ* 41, 1930, pp. 73–93, 145–73.

—— 'Die Lösung des deuterojesajanischen Gottesknechtsrätsels', *ZAW* 55, 1937, pp. 177–217.

SHARPE, S.: *The Book of Isaiah, Arranged Chronologically in a Revised Translation, and Accompanied with Historical Notes*, London, 1877.

SKEMP, A. E.: ' "Immanuel" and "The Suffering Servant of Jahweh": A Suggestion', *ET* 44, 1932–3, p. 94 f.

SKINNER, J.: *The Book of the Prophet Isaiah Chapters XL–LXVI*, Cambridge, 1898; revised ed., 1917.

SMITH, G. A.: *The Book of Isaiah*, 2 vols., London, 1890, ²1927.

SMITH, SIDNEY: *Isaiah Chapters XL–LV: Literary Criticism and History* (Schweich Lectures, 1940), London, 1944.

SNAITH, N. H.: 'The So-called Servant Songs', *ET* 56, 1944–5, pp. 79–81.

STADE, B.: *Geschichte des Volkes Israel*, 2. Bd., Berlin, 1888, pp. 77–82.

—— *Biblische Theologie des Alten Testaments*, Tübingen, 1905.

STÄHELIN, J. J.: *Die messianischen Weissagungen des Alten Testaments in ihrer Entstehung, Entwicklung und Ausbildung*, Berlin, 1847.

STAERK, W.: 'Bemerkungen zu den Ebed Jahwe-Liedern in Jes. 40 ff.', *ZWT* 49, 1909, pp. 28–56.

—— *Die Ebed Jahwe-Lieder in Jesaja 40 ff. Ein Beitrag zur Deuterojesaja-Kritik*, Leipzig, 1913.

—— 'Zum Ebed-Jahwe-Problem', *ZAW* 44, 1926, pp. 242–60.

—— 'Zur Exegese von Jes 53 im Diasporajudentum', *ZNW* 35, 1936, p. 308.

STÄUDLIN, C. F.: *Neue Beiträge zur Erläuterung der biblischen Propheten*, Göttingen, 1791.

STEPHANI, H.: *Meine Gedanken über die Entstehung und Ausbildung der Idee von einem Messias*, Nürnberg, 1787, pp. 89 ff.

STEUDEL, J. C. F.: *Observationum ad Jes. 52, 13–53, 12*, Tubingae, 1825–6.

—— *Disquisitio: de* עֶבֶד יְהוָה*; num et quo sensu ejus idea a (veri nominis) Jesaja mente concipi potuisse videatur?* Tubingae, 1829.

STIER, R.: *Jesaias, nicht Pseudo-Jesaias*, Barmen, 1850.

STORR, G. C.: *Commentatio exegetica, qua insigne de Christo oraculum Es. LII, 13–LIII. 12. illustratur*, Tubingae, n.d. ?1768.

STRACK, H. L.: *Einleitung in das Alte Testament*, 6. Aufl., München, 1906.

—— and BILLERBECK, P.: *Kommentar zum Neuen Testament aus Talmud und Midrasch*, München, 1922, 1. Bd., pp. 481 ff.

TELGE, J. F.: 'Meletemata in carmen fatidicum Jes. LII, 13–LIII, 12', in *Theologische Miscellen, gesammelt und herausgegeben von Georg Alexander Ruperti*, Hamburg, 1816–17–18. (In three parts, in vol. i, pp. 315–38, vol. ii, pp. 289–356, vol. iii, pp. 356–93.)

THENIUS, O.: 'Neue Beleuchtung des leidenden Jehova-Dieners (Jes 52, 13–

53, 12)', in Winer's *Zeitschrift für Wissenschaftliche Theologie*, 2. Bd., Erstes Heft, pp. 105–30, 1832.
THUREAU-DANGIN, F.: *Rituels Accadiens*, Paris, 1921.
TOBAC, E.: *Les Prophètes d'Israël II–III*, Malines, 1921.
TORREY, C. C.: *The Second Isaiah: A New Interpretation*, Edinburgh, 1928.
UMBREIT, F. W. C.: 'Ueber den Knecht Gottes im letzten Abschnitt der Jesaianischen Sammlung, Cap. 40–66, mit besonderer Rücksicht auf Herrn D. Gesenius in seinem Commentar über Jesaias', *TSK* 1, 1828, pp. 295–330.
—— *Der Knecht Gottes. Beitrag zur Christologie des Alten Testaments*, Hamburg, 1840.
—— *Praktischer Commentar über den Jesaja mit exegetischen und kritischen Anmerkungen*, 2 Theile, Hamburg, 1841–2.
URWICK, W.: *The Servant of Jehovah. A Commentary, Grammatical and Critical, upon Isaiah LII, 13–LIII. 12*, Edinburgh, 1877.
VATKE, W.: *Die Religion des Alten Testamentes nach den kanonischen Büchern entwickelt*, Erster Theil, Berlin, 1835.
VISCHER, W.: 'Der Gottesknecht. Ein Beitrag zur Auslegung von Jesaja 40–55', in *Jahrbuch der Theologischen Schule Bethel*, ed. Th. Schlatter, Bethel bei Bielefeld, 1930.
—— *Das Christuszeugnis des Alten Testaments*, 2e Teil, Erste Hälfte, Zürich, 1942.
VOGEL, G. J. L.: *Umschreibung der Weissagungen des Propheten Jesaias*, Halle, 1771.
VOLCK, W.: 'Jes. 52, 13 ff.–K. 53', *Theologisches Literaturblatt*, Leipzig, Jg. 23, 1902, cols. 1 f., 17 ff., 25–30.
VOLZ, P.: 'Jesaja 53', in *Budde Festschrift*, *BZAW* 34, 1920, pp. 180–90.
—— *Jesaia II übersetzt und erklärt*, Leipzig, 1932.
WADE, G. W.: *The Book of the Prophet Isaiah with Introduction and Notes*, Westminster Commentaries, London, 1911.
WARDLE, W. L.: 'Isaiah XL.–LXVI.', in *A Commentary on the Bible*, ed. A. S. Peake, London and Edinburgh, 1924.
WATERMAN, L.: 'The Martyred Servant Motif of Is. 53', *JBL* 56, 1937, pp. 27–34.
WEIR, T. H.: 'A New Theory of "The Servant of Jehovah" in Isaiah 40–55', *Westminster Review*, 169, 1908, pp. 309–14.
WEISSMANN, A. S.: *Ernste Antworten auf ernste Fragen*, 2. Aufl., Wien, 1888.
WELLHAUSEN, J.: *Prolegomena zur Geschichte Israels*, Berlin, 1883, 6. Aufl., 1905.
—— *Israelitische und jüdische Geschichte*, Berlin, 7. Ausg., 1914.
WETTE, W. M. L. DE: *Opuscula theologica: Commentatio de morte Jesu Christi expiatoria*, Berlin, 1830, pp. 34–48.
WHITEHOUSE, O. C.: *Isaiah XL–LXVI*, Century Bible, Edinburgh, n. d.
WINCKLER, H.: *Altorientalische Forschungen*, Zweite Reihe, 3. Bd., Leipzig, 1901, p. 452 f.
—— in *Die Keilinschriften und das Alte Testament*, ed. E. Schrader, 3. Aufl., Berlin, 1903, p. 295.
WORKMAN, G. C.: *The Servant of Jehovah*, London, 1907.
WÜNSCHE, A.: *Die Leiden des Messias in ihrer Uebereinstimmung mit der Lehre des*

Alten Testaments und den Aussprüchen der Rabbinen in den Talmuden, Midraschim und andern alten rabbinischen Schriften, Leipzig, 1870.

ZIEGLER, J.: *Untersuchungen zur Septuaginta des Buches Isaias*, Münster i. W., 1934.

ZIEMER, E.: *Jesaias 53 in der neueren Theologie*, Cassel, 1912.

ZILLESSEN, A.: 'Israel in Darstellung und Beurteilung Deuterojesajas (40–55). Ein Beitrag zum Ebed-Jahve-Problem', *ZAW* 24, 1904, pp. 251–95.

—— 'Jesaja 52, 13–53, 12 hebräisch nach LXX', *ZAW* 25, 1905, pp. 261–84.

ZIMMERN, H.: In *Die Keilinschriften und das Alte Testament*, ed. E. Schrader, 3. Aufl., Berlin, 1903, pp. 384 ff.

—— *Babylonische Hymnen und Gebete*, Leipzig, 1905.

—— Ibid., Zweite Auswahl, Leipzig, 1911.

—— *Zum babylonischen Neujahrsfest*, Zweiter Beitrag, Leipzig, 1918.

—— *Das babylonische Neujahrsfest*, Leipzig, 1926.

ZORELL, F.: 'Das vierte 'Ebed-Jahwe-Lied', *Biblische Zeitschrift*, 1916, pp. 140–6.

SELECTED LIST OF (MAINLY) RECENT WORKS

BENTZEN, A.: *Jesaja fortolket, Bind II, Jes. 40–66*, Copenhagen, 1943.

—— *Det sakrale Kongedømme*, Copenhagen, 1945.

—— *Introduction to the Old Testament* (revised from the Danish ed., 1941), Copenhagen, 1948; Second ed., with corrections and a supplement, 1952.

—— *Messias, Moses redivivus, Menschensohn*, Zürich, 1948; ET *King and Messiah*, London, 1955.

—— 'On the ideas of "the old" and "the new" in Deutero-Isaiah', *Studia Theologica* 1, Lund, 1947, pp. 183–7.

COPPENS, J.: 'Nieuw Licht over de Ebed-Jahweh-Liederen' (with a summary in French), *Analecta Lovaniensia Biblica et Orientalia*, Ser. II, Fasc. 15, 1950, pp. 3–16.

ENGNELL, I.: *Studies in Divine Kingship in the Ancient Near East*, Uppsala, 1943.

HEGERMANN, H.: *Jesaja 53 in Hexapla, Targum und Peschitta*, Gütersloh, 1954.

JOHNSON, A. R.: 'Divine Kingship in the Old Testament', *ET* 62, 1950–1, pp. 36–42.

KRUSE, H.: 'Carmina Servi Jahve', *Verbum Domini* 29, 1951, pp. 193–205, 286–95, 334–40.

DE LEEUW, V.: 'De Koninklijke Verklaring van de Ebed-Jahweh-Zangen' (with a summary in French), *Analecta Lovaniensia Biblica et Orientalia*, Ser. II, Fasc. 33, 1952, pp. 449–71.

LINDBLOM J.: *The Servant Songs in Deutero-Isaiah: A New Attempt to Solve an Old Problem*, Lund, 1951.

—— 'Die Ebed Jahwe-Orakel in der neuentdeckten Jesajahandschrift (DSIa)', *ZAW* 63, 1951, pp. 235–48.

LINDHAGEN, C.: 'De tre sista decenniernas Ebed Jahve-forskning', *Svensk Teologisk Kvartalskrift* 8, 1932, pp. 350–75.

LINDHAGEN, C.: *The Servant Motif in the Old Testament: A Preliminary Study to the 'Ebed-Yahweh Problem' in Deutero-Isaiah*, Uppsala, 1950.

—— 'Ebed Jahve-problemet i svensk exegetik. En översikt', *Svensk Exegetisk Årsbok* 18–19, 1953–4, pp. 32–71.

MOWINCKEL, S.: 'Jesajaboken. II. Kap. 40–66', in *Det Gamle Testamente, oversatt av S. Michelet, Sigmund Mowinckel og N. Messel, III. De Senere Profeter*, Oslo, 1944, pp. 185–283.

—— *Han som kommer: Messiasforventningen i det Gamle Testament og på Jesu tid*, Copenhagen, 1951.

NORTH, C. R.: 'The "Former Things" and the "New Things" in Deutero-Isaiah', in *Studies in Old Testament Prophecy*, ed. H. H. Rowley, Edinburgh, 1950, pp. 111–26.

VON PÁKOZDY, L. M.: *Deuterojesajanische Studien. I. Die neuere Deuterojesaja-Kritik mit besonderer Rücksicht auf die s.g. Ebed-Jahweh-Lieder*, Pápa (Hungary), 1940. *II. Der Ebed Jahweh in der Theologie Deuterojesajas*, Debrecen (Hungary), 1942. (Written in Hungarian, with summaries in German, and very full bibliographies. The author defends the collective interpretation, with particular reference to Eissfeldt).

RIESENFELD, H.: *Jésus transfiguré*, Copenhagen, 1947.

RINGGREN, H.: 'König und Messias', *ZAW* 64, 1952, pp. 120–47.

—— *Messias Konungen*, Uppsala, 1954.

ROWLEY, H. H.: *The Servant of the Lord and other Essays on the Old Testament*, London, 1952.

—— 'The Suffering Servant and the Davidic Messiah', in the preceding volume, pp. 59–88.

SIMON, U. E.: *A Theology of Salvation: A Commentary on Isaiah 40–55*, London, 1953.

SJÖBERG, E.: 'Känna 1 Henok och 4 Esra tanken på den lidande Människosonen?', *Svensk Exegetisk Årsbok* 5, 1940, pp. 163–83.

—— *Der Menschensohn im äthiopischen Henochbuch*, Lund, 1946, pp. 116–39.

SNAITH, N. H.: 'The Servant of the Lord in Deutero-Isaiah', in *Studies in Old Testament Prophecy*, ed. H. H. Rowley, Edinburgh, 1950, pp. 178–200.

TOURNAY, R. J.: 'Les chants du serviteur dans la seconde partie d'Isaïe', *RB* 59, 1952, pp. 355–84, 481–512.

WIDENGREN, G.: 'Konungens vistelse i dödsriket: En studie till Psalm 88', *Svensk Exegetisk Årsbok* 10, 1945, pp. 66–81.

WOLFF, H. W.: *Jesaja 53 im Urchristentum*[2], Berlin, 1950.

YOUNG, E. J.: *Studies in Isaiah*, London, 1954.

ZIMMERLI, H., and JEREMIAS, J.: *παῖς θεοῦ*, in *Theologisches Wörterbuch zum Neuen Testament*, v, herausgegeben von Gerhard Friedrich, Stuttgart, 1954, pp. 653–713.

INDEX OF AUTHORS

Aaron ben Joseph, 10.
Abarbanel, 14 f., 18–21, 27, 192.
Abraham of Cordova, 18 f.
— Farissol, 18.
Akiba, 9.
Alexander, J. A., 45.
Altschuler, *see* Naphtali.
Ammon, C. F. von, 35.
Anonymous author of *Ausf. Erkl. d. mess. Weiss*, 39.
Arnold, M., 32, 62, 127 *n.*, 203.
Augusti, J. C. W., 1, 41, 89.
— and Höpfner, J. G. Ch., 41 *n.*
Aytoun, R. A., 11, 17 *n.*

Bade, J., 43.
Bahrdt, K. F., 39 f.
Bailey, C., 202 *n.*
Balla, E., 75.
Banks, J. S., 43 *n.*
Barnes, W. E., 133.
Baudissin, W. W. Graf, 61 *n.*, 101 *n.*, 147 *n.*, 221 *n.*
Bauer, Br., 45.
— G. L., 40.
Beck, Fr., 20, 32 f., 63, 204.
—, J., 43.
Beer, G., 117.
Begrich, J., 3, 83 ff., 137, 142, 160 *n.*, 179, 195–8.
Bentzen, A., 98 *n.*, 215, 221, 233 ff.
Bertholet, A., 49, 108, 154 *n.*, 169, 193.
Blank, S. H., 192, 204 *n.*
Bleek, F., 36.
Bleeker, L. H. K., 51 *n.*
Böhl, F. M. Th., 102.
Bousset, W., 24, 26.
Brandt, Th., 113.
Braun, H., 43, 46, 127 *n.*
Bredenkamp, C. J., 43, 66, 169.
Brierre-Narbonne, J.-J., 1 *n.*, 15 *n.*, 16 *n.*
Brown, S. L., 61 *n.*
Browne, L. E., 115 *n.*
Brückner, M., 102.
Bruston, E., 204.
Budde, K., 30, 52, 57 f., 60 ff., 104, 107 ff., 114 f., 144, 150 *n.*, 157 f., 182, 204 *n.*
Bühler, L. A., 51 *n.*
Bultmann, R., 24.
Bunsen, C. C. J., 41.
Burkitt, F. C., 23.
Burney, C. F., 62.
Burrows, E., 4 *n.*, 52 *n.*, 91 *n.*, 145 *n.*, 148 *n.*

Cannon, W. W., 138.
Carpenter, L. L., 23 *n.*
Caspari, W., 90, 101, 158.
Cheyne, T. K., 33, 44 f., 101 *n.*, 123, 169, 192 *n.*, 193 *n.*
Chrysostom, St. J., 26, 127 *n.*
Cobb, W. H., 64 *n.*
Cölln, D. G. C. von, 36.
Collins, A., 27.
Condamin, A., 26 *n.*, 68 f., 137 f., 157.
Conway, R. S., 213.
Cook, S. A., 99 f.
Cornill, C. H., 61.
Crampon, A., 69 *n.*, 137 *n.*
Cripps, R. S., 100 *n.*

Dalman, G. H., 7 f., 11, 14 *n.*, 15 *n.*, 16, 42.
Dathe, J. A., 43, 46, 127 *n.*
Davidson, A. B., 20, 33 f., 64 *n.*
— S., 33.
Delitzsch, F., 21, 43 ff., 111, 216.
Denio, F. B., 67 *n.*
Diestel, L., 36.
Dietze, K., 89, 193.
Dillman, A., 35 f., 169.
Dix, G. H., 102 *n.*
Döderlein, J. C., 28 f.
Dodson, M., 43.
Drechsler, M., 43 f., 46.
Driver, G. R., 102 *n.*, 123, 125, 129, 152 *n.*
Driver, S. R., 1, 33 f., 52, 152 *n.*
— and Gray, G. B., 202 *n.*
— and Neubauer, A., 1, 9 f., 12–22
Duhm, B., 2, 4 *n.*, 28, 41 f., 46 f., 49, 57 ff., 64 f., 72, 94, 96, 103, 114 f., 119, 125, 127 ff., 131 *n.*, 137, 149, 152 f., 156 f., 169, 175, 177 f., 180, 182, 184, 187 f., 192, 208, 214 f.
Durkheim, E., 105 f.
Dürr, L., 102, 201, 221.

Eckermann, J. C. R., 31.
Edelkoort, A. H., 98.
Eichhorn, J. G., 28 f., 40.
Eichrodt, W., 201 *n.*
Eissfeldt, O., 3 f., 57 *n.*, 72, 75, 82 *n.*, 103, 105–9, 158, 160, 204 f., 217, 221.
Eliezer, Rabbi, 21, 192.
— of Beaujenci, 10, 20.
Elliger, K., 3, 81–4, 124 f., 130 *n.*, 134 *n.*, 154, 169–77, 195 ff., 198 *n.*, 217.
Emmet, D. M., 216.
Engnell, I., 98 f., 228 ff.
Euler, K. F., 8, 26 *n.*
Ewald, H., 31 ff., 42, 48 *n.*, 62, 123, 169.

Farley, F. A., 192.
Feilchenfeld, W., 19.
Feldmann, Fr., 67 f., 97, 152, 180, 182 *n.*
Fischel, H. A., 1 *n.*
Fischer, J., 4 *n.*, 94–8, 110, 124, 129 *n.*, 137 *n.*, 152 f., 156 *n.*, 166, 179 f., 182 *n.*, 190, 206, 208 f., 211.
Flier, A. van der, 67.
Foakes-Jackson, F. J., Lake, K., and Cadbury, H. J., 23 f., 26 *n.*
Forbes, J., 43.
Friedmann, 42.
Freud, S., 55, 193.
Füllkrug, G., 66 f.

Gadd, C. J., 102 *n.*
Gesenius, W., 30, 36 f.
Giesebrecht, F., 57, 59 ff., 114, 117, 141, 144, 156.
Glahn, L., and Köhler, L., 159 *n.*
Glazebrook, M. G., 61.
Gordon, C. H., 231.
Grensted, L. W., 100 *n.*
Gressmann, H., 4, 69 f., 74, 90–4, 101 f., 129, 135 *n.*, 142, 154 f., 157 ff., 192, 208.
Grotius, H., 1, 27, 41, 127 *n.*
Guillaume, A., 98 *n.*
Gunkel, H., 70, 72, 74 f., 101.

Halévy, J., 63 *n.*
Haller, M., 61, 65, 71, 75–9, 101 f., 125, 133.
Hansi, J. I., 43.
Haupt, P., 63 *n.*, 126.
Hempel, J., 65, 77 ff., 109, 217.
Henderson, E., 43.
Hendewerk, C. L., 39.
Hengstenberg, E. W., 27, 43.
Hensler, C. G., 43, 46, 127 *n.*
Herodotus, 57 *n.*
Hertzberg, H. W., 141.
Hezel, W. F., 43, 46.
Hitchcock, F. R. M., 23 *n.*
Hitzig, F., 30, 58, 114, 127 *n.*, 132 *n.*, 144.
Hoepers, M., 98 *n.*
Hofmann, J. C. K., 39.
Holzhey, K., 4 *n.*
Homberg, H., 13.
Hontheim, J., 68 *n.*
Hooke, S. H., 98 *n.*, 102 *n.*, 116 *n.*, 202 *n.*
Hoonacker, A. van, 53 *n.*, 68, 136 ff., 157.
Hvidberg, F. F., 228 *n.*
Hyatt, J. P., 102.

Ibn Crispin *see* Moses Ibn Crispin.
Ibn Danân, *see* Saadyah Ibn D.
Ibn Ezra, 18, 20 f., 42.
Isaiah ben Mali, 18.
Isaac Orobio, 18.
Isaac Troki, 18.
Itkonen, L., 56, 178.

Jacob ben Reuben, 10, 18.
—Joseph Mordekai Hayyim Passani, *see* Passani.
Jahnow, H., 101 *n.*
James, E. O., 202 *n.*
Jephet ibn 'Ali, 10, 12, 19.
Jeremias, A., 70 *n.*
Jerome, 18 f.
Johansson, N., 107 *n.*, 142 *n.*
Johnson, A. R., 98 f., 229.
Jonah, Rabbi, 9.
Joseph b. Chija, 11.
— b. Nathan, 18.
Josephus, 93.
Joshua Segre, *see* Segre.
Judah b. Balaam, 21.
— han-Nasi, 14.

Kautzsch, E., 57 *n.*
Kelly, W., 43.
Kennett, R. H., 63.
Kimchi, D., 13, 18 f.
—, J., 18.
Kissane, E. J., 159, 193 *n.*
Kittel, R., 3, 55 f., 78, 85, 117, 121, 125, 153, 194.
Klausner, J., 15 *n.*
Kleinert, P., 20, 32 f., 63, 204.
Knabenbauer, J., 43.
Knobel, A., 35 f., 127 *n.*
Knoch, C. A., 55 *n.*
Koch, R., 98 *n.*
Köhler, L., 118, 124, 145 *n.*, 152 *n.*, 158 f., 175 f., 178, 182.
König, E., 62, 156, 182 f.
Koeppler, 72.
Köster, F., 30.
Konynenburg, J., 39.
Koppe, J. B., 28, 43, 46, 127 *n.*
Kosters, W. H., 63, 169.
Kraetzschmar, R., 56, 98 *n.*, 192.
Kruiger, J. D., 43.
Kuenen, A., 36.

Lagrange, M.-J., 15 *n.*, 69 *n.*, 157.
Langdon, S., 147 *n.*, 221.
Lanyado, S., 10, 15 f.
Laue, L., 65 f., 127, 183.
Levy, R., 17 *n.*, 20, 126 f., 204.
Lévy-Bruhl, L., 105 f.
Ley, J., 64 ff., 69, 127, 208.
Lindhagen, C., 220 *n.*
Lindblom, J., 223.
Lippmann, Jom Tob b. Salomo, 19 f.
Lods, A., 116 *n.*
Lofthouse, W. F., 100, 211 f., 214.
Loisy, A., 204.
Lowth, R., 28 *n.*, 43.
Lundborg, M., 63.
Luzzato, S. D., 21, 192.

McCaul, A., 43.
Mackinnon, J., 26 *n.*
Mäcklenburg, A., 67.
Marmorstein, A., 17 *n.*
Marti, K., 60 f., 123, 181 ff.
Martini, C. D. A., 43, 169.
Maurer, F. J. V. D., 36.
Meir b. Simeon, 21.
Menahem Azariah, 16.
Michaelis, J. D., 43, 118.
Milroy, A., 37 *n.*
Minocchi, S., 4 *n.*
Moffat, R. M., 63 *n.*
Moffatt, J., 23, 118, 181.
Moldenhawer, J. H. D., 43.
Monteith, J., 150 *n.*
Moore, G. F., 123.
Moses b. Nahman, 12.
— hak-Kohen, 20, 42.
— Kohen Ibn Crispin, 12, 21.
— el-Shaikh, 12.
Mowinckel, S., 2 f., 41, 47, 53, 55, 57, 65, 72–6, 78–85, 94, 97 f., 105, 108, 111, 114, 130 *n.*, 133, 136 f., 151, 158, 160, 182, 195 f., 204, 217, 220 ff.

Nachmanides, 21.
Nägelsbach, C., 43.
Naphtali b. Asher Altschuler, 13, 16.
Neteler, B., 43.
Nyberg, H. S., 98 *n.*, 223 ff.

Oehler, V. F., 43.
Oesterley, W. O. E., 3, 88, 158, 194.
Orelli, C. von, 43, 137 f.
Origen, 17 f., 20.

Palache, J. L., 89 f., 193.
Parvish, S., 27.
Passani, 21.
Paulus, H. E. G., 35.
Peake, A. S., 3, 60 f., 114 f., 117, 141 *n.*, 200 *n.*
Pedersen, J., 107 ff., 226.
Peters, N., 69 *n.*
Ploeg, J. S. van der, 97, 127, 137 *n.*, 155 *n.*
Praetorius, F., 55, 118, 125, 129, 145.
Procksch, O., 98, 137.

Rashi, 13, 18, 20.
Reinke, L., 27 f., 43.
Reuss, E., 33.
Riesenfeld, H., 227 *n.*, 228 *n.*
Ringgren, H., 232 f.
Robinson, H. W., 1, 3 f., 23 *n.*, 25, 32, 103, 105–8, 110 f., 113, 118, 203 ff., 207, 210 *n.*, 215, 226.
— T. H., 150, 158, 199.
Rodwell, 84 *n.*
Rohling, A., 43.
Rosenmüller, E. F. C., 30, 36 f., 127 *n.*
Roth, O., 63 *n.*
Rothstein, J. W., 51 f.
Rowley, H. H., 124, 126, 207.
Roy, H., 61 f., 94 f., 110, 202.
Rudolph, W., 3, 78, 85 ff., 92, 129 *n.*, 137 *n.*, 153, 194 f., 210 *n.*
Ruperti, G. A., 29.

Saadyah Gaon, 20 f., 27.
— ibn Danân, 21.
Samuel Lanyado, *see* Lanyado.
Schegg, P., 43.
Schelhaas, J., 98.
Schenkel, D., 38, 42, 48 *n.*, 154 *n.*, 169.
Schian, M., 48 f., 65, 131 *n.*, 156, 169, 178, 182.
Schmidt, H., 75 f., 129 *n.*, 133, 135 f.
Schrader, E., 50 *n.*
Schuster, C. G., 4, 29.
Segre, J., 13.
Seidelin, P., 11.
Selbie, W. B., 62 *n.*
Sellin, E., 2 f., 42, 45, 49–55, 69, 79, 81 f., 84, 89 f., 97, 121, 130 *n.*, 134–7, 139, 141 f., 148, 154 f., 160, 169, 174 *n.*, 193, 195 ff., 221 *n.*
Semler, J. S., 28.
Servetus, 26.
Sharpe, S., 42.
Shem Tob b. Shaprut, 18.
Skemp, A. E., 204.
Skinner, J., 20, 63 f., 125, 146 *n.*, 177 f., 185 *n.*, 200 f.
Smith, F. J., 31 *n.*
Smith, G. A., 45.
—, S., 85, 217.
Snaith, N. H., 214 f.
Solomon Astruc, 12, 21.
Solomon Levi, 10.
— de Morini, 21.
Stade, B., 30 f.
Stähelin, J. J., 41 f.
Staerk, W., 52 f., 137 *n.*, 148, 154, 169.
Stäudlin, C. F., 40.
Stephani, H., 28.
Steudel, J. C. F., 43.
Stevenson, W. B., 136.
Stewart, J. A., 211 ff.
Stier, R., 43.
Storr, G. C., 43.
Strack, H. L., and Billerbeck, P., 9 f. *n.*, 14 *n.*
Sutcliffe, E. F., 52 *n.*

Taylor, V., 6, 26.
Telge, J. F., 29.
Thenius, O., 35 f.
Thomas, D. W., 133.
Tobac, E., 68 *n.*
Torczyner, H., 133.
Torrey, C. C., 113 f., 126, 138, 159.

Umbreit, F. W. C., 38, 43 f., 216.
Urwick, W., 43.

Vatke, W., 31.
Vetter, 68 *n.*
Vischer, W., 111 ff.
Vogel, G. J. L., 43, 46, 127 *n.*
Volck, W., 67 *n.*
Volz, P., 78 f., 81 f., 113, 117, 123, 127, 129 f., 137 *n.*, 139, 141, 147, 153 f., 158, 160, 169, 177, 182, 192–5, 197.

Wade, G. W., 61.
Wardle, W. L., 61.
Webb, C. C. J., 212 f.
Weir, T. H., 57.
Weissmann, A. S., 21, 193.
Welch, A. C., 146 *n.*
Wellhausen, J., 30.
Wette, G. M. L. de, 38.
Whitehouse, O. C., 62, 184.
Widengren, G., 223, 228 *n.*, 232.
Winckler, H., 50, 193.
Workman, G. C., 64 *n.*
Wright, C. D., 55–6 *n.*
Wright, W., 145 *n.*
Wünsche, A., 14 *n.*

Ziemer, E., 67.
Zillessen, A., 8 *n.*, 61, 180.
Zimmern, H., 70 f., 102.

INDEX OF SUBJECTS

Adonis, 69 f., 93, 234. *See also* Tammuz.
Akiba, 9 f.
Ancestor, tribal, 107 ff., 226 f.
ardu, 71, 102.
Autobiographical interpretation, 2 f., 72–85, 195–9.

Babylonian court-style, 51, 69, 77.
'Babylonian Job', 71.
Babylonian New-year Festival, 102.
b^erîṯ 'ām, 38, 76, 91 ff., 132 ff.

'Catchword' theory, 80, 85, 160.
Collective interpretation, 2 f., 17 f., 28 ff., 57–64, 103–10, 114 ff., 202–7.
Composite theories, 21 f., 32 f., 36–9, 45 f., 49, 52 f., 56 f., 78 f., 111–14.
Corporate personality, 4, 18, 29, 103–10, 113, 204 ff., 226.
Cyrus, 29, 39 ff., 46, 83, 113 f., 133, 136 ff., 180, 183, 186; relation to Servant, 65, 68, 75–9, 109, 140, 187, 217; as Servant, 2, 26, 57, 101, 192 f.
Cyrus-Songs, 76 f., 83 ff.

Dante, 213.
David, 139; *David redivivus*, 102; Davidic Messiah, 5, 44, 51 f., 71, 139, 218.
Deutero-Isaiah, as Servant, 2 f., 41 f., 72–85, 195–9, 236.
Dying and rising god, 3, 69 f., 100, 102 *n.* 1. *See also* Tammuz.

'Ebed Yahweh, *see* Servant.
— — Psalms, 99, 229 f.
Eleazar, 2, 49, 192 f.
Elijah, 7, 20.
Empirical Israel, 3, 31 f., 35, 62, 182, 202 f.
Ezekiel, 2, 56, 192.

Gentiles, attitude to: in DI, 61, 87, 184; in Songs, 184 f., 197, 206.

Hadad-Rimmon, 70, 93.
Hasîdîm, 63, 203.
Hezekiah, 21, 27, 39 f., 57, 192.
Historico-Messianic interpretation, 3, 55 f., 85–8, 194 f.
History, question of prevision of, 207 f.

Ideal interpretation, 99 ff., 200, 216.
— Israel, 3, 20, 31–5, 41, 62 ff., 107 ff., 182, 203 f.
Isaiah, as Servant, 8, 40, 112, 192.
Israel, as Servant, 2 f., 28–31, 57–64, 103–10, 202–7.

Jehoiachin, 2, 50–3, 112, 192 f.
Jeremiah, 1, 20, 27, 41, 57, 70, 100, 112, 192, 208, 211.
Jesus, Messianic consciousness of, 23 ff., 218.
Job, 21, 89, 192, 208.
Josiah, 4, 21, 93 f., 112, 192.

Keret, 81 *n.* 1.
Kern, Theocratic, 36, 64. *See also* Pious Remnant.
King, sufferings of, 99, 102, 201, 229 ff.

Leprosy, attributed to Servant, 14, 40 f., 48, 125, 149, 200, 220, 225.
'Leprous rabbi', 2, 115, 149, 223.

Mediator, concept of, 213 f.
Menahem ben 'Ammiel, 16.
Meshullam, 2, 89 f., 192 f.
Messiah ben David, 13–17.
— ben Joseph (Ephraim), 15 ff.
—, exilic, 86, 94.
Messianic interpretation, 2, 4, 9, 11, 38, 42–6, 64–8, 90–9, 111, 207 ff., 220.
mišpāṭ, 51, 91, 124, 139 ff.
Moses, as Servant, 2, 9, 13, 20, 53 ff., 112, 192 ff., 236; alleged martyrdom of, 54 f.
Mystery-cult, 69, 101 *n.* 11. *See also* Tammuz.
Myth, philosophic, 212 ff.
Mythological interpretation, 69 ff., 101 ff., 201 f., 220.

Nebuchadrezzar, 139.
Nehemiah, 21, 192 f.

Phinehas, 10.
Pious Remnant, 3, 19 f., 32, 35 ff., 62 f., 202 ff.
Plato's righteous man, 44, 213, 216.
Priests, Order of, 39.
Prophets, Order of, 3, 30, 32, 36–9, 52, 62, 204.
'Pyramid' theory, 21, 44, 216.

Qaraites, 10, 12, 19

Ras Shamra, 81 *n.* 1.
Repetition in DI, 124.
Righteous, community of, 7–10.

Secondary Servant-Songs, 47 ff., 65, 130, 134 f., 189 ff.
Servant, as Akiba, 9 f.; as Cyrus, 2, 26, 57, 192 f.; as DI, 2 f., 41 f., 72–85, 195–9; as Eleazar, 2, 49, 192 f.; as

Ezekiel, 2, 56, 192; as Hezekiah, 21, 27, 39 f., 57, 192; as Isaiah, 8, 40, 192; as Jehoiachin, 2, 50–3, 192 f.; as Jeremiah, 1, 20 f., 27, 41, 57, 192; as Job, 21, 192; as Josiah, 21, 192; as Meshullam, 2, 89 f., 192 f.; as Moses, 2, 9, 53 ff., 192 ff.; as Nehemiah, 21, 192 f.; as Sheshbazzar, 2, 50, 192 f.; as Uzziah, 2, 41, 57, 89, 192 f.; as Zerubbabel, 2, 42, 49 f., 52, 192 f.; as Unknown Teacher of the Law, 47; as Israel, 2 f., 28–31, 57–64, 103–10, 202–7; as Ideal Israel, 3, 31–5, 62, 202 ff.; as Pious Remnant, 3, 19 f., 35 ff., 62, 202 ff.; as Order of Prophets, 3, 30, 37 ff.; as Order of Priests, 39; as Community of Righteous, 7–10; as The Wise, 7 f., 10; as *Hasîdîm*, 63; as the Messiah, 2, 4, 9, 11, 38, 42–6, 64–8, 90–9, 207–19, 220; a soteriological figure, 67, 98, 218; active calling of, 48, 61, 73, 79, 182 ff., 206; anonymity of, in Songs, 110, 178 ff., 205 f.; as ideal figure, 99 ff., 154; as leprous, 14, 40 f., 48, 60, 65, 92, 125, 149, 200; as second Moses, 66, 70, 96; death of the, 51 f., 90, 148 f.; fulfilment in Christ, 97 f., 213–18; kingly features in description of, 67, 91, 121, 139, 194, prophetic features in description of, 67, 86, 91, 139, 194; mission to Israel, 30, 62, 64, 86, 104 ff., 109, 132, 143–6, 203 ff.; world mission of, 87, 92, 108, 132, 143–6, 176, 184 f., 194, 197 f.

Servant-Songs, as allegory, 29, 60; authorship of, 47 ff., 59, 103–6, 156–86; by DI, 186; composed at intervals, 86, 188; consistency of portrait of Servant in, 154 f.; fragmentary character of, 69, 74, 86, 90, 188; influence on N.T., 24 ff.; later than main prophecy, 187 f.; linguistic affinities of, 48, 59, 65, 82, 89, 161–78; political background of, 146, 209 f.; relation to contexts, 47–69 (*passim*), 80, 85, 94, 156–60; style and metre of, 177 f.; theological conceptions of, 178–86; unity of authorship, question of, 47 ff., 52, 65, 95.

Sheshbazzar, 2, 50, 192 f.

Son of Man, Enochic, 7.

Suffering righteous man, 4, 8, 10, 13.

Tammuz, 3, 61, 69 ff., 99, 101 f., 147, 201 f., 223 ff.

Targum Jonathan, 11 ff.

'Tenses' in Servant-Songs, 67, 74, 96, 152, 210 f.

Toralehrer, 49, 63.

Trito-Isaiah, relation to DI, 79–82, 169–77.

Unknown Teacher of the Law, 47 f., 192.

Uzziah, 2, 41, 57, 89, 192 f.

Virgil, 213.

Wise, The, 6 f., 10.

Zerubbabel, 2, 42, 49 f., 52, 87 f., 112, 139, 192 f.

INDEX OF SCRIPTURE PASSAGES AND JEWISH WRITINGS

Note. The references do not include the Servant-Songs themselves, nor the Deutero- (Trito-) Isaianic passages compared therewith in Chapter IX, section 2.

OLD TESTAMENT

Genesis
v. 24 125
ix. 8–17 133
xvi. 12 132
xxxi. 19 168
xxxviii. 12 f. 168

Exodus
ix. 31 162
xv. 25 f. 55
xxxii. 32 54

Leviticus
xiii. 22, 32 149
xvi. 29 171

Numbers
xii. 3 55
7 ff. 54
8 55
xiv. 1 117
xxv 54

Deuteronomy
xv. 19 168
xvii. 9, 11 124
xviii. 15, 18 66
xix. 6 124
xxi. 22 124
xxxiv. 5 54

Judges
iv. 5 140
ix. 7 162

Ruth
iv. 15 146

1 Samuel
iii. 20 140
v. 3 f. 123
vii. 6 140
7–13, 15 140
xxv 168

2 Samuel
iii. 18 139
xiii. 23 f. 168

1 Kings
ii. 34 126
xvii. 21 ff. 211
xix. 16 139
xx. 40 124

2 Kings
ii. 3, 5, 10 125
iv. 34 f. 211
xiii. 21 211
xv. 6 149
xvii. 4 124
26 f. 140
xxiii. 3 93

1 Chronicles
iii. 18 50
iii. 19 89
xvi. 13 139

2 Chronicles
xxvi. 22 41
xxxv. 24 f. 93
xxxvi. 23. 77

Ezra
i. 2 ff. 77

Esther
ii. 1 13

Job
i. 20 168
iv. 16 124
viii. 10 141
xxi. 32 175
xxvi. 13 167
xlii. 16 153

Psalms
ii. 7 . . . . . 5, 25
xvii. 9 129
xviii 98
50 197
xix. 8 146
xxii 6
28, 30 197

Psalms (cont.):
xxiii. 3 145
xxiv. 6 125
xlix. 16 125
20 148
lvi 198
lvii. 10 197
lxvi. 8 197
lxxii 174
11 . . . . . 165, 167
lxxiii. 14 166
24 125
lxxiv. 12–17 201
lxxvii. 11 167
lxxxviii 148
lxxxix 98
4 139
31 141
xciii. 1 135
xcvi 198
c 198
cii 174
16 165
ciii. 20–2 197
cv. 43 139
cvi. 5, 23 139
cvii. 35 166
cxviii 99
cxix 29, 104
cxxxv 174
10 165

Proverbs
iv. 4 142
v. 5 142
vii. 26 127
x. 18 141
xv. 20 132
xxi. 20 132
xxiv. 11 125
xxv. 13 146
xxxi. 11 127
13 168

Song of Songs
v. 1 17

Isaiah
i–xxxix 89
i. 5 f. 29, 104
vi. 1 170
viii. 16 . . . . . 141, 203
ix 5, 8, 218
2 127
5 132

Isaiah (cont.):
xi 5, 8, 218
2 139
xiv. 18 126
19 . . . . . 126, 175
xxvii. 11 135
xxx. 9 f. 141
xxxiv–xxxv 159
xxxviii. 9–20 99
xxxviii. 17 164
xxxix. 7 40
xl 42, 169
xl ff. . . . 33, 43, 53, 101, 193
xl–xlvii (xlviii) 68
xl–xlviii 52, 77, 84 f., 162, 164 f.
xl–lv 42, 52, 57, 61 f., 67 f., 81 f., 85, 94, 96, 137, 158 f., 176, 214 f.
xl–lv (lxvi) . . . 156, 159 f.
xl–lxvi 8, 33, 43, 45, 57, 61, 63 f., 67, 89, 113, 137, 159, 174
xl. 2 . . . . . 116, 181
3 f. 142
3, 6 80
9 . . . . . 80, 84
10 143
19 f. 184
27 . . . . . 143, 181
xli. 1–4 159
1–13 76
2 136
2 f. 76
4 136
6 f. 184
8 . . . . 51, 117, 179, 215
8 f. . . . . . 37, 179 f.
9 . . . . . 133 f., 183
13 134
18 129
19 124
21–8 76
22 50
23 123
25 76
25 f. 136, 159
27 . . . . . 73, 79, 84
29 . . . . . 131 f., 184
xlii. 1–7 47, 50, 61, 67 f., 72, 85, 94 f., 105, 131
5–7 . . . . 47, 49, 65, 184
5–8 56
5–9 76, 83, 85, 90, 101, 113, 113, 128, 131–5, 196
6 . . . . 6, 38, 129 f.
6 f. 209
7 . . . . . 76, 86, 91

Isaiah (cont.):
xlii. 9 50
18 . . . . 73, 136
18–22 136
18–25 . . . . 179, 181
19 . . . 58, 89 f., 179
19–21 . . 50, 128, 135 f.
21 179
22 136
24 179
xliii. 1 . . . 119, 130, 133 f.
1–7 76
3 182
7 133
10 . . . 11. 179, 183 f.
14 130
20 124
21 134
22 ff. 183
xliv. 1 179
2 . . 44, 130 f., 134, 179
3, 5 185
8 . . . . . 183 f.
9–20 184
21 . . . . 134, 179
22 185
23 . . . . 119, 184
24 . . . . 131, 134
24–8 76
26 . . 37 f., 89, 179 f., 183
28 76
xlv. 1 . . . 76, 119, 133 f.
1–4 . . . . 114, 136
1–7 77
1–8 76
3 . . . . 76, 133
4 . . . . 76, 179
9–13 76
11 134
13 . . . 76, 114, 133
14 184
22 f. 185
xlvi–xlvii 67, 184
xlvi. 1–13 76
11 133
xlvii 169
xlviii . . . 68, 76, 182
1 73
1–19 181
4, 8 73
12 . . . . 133, 183
12–16 76
14 114
14–16 . . . 128, 136
15 133
Isaiah (cont.):
xlviii. 16 . . . . 73, 79
20 . . . 28, 119, 179
20 f. 119
xlix 132
xlix–lv . 35, 52, 63, 68, 77, 84 f., 165
xlix. 1–9 . . . 67, 85, 94 f.
1–13 61
7 . . 8, 89 ff., 123, 179 f.
7 ff. . . . 65, 73, 131
7–13 . . . 90, 128 ff., 132
8–13 . . . 83, 129, 196
8 f. . . 6, 50, 86, 91, 134
22–6 184
24 f. 124
l. 1 182
4 128
4–10 90
4–11 72
l. 4–li. 8 61
10 . . . . 38, 136, 179 f.
10 f. . 6, 47, 49, 61, 65, 127 f., 135
li. 4–(6)8 . . . 66, 128, 136 f.
6, 8 124
9 f. 201
9(12)–16 . . . . 128, 136
14 ff. 79
16 73
19 124
lii. 1 80
3–6 182
5 89
11 80
11 f. 77, 112
liv 169
1–8 104
6 134
6 f. 185
lv. 5 129
lvi 159
lvi–lxvi . . . . . 42, 81 f.
lvii. 1 119
lviii. 12 146
lx 184
lx–lxii . . . . 68, 137 f.
lxi 138
1 . . . . 25, 136, 139
1 ff. . . 6, 74, 98, 128, 137 f.
1–6, 10 138
lxv. 9, 15, 22 139

Jeremiah
i. 5 131
6 20
ii. 8 141

Jeremiah (cont.):
v. 4 f. 140
xi. 19 . . . 20, 148, 192
xv. 19 . . . . 141, 143
xvii. 16 121
xviii. 18 141
xxii. 4 100
xxvi. 11, 16 124
xxvii. 6 139
xxx. 18–21 93
xxxi. 15 f. 107
29 100
xxxii. 36 163
xxxiii. 1 124
xxxix. 15 124
xl. 5 . . . . 21, 27
xliv. 7 163
l. 19 146

Lamentations
i. 11, 16, 19 146
ii. 9 141

Ezekiel
iv. 4–8 56
vii. 26 141
viii. 17 119
xiv. 14 200
xvi 106
xviii. 2 100
xxiii 106
xxxii. 10 123
xxxiv. 23 f. 139
xxxvi. 23 167
xxxvii 49
xxxix. 27 146
xliii. 7 126

Daniel
i. 13, 15 166
xi. 33 127
33 ff. 7
xii. 2 20
3 . . . 6 f., 9 f., 127

Hosea
v. 1–2 54
ix. 7 139
7–14 54
xii. 14(13)–xiii. 1 54

Joel
i. 6 129
iv. 16 117

Amos
i. 2 117
iii. 7 139

Jonah
ii 148

Micah
iii. 8 140

Habakkuk
i. 4 141

Haggai
i. 5 163
ii. 4 f. 88
11 141
23 . . . . . 88, 139

Zechariah
iv. 6, 14 88
vii. 12 141
ix. 9 . . . . . 6, 66, 100
xi. 4–xiii. 9 54
8 54
xii. 9–14 93
10 . . . . . 6, 54, 66
10 ff. 70
xii. 14–xiii. 1 55
xiii. 7 54

Malachi
i. 10 135
ii. 6 ff. 141
iii. 24 (iv. 6) 7

APOCRYPHA AND PSEUDEPIGRAPHA

Wisdom of Solomon
ii. 13, 18 8
iii. 1–6 8
v. 1–7 8
ix. 4, 7 8
xii. 19 f. 8

Ecclesiasticus
xlviii. 10. 7

2 Maccabees
vi. 18–31 49

Enoch
xxxviii. 2 7
xl. 5 7
xlv. 3 7
xlvi. 3 7
4 8
xlviii. 4 7
6 8
xlix. 2 7
lxii. 3 8
7 7

OTHER JEWISH WRITINGS

Asereth Memroth 16
Midrash(im) . . . . . 14 ff.
Midrash Rabbah on Ruth ii. 14 . 14
— on Song v 1 . . . . 17 f.
Midrash Ne'lam 10
— *Pesiqta* 14
— *Pesiqta Rabbathi* . . . 16
— *Siphre* on Numbers xxv. 13 . 10
Secrets, Book of 16
Talmud
— *Sanhedrin* . . . . . 14 *n.*
— *Sheqalim*, v. 1 9
Targum Jonathan . . . 11–14
Yalkut Rubeni 10

NEW TESTAMENT

Matthew
ii. 15 24
iv. 8 f. 218
xii. 19 117
xxi. 4–7 24

Mark
i. 11 . . . . . 5, 25
x. 38 f. 24
45 . . . . . 26, 127
xiv. 24 26
36, 41 24

Luke
ii. 29–32 . . . . 9, 133
iv. 5 ff. 218
18 f. 137
21 25
xii. 50 24

John
i. 29 9

Acts
iii. 13, 26 26
iv. 27–30 26
viii. 27–39 26
34 . . . . . 1, 73
xiii. 46 147

Romans
v. 19 127

1 Corinthians
xvi. 13 139

2 Corinthians
xxvi. 22 41

1 Peter
i. 24 166
ii. 22–5 26